# THE ORGANIZATIONAL CONTRACT

# Markets and the Law

*Series Editor:*
Geraint Howells, University of Manchester, UK



Markets and the Law is concerned with the way the law interacts with the market through regulation, self-regulation and the impact of private law regimes. It looks at the impact of regional and international organizations (e.g. EC and WTO) and many of the works adopt a comparative approach and/or appeal to an international audience. Examples of subjects covered include trade laws, intellectual property, sales law, insurance, consumer law, banking, financial markets, labour law, environmental law and social regulation affecting the market as well as competition law. The series includes texts covering a broad area, monographs on focused issues, and collections of essays dealing with particular themes.

*Other titles in the series*

**International Insolvency Law**
Reforms and Challenges
Edited by Paul Omar
ISBN 978 07546 7482 5

**International Responses to Issues of Credit and Over-indebtedness in the Wake of Crisis**
Edited by Therese Wilson
ISBN 978 1 4094 5522 6

**EU and US Competition Law: Divided in Unity?**
The Rule on Restrictive Agreements and Vertical Intra-brand Restraints
Csongor István Nagy
ISBN 978 1 4094 4230 1

# The Organizational Contract

## From Exchange to Long-Term Network Cooperation in European Contract Law

*Edited by*

STEFAN GRUNDMANN
*Humboldt University of Berlin, Germany, and European University Institute, Italy*

FABRIZIO CAFAGGI
*European University Institute, Italy*

GIUSEPPE VETTORI
*University of Florence, Italy*

Routledge
Taylor & Francis Group
LONDON AND NEW YORK

First published 2013 by Ashgate Publishing

2 Park Square, Milton Park, Abingdon, Oxfordshire OX14 4RN
52 Vanderbilt Avenue, New York, NY 10017

*Routledge is an imprint of the Taylor & Francis Group, an informa business*

First issued in paperback 2020



**British Library Cataloguing in Publication Data**
A catalogue record for this book is available from the British Library

**The Library of Congress has cataloged the printed edition as follows:**
The organizational contract : from exchange to long-term network cooperation in European contract law / [edited] by Stefan Grundmann, Fabrizio Cafaggi, Giuseppe Vettori.
p. cm. – (Markets and the law)
Includes bibliographical references and index.
ISBN 978-1-4724-2124-1 (hardback : alk. paper)
1. Commercial law–Europe. I. Grundmann, Stefan, 1958– editor of compilation. II. Cafaggi, Fabrizio, editor of compilation. III. Vettori, Giuseppe, 1949– editor of compilation.
KJC2045.O74 2017
346.402'2--dc23

2013020859

ISBN 978-1-4724-2124-1 (hbk)
ISBN 978-0-367-60112-6 (pbk)

# Contents

**PART IV KNOWLEDGE EXCHANGE IN LONG-TERM CONTRACTUAL COOPERATION**



**PART V REMEDIES AND SPECIFIC GOVERNANCE RULES IN LONG-TERM RELATIONSHIPS**



**PART VI TOWARDS LEGISLATION?**

# List of Contributors

**Yehuda Adar** is Lecturer in Private Law at the University of Haifa, Israel.

**Marc Amstutz** is Professor of Commercial Law and Theory of Law at the University of Freiburg.

**Mireia Artigot i Golobardes** is a Juan de la Cierva Researcher at the University Pompeu Fabra, Barcelona.

**Cesare Massimo Bianca** is Professor Emeritus of Private Law at the University La Sapienza, Rome.

**Roger Brownsword** is Professor of Law at King's College, London.

**Fabrizio Cafaggi** is Professor of Comparative Law at the European University Institute in Florence and Professor of Transnational Law at the SSPA, Rome.

**Hugh Collins** is Blackstone Professor of Private Law at Oxford University and Member of the Board of Secola.

**Moshe Gelbard** is Senior Lecturer of Contract Law at the Netanya Academic College, Israel.

**Clayton P. Gillette** is the Max E. Greenberg Professor of Contract Law at the New York University School of Law.

**Marco Gobbato** is Researcher in Law and Economics at the University of Siena.

**Fernando Gómez Pomar** is Professor of Law and Economics at the University Pompeu Fabra, Barcelona.

**Stefan Grundmann** is Professor of Private Law and Private European Law at Humboldt-University, Berlin, and at the European University Institute, Florence.

**Chantal Mak** is Associate Professor at the Centre for the Study of European Contract Law, University of Amsterdam.

**Michael Martinek** is Professor of Civil Law and Commercial Law at the University of Saarland.

**Florian Möslein** is Professor of Private Law, International Commercial and Corporate Law at the University of Bremen, and Schumpeter Fellow at the Ludwig-Maximilians-University of Munich.

**Jacobien Rutgers** is Professor of Private Law at Amsterdam University and Member of the Board of Secola.

**Pietro Sirena** is Professor of Private Law at Siena University and Member of the Board of Secola.

**Aurea Suñol** is Professor of Commercial Law at the University Pompeu Fabra, Barcelona.

**Gunther Teubner** is Professor of Comparative Private Law and Legal Sociology at the International University College at Torino and Permanent Visiting Professor at Peking University.

**Giuseppe Vettori** is Professor of Civil Law at the University of Florence.

# Preface

## Society of European Contract Law (SECOLA)

Hugh Collins, Fernando Gómez Pomar, Stefan Grundmann (President), Jacobien Rutgers, Pietro Sirena

Contract law is probably the most dynamic area of European private law and also the fundamental private law discipline in all national legal systems. SECOLA was founded to assist the study of European contract law and to enhance its quality. SECOLA organizes an open, truly international and interdisciplinary discussion platform. The focus of the Society is upon newly enacted European Community legal measures, on core concepts in the field of European contract law and on proposals for further legislation. The Society organizes one or two international conferences each year, arranges for the publication of scholarly discussions in the field including books to be published in this series and assists with other network activities. In addition, SECOLA has created a journal dedicated to the same aims: the *European Review of Contract Law* (see www.secola.org and www.degruyter.com).

# PART I
# Overview

Chapter 1

# The Contractual Basis of Long-Term Organization – The Overall Architecture

Stefan Grundmann, Fabrizio Cafaggi, and Giuseppe Vettori

## Introducing the Paradigm of the Organizational Contract

This book broadly introduces the paradigm of the organizational contract in European contract law – which, of course, is not completely unheard-of, but not really developed either, neither in national law nor in European contract law. Bits and pieces of this paradigm are known. There are some particular (restricted) discussion circles, namely in the realm of networks (see section below on the Network Character and Part III), where there is solid ground in economic theory and governance research, namely with respect to long-term contractual relationships (see section below on the Long-Term Character and Part II), and problems such as information in long-term and networks' contractual relationships are seen as highly important in practice (see section below on the Long-Term Character and Part IV). There is, however, no paradigm of an 'Organizational Contract' in national or European contract law.

Such an 'organizational contract' is, of course, not a contract type in the traditional sense within a codified system – one for each type of one particular characteristic duty such as the delivery of a good or a right (sale of goods or of rights) or the providing of the use of a good or right (rental or lease contracts) or of a particular service (works' or services contracts) etc, in most cases with an obligation to pay imposed on the other party. Rather the concept of 'organizational contract' describes a phenomenon and tries to discuss it in its entirety, conceiving the different aspects as core elements which interact. The phenomenon is – broadly speaking – that within contracts a more radical distinction should be made between those which regulate single or spot exchanges and those that organize complex economic activities without creating a new legal entity. This distinction goes beyond that between spot and relational contracts because it focuses on the organizational dimension of contracting and its governance features.[1]

The interaction of heterogeneous elements of contract law and theory is important, because the links between the different elements are seen as being

1 See O. Williamson, 'Transaction-Cost Economics: The Governance of Contractual Relations' 22 *Journal of Law & Economics* 233–261 (1979); and O. Williamson, *Mechanisms of Governance* (New York: Oxford University Press, 1996) ch. 4.

inseverable and characteristic. In terms of traditional contract law, one could say that elements of a specific part of contract law (types of contracts) and of a general part of contract law (general for all types of contracts) interact – namely parts of the law of agency, of service contracts and parts of a more generic kind, such as plurality of contracts, all these complemented by many more elements which are little discussed as such and which certainly are *not* discussed in their interplay. While this phenomenon is certainly not so recent and while it is so important that, in fact, it has to be considered as the second, equally important, pole of contract law besides mere exchange contracts, discussion on this second pole is largely lacking, and still, the organizational contract has become more important as a phenomenon and in the refinement of the clauses used over the last few decades.[2] In its rather holistic approach, research on the organizational contract, of course, owes a lot to governance research whose characteristic is, among others, the holistic approach,[3] and more particularly to contract governance research which at last seems to be evolving over the last few years as an area in its own right.[4]

Three elements would seem to be the cornerstones of the architecture:

---

2 See, for instance, M. Klausner, 'Governance Mechanism in Long-Term Contracts', in S. Grundmann, F. Möslein and K. Riesenhuber (eds), *Contract Governance – Dimensions in Law and Interdisciplinary Research* (Oxford: Oxford University Press, forthcoming).

3 Ground-breaking Williamson (1979), n 1 above; good survey on the booming development of the approach – namely in the 80s and 90s – in P. Behrens, 'Corporate governance', *Festschrift for Drobnig* (Tübingen: Mohr Siebeck, 1998) 491–506; K. Hopt, H. Kanda, M. Roe, E. Wymeersch and S. Prigge (eds), *Comparative Corporate Governance – the State of the Art and Emerging Research* (Oxford: Oxford University Press, 1998); J. McCahery, P. Moerland, T. Raaijmakers and L. Renneboog (eds), *Corporate Governance Regimes – Convergence and Diversity* (Oxford: Oxford University Press, 2002); and (mainly US and economic theory) A. Shleifer and R. Vishny, 'A Survey of Corporate Governance' 52 *Journal of Finance* 737–83 (1997); today, T. Clarke (ed.), *Corporate Governance – Critical Perspectives on Business and Management*, 5 vols (London/New York: Routledge, 2005); K. Hopt 'Comparative Corporate Governance: The State of the Art and International Regulation' 59 *American Journal of Comparative Law* 1–73 (2011); J. Lieder, 'Legal Origins und empirische Rechtsvergleichung – Zur Bedeutung des Rechts für die Entwicklung von Kapitalmärkten und Corporate-Governance-Strukturen' 109 *Zeitschrift für vergleichende Rechtswissenschaften* 216–64 (2010). For the holistic character of governance discussion and research, see in more detail F. Möslein, 'Contract Governance within Corporate Governance', in this volume below 297–319.

4 See F. Möslein and K. Riesenhuber, 'Contract Governance – A Draft Research Agenda' 5 *European Review of Contract Law* 248–89 (2009) ; Grundmann, Möslein and Riesenhuber (eds), n 2 above; A. Habel, *Contract Governance – eine verfassungsrechtliche und rechtsdogmatische Analyse zu vertraglichen und vertragsrechtlichen Regelungsstrukturen in Belangen des Gemeinwohls* (Baden-Baden, Nomos, 2012); and in this volume below § 12 (Möslein, last n above); particularly close before, namely in the English literature, J. Brownsword, *Contract Law – Themes for the 21st Century* (2nd edn, Oxford: Clarendon, 2006); H. Collins, *Regulating Contracts* (Oxford: Oxford University Press, 1999).

*Duration*: This is, first, that the backbone of the organizational contract is its long-term character, its increased stability, as opposed to its characteristic of exchange. With the peculiarities of long-term relationships, the organizational contract may even be more distinct from the exchange contract than from other areas of the law, namely organizations such as companies. The phenomenon of duration is, of course, not monolithic. Even in exchange contracts, there are simultaneous and deferred exchanges (with a time span between formation of the contract and execution), the latter already creating a problem of duration which calls for some governance responses. There are simple and complex exchanges. The phenomenon of (complex) long-term contracts in its largest sense, however, encompasses more. Typically, in long-term contracts, contrary to what is the case in simple exchange contracts ('discrete contracts'), core objects cannot be defined in advance, not even the object of performance itself, or only very vaguely. Long-term contracts – as opposed to short-term contracts – often create the problem that even the object of performance needs to remain open, because the future vicissitudes of the relationship are ignored by the parties. A second distinction largely runs parallel, but has its own merits nevertheless. This is the distinction between discrete contracts and relational contracts, the latter being characterized by a largely increased interdependence of performances – which again implies that the degree of risk sharing is much higher than in traditional exchange contracts and that therefore each party may have additional tools beyond legal sanctions for reacting to ('punishing') poor performance by the other party.

*Number of participants*: The second cornerstone would seem to be that the organizational contract, while in principle also possible between two parties only, would mostly come with a plurality of parties, either as linked contracts or (more seldom) as a genuine multiparty contract. Therefore one traditional foundation of contract law, privity or relativity of contracts, the *credo* that there are effects in principle only between two parties, is questioned in relation to linked contracts among heterogeneous parties.

Finally, the *relationship to company law*: If really the 'organizational contract' forms a second pole besides the traditional exchange contract, not only are we faced with a new pole in contract law, adding a lot of heterogeneity to contract law and its foundations – from 'exchange to cooperation' or more precisely: cooperation supplementing exchanges and common activities as a second paradigm of contract law – but yet another comparison would seem to be needed. If organization is traditionally associated with the law of organizations and companies (so-called 'hierarchies') and exchange with the law of contracts, the concept of an organizational contract would certainly raise the question of its relationship with company law; it would need to be compared to core features of company law. The third 'architectural' question would therefore be what distinguishes the organizational contract from organization via company law, and which are the parallels? Considering cross-sections between company and (this branch of) contract law might even be a field of inquiry in its own right.[5] Along these lines two important issues need to be addressed. Is it possible and desirable to partition assets of the contracting parties so that the resources for the common project will be separated from those deployed for individual projects? Furthermore can contracts with limited liability be created similarly to the partition conventionally adopted in company law where both entities with and without limited liability coexist?

It should be emphasized that organizational contracts are characterized by something more than pure exchanges. Parties can develop a common project (creation of a platform for logistics, creation of a new patent) with the organizational contract. Both in linked contracts and in multiparty contracts, parties often combine exchanges of information and performances with activity in common. For example in research and development contracts, parties perform activities together, but little or no exchanges take place. Slightly differently in supply chains, there are exchanges, but they are instrumental to the production of a final product. Therefore, there is not only the divide between spot contracts and long-term contracts, but – running often in parallel – also the divide between exchange contracts and contracts for cooperation, the latter often even a mix of several types of duties and contracts.

## The Long-Term Character of the Organizational Contract

### *High Practical Importance, Limited Research and Legislation*

Among the important trends in market economies of the last decades, transition from the manufacturing age to a services age (or a combination of both) would seem to be a particularly meaningful one. It seems to be the case that in all modern market economies, the share of services nowadays equals and often exceeds that of industrial production,[6] and that the distribution of industrial production and the networks needed for this typically include an effective sharing of services as well. Ever more sales of goods are complemented by services both at time of sales and after sales. Two types of interdependencies are growing

a. functional interdependence between goods and services exchanged
b. structural interdependence along the supply chain among the different knots providing services in addition to goods (when manufacturers provide know-how to suppliers in order to meet quality standards).

5 S. Grundmann, 'On the Unity of Private Law – From a Formal to a Substance Based Concept of Private Law' *European Review of Private Law* 1055–78 (2010); focusing rather on the interplay than on a comparison, Möslein, n 3 above, 297–319.

6 See, on a summary basis, P. Love and R. Lattimore, in *OECD Insights: International Trade: Free, Fair and Open?* (OECD Publishing: 2009), 51.

Network contracts are long-term relationships characterized by strong interdependence among contractual performances and a shared objective. The two are obviously linked. It is the existence of a shared objective that makes several sales interdependent or more interdependent – even though no common scope (with profit sharing) is formulated. The existence of a shared objective, like exporting a portfolio of products under the same trademark abroad may make production of unrelated goods interdependent. The puzzling question concerns how the governance design is affected by the pursuit of the shared objective even when performances remain separate. Interdependence goes well beyond specific investments and offers an opportunity to revise Williamson's theoretical insights to a much broader range of cases.

In the following, the distinction is made between shared objectives and common objectives/purposes, although not all national laws (or European Company Law) draw the line (exactly) the same way – common purpose implies the agreement to have inputs pooled *and* share profits according to a pre-established ratio, a shared objective implies, primarily, only a common interest (and at least no agreement to share profits): all parties want the network of contracts to succeed. On the other hand, the law can infer (and under many national laws does infer) that, given this shared interest, there are implied duties (i) at least not to obstruct this shared interest (duty to abstain), or also (ii) to promote it actively.

Against this background, it would seem as if transnational legislation and also research rather lagged behind: the contract type paradigmatic of the industrial era, the sales contract, has been the object of extensive international and supranational harmonization, while the same is not true for services contracts. The EC Sales Law Directive of 1999 and the draft for an (Optional) Common (European) Sales Law of 2010 followed by a regulation proposal on EU Sales stand out.[7] And on the international level, the CISG was clearly seen as an overall model for contract law more generally.[8] The EC Services Directive clearly is not of parallel importance for

7 Directive 1999/44/EC of the European Parliament and of the Council of 25 May 1999 on certain aspects of the sale of consumer goods and associated guarantees, *OJEC* 1999 L 171/12. Monographs on the directive by G. de Cristofaro, *Difetto di conformità al contratto e diritti del consumatore – l'ordinamento italiano e la direttiva 99/44/CE sulla vendita e le garanzie dei beni di consumo* (Padova: Cedam, 2000); M. Bianca and S. Grundmann (eds), *EU Sales Directive - Commentary* (Antwerp et al.: Intersentia, 2002); S. Pellet, *La garantie légale des biens de consommation – étude comparée des droits français, anglais et communautaire* (Villeneuve d'Ascg: Presses universitaires, du Septentrion, 2003); A. Orti Vallejo, *Los defectos de la cosa en la compraventa civil e mercantil. El nuevo régimen jurídico de las faltas de comformidad según la Directiva 1999/44/CE* (Granada: Comares, 2002); T. Repgen, *Kein Abschied von der Privatautonomie - die Funktion zwingenden Rechts in der Verbrauchsgüterkaufrichtlinie* (Lübeck: Schöning, 2001). Proposal for a Regulation of the European Parliament and of the Council on a Common European Sales Law of 11 October 2011, *COM* (2011) 635 final.

8 (Vienna) UN Convention on Contracts for the International Sale of Goods of 11th April 1980, United Nations, Official Records, 1981, 178 = (German) *Bundesgesetzblatt*

a services contract law, in fact, its importance as a model for contract law is more than limited.[9] A parallel act to the CISG on the side of services contracts is missing altogether. The picture is similar at the national level in many countries, for instance in the large re-codification endeavour of the German *Schuldrechtsmodernisierung*, in which the general regime on breach of contract has been completely modelled after the (international regime of the) sales contract (transposing, it is true, the EC Sales Directive). Long-term (services) contracts received little attention, basically in one rule on termination (sec. 314 German Civil Code). Irrespective of whether national law has just one overarching type of services contract or distinguishes between service contracts, works contracts and agency contracts – in all cases, the area of services is taken much less into consideration in the general parts of national contract law than the sales (on-the-spot) contract paradigm. Even payment as the 'neutral' obligation in contracts has been taken care of much more intensively, namely with the Payments Services Directive and its transposition into the national laws.[10] And also doctrinal writing is not particularly strong in this field[11] which is so novel in problems and so important in practice.

(1989 II), 588 (English, French, German); for the states adhering to the convention (altogether 58, end 2000) see annex B to (German) *Bundesgesetzblatt* (2000 II), 595 or J.O. Honnold, *Uniform Law for International Sales* (3rd edn, Deventer: Kluwer Law, 1999) 577 (53 in June 1998); J.O. Honnold, *Documentary History of the Uniform Law of International Sales* (Deventer: Kluwer Law and Taxation Publishing, 1989). The Convention is often seen not only as a regulation of (commercial) sales law, but of contract law in general: see, for instance, Honnold (1999), *op cit*, para 2 *et seq.*; H. Magnus, in Staudinger Commentary, *CISG* (Berlin: Sellier/de Gruyter, 1999) Introduction para 2.

9 The EC Services Directive (Directive 2006/123/EC of the European Parliament and of the Council of 12 December 2006 on Services in the Internal Market, *OJEC* 2006 L 376/36) contains little contract law, according to its drafters it (almost exclusively) served the purpose of deregulating administrative impediments (see 4th recital). On the lack of contract law in the directive see, for instance, M. Schauer, 'Contract Law of the Services Directive' 4 *European Review of Contract Law* 1–14 (2008).

10 Directive 2007/64/EC of the European Parliament and of the Council of 13 November 2007 on payment services in the internal market amending Directives 97/7/EC, 2002/65/EC, 2005/60/EC and 2006/48/EC and repealing Directive 97/5/EC [Payment Services Directive], *OJEC* 2007 L 319/1; for this measure, see, for instance: J.-U. Franck and P. Massari, 'Die Zahlungsdiensterichtlinie: Günstigere und schnellere Zahlungen durch besseres Vertragsrecht?' *Wertpapier-Mitteilungen* 1117–28 (2009); S. Grundmann, 'Das neue Recht des Zahlungsverkehrs' *Wertpapier-Mitteilungen*, 1109–17 and 1157–64 (2009). For the question whether financial services cannot serve as a model for services more generally, see also explanations in the following.

11 For the contractual long-term relationship, literature on the continent is not very rich, see J. Jickeli, *Der langfristige Vertrag* (Baden-Baden: Nomos, 1996); F. Niklisch (ed.), *Vertragsnetzwerke komplexer Langzeitverträge* (Munich: Beck, 2001); H.-G. Kern, 'Ökonomische Theorie der Langzeitverträge' *Juristische Schulung* 13–19 (1992); and more specifically on the important issue of termination, H. Oetker, *Das Dauerschuldverhältnis und seine Beendigung* (Tübingen: Mohr Siebeck, 1994); seminal works by I.R. MacNeil

This is all the more remarkable as the case patterns in this area are more varied, as the assessment of quality is typically even more difficult (*obligations de moyen*, obliging only to proper work, and *obligations de résultat*, obliging to reach a defined result), and finally also as non-performance may typically be of existential importance for the other party more often in the area of services. One important exception would seem to be the EC Markets in Financial Instruments Directive, regulating one important service in great detail.[12] While it is true that this directive constitutes the most important exception, it is restricted to one particular service; beyond this, the service regulated here lacks (at least) one highly particular element of long-term (service) relationships.

### *The Long-Term Character and Three Basic Features*

If long-term relationships are still rather neglected in contract regulation and contract law academia, the main reason for this would seem to be that the rules on content, performance and breach are still seen to follow basically that of simple on-the-spot contracts. This underlying idea (the *presumptio similitudinis*) is, however, erroneous. There are a number of basic features which completely differ; the first two have been identified very clearly in the seminal writings by O. Williamson on

(n 15) and S. Macaulay, 'The Use and Non-use of Contracts in the Manufacturing Industry' 9 (7) *Practical Lawyer* 13–40 (1963); see also, for instance, Collins, n 4 above, 140–43; J. Haley, 'Relational Contracting: Does Community Count?', in H. Baum (ed.), *Japan, Economic Success and Legal System* (Berlin et al.: de Gruyter, 1997) 167–84; and, of course, within the DCFR publications: M. Hesselink et al., *Principles of European Law: Commercial Agency, Franchise and Distribution* (Munich: Sellier, 2006).

12 Directive 2004/39/EC of the European Parliament and of the Council of 21 April 2004 on markets in financial instruments amending Council Directives 85/611/EEC and 93/6/EEC and Directive 2000/12/EC of the European Parliament and of the Council and repealing Council Directive 93/22/EEC (MiFID), *OJEC* 2004 L 145/1; for payment services which could be considered as well in this respect, see already above n 10. For the MiFID see namely G. Ferrarini, 'Contract Standards and the Markets in Financial Instruments Directive (MiFID): An Assessment of the Lamfalussy Regulatory Architecture' 1 *European Review of Contract Law* 19–43 (2005); S. Grundmann, Commentary to §§ 31 *et seq*., Bankrecht VI – Wertpapierhandelsgesetz, in K. Ebenroth, C. Boujong, D. Joost and L. Strohn (eds), *HGB-Kommentar*, 2 vols (2nd edn, Munich: Beck-Vahlen, 2009) (with ample further references): Ü. Tekinalp, 'Investor Protection and Investment Firms' Duty of Care and Loyalty Towards Clients', in S. Grundmann and Y. Atamer (eds), *Financial Services, Financial Crisis and General European Contract Law – Failure and Challenges of Contracting* (Alphen: Kluwer International, 2011) 165–77. Still relevant, core literature on the ISD, such as, among many others D. Bliesener, *Aufsichtsrechtliche Verhaltenspflichten beim Wertpapierhandel* (Berlin: de Gruyter, 1998); G. Ferrarini (ed.), *European Securities Markets - the Investment Services Directive and beyond* (London et al.: Kluwer, 1998); P. Lastenouse, 'Les règles de conduite et la reconnaissance mutuelle dans la directive sur les services d'investissement' *Revue du Marché Unique Européen* 79–120 (1995).

(contract) governance.[13] The first and probably most striking stems from the fact that there is uncertainty (lack of sufficient knowledge to plan, often referred to as 'ignorance of the future'). Parties do not know the situations to which the contract will apply and which it will have to provide solutions for. Simple as this statement may be, it nevertheless contradicts completely the *presumptio similitudinis*, because the uncertainty of the future also (often) takes away the possibility to fix the core contents of the contract which makes the basic scheme of problems in long-term contracts fundamentally different from that in on-the-spot contracts. Uncertainty leads to incompleteness and requires procedures to complete the contract after it becomes enforceable. Incompleteness can lead to higher and different opportunism than that typically considered in spot contracts. *Ex ante* uncertainty may concern contingencies that might arise over time. Contractual design may vary depending on how unanticipated contingencies arise and which procedure has to be followed to respond to these. When facing unanticipated contingencies the contract design may simply trigger renegotiation or need a governance architecture beyond renegotiation which would approach organizational contracts. Organizational contracts are needed to govern interdependences with and without uncertainty.[14] When interdependence needs to be governed under uncertainty, parties have to limit opportunistic behaviour especially when it can affect third parties to the contract that are involved in the common project, as it is the case in multiple linked contract networks.

---

13 Vulnerability (and a need for governance schemes) is seen if (1) future developments are unforeseeable, but (2) investments specific to this relationship (and not easily to be re-used elsewhere) are made (creating the risk of sunk cost if the relationship is terminated or if the other side devaluates it by behaving opportunistically [moral hazard]), see Williamson (1979), n 1 above; O. Williamson, *Markets and Hierarchies – Analysis and Antitrust Implications* (New York/London: Free Press, 1975) *passim*; O. Williamson, *The Economic Institutions of Capitalism* (New York: Free Press, 1985) 56–67; and also K.J. Arrow, 'The Economics of Agency', in J.W. Pratt and R.J. Zeckhauser (eds), *Principals and Agents – The Structure of Business* (Boston: Harvard Business School Press, 1985) 37–51; B. Klein, R.G. Crawford and A. Alchian, 'Vertical Integration, Appropriable Rents, and the Competitive Contracting Process' 21 *Journal of Law and Economics* 297–326 (1978); then O. Hart, *Firms, Contracts, and Financial Structure* (Oxford: Clarendon Press, 1997) 27 *et seq.*, 73–85, 87 *et seq.*; J. Tirole, 'Incomplete Contracts – Where do we Stand?' 67 *Econometrica* 741–81 (1999); G.R. Shell, 'Opportunism and Trust in the Negotiation of Commercial Contracts – Towards a New Cause of Action' 44 *Vanderbilt Law Review* 221–82 (1991); E.G. Furubotn and R. Richter, *Institutions and Economic Theory – The Contribution of the New Institutional Economics* (2nd edn, Ann Arbor: University of Michigan Press, 2005) 135–54, 342–51, *passim*; Y. Kotowitz, in S.N. Durlauf and L.E. Blume (eds), *The New Palgrave Dictionary of Economics and the Law*, vol 5 (2nd edn, Basingstoke: Palgrave Macmillan, 2008) 773–7 ('Moral Hazard'); O. Williamson, in P. Newman (ed.), *The New Palgrave Dictionary of Economics and the Law*, vol 2 (London: Macmillan, 1998) 703–10 ('Opportunistic behaviour in contracts').

14 See F. Cafaggi, *Reti di imprese tra regolazione e norme sociali* (Bologna: Mulino, 2004).

The second problem typical for long-term contracts (and which is rather theoretical only for on-the-spot contracts) is investment specificity. That investment is often made specifically for the relationship – for instance, the machinery for a particular supply relationship, moving to another place to take up a work relationship there, investment in the education and training of a long-term partner or handing-on of sensitive information for collaboration. This makes partners in a long-term relationship particularly vulnerable. In fact, after Williamson, relation-specific (or firm-specific) investment is seen as the main reason for the need of (protective) governance arrangements. This is much more precise than 'economically stronger party' and the like. It is, of course, a criterion typically more useful in firms and B2B relationships than in B2C relationships. The Williamson model is focused on bilateral contracting. Here it is suggested that investment specificity matters in multiparty contracts as well but it might require different solutions from those deployed in bilateral contracts – or also offer additional ones. In multiparty contracts, peer monitoring may decrease opportunism; in addition exit threat does not necessarily coincide with the end of the project since in most of the instances parties are replaceable even if at a cost.

A third feature would seem to be highly meaningful: the incentive structure is also substantially different in contracts where each party has to 'perform in continuity', thus giving each party the possibility immediately to 'punish' improper performance on the other side.[15] The incentive structure is determined not only by the allocation of opportunities during the time of contract but also by the regime of termination. From this structure, it also becomes evident why a termination regime which is stringent enough to create a real threat may be important, but may as well be a means by which the party who has invested less can blackmail the other. This structure explains why in fact termination regimes are paramount for long-term relation regimes, but also so difficult to calibrate. As mentioned, differences should be made within long-term contracts between bilateral and multiparty ones. In multiparty contracts exits may have different consequences depending on the resources and liability of the exiting member.

The most solid theory – for all three features – and in fact a genuine field of research responding to these core features has been developed in institutional economics and governance research, namely with the theory of incomplete contracts and their governance as developed by O. Williamson and, for a more narrowly defined, yet paradigmatic setting, also with principal agency theory.[16] The

15 See, for instance, I.R. MacNeil, 'The Many Futures of Contracts' 47 *Southern California Law Review* 691–816, 738–40 (1974); G.K. Hadfield, 'Problematic Relations: Franchising and the Law of Incomplete Contracts' 42 *Stanford Law Review* 927–992 *passim* (1990).

16 See n 1 and 3 above and notes accompanying the text in the following. For a principled overview, bridging already the gap between this theory and concrete legal institutions, see M. Artigot i Golobardes and F. Gómez Pomar, 'Dissecting Long-Term Contracts – A Law and Economics Approach' below 41–75.

common starting point is that the institutional framework does make a difference and is needed – either by party arrangement or by a legislative environment. In both theories named, ex-post opportunism (moral hazard) is a core concern. Ex-post opportunism – i.e. profiting from incompleteness of the contractual arrangement in a way which the other party would not have accepted if the issue had been negotiated – may as well be an issue in some instances of on-the-spot contracts, but given that the object of the contract can mostly be described in very concrete details, this is far less the case here. Conversely for long-term contracts, ex-post opportunism is omnipresent as a risk, given that contracts more systematically (have to) tend to be incomplete and given that there is much more relation-specific investment. While ex-post opportunism was the concern most addressed, it is true that all the schemes and solutions deal – and should deal – with decision taking and control rights more generally – even without any intent of one party to behave opportunistically. Thus, uncertainty ('ignorance of the future') is the basic problem and different theories contribute certain pieces to the governance of relationships created under such a strong shadow of uncertainty.

The theory of incomplete contracts as developed by Williamson approaches the problem of uncertainty ('ignorance of the future') mainly for the setting in which at least one party in the scheme has made investments which can be used specifically within this setting (and less well outside and thus cannot easily be withdrawn and re-used) and other parties can use this situation to 'hold-up'. The principal agent theory approaches the situation in which the diverging interests are aligned in a particular way: it applies in the context of multiparty contracts where there is some degree of delegation to define the common project and specify commitments and obligations. This can happen where one party acting within this scheme is expected (and then also obliged by law) to act in the interest of another party or in the interest of (the pool of) all parties when a multiparty contract is in place. For this situation – typical wherever one party acts on the basis of particular professional expertise or also because of a split of tasks – principal agent theory develops a particular (default) set of governance rules.[17] In this setting again,

17 Groundbreaking M. Jensen and W. Meckling, 'Theory of the Firm: Managerial Behavior, Agency Costs and Ownership Structure' 3 *Journal of Financial Economics* 305–60 (1976); M. Jensen and W. Meckling, 'Separation of Ownership and Control' 26 *Journal of Law and Economics* 301–25 (1983); tracing it back to Adam Smith, Hopt, n 3 above, 4 *et seq*. For a concise contract-based perspective of the problems see U. Schweizer, *Vertragstheorie* (Tübingen: Mohr-Siebeck, 1999) 33–85 and 230–38; much more prolific is the discussion in company law literature which, however, deals with the same basic problem: M. Roe, *Strong managers and weak owners – the political roots of American corporate finance* (Princeton: Princeton University Press, 1994); Shleifer and Vishny, n 3 above, 737–83; J. Tirole, 'Corporate Governance' 69 *Econometrica* 1–35 (2001); pithy description also in Behrens, n 3 above, 494–7; M. Naniwadekar, 'The Law of Agency as applied in Company Transactions' 5 *European Company and Financial Law Review* 280–304 (2008); and M. Ruffner, *Die ökonomischen Grundlagen eines Rechts der Publikumsgesellschaft – ein Beitrag zur Theorie der Corporate Governance* (Zurich: Schulthess, 2000) 131 *et seq.*

behaviour which exploits the initial ignorance of the other party and to which that other party, if informed, would have opposed when the contract was formed (or otherwise renounced the contract), is the question (of agency theory). Yet, another highly prominent approach, rooted in sociological models mainly, the theory of 'relational contracts'[18] stresses the aspect that parties know about the unfairness best (better than judges), but often also have the better tools to retaliate and that therefore long-term relationships are better dealt with outside the courts, with private party arrangements and modes of reaction. In fact, repeated games – and therefore repeated possibilities to react to ex-post opportunism – provide for some corrective tool, but the interplay between higher risk and this additional possibility to react is much more intricate than in on-the-spot contracts, the equilibrium more difficult to reach and to maintain. All approaches can in fact be seen as interacting. Principal agent problems may increase with duration of the relationship and reduction of the possibility to choose anew. In both respects, long-term contracts are typically situated in between the firm and on-the-spot contracts, but are typically closer to the paradigm of the firm. It is evident that the long-term contract on the one hand and the on-the-spot contract ('pure market') on the other are but two extremes with many intermediate arrangements in between. What characterizes relational or long-term contracts is that no specific exchange programme is fixed; by contrast, with complete contracts the duties are quite clearly defined, and the main problem is that of enforcing them. However, relational contracts (or 'relations') establish only framework duties – with the aim that both parties profit ('symbiotically') from the relation. The content of the duties can be defined only vaguely, given the openness for an unknown and rich future. These contracts are arrangements which are designed to handle the problem of uncertainty, that is, arrangements aimed at enabling collaboration (profitable to both) despite uncertainty and anxiety about unknown developments.

Principal agent theory is concerned with the question of which structures can be found in order to reduce opportunistic behaviour by the agent whenever one party can be seen as the agent, that is, having decision power, but being asked to use it for the interests of a party or a group of parties other than itself. This is typical for a good number of long-term relationships, although not all. It is the basic scheme between management and owners in company law, but also in all management relationships where one party, because of professional expertise or because parties split tasks, is expected to act in the interest of others.

In long-term contractual relationships this may either be the one party who has decision power or both parties who should act for the benefit of the other, but also

---

18 S. Macaulay, 'Non-Contractual Relations in Business – a Preliminary Study' 28 *American Sociological Review* 55–67 (1963); MacNeil, n 15 above; O. Williamson, 'Markets and Hierarchies – Some Elementary Considerations' 63 *American Economic Review, Papers and Proceedings* 316–325 (1973); then V. Goldberg, 'Relational Exchange – Economic and Complex Contracts' 23 *American Behavioural Scientist* 337–352 (1980); Klein, Crawford and Alchian, n 13 above.

have the power to act to the other's detriment.[19] In the latter case, often occurring in multiparty contracts, there can be multiple principals and multiple agents, jointly or disjointly completing the contract. Costs (so-called agency costs) are those the agent incurs to make his commitment credible and those incurred by the principal to make contractual arrangements so the agent acts in the way expected and the costs arising from any failure in these attempts.[20] These are the costs of having a long-term relationship rather than many changing (on-the-spot) market transactions (with their search and information costs). Interdependence induces the contracting parties to have one long-term contract rather than a fragmented series of short-term contracts. In the latter case, to induce parties making specific investments would be almost impossible.

The various possible arrangements lead to different agency costs, the most important arrangements being a right to direct the other party and information rights, mechanisms which allow conflicting interests to be reconciled, that is, giving the decision-makers incentives rendering the expected behaviour as being in their own interest, and, often seen as a core device, enhancing market forces which discourage opportunistic behaviour. The latter mechanism depends on whether the parties concerned have the information needed and that situations in which the principal no longer has a choice (namely situations of relation-specific investment, also called hold-up situations)[21] are increasingly taken care of or eliminated. For this aim, the existence of the relevant markets is of core importance, for instance, markets of information exchange on how potential (long-term) partners have behaved in long-term relationships in the past.

The neglect of the three rather straight-forward features exposed at the beginning of this section, or at least the relatively little attention given to them in contract law can probably best be explained by a rather simple point on the sociology of legal scholarship: company lawyers are amazed at the idea that long-term contracts are

19 See, besides the authors quoted in the preceding note, especially Pratt and Zeckhauser (eds), n 13 above, (especially the contributions by Arrow, n 13 above, 37–51, and R.C. Clark, 'Agency Costs versus Fiduciary Duties' 55–79).

20 Groundbreaking Jensen and Meckling (1976), n 17 above, 305–60; today S. Deakin and A. Hughes, 'Economic Efficiency and the Proceduralisation of Company Law' *Company Financial and Insolvency Law Review* 169–89, 176 *et seq.* (1999); Behrens, n 3 above, 499; H. Eidenmüller, 'Kapitalgesellschaftsrecht im Lichte der ökonomischen Theorie' *JuristenZeitung* 1041–1051, 1047–1049 (2001); Ruffner, n 17 above, 131 *et seq.* On legal answers to the Principal Agent problems, see J. Armour, H. Hansman and R. Kraakman, in R. Kraakman, J. Armour, P. Davies, L. Enriques, H. Hansman, G. Hertig, K. Hopt, H. Kanda and E. Rock, *The Anatomy of Corporate Law* (2nd edn, Oxford: Oxford University Press, 2010) 35–53.

21 See references above n 13; and as well V. Goldberg, 'Regulation and Administered Contracts' 7 *Bell Journal of Economics & Management Science* 426–448, especially 439–441 (1986); and again Hart, n 13 above, 27 *et seq.*, 73–85, 87 *et seq.* (basic idea: Property Rights should be attributed to those who invest most intensively in firm-specific values).

seen as just a variant of on-the-spot transactions and are not treated as a second, independent pole of contract law. This is so because for company lawyers, dealing with the long-term nature of relationships is core business. Company lawyers are, however, very rarely contract lawyers, hence discussion of the cross-sections is weak. Publications on networks of contracts or long-term contracts indeed often stem from business or company law scholars – with their particular interest in the 'organizational' and not merely transactional aspect. Change is needed in this respect, perhaps in the wake of the financial crisis in which at least networks, as well as long-term contract-based organization played a major role (and often failed).

*Arranging for the Long-Term Relationship (With Information Regime)*

The three features discussed so far which stand out as cornerstones for a design of long-term contract law are those which have to be considered when asking the question how to arrange for the long-term relationship.

A first sub-question would seem to be whether there is not already the paradigm of a legal regime which arranges for one kind of long-term service relationship. This regime could be seen in financial services law which, at the EU level, is indeed the most thoroughly regulated regime of a particular kind of service – and in fact the only one which is thoroughly regulated. The question is in how far it can serve as a model for long-term services contract law in general. In fact, both payment services and investment services are conceived as 'mandate' or 'agency' relationships, and both are regulated at the EU level so extensively that one can even speak of (mini) codification already.[22] On the other hand, payment services (n 10) – although constituting services – largely lack the core feature specified above: the different steps in a payment transaction and in the payment systems can be forecasted quite precisely since there is a rather well specified number of possible problems arising. To a great extent, payments are mass transactions and they are organized by such highly professional players that a virtually complete contract can be written – despite the fact that the contract reaches into the future and is a service contract. This is not a contract in which the core duties cannot yet be specified very precisely already. Moreover, there is not really relation-specific investment.

At least in one type of payments service, namely in the credit card business, however, there are elements which bring this service much closer to a long-term relationship with incomplete contractual basis. This is the loan element and the element of fraudulent use of credit cards. Gillette investigates this business which,

22 See above n 12 and 14. For the density of EU 'codification' of financial services which exceeds the density of all other areas of contract (and even of company) law at the EU level, see S. Grundmann, 'European Law and Principles on Commercial and Investment Banking Contracts: An Advanced Area of Codification', in A. Hartkamp, M. Hesselink, E. Hondius, Ch. Mak and E. du Perron (eds), *Towards a European Civil Code* (4th edn, Alphen: Wolters/Kluwer, 2011) 787–817.

as suggested by Williamson, has primarily been arranged by the parties affected themselves, not primarily by public legislation, at least in the US.[23] Gillette sees the core problem in that a credible commitment to outsiders (clients) is needed which makes them adhere to the system of contracts. They test clauses in place whether they come up to this standard. The core aim is to find a 'clearly efficient pattern of behaviour or risk allocation that parties might not otherwise adhere to because they anticipate defection by others'. The threat is that, if this standard cannot be reached, outsiders would abstain – at least in the long run: despite the fact that such credit card networks can be beneficial to all parties affected, these networks would not be used because clients cannot negotiate the terms of credit card system – the network is arranged by the suppliers – in other words, the clients have problems to act collectively for their benefit. The network of suppliers would overcome this collective action problem. The authors' analysis is that 'assigning monitoring or other responsibilities to participants best positioned to undertake them, to avoid free riding or other inducements for defection' would be the basic solution reached. Thus, already this first example takes the typical form of a combination of long-term and network relationships and the problems arising from them.

The second type of financial services contract is about investment services as regulated in the MiFID (n 12). Although these are mass transactions as well, they are far less 'mechanical' and 'automated' than payment services. It seems less possible to write a (virtually) complete contract in advance in investment services, namely in contracts on investment advice or portfolio management. Despite this fact, however, investment advice is not primarily about a future behaviour and ignorance of the future does not constitute the core problem in the same way as discussed so far: there is no need to install a governance scheme for future decision taking; rather the provider of investment service has to give a description of the economic situation as it is now and at most, on this basis, a forecast for the future which, given the facts publicly known *now*, *ex ante*, is to be seen as a sensible business judgment. The main distinguishing factor is that unanticipated contingencies which arise in financial markets are *not* the object of the duties of an investment services contract. Investment advice is not primarily about forecasting the future – this risk, whether the investment prospers is, in principle, taken by the client – but about giving information and advice on two core aspects as they stand at the moment of the investment interview: the provider of investment services has to tell about the adequacy of this kind of investment for this particular kind

23 See below C. Gillette, 'Contractual Networks, Contract Design, and Contract Interpretation – The Case of Credit Cards', 77–95; O. Williamson suggested that, because of the high variety of problems encountered, governance by private party arrangement was typically preferable to (more standardized) governance regimes imposed by public regulation; see, for instance, Williamson, *The Economic Institutions*, n 13 above, 18, 20–22, *passim*. The EC Payment Systems Directive (n 10), however, catches also payment by credit cards, thus favouring a regime which tries to give equitable protection to all parties affected.

of client (given his investment aims, the financial means available and so on, 'know your customer') and about the (actual) value of the particular investment instrument (solvency and economic strength and prospects of the issuer etc).[24] Thus, investment services relationships are not primarily about future developments which the parties ignore but here one party, the professional, acquires information *existing today* that can be useful for investment choices to be made by the investor. This is a case of asymmetric information about current knowledge, not future contingencies (i.e. stock market development). Moreover in investment services contracts, relation-specific investment is not typical either. Despite this fact, however, investment services regulation is nevertheless paradigmatic at least in one aspect: it contains a core rule – in great detail – on opportunistic behaviour, the rule on conflict of interests. Providers of investment services must minimize such conflicts and, in case a conflict cannot be avoided, must not act in their own interest and one other person's (also one other client's) interest when acting for a particular client.[25] In part, of course, this also reaches into the future, for instance when acts of execution of a client's order are covered, execution, which typically leaves a lot of different options to the provider (so-called 'best execution' duty).[26] The duty to minimize conflicts of interest and always to act in the client's interest also applies, however, to any giving of investment advice and information. While it is true that asymmetric information at the moment of formation of the contract and contractual responses to uncertainty about future contingencies are different

24 See art 19 MiFID (n 12). On these two duties, see in more detail: S. Grundmann and W. Kerber, 'Information Intermediaries and Party Autonomy – the example of securities and insurance markets', in S. Grundmann, W. Kerber and S. Weatherill (eds), *Party Autonomy and the Role of Information in the Internal Market* (Berlin/New York: de Gruyter, 2001) 264–310; M. Kruithof, 'A Differentiated Approach to Client Protection – The Example of MiFID', in Grundmann / Atamer (eds), n 12 above, 105–62, 123–8 and 147–51; and references above n 12.

25 See art 13 and 18 of the MiFID (n 12). On these duties (and also on the fact that the duties could as well be derived from the old general standard of a duty of loyalty, but are spelled out in much more detail here), see L. Enriques, 'Conflicts of Interest in Investment Services: The Price and Uncertain Impact of MiFID's Regulatory Framework', in G. Ferrarini and E. Wymeersch (eds), *Investor Protection in Europe* (Oxford: Oxford University Press, 2006) 321–238; Th. Möllers, in H. Hirte and Th. Möllers, *Kölner Kommentar zum WpHG* (Cologne: Heymanns, 2007) § 31 para 73–150; N. Moloney, *EC Securities Regulation* (2nd edn, Oxford: Oxford University Press, 2010) 499–522.

26 See art 21 MiFID (n 12). On this duty, see in more detail: G. Ferrarini, 'Market Transparency and Best Execution: Bond Trading under MiFID', in M. Tison, H. de Wulf, C. van der Elst and R. Steennot (eds), *Perspectives in Company Law and Financial Regulation* (Cambridge: Cambridge University Press, 2009) 477–96; Ch. Kumpan, *Die Regulierung außerbörslicher Wertpapierhandelssysteme im deutschen, europäischen und US-amerikanischen Recht* (Berlin/New York: de Gruyter, 2006), esp. 390–94; F. Zingel, 'Die Verpflichtung zur bestmöglichen Ausführung von Kundenaufträgen nach dem Finanzmarkt-Richtlinie-Umsetzungsgesetz' *Bank- und Kapitalmarktrecht* 173–8 (2007).

issues and each requires its own contractual answers, the situation described shows that, structurally, uncertainty about the future – shared by both parties – may in certain cases also have rather similar effects for the sake of contracting as ignorance of a present situation by at least one party (or also both parties). In this case, it is the client who typically is not well equipped for detecting potential biases in the advice given (asymmetric information at the moment of formation). For him, these factors often constitute mere credence goods, which he ignores (and moreover, in case his investment does not prosper, he often also continues to ignore whether the cause was a biased advice or the risk of future development which he has to carry). In order to exclude the adverse effects of such ignorance (the quality of credence goods),[27] first the bias is eliminated as far as possible, second information is owed on this bias (to allow the client to protect himself), and finally a duty is owed to act exclusively in the interest of the client (n 23). This is a typical procedural ('governance') rule, eliminating possibilities for the partner who takes the relevant decisions – in this case the provider of investment services – to behave opportunistically. The procedure is to guide him as clearly as possible in the particular situation of conflicting interests.

Particular attention is given in this book to the problem of information (Part IV). After all, uncertainty about the future is the starting point, the phenomenon which really asks for a particular legal regime in the organizational contract. The three chapters address decisive situations: (i) information at time of formation (M. Bianca), where particular information about potential future risks is needed in the case of entering into long-term relationships, for instance, franchise relationships which are characterized by rather extensive regulation at various levels; (ii) ongoing information transfer of information not protected by (exclusive) intellectual property rights (M. Gobbato), where contracts to produce information and contracts to transfer information are distinguished and the latter are investigated more intensely, namely the pay-off between rendering this information more useful when shared by more partners and the cartelizing effect of the clauses used to protect such information against the risk of complete proliferation; and (iii) the question of how to deal with situations where an employee or partner gets the confidential information on a 'no competition' basis but then quits the relationship and cannot use his other skills without being influenced by the information

---

27 On credence goods and on their effect to hamper the allocative function of markets (and even to make certain markets disappear), see, the pioneering works of P. Nelson, 'Information and Consumer Behaviour' 78 *Journal of Political Economy* 311–29 (1970); M.R. Darby and E. Karni, 'Free Competition and the Optimal Amount of Fraud' 16 *Journal of Law and Economics* 67–88 (1973); and today W. Magat, in Newman (ed.), n 13 above, 307–10 ('Information Regulation'); Furubotn and Richter, n 13 above, 325–30; H.B. Schäfer and C. Ott, *Lehrbuch der ökonomischen Analyse des Rechts* (4th edn, Berlin et al.: Springer, 2005) 502–5.

received or at least without running this risk (A. Suñol).[28] All three chapters show an extended variety of problems in the long-term information regime, namely with respect to tools of private governance (Gobbato) and governance by legislation (Bianca, Suñol).

Organizational contracts are structurally incomplete and need to design mechanisms to acquire and distribute information among parties. There is a structural distinction between contract formation and implementation and the latter is not mere execution of the former. The common project at the basis of the collaborative endeavour often is not *ex ante* well defined; parties define and specify its characteristics after the contract is signed depending on the emerging business opportunities, the availability of resources and competences and the desired allocation of costs and benefits. Two goals have to be pursued in governance design of organizational contracts: to maximize acquisition of information and to distribute it evenly so that benefits coming from private information will not translate into opportunistic behaviour. Asymmetric information may occur among contracting parties and between them and the governance body if that is set up. In the traditional contract world the former issue is considered. For example, in a multiparty contract concerning the research directed to patenting, parties may be asymmetrically informed about the expected value of the patent and its industrial uses. In supply chain network contracts only some parties may have contact and knowledge of the needs of the main buyer while others may not be acquainted with the final market but only with intermediate ones. Asymmetric distribution of information about the potential benefits of the common project can translate into opportunistic behaviour which can either be minimized or enhanced by governance design and enforcement of duties to inform. In the world of company law, focus is primarily on asymmetry of information between principals (shareholders) and the agent (the board). Design in organizational contracting should correlate with the two questions raised above – to maximize acquisition of information and distribute it evenly – since the flow of information between contracting parties and the governing body is often a function of the initial distribution among the parties. If there is delegation to a governing body for the implementation of the project, efficiency requires that the governing body will be required to inform all the contracting parties about the potential benefits of the project regardless of the uneven initial allocation. Incentives to inform will come not only by provisions of duties but also and probably more effectively by accountability mechanisms concerning the activity of the governing body towards the participants to the network. Contractual governance will differ in bilateral, linked contracts and multiparty contracts. The latter will be closer to the corporate model whereas the

28 M. Bianca, 'Good Faith Related Disclosure Duties and a View on Franchising', in this volume 183–198; M. Gobbato, 'Long-Term Relationships, Networks and Exchange of Knowledge in Production and Distribution Contracts', in this volume 235–269; A. Suñol, 'Trade Secrets vs. Skill and Knowledge', in this volume 199–233.

former will probably adopt lighter coordination mechanisms beyond connecting contractual clauses.

## The Network Character of the Organizational Contract

### *High Practical Importance, Limited Research and Legislation*

As with the long-term character of the organizational contract, the network character, which is typical for most instances of organizational contracts is much less prominent in (legal) research than its practical importance would suggest.

The phenomenon as such clearly dominates practice (and has done so for quite some time). It is of prime practical importance. One only has to think not only of production with its manifold supply relationships around the main producer, but also distribution, which is structured around networks. Production and distribution – this is the backbone of economy – are thence both dominated by networks of contracts. Chains and networks are paramount, however, also in large parts of financial services (clearly in all payments systems, but as well in syndicated loans, in the marketing and trading of shares and bonds etc), i.e. on the capital side of market economies.[29]

Despite this importance in practice, in doctrinal thinking, networks of contracts are far less stressed as an area of inquiry than the concept of privity and relativity of contract.[30] Doctrinal discussion is still in its infancy there.[31] There is dispute namely on whether classical contract law should be applied basically unchanged, whether there should be a separate law of networks between company and contract law, nourished in part from the one area and in part from the other, or whether one should take contract law as the starting point, namely the assumption that each member is doing business separately and that, at least in

29 See G. Gereffi, J. Humphrey and T. Sturgeon, 'The governance of global value chains' *Review of International Political Economy* 78–104 (2005).

30 For a comparative analysis see the contributions by S. Grundmann, C. Aubert de Vincelles and S. Whittaker, in F. Cafaggi (ed.), *Contractual Networks, Inter-Firm Cooperation and Economic Growth* (Cheltenham et al.: Edgar Elgar, 2011).

31 R. Buxbaum, 'Is "Network" a Legal Concept?' 149 *Journal of Institutional and Theoretical Economics* 698–705 (1993); F. Cafaggi, 'Contractual Networks and the Small Business Act – Towards European Principles?' 4 *European Review of Contract Law* 493–539 (2008); Cafaggi (ed.), n 30 above; S. Grundmann, 'Contractual networks in German private law', in Cafaggi (ed.), n 30 above, 111–62 (= 'Die Dogmatik des Vertragsnetzes' *Archiv für die civilistische Praxis* 207 708–67 (2007); C. Ott, 'Contract Network in Distribution Systems' 151 *Journal of Institutional and Theoretical Economics* 212–17 (1995); G. Teubner, *Netzwerk als Vertragsverbund - Virtuelle Unternehmen, Franchising, Just-in-time aus sozialwissenschaftlicher und juristischer Sicht* (Baden-Baden: Nomos, 2004); G. Teubner, *Networks as Connected Contracts* (Oxford: Hart, 2011), with a preface by H. Collins.

principle, efforts are not pooled and gains are not shared, but, on the other hand, also use contract law instruments to respond to the peculiarities of networks and of the integration of contracts into them.[32] After all, all members of the network, even though doing business separately, have a shared interest in a functioning of the network.[33] The success of the network creates the cooperative advantage of the members participating in it, and also for contributions outside Part III, focusing on this phenomenon, the cooperative advantage is key, for instance in the line of arguments advanced by Gillette (77–95) or by Gobbato (235–269). So far, networks of contracts have been an area of research mainly for specialists in the subsets named – for instance, the area of franchising and distribution more generally – and only a few more general studies.

There is, however, some considerable input from supranational legislation (and its transposition into national laws). Both the EC Sales Directive (n 7) – for industrial production and distribution chains – and the EC Payments System Directive (n 10) – for payments chains – contain important rules on a right of redress within the chain in their Articles 4 and 75–78 respectively. The model is that the member of the chain which is linked by contract to the customer is liable for any breach for which one member of the chain (or a part of the system) is responsible, but that, as compensation, this last link (or member) in the chain has a right to redress against the next member of the chain – this series of claims continuing up to the one member which really was responsible for the breach (and therefore no longer has a right to redress to any other person). But the links among contracts are manifold; they may relate to interpretation, invalidity or also termination. For example in the unfair contract term directive unfairness can be evaluated in the light of contracts linked to that whose terms are under scrutiny.

### *The Network Character and Its Basic Problems*

Networks of contracts are highly diverse in shape:[34] stars and chains and other patterns, also combinations of stars and chains etc, can be distinguished; insiders organizing the network and outsiders only using the network can be distinguished;

32 In the first sense the large majority of traditional contract law writing which, even more often, is completely tacit on the issue. In the second sense most prominently Teubner (last footnote). In the third sense my own contributions (last footnote).

33 That there is such a 'shared objective of the network' ('*Netzzweck*'), i.e. that it forms the basis of the collaboration of all partners and that the partners are aware of this is not really disputed. See, for instance Teubner (2004), n 31 above, 86–8, *passim*; this is true as well for authors who are critical about the idea of a specific legal regime for networks of contracts, for instance, F. Niklisch, 'Vernetzte Projektverträge und vernetzte Streitbeilegungsverfahren' *Betriebs-Berater* 2166–69, 2166 *et seq.* (2000); M. Wellenhofer, 'Drittwirkung von Schutzpflichten im Netz' *Kritische Vierteljahresschrift* 187–207, 188 (2006).

34 Cafaggi, n 31 above, 501–13 and before Cafaggi, n 14 above; Wellenhofer, n 33 above, 187; M. Wolf, 'Schutz von Netzwerken gegen Eingriffe Dritter' *Kritische Vierteljahresschrift* 253–65, 253 (2006) (star patterns described as networks).

networks organized at the same production or distribution level can be distinguished from networks linking the different levels downstream or upstream. Despite this diversity, however, both the starting point and the two questions that seem to be the most fundamental ones, in principle always remain the same.

The starting point would seem to be the following: these networks in their high diversity are, of course, all distinctly formed as a conglomerate of individual relationships; in the majority of instances the network is composed of linked, connected contracts where the common aim is hard to identify (often parties do not even know the content of the other contracts), but in a minority of instances there are multiparty contracts where shared objectives and perhaps even a common aim are defined in the contract although their incompleteness may require further specification of the project and the objectives at the implementation stage. When legislation is in place the proportion might change. The new Italian legislation on network contracts provides a good illustration for this, designed more directly to multiparty contracts. This legislation illustrates the co-existence of these two models and the first empirical research shows that, under this legislation, the ratio has been inversed and out of three hundred contracts, four fifths are multiparty and one fifth is bilateral.[35]

Therefore in the connected contract model, a joint purpose is not expressly defined. Conversely, however, the parties nevertheless have the intention that contracts are linked to each other in a network, because without such a network the economic purpose could not be reached – no production, no marketing, no payment and no loan. Thus, with respect to the aim of the arrangement – no joint purpose is defined, no pooling of investments is explicitly organized but success of the network is still desired by all members (n 30) – the network of contracts is indeed a 'hybrid' between contracts and associations. Even in the connected contract model investments are interdependent. This is the case when one supply chain adopts the same regulatory requirements concerning quality management and product safety. Parties are all required to comply with the same standard and coordination takes place even when contracts remain bilateral.

Given a lack of a joint purpose no firm structure is created; the core question is which modifications to general contract law are needed because all members nevertheless have the shared objective that the network works successfully. The shared objective may affect the interpretation of individual contracts and influence how frustration or impossibility operates when contractual performance becomes impossible or impractical. Similarly in the event of breaches upstream, the costs of the final product downstream increases. It is conceivable on the one hand that the content and the interpretation of each single contract in the chain may change, albeit only in certain aspects, that, for instance, prescription may only start to run in every sales contract in a chain once the last sale downstream is made. It is conceivable on the other hand that because of this circumstance (fact), that is, because there is the shared objective to have the network succeed, direct claims

35 See F. Cafaggi, 'Learning by doing' *Contratti* 2010, pp. 1143–54.

have to be given to members of the network also outside contractual relationships, that is, to a member of the network against another member of the network with whom he does not have a contract. Thus, in both hypotheses, general contract law is modified because of the existence of a network.[36]

In fact, on the basis of this hybrid formulation of the 'shared aim', two questions would seem to stand out: the first question would seem to be whether each member of the network (or which member?) should have direct claims and liabilities against or towards other members of the network, even in cases where the two are not directly and mutually linked by contract. Whether, for instance the intended beneficiary of a credit transfer should have a direct claim against the payer's bank if this bank did not perform in time (and the payer himself may be bankrupt now or difficult to seize). This is the question of whether new (quasi-contractual) relationships should be inferred from the existence of a network of linked contract. Clearly, in the case of multiparty contract this is not an issue since each member is bound towards every participant and often to the group even if the latter does not have a legal personality. In the context of linked contracts, the legal rules existing so far – at least on the supranational level – would seem to point to an alternative way of proceeding (see below).

The second question would seem to be whether additional gains or risks which are derived from the (existence of the) network and which are made or incurred by one member of the network should be distributed to or placed upon all members of the network or – conversely – whether (absent private arrangement dealing with the question differently) all members are free to use the network and profit from its potential where they can, if this does not diminish the use of the network by others. One famous German example is whether discounts from which the franchisor profits (when he is responsible for the purchase of goods for the network and the size of the network established increases) have to be distributed proportionally to all franchisees (or whether, conversely, they have to pay the fees and prices unchanged, as fixed at the outset).[37]

36 See (also for the different opinions referred to in the text) references above n 28 and (more precisely): M. Amstutz, 'Vertragskollisionen: Fragmente für eine Lehre von der Vertragsverbindung', in *Festschrift for Rey* (Zurich: Schulthess, 2003) 161–76, esp. 168–70; Cafaggi, n 31 above, 493–539; Grundmann, n 31 above, 111–62, esp. 115–125; F. Cafaggi, in Cafaggi (ed.), n 30 above; Teubner (2004), n 31 above, 25–8, 141–3, 161, *passim*; G. Teubner, 'And if I by Beelzebub cast devils, …: An Essay on the Diabolics of Network Failure', in this volume below 113–135; Wellenhofer, n 33 above, 192, 194 and 196 *et seq., passim.*

37 See, under the case law of the German (Private Law) Supreme Court, where a separate agreement to share these profits would be needed, but has sometimes been inferred from rather general clauses in standard contract terms if they stated a duty to further the success of the network: BGH *Neue Juristische Wochenschrift* 2671, esp. 2675 *et seq.* (1999) (*Sixt*) and BGH *Neue Juristische Wochenschrift – Rechtsprechungsreport* 1554, esp. 1556 (2002) (*Hertz*); BGH *Zeitschrift für Wirtschaftsrecht* 2030 (2003) (*Apollo* – interpreting standard contract terms).

With respect to direct claims in linked contracts, the prevalent trend – both between outsiders using the network only and members of the network and between insiders all participating in the organization of the network – would seem to be indicated by the two rules at the EU level mentioned. Both Article 4 of the EC Sales Directive and Articles 75–78 of the EC Payment Systems Directive state that the client has a claim (only) against his contractual partner, but that this claim covers any breach committed by other members of the network. Conversely, both rules do not give a direct claim against other members of the network – excluding such claims also at the national level at least in the second case, given that the EC Payment Systems Directive follows the full harmonization approach. The same is true for the right of redress: the seller or bank which had to respond to the client for breach committed by a member of the chain, again does not have a direct claim (right to redress), but a claim against the direct contractual partner. One can compare the chain approach with one where there is a direct claim against the producer (where the advantages which proponents see for the chain approach are more evident), but as well with one where the chain approach is combined with a direct claim against the producer. While in some countries, namely Germany, the approach taken at the EU level is clearly favoured also from a policy perspective to strongly favour the 'chain approach only', giving only the possibility to add on a contractual basis a direct warranty against the producer,[38] there are proponents of the 'action direct' approach in other countries. This is certainly the case in France, but it has to be taken into consideration that nowadays this approach really is an approach cumulating both remedies, as the EU directives ask at least for the (mandatory) remedy against the final seller and a right of redress. These differences in policy approach need not be discussed further here, namely because the two chapters devoted to these questions are quite diverse: Teubner advocates an intuitive approach, inspired by the model of a hybrid and combining parts of the law of associations with parts of the law of contracts, advocating much more openly direct claims,[39] while, conversely, Brownsword's contribution would seem to be more reluctant to assume particular and far-reaching network effects without explicit terms or also implied terms derived from business practice (for commercial contracts) or explicit EU regulation (for consumer contracts).[40] The important

38 The core argument is seen in that this would further the smoother functioning of the chain and that the client has the possibility to choose his final seller (often with the option given that he has a direct warranty in addition). For a development of these arguments, see Grundmann, n 31 above. See there as well for the question of whether additional profits (for instance on the basis of discounts) should always be shared between all parties to a network of contracts.

39 See already references above n 28 and 32; and Teubner, n 36 above, 113–135, also on the question of whether additional profits should be shared be the network as a whole (see also last n).

40 R. Brownsword, 'Contracts with Network Effects – Is the Time Now Right?', in this volume below 137–163, and in particular 162: Contracts can (and should) be 'treated as having network effects (where this is necessary in order to give effect to the implicit

result for this chapter on the overall architecture would seem to be the following: irrespective of the disputes named, all those inquiries dealing specifically with networks of contracts are in favour of some kind of a modification of traditional contract law – in one way or another. Also, such young and Europe-wide accepted rules as the one on redress in the distribution chain (contained in Article 4 of the EC Sales Directive) would seem to indicate that European legislatures (including those of the Member States) in principle concur as well. Rather, what is disputed is whether direct claims should be the rule or only the exception or, conversely, mere modification within the single contractual link.

*Arranging for Network Relationships*

With respect to networks – as with respect to the arrangement of long-term relationships – the first question is whether a *private party arrangement* exists – and how far legislative arrangements should supplement it (as a default or even as a mandatory regime). There is a powerful policy argument which takes as its starting point the high variety of types of relationships and tasks existing in practice. The policy recommendation made on this basis is that the parties should mainly design their own governance scheme[41] – which would imply that only general framework standards (such as duty of loyalty, a duty to renegotiate when circumstances are considerably changed, or a strong equitable power of judges) are needed. Two examples of such private party arrangements are discussed in more detail in this volume: one is about the endeavour (and collaboration) within the network to offer an attractive network design and set of clauses to credit card clients (Gillette), the other is about an arrangement protecting the value of (secret) information transferred within the network while using it to the greatest shared benefit for the network (Gobbato). In both cases, the cooperative (overall) advantage is paramount; less discussed is the distribution of the benefits derived.

Such private arrangements can be supplemented by default rules which then typically serve as well as the 'shadow' under which a diverging private party arrangement is negotiated.[42] Such default rules are, however, less developed than *mandatory boundaries* to such arrangements or cornerstone regulations. The traditional field of mandatory law is antitrust law which considers networks of contracts under the paradigm of cartelizing (and restricting) competition. Its supranational and national level and its impact on the private party relationships are the subject of Martinek's chapter.[43] The traditional perspective of challenging

reasonable expectations of the parties), the occasions for having to rely on such a discretion might be (and should be) minimized.'

41 Prominently in this sense, already Williamson, for instance: n 13 above, 18, 20–22, *passim*.

42 Ground breaking R. Mnookin and L. Kornhauser, 'Bargaining in the Shadow of the Law: The Case of Divorce' *Yale Law Journal* 88 950–97 (1979).

43 M. Martinek, 'Networks of Contracts and Competition Law', in this volume 165–180.

networks of contracts, mainly because of their cartelizing effect, has first been vigorously attacked by Williamson. He stresses the beneficial aspect of cooperation gains and sees them even in the forefront in most cases.[44] Today, the dominant view, also supported by rules such as Article 101 para. 3 TFEU, is that the cartelizing effects are to be taken seriously, but that they have to be balanced against the cooperation gains (in this sense see also the chapters by Gillette and Gobbato). There are, however, increasingly other types of mandatory law for networks, typically justified as protection of weaker parties. They primarily affect professional players within the network considered in need of protection, not consumer law (which may, however, loom in the background). The most prominent rule on the supranational level – for the whole of the European Union – is that already discussed on redress, which is mandatory, at least in principle, imposing that such a right to redress cannot be contracted out. As already discussed, this is a rule in B2B relationships, but it has been enacted as a rule (also) enhancing the position of the final (consumer!) client.[45] In several national laws, very prominently in Italy, legislation has been introduced to protect professionals mostly confronted with (presumably) much more powerful professional partners – namely franchisees in their relationship to franchisors.[46]

## Organizational Contract and Company Law

### *Contract and Firm: The Two Modes of Party Autonomy Based Organization*

Contract and company ('market and firm') are the two – often alternative – basic instruments of economic planning and arrangements:[47] They are the two core areas where economic players are invited to create their own designs via party autonomy, and conversely, they are also the two core areas where business regulation sets limits to (and thereby also additionally empowers) the use of party autonomy.[48] Thus, both for party autonomy and for its limits, these are really the

44 Williamson, for instance: n 13 above, 23–9.

45 The argument for the introduction of this rule into the EC Consumer (!) Sales Directive (n 7) was that the consumer could be more confident really to have his legal warranties respected by the final seller if the final seller had at least in principle a right to redress – presumably a mandatory right; for this line of arguments, see COM(95) 520 final, 14; M. Bridge, in Bianca and Grundmann (eds), n 7 above, art 4 para 7.

46 F. Cafaggi, 'Contractual Networks and Contract Theory: A Research Agenda for European Contract Law', in Cafaggi (ed.) n 30 above.

47 Groundbreaking R. Coase, 'The Nature of the Firm' 4 *Economica* 386–405 (1937).

48 More in detail on the following see Grundmann, n 5 above, 1057–66; for parts of the text in the following see also S. Grundmann, F. Möslein and K. Riesenhuber, 'Contract Governance: Dimensions in Law and Interdisciplinary Research', in Grundmann, Möslein and Riesenhuber (eds), n 2 above, forthcoming; and also focusing rather on the interplay than on a comparison: Möslein, n 3 above, 297–319.

two paradigmatic areas. This is clearly so with respect to the party autonomy side. With respect to the regulation side, the paradigmatic character of these two areas is no less obvious and can be specified for the two most important branches or waves of regulation as follows: the dominant form of regulation with respect to competition is antitrust law and this is a law with mainly two branches, one concerning the control of cartels and the other merger control, i.e. contracts and companies. The dominant form of regulation with respect to information problems and asymmetries are again two areas which are clearly related to firm and market and both developed because of this source of market failure. They are, on the one hand, capital market and accounting law (in the area of firms) and, on the other hand, consumer law with its information model in the area of contract law.[49] Both – and their imposition worldwide – follow important developments in economic theory with respect to the effects of competitive markets from the 1930s to the 1950s (highly influential for Europe is the Freiburg School) and with respect to information economics in the 1960s and 1970s (Stigler, Akerlof and Spence).[50] Thus, both contract and company are equally about individual, private party driven design *and* market regulation and stability or, more generally, stability of organization forms and institutions. An important difference is that this is sensed much more in company law: creditor protection in company law is a key dimension, while the third party impact in contract law is not (yet). In

49 On information problems, see for the law of contracts: H. Fleischer, *Informationsasymmetrie im Vertragsrecht* (Tübingen: Mohr, 2001); S. Grundmann, 'Information, Party Autonomy and Economic Agents in European Contract Law' 39 *Common Market Law Review* 269–93 (2002); for company law see S. Grundmann, 'Information und ihre Grenzen im Europäischen und neuen englischen Gesellschaftsrecht', in *Festschrift für Lutter* (Cologne: Schmidt, 2000) 61–82; U. Grohmann, *Das Informationsmodell im Europäischen Gesellschaftsrecht* (Berlin et al.: de Gruyter, 2006); H. Merkt, *Unternehmenspublizität – Offenlegung von Unternehmensdaten als Korrelat der Marktteilnahme* (Tübingen: Mohr, 2001); for labour law, K. Riesenhuber, 'Nachweispflichten – Ansprüche auf Information über Vertragsbedingungen im Europäischen und deutschen Vertragsrecht', in *Festschrift für Bezzenberger* (Berlin: de Gruyter, 2000) 721–743. And for all areas named and the general approaches: Grundmann, Kerber and Weatherill (eds), n 24 above; also W. Schön, 'Zwingendes Recht oder informierte Entscheidung – zu einer (neuen) Grundlage unserer Zivilrechtsordnung', in *Festschrift für Canaris* (Munich: Beck, 2007) 1191–1211. It is evident that in certain sectors, namely investment services, the information paradigm reaches well beyond B2C relationships only and constitutes a true market order for all investment services (also in B2C). See, for instance, Kruithof, n 24 above, 105–162.

50 G. Akerlof, 'The Market for "Lemons": Quality Uncertainty and the Market Mechanism' 84 *Quarterly Journal of Economics* 488–500 (1970); A.M. Spence, *Market Signaling - Informational Transfer in Hiring and Related Screening Processes* (Cambridge: Harvard University Press, 1974); G. Stigler, 'The Economics of Information' 3 *Journal of Political Economy* 213–25 (1961); today, for instance, Magat, n 27 above, 307–10 ('Information Regulation'); and also Grundmann, Kerber and Weatherill (eds), n 24 above.

fact, contractual networks suggest that creditor protection is an important area for mandatory rules, including bankruptcy.

*Long-Term and Network Contract and Firm: A More Focused Couple*

The organizational contract as a particular area of contract law with its own features – as second 'pole' of contract law – comes even closer to company law. Now it is not only party autonomy – private party driven design – *and* market regulation and stability which are common pillars of the two areas, but the long-term and network character are shared as well.

This does not imply that the solutions to particular questions are often or even necessarily the same. It does, however, imply that the basic problems are still more related to each other (than between contract and company generally). Three cross-sections and common problems for long-term contractual relationships and firms can be specified as follows. Although, of course, they do not exhaust the range of common questions for which both areas can very fruitfully be compared, these three cross-sections are issues of overarching structural importance in both areas, i.e. for all long-term relationships designed by the use of party autonomy.

*Some Examples For Long-Term and Network Contract and Firm*

The common basic problems – or at least some of the most fundamental common problems – have been identified: the long-term character of the relationship brings about the problem that parties ignore the future, making it very difficult to specify *ex ante* the content of the contract. Therefore, procedures and arrangements are spelled out instead of describing particular qualities of the object of the duty. For the organizational contract, the network character of the relationships is omnipresent while in discrete exchange relationships it is possible, for instance in linked loans and sales transactions (which do form networks), but it is by no means omnipresent or even highly characteristic. A third problem – not particularly discussed in this book – is related to third party effects.[51] Again this is much more typical in the organizational contract than in the normal discrete exchange contract. Thus the long-term relationships designed by the use of party autonomy have an inside dimension and an outside dimension. The impact most discussed is probably negative external effects of the organizational scheme – contract or firm – on third parties, but there are negative effects of third parties' actions on the firm or the (long-term) contract and there are positive external effects in both senses as well.

---

51 See more extensively Part 2 in Grundmann, Möslein and Riesenhuber (eds), n 4 above, with contributions by T. Kameda and by P. Zumbansen (biological and behavioural foundations), by B. Frey and R. Cueni and by G. Teubner (economic and sociological theory), and H. Micklitz (legal consequences); and systematic discussion on the contract side in S. Grundmann and M. Renner, 'Vertrag und Dritter – System der Wechselwirkungen zwischen Vertragsrecht und Regulierung' *Juristenzeitung* (2013) 379–88, esp. 384–5.

The common feature – between contract and firm – is that the scheme is primarily designed by partners, but that the effects are born by third parties or the other way around and this peculiarity raises characteristic problems of opportunism and of alignment of incentives.[52]

a) Taking up the third example first – the *organizational scheme and third parties* – the parallels in the problems raised, as well as the difference in approaches in contract law and company law (research and practice) become particularly visible. In all the questions discussed in this respect, both the interests of those inside the organization (firm or partners to the contract or network of contracts) and the interests of those outside the organization (third parties) have to be taken into consideration. There are negative external effects of (long-term) contracts and there are negative external effects of organizations (firms) on outsiders (third parties), for instance, the negative external effect of a cartel (antitrust) or of awarding a security to the contract partner in a (hidden) way which is not visible for other creditors or the negative external effect of a merger (antitrust) or of limited liability. The (contractual or firm) arrangement may produce a negative impact on third parties. In both cases, i.e. on the side of the contract and of the firm, traditional civil law concepts have been used initially – namely the general clause which avoids legal acts which are contra *bona mores* – but more specific (public) regulation has evolved for particularly meaningful cases with a view to overcome particular problems of a civil law approach. Such problems of a mere civil law approach stem more generally from the fact that the general standard is too vague. Even more important are more particular problems, such as – for instance in the area of antitrust – that particular harm may be difficult to prove or that it may be too small and legal proceedings may be too risky so that private enforcement is weak. In both cases, the basic form of market failure is pretty much the same, i.e. that those designing the organizational scheme do not bear the burden of it,[53] and as well that this phenomenon alone does not necessarily justify prohibitions (grounds for avoidance) or regulation, rather the burden imposed

52 There are examples where the creditors, banks in particular do affect the governance design in their covenants. But for the purpose of the chapter, it is imagined that third parties have no direct influence in governance design.

53 For antitrust law, see: White Paper on Damages for Breach of Competition Law; *COM*(2008) 165 (considering also remedies such as collective actions); on this development see J. Basedow, 'Incentives and Disincentives for the Private Enforcement of EC Competition Law', in T. Eger, J. Bigus and G. von Wangenheim (eds), *Internationalisierung des Rechts und seine ökonomische Analyse* (Wiesbaden: Gabler, 2008) 499–508; G. Wagner, 'Should Private Enforcement of Competition Law be Strengthened?', in D. Schmittchen and M. Albert (eds), *The More Economic Approach to European Competition Law* (Tübingen: Mohr, 2007) 115–29; J. Zöttl, 'Weißbuch der Europäischen Kommission zu Schadensersatz in Kartellfällen' *Der Betrieb* 1200–1202 (2008); for the latest developments: V. Pinotti and D. Stepina, 'Antitrust Class Actions in the European Union: Latest Developments and the Need for a Uniform Regime' 2 *Journal of European Competition Law & Practice* 24–33 (2011).

on third parties and the value of party autonomy and of individual design based on it have to be balanced against each other. In cases where the burden is made transparent to third parties and they can avoid it by not entering into transactions with partners of the organizational scheme or the organizational scheme itself, regulation is more difficult to justify. Therefore, in many countries nowadays, the basic question is only whether the security taken is visible to other creditors and whether the amount of company capital subscribed (even if minimal) is visible to creditors. One particular difference between contract law and company law, with respect to the treatment of negative external effects, is that regulation much more specific than a mere general standard (*bona mores*) seems to be seen much more naturally as an integrative part of company law than of contract law: creditor protection is a good example. Company lawyers also tend to discuss bankruptcy in a more integrated way with company law, moreover the same scholars discuss company law and regulation, namely capital market, but also antitrust law. Often the same legislative bodies have the competence to do this. All this is much less true for contract law. There, those discussing and those setting the rules on the civil law side and those on the side of (market) regulation are typically not the same. This gives contract law a 'competitive' disadvantage with respect to an integrated research of functionally interlinking problems and functionally equivalent sets of rules.

Negative external effects of the organizational scheme on third parties are, however, by no means the only dimension of the third party relationship, but only one out of four: conversely also action by third parties – including via legal transactions – which adversely affects the organizational scheme has to be considered, for instance the headhunting of other firms' labour force or the taking of corporate opportunities. This is the setting in which negative external effects *on* the organization (contract or firm) are at stake. The problems and approaches would seem to be rather similar in this case as in the case of negative external effects *of* the organization (discussed above). Even more interesting are therefore positive effects, first by the organizational scheme, for instance the contract, on third parties (contract to the benefit or to the protection of third parties), a field in which the solutions found under German (contract) law would seem to be particularly rich and nuanced.[54] The other set of positive effects is that caused by third party action which influences the success of the organizational scheme. The most prominent example comes from company law and would seem to be takeover regimes: the rationale is seen in that the possibility of a hostile bid (for a takeover)

54 See surveys by B. Markesinis, H. Unberath and A. Johnston, *The German Law of Contract – A Comparative Treatise* (2nd edn, Oxford et al.: Hart, 2006) 186–225; and Grundmann, n 31 above, 111–62, 125 *et seq*., and 143–52; for the much narrower approach, for instance, under English Law (also after the Contracts [Rights of Third Parties] Act 1999) see R. Merkin (ed.), *Privity of Contract – the Impact of the Contracts (Rights of Third Parties) Act 1999* (London: LLP Professional Publishing, 2000); R. Stevens, 'The Contracts (Rights of Third Parties) Act 1999' (2004) 120 *Law Quarterly Review* 292–323; Markesinis, Unberath and Johnston, op cit, 181–86.

already has a disciplining effect on the board members currently in charge. This effect is based on their wanting to prevent such bids which are likely to oust them (or wanting to render such bids less likely to happen) and that, for this reason, they try to perform well, thus contributing to the rise of the stock prices of their own firm (which then would render takeover bids less likely to happen).[55] Because of these positive effects, the core question is whether these positive effects should be protected against defensive measures which would try to avoid them and whether the mechanism as such should be protected against the inherent dangers – all this by regulatory measures. The European Union has given this question an affirmative answer.[56] For contract law, the interesting question is whether similar positive effects could be imagined and furthered or protected via regulation[57] – one such example (in German Law) is that cession of receivables may not be excluded in commercial transactions, thus guaranteeing the creditor the chance to hand over the task of enforcement against renitent debtors to a more professional debt-collecting enterprise. More professional debt-collecting enterprises could, of course, also influence market structures where (some) suppliers on consumer markets heavily rely on just not responding to legal obligations, for instance in the area of e-commerce or also air transportation. In such areas it may well be a business model to decline responsibility in all cases, even if legally beyond doubt, in the hope that most consumers will not sue. Therefore, in such areas, the 'risk' that a stronger creditor steps in (enforcing consumer claims transferred to them) should perhaps be maintained via mandatory regulation.

b) With respect to the *characteristics of long-term relationships*, parallels between firm and long-term contract have already been mentioned above when discussing the three features of ignorance of the future, firm- or relation-specific investment and repeated games (see section above on the Long-Term Character and Three Basic Features). These cross-sections between firm and long-term contract can be taken up in a slightly more focused way here. The starting point – uncertainty and high level of relation/firm-specific investment – is strikingly similar in long-

---

55 For the concept of a market for corporate control, namely with respect to takeover, and their disciplining effect, see ground-breaking H.G. Manne, 'Mergers and the Market for Corporate Control' 73 *Journal of Political Economy* 110–20 (1965); the concept has been applied to private control transactions (see in the following) mainly by J.C. Jr. Coffee, 'Regulating the Market for Corporate Control – a Critical Assessment of the Tender Offer's Role in Corporate Governance' 84 *Columbia Law Review* 1145–1296 (1984); F.H. Easterbrook and D.R. Fischel, 'Corporate Control Transactions' 91 *Yale Law Journal* 698–737, especially 714–721 (1981/82).

56 Directive 2004/25/EC of the European Parliament and the Council of 21 April 2004 on takeover bids, *OJEC* 2004 L 142/12. For literature and a condensed description of the Act and legal and economic theory behind it, see S. Grundmann, *European Company Law – Organisation, Finance, and Capital Markets* (2nd edn, Antwerp et al.: Intersentia, 2012) § 30.

57 For the following, see more extensively again Grundmann and Renner, n 51 above, 379–88.

term contracts and firms (companies) but the combination between hierarchy and cooperation might differ.

The core conflict to be dealt with in company law is the principal agent relationship between owners and management. This implies that the parallelism is with a particular kind of long-term contract relationship: that of agency structure where the basic duty of one side is to take the interests of the other side as the guideline for their own actions, particularly relevant in multiparty contracts where the implementation of the project is delegated to an appointed body. This is the model of pure agency (mandate). A second important model is that of parties deciding jointly in the pursuit of a shared objective. In company law the first issue is associated to the relationship between management and shareholders whereas the second is related to the relationship among shareholders and the duties owed by a majority towards a minority. The latter point is conceived more as an incomplete contracting problem than as an agency question. Conversely, the agency dimension is strong where there is a delegation in the execution of the contract to a separate body as also often happens in network contracts. Not all long-term contract relationships are of either type – quite a few are rather ongoing exchange relationships, for example, supply chains etc. On the other hand, elements of agency – or trust – partly also of joint decision taking in a shared objective, are important in these other relationships whenever one party hands over assets or positions to the other with a view to make collaboration more efficient, as in the case of project financing. Valuable information (for instance trade secrets), if provided by one side, may be an example (see Part IV). If the principal agent relationship and the principal agent theory is one common starting point – at least for the agency type relationships – the most important difference between firm and long-term contract in this respect would seem to be that principals are more difficult to define in company law, more heterogeneous, given the multitude of stakeholders (if a particular company law obliges the board to take their interests into account) or also given the heterogeneous structure of shareholders (if only their interests count).[58] A pure shareholder value approach would even seem to

58 Whether only shareholders are considered to be included or also other stakeholders is, of course, one of the core divergences which can be sensed in the corporate governance debate in different parts of the world, namely between Europe and the US. See for this and an increasing trend towards stakeholderism recently: R.E. Freeman, 'A Stakeholder Theory of the Modern Corporation', in L. Hartman (ed.), *Perspectives in Business Ethics* (3rd edn, New York: McGraw-Hill, 2004) 112–22; A. Keay, 'Moving Towards Stakeholderism? Constituency Statutes, Enlightened Shareholder Value, and More: Much Ado About Little?' 22 *European Business Law Review* 1–49 (2011); A. Keay, 'Shareholder Primacy in Corporate Law: Can it Survive? Should it Survive?' 7 *European Company and Financial Law Review* 369–413 (2010); or, describing more objectively the main stream in the different countries: *Modern Company Law – For a Competitive Economy – The Strategic Framework – A Consultation Document from the Company Law Review Steering Group*, (2/1999) 37–51, available at http://www.bis.gov.uk/; K. Hopt, 'Common Principles of Corporate Governance in Europe?', in B. Markesinis (ed.), *The Clifford Chance Millennium Lectures – The Coming*

come closest to the often simpler model of long-term contracts with one clearly defined principal. This difference, however, while being striking when firms and bipolar long-term relationships are compared, may well diminish when networks of long-term relationships are taken into account and when the problem arises also in the contractual setting to define whose interest as a principal is to be taken into account by an agent taking decisions. There is evidence that in global value chains external stakeholders influence both the design and the implementation of network contracts.[59]

If ignorance about the future and firm-/relation-specific investment are common starting points, the solutions which the law finds to solve the problems for long-term contracts would often seem not to go as far as in company law. Stringent rules on termination, for instance, may protect firm-/relation-specific investment. There is, however, also the danger of keeping the other partner too extensively to the agreement – for instance, with respect to the conditions of termination of labour contracts or credit contracts or also partnership agreements. A termination regime which is too protective increases this danger. The regimes diverge quite considerably, and this would certainly be yet another important feature on a comparative research agenda for long-term contractual and long-term firm relationships. Typically, company law opts for termination rights as very exceptional remedies only: in the law of partnerships, typically universal consent or a very serious cause is asked for; in the law of limited liability firms, in many countries the withdrawal of capital (exit) is possible only in a winding-up procedure. If a shareholder wants to 'exit' before this, he can do so only indirectly via a sale of his share to another investor. However recent law reforms have relaxed these requirements in some countries and widened exit opportunities. Conversely, the law on long-term contracts typically even gives the right to termination after a certain period of time without particular reason – putting an end not only to all duties, but also to the use of investment made by the other party. In other words, even though the starting point is the same, the legal regime on long-term contracts law typically still contains more of a market element. This trend can be seen in other aspects as well, for instance with respect to how far information is shared by all parties, and how far instruction rights and other elements of hierarchy

*Together of the Common Law and the Civil Law* (Oxford: Hart, 2000) 105–32, 118 *et seq.*; comparative law survey in E. Wymeersch, 'A Status Report on Corporate Governance Rules and Practices in Some Continental European States', in Hopt, Kanda, Roe, Wymeersch and Prigge (eds), n 3 above, 1045–1199, 1079–87 (recognizing consensus in that there should be scrutiny always only when clearly defined procedures have been violated). Even in the US, in principle, stakeholder interests may at least be taken into account: groundbreaking *Shlensky* v *Wrigley*, 237 NE2d 776, 778–780 (IllAppCt 1968).

59 For a broader analysis see F. Cafaggi, 'Compliance and remedies of regulatory provisions in transnational commercial contracts', paper presented at the HIIL conference held in Firenze, April 2012, showing how private regulators and certifiers affect contractual design and supplement remedies for breach of contract which constitutes at the same time breach of regulatory and certification provisions.

are woven into the relationship. This trend is indeed a common denominator – gradually distinguishing both regimes. Of course, many solutions are only default solutions so that firm and long-term contract can be modelled after each other via party agreement to a large extent. At the core of the distinction is the different protection of stability. In company law, exit is limited – also on behalf of creditors. In network and organizational contracts, the absence of limited liability grants higher protection and makes individual exits less destabilizing. Often, as shown by the Italian case law on network contracts, individual withdrawal is not combined with the right to take back the resources that had been supplied.

Also the procedure on how to reach decisions responds to the same problem – the need to adapt to the future development once it is known – and therefore it is not astonishing that again solutions are similar to a certain extent, yet also different in other respects. If the duty to be performed cannot be fixed in advance, procedures have to be established to reach decisions once the moment has come. There are many possible mechanisms for doing so. It is a core question of the law of long-term relationships – both contractual and in the company law setting – how they are fixed. In all cases, procedure becomes paramount. Agency is a core instrument in this context, especially when there is delegation – the basic model of a duty to decide in the interest solely of the principal which also applies in company law. This basic model brings about far-reaching similarities between the treatment of a contractual long-term relationship and long-term relationships in companies in agency relationships, namely of the duty of the board to further the interests of the company/shareholders. The discussion of this duty in company law, however, is refined in all details; for that of contractual long-term relationships of the agency type, much less so. In other words, the principal agent theory which deals in particular with the question of how actions have to be taken in the interest of another person (or pool),[60] must be seen as a theory of company *and* contract law. The core difference between firm and long-term contract in this respect is that the right of the principal to instruct the agent is typically less direct in the law of the firm, at least for the corporation, and that there is a (majority) regime in the law of the firm for principals' decision making – a regime which in networks of long-term relationships needs to be planned for in advance, for instance if indeed the 'principal' is a multiparty body in this context as well.

Differences might arise if there is no delegation in network contracts. In this instance, contracts are incomplete due to uncertainty, but completion is not delegated to a body. Rather the same contracting parties define procedures, including renegotiation, to complete *ex post* the contract. The company and contract law models might here diverge in the combination between transaction and monitoring costs to complete contracts. In the company law model, the benefits of delegation have to be balanced with the costs of monitoring agents to avoid

60 Path-breaking Jensen and Meckling (1976), n 17 above, 305–60; Jensen and Meckling (1983), n 17 above, 301–25; see also other references above n 16.

moral hazard. In the contractual network model, without delegation, transaction costs are higher while monitoring costs are lower.

In the overall panorama, however, namely with respect to risks (and chances) stemming from long-term duration of the relationship, the similarities between the setting of company law and the setting of long-term contractual relationships are particularly evident and striking. The examples given can all be formulated as contractual ones – as in Williamson's famous example of a work force hired for a place in Alaska, asking how ownership rights and investment in housing should be arranged and how the same rights apply in the local retail store. The model of low search costs and high agency costs (Jensen/Meckling, last note) is well adapted both to the company law setting and to long-term contractual relationships – more or less depending on the degree of stabilization, for instance via termination prerequisites. It is always the legal shaping of the relationship – in the company law setting *or* in a contractual setting – which makes it adopt more of one characteristic or of the other, but the particular mix can be largely identical in contractual long-term relationships and in partnerships/companies: with respect to termination prerequisites, with respect to the important question of compensation, with respect to inspection rights into the other actor's actions, and with respect to decision-taking rights – albeit only on the basis of individual party arrangement.

c) Also with respect to the *network character of (many) long-term contracts* (see the section above on the network character), the comparison between firm and long-term contract can be taken up a bit more systematically here. While networks of contracts are not intensively discussed in legal scholarship, their existence is evident and not disputed. Conversely, the network concept in company law is one which is used only by a particular strand of (economic) theory. The company/corporation is conceived as a network of (bilateral, 'contractual') relationships between all members (shareholders), potentially even with the stakeholders whose interests enjoy legal protection under company law. This configuration is best reflected in the idea of company as a nexus of contracts. This is the perfect model for methodological and normative individualism[61] and explains beautifully why there should be a claim if a legally protected interest or even right of one member should give rise to a claim against another member if harmed by this other member's action.[62]

---

61 Ground-breaking for the theory of a '*nexus of contracts*': A. Alchian and H. Demsetz, 'Production, Information Costs, and Business Organization' 72 *The American Economic Review* 777–95 (1972); Coase, n 47 above; S. Cheung, 'The Contractual Nature of the Firm' 26 *The Journal of Law and Economics* 1–21 (1963); Jensen and Meckling (1976), n 17 above, 305–60; W.A. Klein, 'The Modern Business Organization – Bargaining under Constraints' 91 *Yale Law Journal* 1521–64 (1982); O. Williamson, 'Corporate Governance' 93 *Yale Law Journal* 1197–1230 (1984).

62 In this respect, it is an interesting development, for instance, that under the German Law on the Plc, in particular situations a fiduciary duty may even be owed by small shareholders to large shareholders: see mainly Bundesgerichtshof/Supreme Court – *Official*

Taking up the two core questions raised above on the arranging of network relationships, namely whether (i) direct claims and liabilities should be presumed between members of the network not directly linked by a contract, also a multiparty contract between them and whether gains or risks resulting from the increase or the shape of the overall network should be shared ('communitarized') – it would seem as if the starting point was clearly different: costs and gains are pooled as a matter of principle in company law, for both of them there is a share fixed for each member, and even if this share may be very different – up to the extreme of a *societas leonina* – yet it is a share of a pooled investment and a pool of gains which is then distributed. The basic assumption in most laws would seem to be that each member has the right to keep the 'same' proportional share in the profits (and, as a starting point, also in the decision making power) and that each (other) member has the duty to respect this principle and not to gain hidden additional profits.[63] Conversely, the starting point in networks of contracts is no such pool, but individual separate accounts. Of course, there are also arrangements of multiparty contracts – based on one common agreement – where the scope is really common to all parties or at least to a specified extent is common to all parties. In this case, the seemingly contractual arrangement, of course, follows more closely the model on which partnerships and companies more generally are based. In theory, the distinction is preserved claiming that in contract the common objective is instrumental to the individual interests while in company law individual interests are subject to the primacy of the common objective. In practice in company arrangements, shareholders participate in the common project to achieve individual objectives. Hence the distinction is a matter of procedural balance rather than substantive interests; it allows for the application of different sets of rules and arrangements for diverging preferences, namely with respect to sharing of profits.

One consequence from the difference in principle sketched above is that, in company law, any profit made by only one member on the basis of the pooled investment, for instance the taking of a corporate opportunity which the company has received because of investing in good partner relationships, coincides necessarily with a decrease of the assets in the pool and thus in the harm done to the share of all other members. This speaks in favour of some divergence also in the solutions to the two core questions asked: While the division among all members of any added income (but also loss) is evident in the setting of firms, the same is at least not evident in the setting of networks of contracts. In fact, the majority view (see section above on the network character and its basic problems)

---

*Reports: BGHZ* 103, 184, 194 (*Linotype*); case law of long standing tradition today, see for instance *BGHZ* 129, 136, 142–144 (*Girmes*) (also small investors); *BGHZ* 142, 167, 169 *et seq*. (*Hilgers*).

63 In some legal systems, it is possible to correlate the gains and profits made by each company to the activities and participation of individual members rather than the resources transferred to the company. This is often the model in cooperatives and similar forms.

would seem to be that, absent an agreement in this sense, these additional gains and losses remain with the party who has made them. This criterion may be at odds with incentives to engage into cooperative behaviour. Parties would be induced to act only to the extent they can appropriate gains from the activity. On the other hand, it may as well be that most of the input comes from one player. If gains and losses are attributed to the entire network, two different default rules are available: one which divides equally among the members, the other which correlates the amount of profit or losses to the resources each party has contributed to the common project.

And with respect to direct claims between members not linked by contract, the majority view at least in supranational legislation (see section above) would seem to not include direct contractual warranties etc. Where this line is followed, all claims are to be made within the contractual relationships; a right to redress, however, largely bridges this gap between members not directly and mutually linked by contract. Conversely, in the setting of firms, direct claims would seem to follow from the common entitlement in the common pool. This is not questioned by the fact that, in many jurisdictions, claims attributed to the pool (firm) are to be made primarily by the management of the joint pool, and members' direct claims (so-called derivative suits) are to be seen as the exception which applies only if the management abusively refuses to act. This modulation does not contradict the direct entitlement of all members against all members in principle, but rather streamlines collective action: as in the setting of firms, all other members would have the direct claim in principle against the member taking corporate property rights, and their claims would need to be coordinated anyway.

As a final result, however, it should be stressed that while core questions may have to be solved in different ways in the settings of firms and of networks of contracts – for instance sharing of profits as the core principle in company law and rather a principle of split accounts, costs and income in the network of (individual) contracts, with some deviation in the case of a genuine multiparty contract – all core questions have to be asked in a very similar way both in the company law and in the (network of) contracts setting: whether an added income which the network creates or added costs which it incurs should be shared by all – albeit not necessarily in the same proportion; which decision mechanisms should apply (majority, unanimity/consensus) with which management powers delegated to one core decision body (such as the franchisor or the board); and in how far there should be direct claims between the members. And because of extended party autonomy, in each setting the default rule of the other setting – insofar as it diverges – can also be integrated by drafting of the contract or the charter.

## Summary

The organizational contract is a phenomenon of such high practical importance that a solid research agenda is needed and proposed. Its two core features – the long-term and the network character – have both received considerable attention in interdisciplinary theory. Research can also profit from a comparison with parallel problems in other organizational schemes of private law, namely in the organization of the firm (company law) where discussion is much more extensive. It can profit from such comparison despite the fact that answers – to similar questions – may be different nevertheless. One obstacle in traditional contract law thinking has, however, to be removed: this is the *presumptio similitudinis* with the on-the-spot contract. The core characteristics of long-term organizational relationships diverge too much from those of on-the-spot contracts, namely the impossibility to forecast the future and the content of the core duty – provoking a need for other types of rules, namely procedural or 'governance' rules – and the importance of relation- or firm-specific investment. Conversely, the repeated games paradigm can play an increased role in establishing the equilibrium needed. It may well be that these characteristics also ask for a more nuanced interplay between default rules (rather than framework rules) and specific private party arrangements, i.e. for an increased need for the latter.

# PART II
# The Structure of Long-Term Contractual Cooperation

# Chapter 2
# Dissecting Long-Term Contracts: A Law and Economics Approach

Mireia Artigot i Golobardes and Fernando Gómez Pomar

## Introduction

Contracts are legal instruments that allow parties to cooperate by making binding commitments both more credible and less costly in economic and social interactions. Such cooperation may take place in relationships over extended periods of time creating what has been identified in the economics literature[1] as long-term contracts or contracts that extend over a long period of time, often referred to as relational contracts.[2]

Relationships that last a long time do not necessarily require a certain type of contract, a given contract length or even a formal contract at all and hence may be governed by a long-term contract or by successive short contracts. All long-term contracts are contracts that aim at structuring the relationship between the contracting parties over a long period of time but not all contractual relationships that have certain duration are structured around a long-term contract.

The Law and Economics[3] literature has highlighted three major dimensions of long-term contracts: the existence of specific investments, the inherent incompleteness of long-term contracts and the complexities arising from breach and termination that directly affect the drafting of the long-term contract.

Specific investments are investments that one party – or both, in certain cases – may undertake in order to enhance the value and/or reduce the cost of performing his or her obligations under the contract. The main characteristic of this kind of investment is the fact that their value depends on whether they are used by parties within the contractual relationship or outside of it.[4] Whenever such investments have value in the contract between the parties but are worth nothing outside of it or when the contract ends, these investments are called pure specific investments. In cases where pure specific investments are involved, the party undertaking such investments is particularly vulnerable to what is called the hold-up problem that might be subject to the strategic behaviour of the other party in the contract

1 Williamson (1985).
2 Hviid (1999).
3 De Geest (2006).
4 Becker (1962).

once these investments have been done. Consequently, such specific investments strongly influence the parties' strategies and incentives to cooperate between them.

A second major characteristic of long-term contracts is their inherent uncertainty linked to the time frame of the contract and the resulting impossibility of drafting a complete contract that could foresee and solve all potential contingencies that could arise during its life span.[5] When any contract is designed, parties face the *ex ante* challenge of foreseeing and including all clauses to address the potential issues that may affect the contractual relationship between the parties.[6] In other words, all contracting parties face the challenge of addressing uncertainty and aiming at drafting a complete contingent contract. This challenge is especially difficult in long-term relations because of the time frame they try to cover. For that reason, long-term contracts often include renegotiation clauses so that parties can adjust the contract terms to the new circumstances of the contract during its life span.[7] Incompleteness characterizes all contracts, not solely long-term contracts, but is especially critical in the context of long-term contracts.

Finally, long-term contracts present great difficulties regarding the determination of adequate remedies for breach of contract. Due to the long duration of the interaction, the multiplicity of types and events of relevant contractual conduct, the proliferation of instances of potential shading and shirking by the parties, the chances that these non-complying contractual behaviours can be shown, in a sufficiently convincing manner, to a court or other external adjudicator, is significantly lower than in a spot contract with a smaller range of contractually relevant behaviours. Further, typical remedies such as specific performance and damages are more difficult to assess and enforce in a long-term contract. The capacity of contract clauses to address these issues and appear as adequate remedies for breach so far has been low.

This chapter will be structured as follows: section two will present the major features that differentiate between long-term and short-term contracts; section three will discuss the most important parameters affecting the optimal contract length; section four will present other questions inherent to long-term contracts; section five will describe the major aspects on contract drafting and design; section six will discuss the major issues concerning contract renegotiation and breach;

5 Schwartz (1992).

6 Salanié (1997) defines a complete contract, one that considers 'all variables that may have an impact on the conditions of the contractual relationship during its whole duration have been taken into account when negotiating and signing the contract'. It should be noted that under this definition, a contract would be complete, despite not regulating all potential foreseeable circumstances, if there were not a change of circumstances that would affect the contract.

7 Some authors consider that whenever parties do not have the need to revise or renegotiate the contract, such contracts could be considered comprehensive contracts. Hart (1995).

section seven will present the consequences of termination and breach. The article will end with brief conclusions.

## Long-Term versus Short-Term Contracts

The legal nature and regulation of long-term contracts does not significantly differ from the regulation of short-term contracts or contracts in general even though long-term contracts present special features and complexities.

Contracts are legal instruments that allow parties to establish binding commitments that serve as mechanisms for creating value, as well as for deciding how it will be divided.[8] Legal systems typically establish – not entirely in the same way across legal traditions – a set of requirements in order to have a legally enforceable contract beyond what could be a simple agreement between two parties. Among these elements there is one that requires that the agreement meets a minimum level of definiteness[9] so that parties, for the contract to be enforceable, need to be in a reasonable position and have enough information to understand and agree on the contract terms, and in the case of breach or disagreement between them, that the courts have sufficiently precise information on what the contract required, so as to be able *ex post* to solve the grievances of the contract parties and award damages, if suitable.

Protracted relationships may be governed by long-term contracts or by a series of short-term contracts. Their content, though, will be quite different. Both kinds of contractual structures – long-term or short-term – would include essential contract requirements such as a reasonably defined contract object, and include a contract price – even though it is not a mandatory element in some jurisdictions. Additionally, long-term contracts may also include contract governance provisions over the long term, renegotiation provisions, contract remedies in case of breach, and parameters that may affect the parties' bargaining position within the contractual relationship.

The choice between a short-term contract – or a series of them – or a long-term contract depends on which type of instrument fits best the nature of the parties' relationship and the context in which the contractual relationship takes place. Several elements of the contract will be different depending on whether the contract used is a short-term or a long-term contract.

Despite the shared essential legal requirements of any contract – short-term or long-term – issues such as definiteness, uncertainty and specific investments will appear differently depending on the chosen contract length. For example, long-term contracts may not require a level of definiteness as high as short-term contracts need, and might leave a bigger scope of discretion for the contracting

8 Goldberg (1995).

9 In general see also Zweigert and Kötz (1998). For French law see Philippe (2005); for Dutch law, Asser-Hartkamp (2000).

parties in order to be able to adjust the contract terms to the circumstances and needs of the contracting parties. Hence, long-term contracts tend generally to be more open-textured than short-term contracts. In contrast, long-term contracts may include many elements and parameters that might not be considered necessary in the context of short-term contracts. For example, given that parties are aware of the risk arising from specific investments, they will also be more interested in defining the consequences of breach in the case where one party has already undertaken specific investments.[10]

Some voices in the literature have discussed whether long-term contracts require different contract rules because of the specific issues presented by them regarding specific investments parties must make or their inherent incompleteness that derives from the lack of information available to contracting parties when the contracts are drafted.[11] But up to now, long-term contracts seem to share in most legal systems the same basic regulatory framework as short-term contracts.

There is no general rule to determine generally whether certain relationships should be governed by a long-term or by a series of short-term contracts. Such decision will depend on the nature of the parties' relationship and the nature and goals of the contract they entered into.

But certain issues on the performance of short-term and long-term contracts have been discussed in the literature and will be presented here. First, whether parties have complete or incomplete information; second, whether the parties' commitment is important for the contractual relationship; and third, whether specific investments are essential elements of the contract.[12]

These elements are developed below.

### *Information Available to the Contracting Parties*

We should distinguish between two different situations: first, where contracting parties have perfect information available to them, and second, where contracting parties have incomplete information.

When parties have perfect information, parties considering entering into a long-term contract would be able to foresee and contract over all potential contingencies that may take place during the contractual relationship. Given that all potential contingencies could be considered, renegotiation would not be

10 Goldberg and Erickson (1987), Joskow (1988) and Solís-Rodríguez, and González-Díaz (2009).

11 De Geest (2006).

12 Fudenberg, Holmstrom and Milgrom (1990) identified sufficient conditions – all public information is contractible, there is no information asymmetry when the contract is entered and contracts are renegotiated – for short-term contracts to achieve the same outcomes as long-term contracts. See also Salanié and Rey (1990) and Chiappori, Macho, Rey and Salanié (1994).

necessary.[13] In such a situation contract terms could be governed either through a series of short-term contracts or with a long-term contract. Further, if commitment was irrelevant for the contracting parties, short-term contracts could be equivalent to long-term contracts when information was perfect.

Sometimes specific investments are a decisive parameter for entering into a long-term contract. One of the problems presented by specific investments is that they are often not contractible. Whenever information is perfect and specific investments are verifiable, the incentives on making such investments will depend on them being verifiable and not on the contract length – and on whether the contract entered into is a short-term or long-term contract.[14]

Consequently, whenever parties have perfect information and can negotiate contract terms at no cost, a short-term contract can be as efficient as and the equivalent of a long-term contract.[15]

In contrast, when there is incomplete information either by both parties of by one of them, the performance and outcomes of short-term or long-term contracts may be significantly different. Further, the possibilities of renegotiation and its cost may be relevant for the performance of short-term and long-term contracts.[16]

One of the major advantages presented by short-term contracts is the possibility they offer of inter-temporal smoothing so that parties can adjust to the information asymmetries between them. When some future outcomes are uncertain, when there are risks involved during the life of the contract, or unobservable actions by the parties that may affect the outcome of the contract, short-term contracts seem to present significant advantages.[17] However, the advantages are not always so clear cut.

But when other elements, such as commitment – present in long-term contracts – is an essential element of the contract, a long-term contract strictly dominates a short-term contract.[18] This advantage ensues from the fact that the incentive problems created by private information not revealed by contracting parties, are generally better overcome through *ex ante* commitment than through

13 If parties had perfect information and renegotiation were not costly long-term contracts would be preferred whenever one of the parties' investment was a sunk cost and the contract could be a way to smooth consumption. In these cases, some have suggested that long-term contracts would serve as a substitute for an efficient credit market. Crawford (1988).

14 Dutta and Reichelstein (2003), using a single variable model in a multi-period contract, concluded that in these cases the hold-up problem present in long-term contracts is significantly mitigated.

15 See Rey and Salanié (1990) noting that this result is achieved using a multi-period agency model where at the beginning of each period one of the parties (the principal) can propose a contract to the other (the agent), on a take-it-or-leave-it basis.

16 Freixas, Guesnerie and Tirole (1985).

17 Rey and Salanié (1990).

18 Rey and Salanié (1990).

solving conflicts *ex post* that will result in inefficiencies.[19] However, because long-term contracts can rely on and observe in the second period the returns of the investment made, this could generate incentives to invest, which could result in a better performance of long-term contracts in such a context.[20]

The problems presented by private information may be overcome by eliminating the possibility of renegotiation. Even where there is asymmetric information, short-term contracting could implement optimal renegotiation-proof contracts.[21] Leading indicator variables may become useful if the principal is confined to renegotiation-proof contracts even though there are authors who still prefer long-term commitment whenever possible than the information provided by indicator variables.[22]

*The Importance of Commitment in the Parties' Decision on Contract Length.*

One of the elements that may be crucial when determining the choice between short-term and long-term contracts is the importance of commitment in the context of the contract and related to this, whether renegotiation if feasible and if so, how costly.[23]

Long-term contracts entail a higher level of commitment so that renegotiation is not so essential and may be avoided.[24] Whenever renegotiation is costly, the commitment element of long-term contracts may imply important savings in transaction costs.[25] But even if renegotiation is not costly, long-term contracts can still be preferable to a series of short-term contracts whenever the parties' investment may be a way to smooth consumption.[26]

Under conditions of perfect information, commitment solves the parties' inter-temporal trade-offs. Hence, long-term contracts will be preferred to short-term contracts whenever they cannot solve such trade-offs outside of the relationship and

19 For an analysis of long-term contracts with private information, Baron and Besanko (1984).

20 Dutta and Reichelstein (2003).

21 Malcomson and Spinnewyn (1988).

22 Sliwka (2002).

23 The value of commitment has been widely discussed in the literature. Williamson suggested that short-term contracts have emerged in order to avoid the difficulties of specifying and enforcing the contingencies inherent in long-term contracts. See Williamson (1985), Dye (1985) and Hart and Holmstrom (1987).

24 Malcomson and Spinnewyn (1988) in the context of a principal agent model under asymmetric information show that, whenever there is no renegotiation, a long-term contract can perform better than a short-term contract when one of the parties – principal or agent – commits to a payoff which is lower than the potential outcome under a short-term contract. Therefore, long-term contracts have some commitment element that makes them preferable to a series of short-term contracts.

25 Hart and Holmstrom (1987).

26 Crawford (1988). Some have suggested that in these cases long-term contracts serve as a substitute for an efficient credit market.

hence commitment was necessary to achieve long-term efficiency.[27] The same result would be true in cases where risk-sharing between the contracting parties presents moral hazard problems.[28] But if inter-temporal trade-offs or commitment is not that important, short-term and long-term contracts could be equivalent.[29] Accordingly, long-term contracts will in general dominate sequences of spot contracts.

*The Possibility of Parties' Renegotiation*

In light of the commitment element inherent to long-term contracts, the need for renegotiation is reduced significantly.[30] When renegotiation is costly, transaction costs of long-term contracts are lower than short-term contracts and therefore long-term contracts are preferred.[31] But if, instead, renegotiation is costless and parties have perfect information, long-term contracts are still preferred whenever the contract represents a way to smooth consumption for at least one of the parties involved.[32]

*The Importance of Specific Investments*

The literature[33] has identified the conditions under which optimal long-term contracts induce larger investments and less reliance on indicator variables compared to short-term contracts, and the conditions under which parties do better with a series of short-term contracts than with a long-term contract.

---

27 There is abundant literature discussing the importance of commitment as a mechanism to solve inter-temporal trade-offs whenever there is no access to credit markets. If both parties had access to perfect credit markets they would only care about the present value of the outcome and not about the time frame, there would exist a number of optimal contracts, all of which would have the same present value of the contract outcome in every state of nature, at least one of the contracts would meet all conditions for an optimal short term contract and therefore would be equivalent to a long-term contract with commitment. See Rey and Salanié (1990).

28 Lambert (1983) and Rogerson (1985).

29 Rey and Salanié suggest that short-term contracts could be interpreted as loan contracts which could enable the principal of the contract to implement the optimal long-term contract without being limited by short-term constraints. Rey and Salanié (1990).

30 Malcomson and Spinnewyn (1988) in the context of a principal agent model under asymmetric information show that, whenever there is no renegotiation, a long-term contract can perform better than a short-term contract when one of the parties – principal or agent – commits to a payoff which is lower than the potential outcome under a short-term contract. Therefore, long-term contracts are endowed with some commitment element that may make them preferred to a series of short-term contracts.

31 Hart and Holmstrom (1987).

32 Crawford (1988). Some have suggested that in these cases long-term contracts serve as a substitute for an efficient credit market.

33 Dutta and Reichelstein (2003).

In the context of principal agent contracts, long-term contracts create incentives for the agent to overinvest – or to invest inefficiently – due to an existing moral hazard problem by which the agent knows that he will not assume any risk of over-investing or of not making the most efficient investment decision for the principal's benefit. In these cases, the principal does better with several short-term contracts that may entail agent rotation; that is, there may be a new agent in the second period. As a consequence, the agent's incentives to overinvest are controlled because he knows he may be replaced in the next period.

In order for the performance of short-term and long-term contracts to be equivalent, two conditions are necessary: renegotiation should not be possible so that the commitment value of long-term contracts would not be reduced and short-term contracts should allow smoothing of consumption.[34]

It should be noted that the length of long-term contracts is not the most important or essential parameter; what is important is to what extent a contract of a given length locks the parties into the relationship.[35]

## Factors to Consider when Determining the Optimal Contract Length

As explained above, there is no general optimal contract for all situations but an optimal contract and an optimal length for each kind of relationship depending on the context, the parties' interests, their size, characteristics, informational structure, and their attitude towards risk.

The relationship between performance and contract length has been widely studied.[36]

### *Contract Length/Contract Price Trade-Off*

When contracting parties value certainty, they will prefer the higher certainty provided by a longer contract and hence will be willing to trade a lower consideration for a longer contract.[37]

---

34 Chiappori, Macho, Rey and Salanié (1994); Fudenberg, Holmstrom and Milgrom (1990); Malcomson and Spinnewyn (1988) and Rey and Salanié (1990).

35 The length that should be considered is the nominal length of the contract. See Aghion and Bolton (1987).

36 Particularly in the context of sports' contracts: Krautmann and Oppenheimer (2002), Maxcy (2004) and Maxcy (1997).

37 Krautmann and Oppenheimer looked at the relationship between player salaries and contract length, and suggested that when players are more risk averse than club owners, they are willing to receive a lower salary in exchange for a longer contract. Krautmann and Oppenheimer (2002).

*The Parties' Attitudes Towards Risk and Contract Length*

The attitude of contracting parties towards risk also has an effect on the contract length. The more risk-averse one of the contracting parties is, the more this party will want certainty and will be willing to insure.[38] This means that when a contract party is risk-averse, she will prefer a long-term contract over a series of short-term contracts.

*The Parties' Incentives to Invest and Length of Contract*

From a theoretical perspective, a long-term binding contract should be able to induce more investments from the parties in light of the elements of certainty and commitment present in this kind of contract. The literature, though, suggests that the evidence is not so conclusive.[39] Even though short-term contracts result in underinvestment, the optimal long-term contract may result in under- or overinvestment depending on the importance of agency problems.[40]

What seems to be unanimous in the literature is the fact that contract length is determined by the trade-off between the costs of entering into a new contract – the costs of re-contracting – and the costs associated with the incompleteness of the contract.[41]

*The Parties' Performance and Length of Contract.*

Contract length may also affect the parties' incentives to perform.[42] The unverifiability of performance regarding many dimensions of the parties' obligations, the use of quasi-rents within the relationship, enhanced by the presence of specific investments, require indefiniteness in the contract terms which is easier to obtain with a longer-term contract with the possibility of termination.[43]

Further, parties' performances may not be smooth across all contract phases and tend to vary depending on the moment of the life of the contract, so that the longer the contract lasts, the more variable parties' performance may be.[44]

---

38 Maxcy (2004) and Maxcy (1997).

39 Dutta and Reichelstein (2003).

40 Dutta and Reichelstein (2003).

41 Williamson (1985) and Aghion and Bolton (1987).

42 Krautmann and Oppenheimer analysed the players' return to performance to vary with the contract length and concluded that the returns in performance decline with contract length. Krautmann and Oppenheimer (2002).

43 See, *infra*, section 6 on contract renegotiation and breach and section 7 on termination and remedies.

44 Maxcy, Fort, and Krautmann compared performance for a three-year average contract length in both the year before or after the new contract is negotiated and concluded that there was a high performance in the year before a new contract is signed and such performance would diminish after the first year after the contract is signed. In light of

## Other Important Issues Inherent in Long-Term Contracts.

### *Long-Term Contracts and the Creation of Barriers to Entry*

The first to note the competition dimension of entering into long-term contracts were Aghion and Bolton.[45] In a well-known 1987 paper they noted that an implicit effect of long-term contracts is the bilateral monopoly created by this kind of contract between the parties. By locking themselves into a long-term contract, parties significantly reduce the probability of entry of third parties so that competitors may be denied market access. Therefore, the size of the market of the other contracting party is reduced where each contracting party may become a monopolist with respect to each other. This situation may be exploited by the other party in order to maximize the surplus obtained from the other contracting party.

This has led many authors in the economic literature to consider long-term contracts as possessing strong anti-competitive elements, because the monopoly created by parties implies a negative externality to the market of other parties that could have offered a competitive alternative on the object of the contract.[46]

Aghion and Bolton[47] first claimed that long-term contracts were in general socially inefficient because they were frequently signed for entry-prevention purposes so that they would block and deter entry. They showed that the contract length will depend on the informational assumption about the incumbent's costs and finally, whenever there is asymmetric information, the length of the contract will signal the incumbent's cost. Long-term contracts would be preferred by sellers who faced a threat of entry into the market in order to prevent the entry of more cost-effective producers.

One of the key assumptions of Aghion and Bolton was that the entrant could observe the incumbent's costs when making any entry decision. Poitevin[48] showed that by changing this assumption and considering that the incumbent signals both to the buyer and to the entrant, the results of Aghion and Bolton changed significantly. If, instead, the entrant cannot observe the incumbent's cost,[49] Poitevin shows that the nominal length of the contract does not signal the incumbent's cost

this, they presented a theoretical model in which long-term contracts are desirable to sport clubs in order to mitigate both market uncertainty and uncertainty about athletes' future productivity. See Maxcy, Fort and Krautmann (2002).

45 Aghion and Bolton (1987).

46 Sibley (2002).

47 Aghion and Bolton (1987).

48 Poitevin (1992).

49 Poitevin justifies modifying this assumption and considers, as Milgrom and Roberts (1982) and based on the literature on 'expectational entry deterrence', a case where the entrant cannot observe the incumbent's cost.

since the incumbent always signs a contract regardless of its cost level; second, entry will be completely deterred.[50]

Rasmusen, Ramseyer and Wiley[51] noted that long-term contracts should not be interpreted as exclusionary instruments based on parties' being a monopoly and therefore having market power, but as exclusionary agreements that enable an incumbent monopolist to exclude its rivals cheaply by exploiting the customers' inability to coordinate their actions.[52]

Segal and Whinston[53] extended Aghion and Bolton's analysis and assumed that long-term contracts were complete barriers to entry so that contracting parties could monitor and enforce a full exclusionary contract. The resulting bilateral monopoly between contracting parties and the risk created by specific investments leads to a contractual dynamic that directly impacts on third parties, such as financial partners or banks, for example.[54] Anticipating such a scenario, contracting parties are hesitant to make relationship-specific investments without adequate contractual protection.[55]

A common assumption of the above-mentioned contributions is that the exclusive contract between the incumbent and a final consumer exerts some externality on third parties so that exclusive dealing is extremely powerful in deterring entry. Fumagalli and Motta[56] modified a major assumption of the literature and assumed that one of the parties, instead of being a final consumer, was a firm that used the input bought either from the potential entrant or from the incumbent in order to resell it to a final market.[57] Hence, these firms would compete in a downstream market where its profits would depend on one side on the input price, that would determine their input demand, and on the price paid by the other competing buyers. In their model, they showed that downstream competition could eliminate the incumbent's incentives to exclude based on two effects: first, by making the demand of a single buyer large enough to attract entry, the negative externality that a buyer would exert on the others by accepting an exclusive agreement would disappear, and second, it could enhance profitability when being more efficient than rivals. Consequently, they noted that the potential

50 Poitevin (1992).

51 Rasmusen, Ramseyer and Wiley (1991).

52 In Rasmusen et al.'s model, they consider a scope of entry deterrence by allowing more than one customer so that fixed costs are covered. Under these assumptions they found two pure-strategy Nash equilibria in which either enough customers signed an exclusionary agreement and deterred entry or no customers signed the agreements. See Rasmusen, Ramseyer and Wiley (1991).

53 Segal and Whinston (2000).

54 Dailami and Hauswald (2000).

55 Dailami and Hauswald (2000).

56 Fumagalli and Motta (2006).

57 Fumagalli and Motta (2006).

for using long-term contracts as anti-competitive instruments would significantly depend on the intensity of competition in downstream markets.[58]

*Specific Investments and Contracting Forms*

In a contractual relationship both parties may need to make certain investments in order to fully exploit the gains from trade. These investments may be necessary for any, or almost any, kind of contractual relationship or they may be specific to the obligations imposed by the contract itself, so that they will not be valuable outside of the contract or outside of the parties' relationship. Specific investments, thus, once made, cannot be used in other relationships or businesses or have no or little value outside the contract or the parties' relationship. Hence, their value within the contract is always higher than it would be in any other alternative use.

The consequences and risks for the contracting parties inherent in making investments in a relationship are very different depending on whether the investments are general or specific. So, while general investments may be used in other contractual relationships and, therefore, do not entail an inherently high risk, specific investments are very risky because they are not valuable in other contractual contexts and become sunk costs.[59] These specific investments are especially important in the context of long-term contracts because the discrepancy of the value of the assets within or outside the relationship often tends to be positively associated with the length of the contract. Moreover, in a long-term contract, due to a higher lock-in effect, one would expect more acute conflict between the parties in the contract,[60] given that the party who has made higher specific investments is in a more vulnerable position than the other and will be more likely subject to the possibility of hold-up.[61] Of course, in some, or even many, settings, specific investments are crucial for adequately exploiting the gains from the interaction, and are essentially unavoidable.

Williamson[62] distinguished between four different kinds of specific assets: physical capital specificity, that stems from investments that involve tools or other physical assets that have higher value in their intended use than in any other; human capital specificity, that results when individuals enhance their human capital, the value of which is higher in the relationship than outside of it; dedicated assets, that are used – in a factory plant, for example – because they have a certain value where they are invested and not in any other place and site specificity, that refers to the quasi-rents generated by savings in inventory and transport costs under vertical

58 Fumagalli and Motta (2006).

59 For an application of specific investments in the natural gas context see Hubbard and Weiner (1986).

60 See Klein (1980) and Williamson (1985).

61 De Geest (2006).

62 Williamson (1983).

integration, for example. A fifth kind of asset specificity, time specificity, refers to assets that must be used in a certain order or under a certain schedule.[63]

The most important hold-up risks are manifest in breach of contract or in unilateral renegotiation.[64] Goldberg points out that the exposure to the risk of hold-up depends on the access to market alternatives so the more difficult it is for contracting parties to have access to alternative markets, the more significant the risk of opportunistic behaviour would be. If, instead, parties had access to market alternatives they would not be that vulnerable to the other parties' strategic behaviour and this could minimize the price divergence between the contract price and the opportunity costs of the parties.[65]

From a structural perspective, Joskow examines the role of specific investments in the choice of vertical integration or entering into long-term contracts, and notes that the relevance of specific investments in vertical relationships strongly determines the decision of integrating vertically or entering into contracts.[66]

In general, there are two instruments that the literature has discussed in order to minimize the expected costs of making relationship-specific investments: vertical integration[67]or entering into a long-term contract.[68] It should be noted that neither of them is generally better than the other. Coase famously suggested that when the relationship between transaction costs and organizational form is not precise, there is more than one organizational response to a transaction costs problem.[69]

Further, Holmström and Roberts claim that the relationship between transaction costs and organizational form is many-to-many: there are different governance tasks and various instruments for managing them. Each task can be addressed by more than one instrument, and each instrument can, alone or in combination with others, be used to address more than one task.[70] However, the two major instruments used to minimize the risks involved in making specific investments will be discussed now.

i) *The temptation of vertical integration* There is an important relationship between specificity and the structure of vertical relationships.[71] Specific investments

---

63 Masten et al. (1991); Pirrong (1993) and Williamson (1991).

64 See *infra*. These risks do not only affect contracting parties, given that they are also transferred to debt-holders of contracting parties who would be indirectly vulnerable to opportunistic and strategic behaviour of the contracting parties. See Dailami and Hauswald (2000).

65 Goldberg (2000).

66 Joskow also considered that the allocation of risk between buyers and sellers is also an important factor in the context of vertical relationships. See Joskow (1990).

67 Joskow (1990).

68 In the context of coal markets, see Joskow (1990).

69 Coase (1988).

70 Gilson, Sabel and Scott (2009).

71 Hart (1988); Williamson (1985); Klein (1980) and Joskow (1988).

made by contracting parties often affect the structure of vertical relationships,[72] and even the risk of opportunism will sometimes drive contract parties away from contracts and towards vertical integration.[73]

When the value of the investments made by contracting parties is mutually dependent, each investor tries to induce the other to invest first in order to extract more favourable terms once an irrevocable commitment has been made and the specific investments are sunk costs. In order to avoid that, many parties understand that placing both assets under the control of a single owner and therefore vertically integrating, unblocks this situation because the incentives and risk of hold-up disappear.[74]

This situation is what happened with the famous General Motors' acquisition of Fisher Body where General Motors merged vertically with Fisher Body, a maker of auto bodies. When this case was analysed, the early literature interpreted that the merger reflected a market failure of contracts as a result of asset specificity – specific investments – and opportunistic behaviour.[75] This discussion evolved showing that the vertical integration between the two companies responded to an interest in improving the coordination of production and inventories as well as assuring General Motors an adequate supply of auto bodies as well as access to the talent of Fisher Body officers.[76] However, opinions today are not unanimous and there is still discussion regarding the motivation that resulted in the merger between General Motors and Fisher Body.[77]

ii) *Contractual solutions to the hold-up problem* When a contract is used to govern a transaction in which the consequences from hold-up are significant due to the presence of relationship-specific investments, contracting parties, aware of the problem, may well try to solve it *ex ante* and incorporate safeguards in the contract in order to protect these investments from opportunistic behaviour by the other.[78]

Parties will aim at drafting a sufficiently complete contract so as to adequately mitigate the risk of appropriability of the specific investments made by one of

72 Joskow (1990).

73 Industrial organization theory predicts that when parties in the supply chain have to make transaction-specific investments, they will vertically integrate. See Gilson, Sabel and Scott (2009).

74 Gilson, Sabel and Scott (2009).

75 Klein, Crawford and Alchian (1978); Williamson (1985) and Hart (1995).

76 Casadesus-Masanell and Spulber (2000).

77 See Coase (2006); Coase (2000) and Klein (2007) where the author claims that the contract adjustment between General Motors and Fisher Body demonstrates the importance of distinguishing between a threat of an inefficient hold-up and the economically efficient way in which it takes place.

78 Poppo and Zenger (2002); Goldberg and Erickson (1987) and Joskow (1988).

them.[79] But drafting a suitable contract to solve the contract risks or hold-up problem presented by specific investments and the parties' incentives to appropriate them is a challenging task. Contract drafting and completeness allows anticipating potential contract risks – including the risk of appropriability – but also reduces the flexibility so that adjusting to potential unforeseeable contract risks is more difficult.[80] Thus, there is a conflict between the commitment necessary to create incentives for parties to make specific investments that increase the contract surplus, and the completeness that reduces the necessary flexibility in long-term transactions.[81]

Additionally, the contractual solution to relationship-specific investments could also entail significant costs in terms of litigation[82] and may not be a perfect instrument.[83]

Despite the challenges presented by the contract solution to hold-up problems, it is worth noting that the transaction cost theory claims that learning between contracting parties improves contract design and the final outcome and performance of the parties.[84] When firms learn and gain experience from each other they are able to assess the risk of opportunistic behaviour of the other, and learn to design more complete contracts. Hence, they do not need to anticipate and contract *ex ante* over such contingencies but may cooperate and solve the situation when it appears. Thus, by cooperating and learning from each other, parties gain experience to identify the risks involved in the relationship and how to efficiently address such risks when they occur.[85] This may be particularly relevant in industries with high investment costs and high innovation elements.

Gilson et al. summarize the evidence on vertical disintegration in technology-based industries.[86] Producers cannot innovate in cutting-edge technology in every field required for the success of their product, and increasingly companies choose to buy innovation from other companies through contracts.[87] But specific investments *ex ante* are significantly high, and collaboration and a long-term

79 Joskow (1988); Goldberg and Erickson (1987); Poppo and Zenger (2002) and Reuer and Ariño (2007), showing that the existence and relevance of specific investments is positively correlated with contractual completeness.

80 Solís-Rodríguez and González-Díaz (2009).

81 Gilson, Sabel and Scott (2009).

82 Some evidence in Solís-Rodríguez and González-Díaz (2009).

83 Joskow (1990) noted that a long-term contract could help protect specific investments made by buyers and sellers but it is very imperfect given the impossibility of drafting a complete contract that, once signed, and specific investments are sunk, cannot adapt to changes in market conditions, and therefore is not entirely able to avoid the hold-up problem for the party making the investment.

84 Williamson (1985).

85 Solís-Rodríguez and González-Díaz (2009).

86 Gilson, Sabel and Scott (2009).

87 Gilson, Sabel and Scott (2009).

relationship between both parties are necessary. This environment is what Gilson et al. characterize as contracting for innovation.

Thus, cooperation *ex post* is necessary in order to interpret the uncertainties contained in the contract and to renegotiate contract clauses when necessary. The long-term nature of the contract may increase with associated uncertainty and risk, albeit it will be compensated by the learning process about the parties' propensities to behave opportunistically that will be significantly reduced and therefore the relationship between the contracting parties will strengthen. Through ongoing cooperation contracting parties can design governance and dispute resolution mechanisms in those long-term contracts that will increase contract surplus.

Cooperation and learning will directly impact the contract design through creating knowledge and routines that raise the parties' switching costs and a dispute resolution mechanism that builds mutual knowledge of the propensity to reciprocate while deterring opportunistic behaviour that could undermine the cooperative equilibrium.[88] Consequently, the collaboration process itself raises the costs of taking advantage of the other party's specific investments.[89]

## Contract Drafting and Design

Perfectly complete contracts do not exist.[90] They are 'hypothetical contracts that describe what action is to be taken and payments made in every possible contingency'.[91] But whenever contracting parties do not have perfect information, it becomes too costly for them to foresee and contract over all potential contingencies that could take place during the contract life. The costs of drafting a contract take place *ex ante*, when anticipating contract contingencies and *ex post*, when the contract has to be enforced. It is very costly for contracting parties to anticipate all potential situations that contracting parties should take into account and further prove that one of them took place. Uncertainty about the future and the cost of writing complete contracts are essential elements when determining the contract length.[92]

The challenge presented by uncertainty does not necessarily imply that parties have no incentives to anticipate as many contingencies as possible and

88 Gilson, Sabel and Scott (2009).

89 Contracting for innovation fits into the more general hypothesis presented in the transaction cost literature concerning how firms develop governance mechanisms in their inter-firm relationships in order to reduce transaction costs and become more efficient. See Williamson (1985).

90 Williamson (1985).

91 Milgrom and Roberts (1992).

92 The key question when analysing the relationship between contract length and contractual incompleteness is determining what contingencies parties should leave out of the contract. Aghion and Bolton (1987).

foresee their contractual consequences. Contracts generally include the rights and obligations of each party, the solution to potential contract contingencies, and how the relationship between contracting parties will be structured and governed. As contracting parties gain experience and learn from each other, they are able to design more complete contracts.[93]

The challenge presented by long-term contracts is that they cannot determine in advance all the obligations of both parties during the life of the contract, and it might be necessary to give to one of the parties or to both of them the discretion necessary to best respond to new circumstances as new information or situations become available.[94] As mentioned earlier, increased contract completeness in long-term contracts, when possible, is no panacea given that it allows contracting parties to anticipate potential contract risks but at the same time reduces the contract flexibility, so that the contract cannot adjust to new contingencies and circumstances that could undermine the parties' commitment necessary for making specific investments and maximize the contract surplus.[95]

When drafting a contract, or more specifically a long-term contract, parties have to define contract terms either before or after specific investments are made. When a contract is defined before specific investments are made, parties may require information that may or may not be available to them. In contrast, drafting a contract after the specific investment is made may distort the power structure of the relationship between contracting parties given that one of them, the one that has invested specifically, will not be able to freely decide, because the specific investment is already sunk in the contract. As a result, when drafting a long-term contract, contracting parties have to choose between an uninformed decision or a subsequent distorted or conditioned decision, specially for the party that has already made the specific investments.

Parties may not respond in the same way to informational problems of contract completeness. There is a classification[96] of responses that looks at over-completeness, under-completeness or a mix between these two. Over-completeness reflects the parties' intent to draft an extremely detailed contract in order to anticipate most contingencies. This strategy allows parties to negotiate the terms, obligations, solutions and safeguards in the contract before any specific investment has been made. At the same time, given the long-term relationship between the contracting parties, some contract provisions will be likely interpreted and enforced under different circumstances from the ones contemplated when they were drafted, and this may result in courts reinterpreting, and even not enforcing them. Sometimes parties may consider that leaving some contingencies or

93 Contracts cannot be completed without having previous experience of different problems and contingencies arising from former exchanges. See Solís-Rodríguez and González-Díaz (2009).

94 Goldberg (2000).

95 Gilson, Sabel and Scott (2009).

96 De Geest (2006).

circumstances open would allow them to renegotiate the contract terms according to their evolving contract conditions or even allow a third party, such as a court, to fill the gaps left by them. In contrast, under-completeness results in parties renegotiating contract terms or in third parties filling the contract gaps once the specific investments have already been made and a monopoly between them has been created.[97] Many mechanisms, such as flexible contract pricing, for example, have been suggested in order to decrease the return of opportunistic behaviour by the party not making the specific investments.[98]

The inequality in the parties' position concerning the need and cost of specific investments has also been discussed. Some argue[99] that if both parties symmetrically invested in the contract relationship, opportunistic behaviour and incentives to renegotiate would decrease, especially in cases where if renegotiation took place, the party who invested the most should receive the most.[100] This argument, though, does not consider that even in cases where parties make symmetrical investments, their different size, market share, market position or reputation would still give them incentives to renegotiate or reject renegotiation.[101]

## Parties' Renegotiation v. Court's Adjustment for Contract Breach

As mentioned above, incompleteness is an inherent characteristic to contract drafting, especially in long-term contracts. Consequently, parties, aware of the fact that the circumstances of the contracting parties may change during the life of the contract and of the high costs involved in foreseeing and allocating contract risks, may decide to leave certain contingencies to be negotiated whenever they may or may not take place.[102]

97 See Hubbard and Weiner (1986) modelling a contract that could solve the bilateral bargaining problem in the natural gas context where there was a high amount of transaction-specific capital with little value outside the relationship. Once the gas well development costs are sunk a pipeline faces the temptation to appropriate some of the rents from production. In light of this, the producer demands a long-term contract with adjustment clauses beforehand.

98 Goldberg (2000).

99 De Geest (2006).

100 Becker (1962) and De Geest (2006).

101 See Dailami and Hauswald (2000) analysing how whenever there is contractual incompleteness, contract risks would be transmitted and allocated between different contracts and investors, in particular in the contract of relationships between the off-take and in financial contracts, because the former would serve as security for the latter. In such cases, long-term supply contracts would be necessarily incomplete and subject to opportunistic behaviour.

102 Sometimes, even when parties do not expressly state it, it is clear from the contract terms that they intended to do so. See Goldberg (1985).

Such prospect negotiation during the life of the contract arises as a potential conflict and disagreement between the parties whenever these contingencies take place, even in long-term contracts, where commitment is an inherent element.[103] When there is non-performance by one of the parties that may or may not amount to a breach of contract, it is possible to differentiate between voluntary and involuntary renegotiation.[104] In the first case, when both parties voluntarily want to renegotiate contract terms, it will not be possible to hold parties to the initial contract.[105] In the second situation, the case of breach, the non-breaching party may have different remedies available in the form of either enforcing the contract whenever possible or seeking damages, depending on the situation, the costs of using the legal system and on the court's determination.[106] Hence, either party may decide to renegotiate and agree over the solution of the contingency or accept the court's remedy for breach of contract. It should be noted that the incentives and consequences of an incomplete contract are different depending on whether parties reached a voluntary agreement for the new contingency or accepted the solution provided by the courts.

### *Voluntary Renegotiation: Agreeing Over Unforeseen Contingencies*

Under perfect information, contracting parties could foresee all potential circumstances and contingencies that could take place during the life of the contract and define and determine the circumstances for renegotiation or reject renegotiation, if parties decided to do so.[107] So if complete information were available, parties could draft a complete contract and could agree on the circumstances for renegotiation or exclude it, so that the contract would be renegotiation-proof.[108]

But generally it is not possible for contracting parties to draft a complete contract, and incomplete contracts entail the possibility of renegotiation whenever

103 Salanié (1997).

104 Joskow (1990).

105 See generally Encyclopedia in Law and Economics Chapter 4600 Contract Remedies: General.

106 For example, if the remedy were specific performance, the contract could only be enforced if both parties agreed on such remedy because otherwise specific performance will not be an available alternative. See Jolls (1997).

107 Hart and Moore show how the contract *ex ante* can be constructed to affect the bargaining power of the two parties *ex post*. See Hart and Moore (1988).

108 Contracts which are renegotiation proof can still improve the *ex ante* vs. *ex post* problem – *ex post* sharing of the contract surplus may not be *ex ante* efficient – presented by the possibility of renegotiation by designing the environment of the renegotiation in the unverifiable state by a third party and where the information between parties is symmetric. See Hart and Moore (1988) and Dewatripont (1989).

unforeseen contingencies take place.[109] Relying on the commitment inherent in long-term contracts, each party will make specific investments and rely on renegotiation over the unforeseen circumstances not specifically addressed in the contract.[110] There may be scope for renegotiation when *ex ante* efficiency may determine *ex post* inefficiency.[111]

Parties' incentives for renegotiation might not be symmetric when their reputation is considered. Reputation may constrain a contracting party's incentives to renegotiate or unilaterally adjust contract provisions and hence reduce the incentives for opportunistic behaviour. In light of this constraint, the other contracting party, with less reputation interest may benefit from greater reliance from the other party and may enjoy greater discretion in determining the desired performance.[112]

The prospect of renegotiation presents advantages and disadvantages for parties. A clear advantage is the flexibility of achieving *ex post* efficiency without having to incur *ex ante* the high costs of foreseeing all the potential contingencies during the contract life.

When contracting parties take into account the possibility of renegotiation while drafting the contract, *ex post* opportunistic behaviour may be reduced or even eliminated given that they may be able to determine how they will share the contract surplus and assure *ex ante* and *ex post* efficiency, whenever possible.[113]

The possibility of achieving *ex post* efficiency through renegotiation was advanced as one of the predictions of the Coase theorem:[114] if the contract were profitable for one of the parties, the other party, not interested in enforcing the contract could bribe the other in order to withdraw from the contract and hence not enforce it. Through renegotiation parties may decide to perform the contract, modify its terms, withdraw from the transaction or write a new contract depending on their circumstances.

Renegotiation also presents remarkable disadvantages from the perspective of the hold-up problem arising from the relationship between commitment and the incentives to make specific investments; the moral hazard problem present in principal–agent relationships; the incentives to reveal private information; and finally, the costs renegotiation itself entails.

---

109 When information costs are high, parties may emphasize *ex post* rather than *ex ante* efficiency and will seek to balance both elements and draft a formal contract with vague standards so that *ex post* it may be renegotiated and adjusted to the contingencies that may take place during the life of the contract. See Gilson, Sabel and Scott (2009).

110 Salanié (1997).

111 Bolton (1990).

112 This result was obtained by Arruñada, Garicano and Vazquez (2001) in the context of the automobile distribution industry in contracts between manufacturers and auto dealers.

113 See Gilson, Sabel and Scott (2009) arguing that when parties regulate the potential renegotiation between them, the risk of hold-up is reduced.

114 Coase (1937).

As noted earlier, if the contract allows for renegotiation, this would most likely take place and hence a breach of contract and litigation might be avoided. But when parties are aware that renegotiation is likely, long-term contracts lose efficiency as an instrument because commitment – inherent and essential to long-term contracts – will significantly diminish and with it the parties' incentives to make efficient specific investments because the chances of hold-up increase.[115] In light of the incomplete information and the parties' future renegotiation, parties will aim at minimizing contracting costs and will balance the benefits of commitment and the flexibility provided by renegotiation with the costs of uncertainty and the increased risk of hold-up of one of the parties.[116]

In the context of principal–agent relationships, the *ex post* inefficient outcome results from the moral hazard problem of the level of effort chosen by the agent. If the agent chose first, the principal would not be able to create incentives for the agent to choose optimally and hence renegotiation *ex post* would result in an inefficient result.[117]

Additionally, the literature has shown that whenever parties are aware that renegotiation may take place in the future, the revelation of private information between the contracting parties is reduced.[118]

Finally, renegotiation is costly. Given that parties anticipate that renegotiation is likely, they may anticipate the potential costs derived from it and introduce price mechanisms in the contract in order to dilute the incentives to renegotiate and increase the expected value of the long-term contract without renegotiation.[119] Further, the larger the variance of the contract outcomes, the more effort parties will devote to drafting the contract.[120] Consequently, assessing future renegotiation costs and creating price mechanisms to avoid renegotiation may increase the contract drafting process.[121]

### *Involuntary Renegotiation: Court Adjustment for Contract Breach*

Reaching a renegotiated solution between the contracting parties is not always possible,[122] so whenever parties are not able to reach an agreement over a contract

115 Gilson, Sabel and Scott (2009).

116 Gilson, Sabel and Scott (2009).

117 Chiappori, Macho, Rey and Salanié (1994).

118 See in general Dewatripont (1989); Hart and Tirole (1988) and Laffont and Tirole (1990).

119 Goldberg (1995).

120 Goldberg (1995).

121 Goldberg and Erickson (1987).

122 Hillman (1987).

term and address an unforeseen contingency, a court will have to interpret, adjust or fill the gap in the contract.[123]

In order to have a successful intervention of courts in providing a contract solution parties did not manage to attain by themselves, a certain level of contract definiteness will be needed.[124] When and if contracts include clear terms and define parties' obligations, parties may be able to avoid many disputes of interpretation.[125] But clear and identifiable provisions will also be useful when courts have to adjust or interpret a contract term because whenever contract clauses are not definite or clear enough, some courts will disregard them and invoke the parties' good faith when determining the solution of the parties' dispute[126] and if they could not enforce a contract term, some efficient transactions may be deterred and inefficient *ex post* negotiations may take place.[127]

Whether and how courts should interpret incomplete contracts is a highly controversial matter. Some suggest that any analysis of contractual interpretation should address two major issues: first the level of evidence – broad or narrow – that courts should base their interpretations of the contract's language on and second, the possibility of courts accepting that parties wrote in a private language and hence should be allowed to provide their own interpretation of the contract.[128]

The first question refers to the evidence admitted to interpret an incomplete contract. When courts interpret incomplete contracts, they generally pursue three strategies:[129] protecting process values, interpreting language and filling the contract gaps so that they supply terms when the parties' contract fails to provide for the dispute that divides them. There is a general tendency in the Law and Economics literature to favour restricting the evidence that courts may use to interpret contracts, understanding that parties should be able to save costs of contract interpretation by just requiring minimal evidence.[130]

With respect to the language that should be used in order to decide contract cases – the parties' language or the court's interpretation of the parties' language –

123 It is often argued that the party making the highest specific investment faces a higher cost the more specific the investment is, because of its exposure to the risk that the other contracting party will walk away from the contract, especially when there are other suppliers available in the market. Therefore, one of the parties – the one assuming a lower specific investment – has an implicit real option through breach of contract. See Dailami and Hauswald (2000) discussing this situation in the context of the Ras Gas Project.

124 Joskow (1990).

125 Hillman (1987).

126 See Goldberg (2000) regarding contract clauses concerning quantity boundaries. Goldberg claims that contract tailoring by parties may create an incentive for them to take into account and hence internalize their reliance interests, which could be much more efficiently done by parties than using the good faith standards by courts.

127 Joskow (1990).

128 Schwartz and Scott (2003).

129 Schwartz (1992).

130 Schwartz and Scott (2003).

the literature on the issue is not unanimous: while some understand that courts should be able to use norms beyond the contractual relationship such as fairness considerations, others understand that the norms used should be provided by the parties, who should be the only ones able to vary the terms of their relationship.[131]

Different factors may predispose courts to activism when adjudicating incomplete contracts:[132] process values are offended in the contract formation or in the course of performance; enforcement of the contract adversely affects third parties; the contract directs a result that is substantially unfair to one of the parties and the contract is incomplete and the court can complete it with a term that parties will accept and courts will be able to apply. In contrast, the literature which defends the role of parties as main interpreters of the terms of their contract relationship argues that the role of parties and courts in enforcing contracts should be clearly differentiated: courts should and are able to ensure the broad structure within which parties' contracts fit while parties are suited for creating and defining their own contracts. Consequently, parties' sovereignty in the contract requires courts to delegate to them the choice of the contract's substantive terms and the interpretation of such terms when enforcing them.[133]

Parallel to the discussion over how courts should interpret contract terms, there is also the discussion over what the goal of the court's contract interpretation should be. Some authors understand that the goal of the court's interpretation of contracts should be to enhance the efforts of contracting parties to maximize the contract surplus.[134] In contrast, some understand that courts should provide a literal interpretation of contract terms and not go beyond that.

These two doctrinal lines of discussion are reflected in the different ways of interpreting contracts in Europe and in the US. In Europe, the Principles of European Contract Law suggest taking into account the intention of the parties regardless of whether such intention is reflected in the words used.[135] In the US, the majority of jurisdictions apply the plain meaning rule and hence a literal interpretation of contract terms.[136]

---

131 Schwartz (1992).

132 Schwartz (1992).

133 Schwartz and Scott (2003).

134 Schwartz and Scott (2003).

135 Article 5.101(1) of the European Principles of Contract Law provides that

(1) A contract is to be interpreted according to the common intention of the parties even if this differs from the literal meaning of the words.

(2) If it is established that one party intended the contract to have a particular meaning, and at the time of the conclusion of the contract the other party could not have been unaware of the first party's intention, the contract is to be interpreted in the way intended by the first party.

(3) If an intention cannot be established according to (1) or (2), the contract is to be interpreted according to the meaning that reasonable persons of the same kind as the parties would give to it in the same circumstances.

136 Scott (2000) justifying formal interpretations understanding that they allow maximizing the value of the contractual relationship, especially considering that 'contract

Whether court-imposed solutions present advantages or generate serious disadvantages is a greatly debated issue. Some consider that courts enjoy an excessively unlimited discretion to create a new contract and hence argue against court interpretations understanding that they lack the necessary instruments to determine *ex post* what parties would have done *ex ante*.[137] But the court's scope of discretion is not unlimited. The parties' bargaining over a contract term and the parties' purpose in including a certain provision are crucial in determining whether the court adjustment should trump an express contract provision.[138]

## Looking Into the Content of the Contract: Determining Breach, Termination, Remedies and the Introduction of Non-Competing Clauses

### *When Performance is Not Verifiable*

As explained earlier, some degree of incompleteness is inherent to any contract, but perhaps especially in long-term contracts where incompleteness is stronger and more decisive. Long-term relationships have, by their nature, a more extended time horizon than spot or short-term contracts. As a result, the number, influence, complexity, difficulty and cost in anticipation of contingencies that can, in one way or the other, have an effect on the contractual outcomes, dramatically increases. This is why economists, when approaching long-term contracts, have routinely assumed that contracts between the parties are incomplete.

This inherent nature of long-term relationships typically makes them relational: many of the relevant actions cannot be foreseen and determined when the contract is drafted and entered into, and it is in the course of the ongoing relationship that the parties will adapt those actions to the formal and legal rules in contract law. A relational contract cannot be enforced strictly as written[139] by a court or an arbitrator.[140] This does not mean that no contractual clause or contractual behaviour by the parties can ever be legally enforced. Some situations will amount to a breach

interpretation often finds competent parties together with incompetent courts'.

137 Hillman analysed the different approaches of the literature to court interpretation and adjustment of incomplete contracts. See Hillman (1987).

138 Courts face difficult challenges because good faith is the parameter applicable to parties when they interpret a contract term and such principle is based on business expectations but courts face the challenge of determining the content or interpretation of a contract term in circumstances different from the ones of the moment when the contract was entered into. See Hillman (1987).

139 On many occasions nothing is written, and the contractual intention has to be inferred from the behaviour of the parties, prior or posterior to the initiation of the relationship.

140 This is the reason why the quest, in this area of relational contracts, of the economic literature has been how to design self-enforcing relational contracts, that is, contracts in which the parties are induced to adopt the best available actions for the common good, based on their own strategies, but checked by reciprocity, reputation, or

of contract – lack of performance or non-cooperation when performing – and might be detected by the other contracting party and easily verified before a court. When breach is observable, it can be deterred by using the available legal remedies such as specific performance or damages.

But sometimes determining breach is not observable or clear. There is a wide range of non-cooperative behaviours within the contractual relationship that present insurmountable measurement problems, especially when these behaviours are multidimensional. In these cases, the chances that contracting parties may be able to show before a court or a third party adjudicator that the other party has breached the contract terms is very low. Additionally, the amount and scope of unverifiable breaches of contract would increase the chances that a breaching party would not be detected and hence subject to contractual remedies but also might imply that consumers would not be able to detect or punish the defective contract performance of that contracting party.

Parties to a long-term contract have imperfect-substitute alternatives to a court determination of a non-verifiable breach of contract.[141] First, courts can use a verifiable dimension to determine whether the parties' behaviour amounted to contract breach and then impose the adequate remedy for breach. Second, parties may introduce contract clauses that may serve as mechanisms to create incentives for being interested in enforcing the contract. Hence, incentive mechanisms could eventually increase the costs of breach and encourage parties to perform and hence not breach the contract. The most important self-enforcing mechanism, in the context of distribution contracts, for example, is the use of future quasi-rents for one of the contracting parties linked to the continuation of the relationship:[142] if the contract terms are adjusted so that one of the parties is able to earn quasi-rents on its investment only if the existing contractual relationship continues, that party has great incentives to remain in the contract and hence avoid any kind of behaviour that could amount to a breach of contract. It should be noted that in order to allow future quasi-rents to be an effective self-enforcing mechanism and achieve cooperation in non-verifiable dimensions, maintaining the threat of termination of the contractual relationship is crucial.[143]

---

other intrinsic motivators. This is, as well, the reason why economists often view with mixed feelings the function of the law in this sort of setting.

141 See Mathewson and Winter (1985); Klein and Murphy (1988); Klein (1995) and Paz-Ares (1997 and 2003).

142 The pioneering analyses along this line are Rubin (1978); Klein (1980); and Klein and Leffler (1981).

143 Klein (1995) underlines the importance of termination-at-will for the effectiveness of self-enforcing mechanisms, and how legal constraints – mandatory severance payments or compensation, or good cause requirements – severely limit this option. See also Paz-Ares (1997 and 2003).

### *The Decision Over Specific Investments and Remedies for Breach of Contract*

Specific investments are investments related to the relationship in that their value depends on whether parties are within or outside of the contract. Whether these investments are specific or general affects the parties' decisions to perform or to breach, and to terminate or continue with the relationship.

The hold-up problem arising from the specific investments made by one of the parties in the relationship makes that party more vulnerable in all dimensions of the relationship.[144] As a result, the more relation-specific the investments are, the higher the costs of ending the contract for the party who made the investments or who invested the most. In contrast, whenever investments are general and hence may be used in other relationships outside the contract, the incentives to terminate the contract will increase. Further, the need for making specific investments will also affect the choice of standard legal remedies for breach of contract.

When considering the parties' incentives to perform or invest, two kinds of specific investments should be differentiated: selfish investments and cooperative investments.[145] Selfish investments are ones that benefit the party making them but not the other. For example, if a buyer makes an investment, it increases the value of his performance but does not provide any positive effect on the performance of the seller and conversely the same would be true. Cooperative investments, on the other side, confer benefits to the other contracting party and not to the party making the investment.[146] So if, for example, a buyer made the investment, it would increase the seller's value of performance – or reduce the seller's costs of performance – without modifying the value of performance of the buyer, who made the investment. The contrary would also be true.

Two lines of analysis have been explored in order to deter opportunistic behaviour by the non-investing party. A first analysis focuses on the design of efficient mechanisms in terms of trade and in terms of specific investments such as, for example, defining the bargaining conditions in the renegotiation phase of the contract so that the investing party receives full value for the already made investments. Another possibility would be placing external conditions on the renegotiation phase[147] or using options and appropriate strike prices for their

144 See Williamson (1985) and Hart and Moore (1988).

145 It should be noted that there are also hybrid investments whenever they benefit both contracting parties but such investments will not be the object of this section. Few papers explore hybrid investments: Che and Hausch (1999); Segal and Whinston (2000); Göller and Stremitzer (2009).

146 The first treatment of cooperative investments is MacLeod and Malcomson (1993). The standard treatment of these investments, in Che and Chung (1999) and Che and Hausch (1999). A very interesting recent contribution on contract remedies and specific investments, showing that the dismal result – concerning expectation damages – of Che and Chung (1999), is but an extreme case, Stremitzer (2008).

147 Chung (1991).

exercise.[148] Other approaches, though with limited applicability, rely on contracts determining intermediate quantities to trade so that after renegotiation the investing party receives more or less than the marginal social value of the investment or, if the quantity chosen in the contract turns out to be efficient, an efficient level of investment may result.[149]

The other line of analysis of selfish investments focuses on the legal remedies for breach and their effect on the *ex ante* investment decision by the parties. The foundational first contribution in this literature is by Shavell,[150] who addressed two different scenarios: The first scenario is one where the investing party could be the one that could be the victim of breach. In such case, expectation damages could induce excessive specific investments by the potential victim of breach – who also decides the amount to invest. This result is due to the fact that expectation damages fully insures the investing party against the possibility of losing the return on the investment, even beyond the optimal level of investment. A second kind of damages, reliance damages, perform worse than expectation damages given that in addition to the over-reliance problem presented by expectation damages – the investing party obtains at least the cost of the investment made – there is a performance inducement problem: by investing more in specific assets, the investing party increases the damage award that may obtain from the other in the case of breach and such additional breaching cost increases the incentives of the non-investing party to perform.[151]

The second scenario is one where the investing party is the one who can decide whether to breach or perform the contract. In this context expectation damages would result in an efficient level of investments given that in this case, the breaching party is the residual claimant of the value of the investment because the damage award he has to pay does not depend on the level of investment. As in the former case, reliance damages also perform worse than expectation damages but for different reasons than in the former situation. Given that reliance damages generally induce suboptimal performance with respect to the efficient level, the investing party will get a lower return on the specific investment than what is optimal and therefore the incentives to invest would be too low.[152]

The first scenario, where the investing party is not the one deciding between breach or performance, has been extended along two different lines in the literature. First, showing that the parties' renegotiation after breach does not alter the inefficient incentives for investment both under expectation and reliance damages as well as claiming that reliance damages are less attractive than expectation

148 Nöldeke and Schmidt (1995).

149 Edlin and Reichelstein (1996).

150 Shavell (1980).

151 These results have been to an important degree confirmed by experimental tests of contracting behaviour in a controlled laboratory setting. See Sloof, Leuven, Oosterbeek, and Sonnemans (2003).

152 Shavell (1980).

damages regarding the creation of efficient incentives to invest.[153] Second, the analysis of the potential instruments to transform the first scenario into the second – where the investing party is the one who decides whether to breach or perform – through a large payment up-front from the buyer to the investing seller. Through this payment that is sunk when the decision of performing or breaching must be adopted, the buyer would never want to breach because he would get performance for a price close to zero. Consequently, any decision to breach would be decided by the investing party who would have efficient incentives for breach when the remedy would be expectation damages.[154] Even though the up-front payment could have problems on its own – liquidity problems for the party having to make the payment – this mechanism arises as a solution to the investment problem by concentrating the decision to breach and to invest in the same party.

But if the specific investments were not selfish, but cooperative, it is not possible to design contract mechanisms that would create efficient incentives.[155] In fact, it is striking to see that when cooperative specific investments are involved, an incomplete contract does not arise as a better mechanism than no contract at all.[156] The role of legal remedies against breach has also been explored when renegotiation is feasible or when it has been excluded.[157] When *ex post* renegotiation is available, expectation damages perform very poorly and reliance damages neither can achieve efficient outcomes by creating incentives to both perform and to make efficient cooperative specific investments. In contrast, whenever renegotiation has been excluded, expectation damages perform poorly because they induce zero cooperative investment. Reliance damages, in turn, perform much better in that they provide better incentives for making specific investments and improve the contractual surplus when compared to expectation damages.

As can be seen, expectation damages perform very poorly in this context. It should be noted that when expectation damages, instead of being paid by one party to the other, are bilateral, that is, the party who can breach may be subject to paying expectation damages to the other, the investor, who may also be liable to the former if the investment level falls short of the investment level set by the contract, bilateral expectation damages induce efficient cooperative specific investments as long as the level of investments are verifiable by a court and the required level of cooperative investments are determined by the parties in the contract, which is an implausible – but not impossible – assumption.[158]

153 Rogerson (1984).

154 Edlin (1996).

155 Che and Hausch (1999) and Maskin, and Moore (1999).

156 Stremitzer (2008) shows that if the contract can be conditioned (i.e., courts are able to verify) on whether performance is above or below a given threshold – of quality, as a paramount example – under certain conditions first best can be attained.

157 Che and Chung (1999).

158 Schweizer (2006).

A further argument to explain the poor efficiency performance of expectation damages – that result in zero cooperative investments – is due to the implicit assumption that the contract does not contain any threshold of performance and that the court cannot determine such threshold either.[159] If contracting parties or courts were able to compare the parties' performance with a verifiable legally binding threshold, expectation damages would induce a positive – albeit suboptimal – level of cooperative investments and could even, under certain conditions, provide incentives for efficient investments of a cooperative nature.[160] When renegotiation is possible,[161] an optimal remedy for breach for the non-investing party[162] consists in the choice between specific performance and termination – with restitution of any payment made, if any – if performance of the investing party falls below the legally enforceable threshold. Above such threshold, only specific performance should be available for either party.

## Conclusion

Drawing general conclusions over long-term contracts seems unfeasible when the different issues presented by them and the different approaches and results in the literature are considered.

Long-term contracts present particular issues – specific investments, additional incompleteness and the difficulties arising from determining adequate remedies for breach in light of the often non-verifiable non-cooperative behaviour of the parties. These are issues that are also present in contracts in general – and also in short-term contracts – but they are specifically challenging in the context of long-term contracts in light of the time frame of the relationship of the contracting parties it aims at regulating. It is not possible to generalize over whether parties should enter into short-term or long-term contracts from a general perspective. Each transaction, context and goal of the contracting parties will require one kind of contract or another.

What one can note here is that from a general perspective, any contract requires cooperation from the contracting parties and such cooperation often is not self-enforcing and calls for the introduction of incentive mechanisms that encourage it. Further, when the open-ended nature of long-term contracts is considered, ongoing cooperation between the contracting parties becomes an essential element of the contract. Commitment, which is an element present in long-term contracts but

159 Stremitzer (2008).

160 Those conditions are the so-called maximum quality or Cadillac contracts. See Edlin (1996).

161 It is well known that in the absence of renegotiation, specific performance is likely to produce inefficient trade and thus undesirable results. Shavell (2004).

162 The use of optional regimes has not often been considered in the literature. An exception is Avraham and Liu (2006 and 2008).

not necessarily in short-term contracts, may result in the parties' cooperation that may lead to compliance with contractual obligations without the need to rely on formal legal remedies for breach. When long-term contracts can define the parties' contractual obligations to ensure commitment and encourage cooperation, is when they can take full advantage of the potential benefits presented by them.

**References**

Aghion, Philippe and Patrick Bolton (1987), Contracts as a Barrier to Entry, *American Economic Review* 77(3), 388–401.

Arruñada, Benito, Luis Garicano, and Luis Vazquez (2001), Contractual Allocation of Decision Rights and Incentives, The Case of Automobile Distribution, *The Journal of Law, Economics & Organization*, 17, 1, 257–84.

Asser-Hartkamp (2000), *Verbintenissenrecht*, part 2, 11th edition, Deventer, Kluwer, chapters V–VII, X.

Avraham, Ronen and Zijhong Liu (2006), Incomplete Contracts with Asymmetric Information: Exclusive versus Optional Remedies, *American Law and Economic Review*, 8, 523–61.

— (2008), Should Courts Ignore Ex-Post Information when Determining Contract Damages?, Working Paper, Northwestern University School of Law.

Baron, David P. and David Besanko (1984), Regulation and Information in a Continuing Relationship, *Information, Economics, and Policy*, 1 (3), 267–302.

Becker, Gary S. (1962), Investment in Human Capital: A Theoretical Analysis, *Journal of Political Economy*, 70, 9–49.

Bolton, Patrick (1990), Renegotiation and the Dynamics of Contract Design, *European Economic Review*, 34, 303–10.

Casadesus-Masanell, Ramon and Daniel F. Spulber (2000), The Fable of Fisher Body, *Journal of Law & Economics*, 43 (1), 67–104.

Che Yeon-Koo, and Tai-Yeong Chung (1999), Contract Damages and Cooperative Investments, *Rand Journal of Economics,* 30, 84–105.

Che, Yeon-Koo and Donald Hausch (1999), Cooperative Investments and the Value of Contracting, *American Economic Review*, 89, 125–47.

Chiappori, Pierre, Ines Macho, Patrick G. Rey and Bernard Salanié (1991), Incomplete Contracts, Specific Investment, and Risk Sharing, *Review of Economic Studies*, 58, 1031–42.

— (1994), Repeated Moral Hazard: The Role of Memory Commitment, and the Access to Credit Markets. *European Economic Review*, 38, 1527–53.

Chung, Tai- Yeong (1991), Incomplete Contracts, Specific Investment, and Risk Sharing, *Review of Economic Studies*, 58, 1031–42.

Coase, Ronald, H. (1937), The Nature of the Firm, *Economica*, 4 (16), 386–405.

— (1988), The Nature of the Firm: Origin, Meaning, Influence, *Journal of Law & Economics*, 4 (1), 3–47.

— (2000), The Acquisition of Fisher Body by General Motors, *Journal of Law & Economics*, 43, 15–31.

— (2006), The Conduct of Economics: The Example of Fisher Body and General Motors, *Journal of Economics and Management Strategy*, 15, 255–78.

Crawford, Vincent P. (1988), Long-Term Relationships Governed by Short-Term Contracts, *American Economic Review*, 78, 485–99.

Dailami, Mansoor and Robert Hauswald (2000), Risk Shifting and Long-Term Contracts: Evidence from the Ras Gas Project, World Bank Policy research working paper 2469.

Dewatripont, Mathias (1989), Renegotiation and Information Revelation over Time: The Case of Optimal Labor Contracts, *Quarterly Journal of Economics*, 103, 589–619.

Dutta, Sunil and Stefan Reichelstein (2003), Leading Indicator Variables, Performance Measurement, and Long-Term Versus Short-Term Contracts, *Journal of Accounting Research*, 41(5), 837–66.

Dye, Ronald A. (1985), Costly Contract Contingencies, *International Economic Review*, 26 (1), 233–50.

Edlin, Aaron (1996), Cadillac Contracts and Up-Front Payments: Efficient Investment Under Expectation Damages, *Journal of Law, Economics & Organization*, 12, 98–118.

Edlin, Aaron and Stefan Reichelstein (1996), Holdups, Standard Breach Remedies, and Optimal Investment, *American Economic Review*, 86, 478–501.

Freixas, Xavier, Roger Guesnerie and Jean Tirole (1985), Planning under Incomplete Information and the Ratchet Effect, *Review of Economic Studies*, 52, 173–91.

Fudenberg, D., B. Holmstrom and P. Milgrom (1990), Short-Term Contracts in Long-Term Agency Relations, *Journal of Economic Theory*, 51, 1–31.

Fumagalli, Chiara and Massimo Motta (2006), Exclusive Dealing and Entry, when Buyers Compete, *American Economic Review*, American Economic Association, 96 (3), 785–95.

De Geest, Gerrit (2006), Long-term Contracts and Distribution Chains: Binding Force, Mimeo, Washington University Working Paper Saint Louis School of Law.

Gilson, Ronald J., Charles F. Sabel and Robert E. Scott (2009), Contracting For Innovation: Vertical Disintegration and Interfirm Collaboration, *Columbia Law Review*, 109 (7), 431–502.

Goldberg, Victor P. (1985), Price adjustment in long term contracts, *Wisconsin Law Review*, 1985, 527–43.

— (1995), Risk Management in Long-Term Contracts (http://ssrn.com/abstract_id=805184)

— (2000), Discretion in Long-Term Open Quantity Contracts: Reining in Good Faith, Columbia Law & Economic studies Working Paper 176. http://papers.ssrn.com/paper.taf?abstract_id=234705.

Goldberg, Victor and John R. Erickson (1987), Quantity and Price Adjustment in Long Term Contracts: A Case Study of Petroleum Coke, *Journal of Law and Economics*, 30, 369–98.
Göller, Daniel and Alexander Stremitzer (2009), Breach Remedies Inducing Hybrid Investments, Working Paper, University of Bonn.
Hart, Oliver (1988), Incomplete Contracts and the Theory of the Firm, *Journal of Law, Economics, and Organization*, 4, 119–39.
— (1995), *Firms Contracts and Financial Structure Clarendon Lectures in Economics*, Oxford and New York, Oxford University Press, Clarendon Press.
Hart, Oliver D. and Bengt Holmstrom (1987), The Theory of Contracts, in Bewley, T. (ed.), *Advances in Economic Theory*. Fifth World Congress, Cambridge, Cambridge University Press.
Hart, Oliver, and John Moore (1988), Incomplete Contracts and Renegotiation, *Econometrica*, 56, 755–85.
Hart, Oliver D. and Jean Tirole (1988), Contract Renegotiation and Coasian Dynamics, *Review of Economic Studies*, 55, 509–40.
Hillman, Robert A. (1987), Court Adjustment of Long-Term Contracts: An Analysis Under Modern Contract Law, *Duke Law Journal*, 36, 1–33.
Hubbard, R. Glenn and Robert J. Weiner (1986), Regulation, Long-Term Contracting in US Natural Gas Markets, *The Journal of Industrial Economics*, 35 (1), 71–9.
Hviid, Morten (1999), Long-Term Contracts and Relational Contracts 4200, 46–72, http://encyclo.findlaw.com/4200book.pdf)
Jolls, Christine (1997), Contracts as Bilateral Commitments: A New Perspective on Contract Modification, *Journal of Legal Studies*, 26 (1), 203–37.
Joskow, Paul L. (1988), Asset specificity and the structure of vertical relationships: empirical evidence, *Journal of Law, Economics & Organization,* 4, 95–117.
— (1990), The Performance of Long-Term Contracts: Further Evidence from Coal Markets, *The Rand Journal of Economics*, 21 (2), 251–74.
Klein, Benjamin (1980), Transaction Cost Determinants of 'Unfair' Contractual Arrangements, *American Economic Review*, 70, 356–62.
— (1995), The Economics of Franchise Contracts, *Journal of Corporate Finance*, 2, 9–37.
— (2007), The Economic Lessons of Fisher Body – General Motors, *International Journal of the Economics of Business*, 14 (1), 1–36. http://ssrn.com/abstract=937510
Klein, Benjamin, Robert G. Crawford and Armen A. Alchian (1978), Vertical Integration, Appropriable Rents, and the Competitive Contracting Process, *Journal of Law & Economics*, 21 (2), 297–326.
Klein, Benjamin and Keith Leffler (1981), The Role of Market Forces in Assuring Contractual Performance, *Journal of Political Economy*, 89, 615–41.
Klein, Benjamin and Kevin Murphy (1988), Vertical Restraints as Contract Enforcement Mechanisms, *Journal of Law & Economics*, 31, 265–297.

Krautmann, Anthony C. and Oppenheimer, Margaret (2002), Contract Length and the Return to Performance in Major League Baseball, *Journal of Sports Economics*, 3, 6–17.

Laffont, Jean-Jacques and Jean Tirole (1990), Adverse Selection and Renegotiation in Procurement, *Review of Economic Studies*, 75, 597–626.

Lambert, Richard A. (1983), Long-Term Contracting and Moral Hazard, *Bell Journal of Economics*, 14, 441–52.

MacLeod, W. Bentley and James M. Malcomson (1993), Investments, Holdup, and the Form of Market Contracts, *American Economic Review*, 83, 811–37.

Malcomson, James and Frans Spinnewyn (1988), The Multiperiod Principal-Agent Problem, *Review of Economic Studies*, 55, 391–407.

Maskin, Eric and John Moore (1999), Implementation and Renegotiation, *Review of Economic Studies*, 66, 39–56.

Masten, Scott E., James W. Meehan Jr., and Edward A. Snyder (1991), The Costs of Organization, *Journal of Law, Economics, and Organization*, 7 (1), 1–25.

Mathewson, George and Ralph Winter (1985), The Economics of Franchise Contracts, *Journal of Law & Economics*, 28, 9–37.

Maxcy, Joel G. (1997), Do Long-Term Contracts Influence Performance in Major League Baseball? in Hendricks, W. (ed.) *Advances in the Economics of Sport*, 2, 157–76, Greenwich CT., JAI Press Inc.

— (2004), Motivating Long-Term Employment Contracts: Risk Management in Major League Baseball, *Managerial and Decision Economics*, 25, 109–20.

Maxcy, Joel G., Rodney D. Fort, and Anthony C. Krautmann (2002), The Effectiveness of Incentive Mechanisms in Major League Baseball, *Journal of Sports Economics*, 3, 246–55.

Milgrom, Paul, and John Roberts (1992), *Economics, Organizations and Management*, Homewood, Prentice-Hall International Editions, 597.

— (1982), Limit Pricing and Entry under Incomplete Information: An Equilibrium Analysis, *Econometrica*, 50, 443–59.

Nöldeke, Georg and Klaus Schmidt (1995), Option Contracts and Renegotiation: A Solution to the Hold-Up Problem, *Rand Journal of Economics*, 26, 163–79.

Paz-Ares, Cándido (2003), La terminación de los contratos de distribución, *Advocatus*, 8, 31–63.

— (1997), La indemnización por clientela en el contrato de concesión, *La Ley*, D-105 T. 2.

Philippe, Julie M. (2005), French and American Approach to Contract Formation and Enforceability: A Comparative Perspective, *Tulsa Journal of Comparative and International Law*, 12, 357.

Pirrong, Stephen Craig (1993), Contracting Practices in Bulk Shipping Markets: A Transactions Cost Explanation, *Journal of Law & Economics*, 36 (2), 937–76.

Poitevin, Michel (1992), A Note on 'Contracts as a Barrier to Entry', Mimeo, *University of Montreal.*

Poppo, Laura and Todd Zenger (2002), Do formal contracts and relational governance function as substitutes or complements?, *Strategic Management Journal*, 23, 707–25.

Rasmusen, Eric B., J. Mark Ramseyer, and John S. Jr, Wiley (1991), Naked Exclusion, *American Economic Review*, 81 (5), 1137–45.

Reuer, Jeffrey J. and Africa Ariño (2007), Strategic Alliance Contracts: Dimensions and Determinants of Contractual Complexity, *Strategic Management Journal*, 28 (3), 313–30.

Rey, Patrick and Bernard Salanié (1990), Long-term, Short-term and Renegotiation: On the Value of Commitment in Contracting, *Econometrica*, 58 (3), 597–619.

Rogerson, William P. (1984), Efficient Reliance and Damage Measures for Breach of Contract, *Rand Journal of Economics,* 15, 39–53.

— (1985), Repeated Moral Hazard, *Econometrica*, 53, 69–76.

Rubin, Paul (1978), The Theory of the Firm and the Structure of the Franchise Contract, *Journal of Law and Economics*, 25, 223–33.

Salanié, Bernard (1997), *The Economics of Contracts*, London, MIT Press.

Salanié, P., and P. Rey (1990), Long-Term, Short-term and Renegotiation: On the Value of Commitment in Contracting, *Econometrica* 58, 597–618.

Schwartz, Alan (1992), Relational Contracts in the Courts: An Analysis of Incomplete Agreements and Judicial Strategies, *Journal of Legal Studies*, 21 (2), 271–318.

Schwartz, Alan and Robert E. Scott (2003), Contract Theory and the Limits of Contract Law, *Yale Law Journal*, 113, 541–619.

Schweizer, Urs (2006), Cooperative Investments Induced by Contract Law, *Rand Journal of Economics*, 37, 134–45.

Scott, Robert E. (2000), The Case for Formalism in Relational Contract, *North Western University Law Review*, 94, 847.

Segal, Ilya and Michael Whinston (2000), Naked Exclusion: Comment, *The American Economic Review*, 90 (1), 296–309.

Shavell, Steven (1980), Damage Measures for Breach of Contract, *Bell Journal of Economics*, 11, 466–90.

— (2004), *Foundations of Economic Analysis of Law*, Cambridge (MA), London, Harvard University Press.

Sibley, David S. (2002), Comments made at the DOJ/FTC Hearings on Competition and Intellectual Property Law and Policy in the Knowledge-Based Economy, May 14.

Sliwka, Dirk (2002), On the Use of Nonfinancial Performance Measures in Management Compensation, *Journal of Economics and Management Strategy*, 11 (3) 487–511.

Sloof, Randolph, Edwin Leuven, Hessel Oosterbeek, and Joep Sonnemans (2003), An Experimental Comparison of Reliance Levels Under Alternative Breach Remedies, *Rand Journal of Economics*, 34, 205–22.

Solís-Rodríguez, Vanesa and Manuel González-Díaz (2009), Performance and Completeness in Repeated Inter-firm Relationships: The Case of Franchising, Working paper.
Stremitzer, Alexander (2008), Standard Breach Remedies, Quality Thresholds, and Cooperative Investments, Columbia Law and Economics Working Paper 335.
Williamson, Oliver E. (1983), Credible Commitments: Using Hostages to Support Exchange, *American Economic Review*, 73 (4), 519–40.
— (1985), *The Economic Institutions of Capitalism*, New York, Free Press.
— (1991), Comparative Economic Organization: The Analysis of Discrete Structural Alternatives, *Administrative Science Quarterly*, 36 (2), 269–96.
Zweigert, Konrad and Heinz Kötz (1998), *An Introduction to Comparative Law*, Third edition, translated by Tony Weir, Oxford University Press, ch. 25–31.

# Chapter 3
# Contractual Networks, Contract Design, and Contract Interpretation: The Case of Credit Cards

Clayton P. Gillette

Transaction cost economics predicts that firms join together in a network when doing so reduces the costs of exchange or otherwise enhances value for those who participate in the network. Caffagi's (2008) taxonomy of networks[1] indicates that network participants may employ various forms to accomplish these objectives, including serial or linear contracts (A-B, B-C, C-D) or concentric contracts in which one central party simultaneously contracts with multiple others, who may or may not contract with one another, but who are dependent on each other for success. Participants in a supply chain, for example, may engage in linear contracting. Concentric contracting, on the other hand, may be used by franchisors who transact individually with each franchisee, while franchisees are unlikely to transact with each other; nevertheless, the success of each franchisee depends to some extent on the performance of others. In each case, the network device is appropriate if it enhances the ability of participants to realize benefits not otherwise available or to induce cooperation among network participants that might otherwise be difficult to obtain if parties acted unilaterally or if obligations were restricted to those with whom they transacted bilaterally.

In each of these examples, the potential participants in a network include multiple firms within the same industry. The likelihood that firms will participate in a common network poses an interesting contracting problem. One traditionally thinks of different firms within an industry as competitors who seek to gain an advantage over each other with respect to common customers and suppliers. The success of the network of which the potential competitors are members, however, depends critically on the willingness of participants to cooperate. Self-interested competition in all respects may ultimately, in classic prisoners' dilemma fashion, redound to the detriment of all participants. Thus, the fledgling literature on networks notes that they are often characterized by an interesting mix of competition and cooperation. Indeed, the mixture of cooperation and competition

---

1 F. Cafaggi, 'Contractual Networks and the Small Business Act: Towards European Principles?', EUI Working Paper LAW No 2008/15, available at http://cadmus.eui.eu/dspace/bitstream/1814/8771/1/LAW_2008_15.pdf.

at least partially explains why a single, global contract may not be employed to govern the relationship among all participants in a network. Cooperation may be necessary to capture certain gains that any given firm could not generate by unilateral action. But the possibility of competition means that parties will not want common terms to apply to all aspects of the relationship, since some participants will desire to exploit an advantage they have over other participants by employing different contract terms than would be possible in a global agreement.

What determines when network participants should cooperate and when they should compete? Law external to contract will dictate some of the boundaries, since cooperation over some aspects of the relationship, such as the setting of prices, may violate antitrust or other regulatory mandates. But even where cooperation is permissible, parties may avoid instantiating that result in a set of contractual obligations, perhaps out of concern that cooperation will induce lock-in effects that make subsequent change in industry practices more costly and more difficult, or perhaps because cooperation is more efficiently induced by informal reputational mechanisms than by threat of legal sanction for defection. At the very least, however, one would expect that the scope of contractual cooperation will be linked to the value of the network itself. That is, cooperation should be embodied in legal obligations where joint efforts that might not otherwise occur could increase the value of the network itself. This does not necessarily mean that all participants will benefit from any particular act of cooperation. The prisoners' dilemma predicate for the network implies that, absent a contractual agreement, some parties would be better off if they did not cooperate, but rather defected from the cooperative solution. It is for that reason that some form of contractual obligation is necessary to induce cooperation. If all parties benefited from cooperation *ex post*, then arguably no contractual obligation would be necessary to induce that behaviour. Contracting permits parties to share expectationally in the gains from cooperation: those who might do better *ex post* by defecting have opportunities to contract *ex ante* for a share of the enhanced value of the network that cooperation generates.

Intranetwork contracts for cooperation, therefore, should exist in at least the following cases. First, one would expect to find obligations to cooperate where there is a dominant solution to the multiparty prisoners' dilemma, such as a clearly efficient pattern of behaviour or risk allocation that parties might not otherwise adhere to because they anticipate defection by others. Second, cooperation should exist to specify a solution to a coordination problem. Here, participants would presumably be willing to cooperate as long as they are aware of the solution to which all other participants will also migrate. Third, one would expect to find obligations to cooperate where doing so takes the form of assigning monitoring or other responsibilities to participants best positioned to undertake them, and thus to avoid free riding or other inducements for defection.

At the same time, these obligations may define the outside boundaries of cooperation within the network. While one might expect to find common or consistent terms in all contracts within a network with respect to terms that enhance the value of the network, one would not necessarily expect similar commonalities with respect to terms that do not enhance the size of the network pie. Specifically, many of the issues that affect the distribution of the surplus generated by the network, rather than the size of that surplus, are likely to be the subject of competition rather than of cooperation. Thus, the allocations of risks with respect to those issues may vary dramatically from contract to contract within the network.

In this chapter, some initial efforts are made towards testing these hypotheses by making a preliminary examination of a particular network. That network involves the series of arrangements, contractual and otherwise, that constitute credit card transactions. Participants within this network, such as banks that issue credit cards, appear to cooperate on some, but not all aspects of their relationship. For instance, they do not cooperate on interest rates that they charge cardholders, perhaps because of antitrust concerns, but also perhaps because some issuers would seek a competitive advantage even if cooperation were possible, and interest rate cooperation would not necessarily increase the value of the network. But cooperation in processing transactions among the participants more clearly increases the value of the network for all participants by reducing transaction costs and by assigning responsibilities for performing and monitoring functions related to payment processing to those best positioned to fulfil them.

The claims made here are both positive and normative. On the positive side, it is predicted that the explicit contracts that constitute the credit card network will tend to include common and consistent clauses that induce cooperation where doing so would enhance the value of the network. The normative claim is both more tentative and more controversial. It is suggested that the same principle that informs the positive claim – using contracts to enhance network value – should also be used to interpret the reach of contracts that involve network participants, even when the affected participants are not express parties to the contract being interpreted. While one may be reluctant to inject courts into the business of interpreting contracts in any manner that invites imposing obligations or allocating risks in a manner inconsistent with the parties' intentions, there may be circumstances in which the intent to benefit all participants in the network is relatively determinable, notwithstanding contractual silence.

Implicit in this normative claim is a limited conception of the judicial role in enforcing contractual intent in commercial transactions. When courts interpret terms so as to enhance the value of the contract, they are not imposing a solution to a contracting problem on network participants. Rather, they are reaching the solution that the participants themselves would have preferred had they been able to bargain explicitly about the term. Thus, incorporating the value of the network into the interpretive process is consistent with a well recognized objective of commercial law – to do for the parties what they could not have done for themselves. That objective, of course, is fully consistent with the goal of contract interpretation that is traditionally phrased in terms of honouring contractual intent. What makes the claim unique in the context of networks is the realization that the relevant relationship is not limited to those who are explicit parties to the contract. Instead, the admonition to enhance the value of the network may have implications for obligations that parties to the contract under review have to non-parties who also are participants in the network.

Indeed, recognizing the interdependent nature of contracts within the network both highlights and justifies a necessary distinction between interpretation of contracts used in a network from the standard mode of contract interpretation. Traditionally, interpretation of bilateral contract is predicated on an assumption of no external effects. Thus, courts look only at the intent of the immediate parties to the contract. The very presence of the network, however, makes it abundantly clear that any contract among fewer than all participants generates externalities for other participants. Relaxing the traditional assumption permits a judicial approach that is more attentive to the external consequences intended by parties to bilateral contracts.

## The Credit Card Transaction

For most people, a credit card transaction entails little more than paying for a good or service by providing the seller with a tangible card or information provided on that card. The cardholder subsequently is billed for the transaction by the issuer of the credit card. The cardholder makes payment to the issuer after receiving a statement from the issuer on which the transaction is indicated. Payments made within a stated time of mailing of the statement bear no additional cost, so that the cardholder benefits from the 'float' between the time of purchase and the time of payment. Payments less than the full balance of the statement, however, may require payments of interest and, if insufficient payment is made within a stated time, may also carry additional penalties. The merchant receives the benefit of immediate payment for goods from the card issuer and, as long as the merchant obtains proper authorization, the assurance that payment will be forthcoming.

This relatively simple transaction, however, masks a more complicated set of arrangements that involves cardholders, issuers, merchants, acquirers, and network operators. The largest credit card network operators, Visa and MasterCard, are typically referred to as 'networks'. The term is used in a broader sense, however, to include all the participants in the credit card transaction. When intending to refer only to Visa or MasterCard, the term 'network operators' is employed. The network operators do not issue cards. Instead, they are organizations composed of member banks who do issue the cards and who otherwise serve to channel payments to merchants who are authorized to accept a network operator's credit cards. The network operators themselves engage in a variety of functions that facilitate the use of credit cards. They authorize banks to issue cards, and provide a platform to authorize, clear, and settle transactions conducted with the card issued under their name.

A specific credit card transaction is authorized after the cardholder provides account information to a merchant. Merchants do not process payment for transactions directly with the platform of the network operators. Rather, they are allowed to accept credit cards after entering into an agreement for the processing of transactions with a bank, known as an acquirer, that is a member of a network operator. The merchant who receives a credit card in payment for a transaction seeks approval for the transaction, typically by sending electronic messages to the network operator. The network operator sends that request to the issuer for approval. The network operator sends notice of approval to the acquirer, which notifies the merchant. The cardholder is then permitted to complete the purchase.

Within a day of authorization, the transaction typically 'clears' (the process of making appropriate debits and credits among the relevant actors) when the merchant provides information, either electronically or through physical purchase slips, to the acquirer. The acquirer then sends the information to the network operator, which transmits the information to the issuer. Both the acquirer and the issuer will have accounts with the network operator. Thus, with respect to any transaction, the network operator will credit the acquirer and debit the account of the issuer. In practice, this settlement process involves daily netting of all transactions for any acquirer or issuer. The issuer uses information provided by the network operator to prepare a monthly statement for each cardholder. The cardholder can then elect whether to pay the outstanding balance each month in full or to make partial payments. If the cardholder elects the latter alternative, she will pay a finance charge.

The costs of using the network, which affects prospective members' incentives to participate, are allocated among the parties. When the acquirer receives (acquires) a record of the transaction from the merchant, it credits the merchant the amount of the transaction less certain fees. Those fees, known as merchant discount fees, consist of an interchange fee that the acquirer pays to the issuer of the card and a per transaction fee that the acquirer retains for its role in processing. Interchange fees are set by the networks and have been the focal point of substantial criticism. Some literature suggests that they reflect supracompetitive rents and thus force merchants to charge consumers a greater than competitive price for goods. Allegedly the 'excessive' amount of the price is subsidized by consumers who pay cash and receive no discount that reflects the absence of a fee for their transaction.[2] Fees may also reflect the size and type of transaction, with transactions of a type that are more susceptible to fraud (e.g., those that are executed through mail order rather than through presentation of a card that allows the use of security features) commanding higher fees. Thus, acquirers receive revenues from the discount they pay to merchants, merchants receive revenues from additional transactions they complete because they accept credit cards and from cost savings over processing other forms of payment, and issuers receive revenues from interchange fees and from finance charges, annual fees, and other fees (such as late fees) that are paid by cardholders.

---

2 J. Wright, 'Pricing in Debit and Credit Card Schemes' 80 *Economic Letters* 305–309 (2003).

For current purposes, what is most notable about the credit card network is that it operates through a series of serial bilateral contracts among the different participants. The network operators enter into agreements with issuers and acquirers for the processing of transactions. Those contractual obligations take the form of network operating rules that the network operator promulgates and to which other participants agree to adhere. Issuers enter into agreements with cardholders to allow the latter to use cards for payment at merchants that accept them. Merchants enter into agreements with acquirers to allow the latter to process transactions. Merchants also enter into agreements with the network operators, including the network operating rules, to set terms under which the merchant is permitted to accept cards.

As indicated by this description, credit cards are part of a multi-sided market, wherein credit card network operators attract both merchants who are willing to accept credit cards and individuals who are willing to use them as payment mechanisms for goods and services.[3] Indeed, much of the literature on two-sided markets developed largely from studies of credit card networks. That literature is largely concerned with pricing strategies that reflect the network externalities created by use of the platform and regulation to avoid exploitation of the platform's position in creating the exchange between end users. A related literature concerns the incentives of each participant to use the credit card network and the presence or absence of cross subsidies in the payment of the network's costs.

Our emphasis here, however, is less on the pricing formula that the credit card networks utilize than on the contractual arrangements that define the obligations of the multiple players in a credit card payment transaction. It is useful to note, however, that a primary objective of those contracts is to capture the benefits available to parties in a two-sided market as a consequence of network externalities. The more people who are willing to use credit cards to make payments, the more merchants will be willing to incur the costs necessary to accept and process payments, and the more banks will be willing to incur the costs of issuing them. At the same time, the more merchants who are willing to accept credit cards, the more individuals will be willing to incur the costs of obtaining them in order to facilitate purchases. Thus, all participants in the network benefit as trust in the use of credit cards induces more participants to enter at each level. Left to their own devices, however, few merchants or issuers or cardholders would publicize the benefits of widespread use and acceptance of credit cards, since publicity is costly and, once those costs are incurred, it has the characteristics of a public good. As a result, potential publicists have incentives to free ride on the investments of another party who pays the costs of publicity. Visa and MasterCard solve this dilemma by incurring advertising costs to promote the use of their cards. The network operators can then recover their costs from all participants in the network by assessing fees and charges that reflect their advertising costs. In addition, Visa and MasterCard provide a single

---

3 J.-C. Rochet and J. Tirole, 'Two-Sided Markets: An Overview' (March 12, 2004), available at http://web.mit.edu/14.271/www/rochet_tirole.pdf.

platform for processing and clearing payments among the relevant parties to the transaction. Presumably this function reduces transaction costs that parties would otherwise incur in bilateral payment processing.

Given the nature of the transaction, it becomes clear that the credit card network presents opportunities for both cooperation and competition. Cooperation among issuers is suitable to promote the use of cards, to ensure the safety and ease of issuing, using, and accepting credit cards, and to facilitate smooth processing of transactions. Nevertheless, acquirers will compete for merchants, and both issuers and merchants will compete with other issuers and merchants for the business of cardholders. One would expect that the terms of the bilateral agreements will reflect both the cooperative and competitive features. For instance, since all participating issuers (and all merchants) benefit from promotion of the network operators' brand through advertising, the creation of affinity programmes, and smooth clearing, one would anticipate cooperation along these dimensions. All participating issuers (and all merchants) suffer costs to the extent that the value of cards is diluted as a consequence of fraudulent use. As a result, one would again expect cooperation along that dimension. However, different merchants may have different exposure to unauthorized credit card use. As a result, one would expect that different acquirers would offer different terms to different merchants, depending on the level of risk the acquirer desired to accept and the acquirer's own capacity to detect or deter unauthorized use.

There does appear to be significant competition among issuers and acquirers. Evans and Schmalensee present evidence of significant distinctions among major credit card issuers along various dimensions, including interest rate, grace period, annual fees, late fees, over limit fees, and cash advance fees.[4] Some of these fees have generated controversy on the grounds that they are insufficiently salient to consumers, or that they exploit high switching costs. Recent changes in federal law may decrease distinctions among issuers, as they prohibit or greatly restrict certain practices. But those changes do not significantly affect many of the characteristics that Evans and Schmalensee suggest are the focal point of competition. In addition, issuers compete with respect to affinity programmes and status, such as the offer of 'Platinum' cards at higher fees to cardholders who have high incomes or creditworthiness.

### *Cooperation to Enhance Network Value*

Bilateral contracts between various participants to credit card transactions are appropriate in part because it would be impossible to create a single, multiparty contract that comprised all participants in the network. But more than the practical difficulties, bilateral contracts are appropriate because they can instantiate many of the competitive features offered by acquirers and issuers that would be lost

4 D.S. Evans and R. Schmalensee, *Paying with Plastic* (2nd edn, MIT Press, Cambridge/Mass. 2005).

in a universal contract. Nevertheless, a contract network would be appropriate if it can induce parties to cooperate in achieving a joint maximizing solution on some aspects of the multiparty relationship that parties might otherwise eschew. This theory of networks predicts that virtually all the bilateral contracts within the credit card network would be similar in one respect: where certain cooperative measures enhance the value of the network, each of the bilateral contracts will explicitly create cooperative obligations to constrain the parties from acting in a self-interested manner that would diminish the value of the network. As noted above, cooperation should exist where there is a clear efficiency to be realized by allocating an identifiable risk to a certain party, where all parties seek a single coordination point, or where monitoring or similar functions need to be assigned in order to avoid free riding.

To test this prediction, the contractual allocation of risks that result from fraudulent use of a credit card has been examined. Fraudulent use may occur in a variety of ways. A card, or information taken from a card, may be stolen from the cardholder and used by an unauthorized person to complete an unauthorized transaction. Alternatively, a merchant or an employee of the merchant may use information obtained in an authorized transaction to complete an unrelated, unauthorized transaction. One would imagine that all participants in the network would benefit from fraud reduction because of greater trust in the network. Cardholders will be more willing to use credit cards if they believe that they will not be held responsible for unauthorized use that is not due to their own misconduct. Merchants will be more willing to accept credit cards if they believe that they are not responsible for unauthorized charges that they could not easily detect. Issuers will be more willing to issue cards if they believe they will not ultimately be responsible for charges that other participants could have avoided.

Notwithstanding the benefits from fraud reduction to the network participants as a group, the participants have very different abilities to avoid fraudulent use of a credit card. Cardholders can reduce fraudulent use by taking precautions against loss or theft of cards and by monitoring monthly statements to detect fraudulent use before the fraudster can engage in additional transactions. Issuers can reduce fraudulent transactions by verifying the identity of applicants for cards and by including security information on the cards that they issue. Merchants can reduce fraudulent use by verifying the identity of cardholders and by using security information before accepting a credit card as payment for a transaction. Acquirers can reduce fraudulent charges initiated by merchants by monitoring merchants who are the subject of a significant number of chargebacks, which may indicate improper behaviour by the merchant and subsequent complaints by cardholders to their issuers. At the same time, there are significant disincentives for each party to exploit its advantage, because doing so is costly, and the same fraud can be avoided if some other, albeit less well positioned, party detects or deters the fraudulent activity. For instance, monitoring merchant chargebacks is costly and monitoring itself has the characteristics of a public good among the network participants – monitoring against fraudulent use by one of the parties dilutes the incentives of the others similarly to monitor. As a result, left to their own devices, all participants may underinvest in monitoring.

Our theory of contractual networks predicts that clauses within each of the bilateral contracts in the network will explicitly assign the risk of fraud and monitoring to the party best positioned to take specified actions that can reduce the risk of fraud, since doing so will minimize the costs of unauthorized transactions, thus enhancing the network's value to all participants. A variety of bilateral contracts within the network has been considered to test these predictions. These bilateral contracts include cardholder agreements with issuers, agreements between acquirers and merchants, and the operating rules of the network operators that govern their relationships with issuers, acquirers, and merchants. The preliminary results are consistent with predictions.

Of course, any contractual allocation of losses from unauthorized transactions must be set against the background of mandatory legal rules. In the credit card context, a statutory rule enacted by the United States Congress limits the ability of issuers to impose losses from unauthorized use on cardholders, even negligent ones, as long as cardholders provide timely notice of the unauthorized charge. This may or may not be an efficient allocation of losses, though there is some evidence that it is. It is the current practice of the network operators to impose even *less* liability on cardholders than the legal rule allows. Network operators impose no liability on cardholders, even if the loss or theft of a card was due to their own negligence, as long as the cardholder provides timely notification of the unauthorized use. This feature arguably reflects a belief that, even with respect to cards that are stolen or lost, parties other than cardholders are best positioned to avoid subsequent unauthorized use. It is, of course, also plausible that the network operators accept the greater liability in order to induce more individuals to become cardholders or for cardholders to use their cards more frequently, because the fees and charges that those additional transactions generate exceed the marginal losses from unauthorized use.

Against that legal background, however, the bilateral contracts in the credit card network do appear to obligate each participant to take those measures against unauthorized use that it is best positioned to enforce. A review of agreements indicates that cardholder agreements tend to impose obligations on cardholders to notify the issuer of loss, theft, or unauthorized use, and to cooperate with the issuer in efforts to recover stolen cards and amounts from unauthorized users. Shorn of that contractual obligation, cardholders who bear no legal liability for unauthorized debts would have little incentive to take costly measures to notify or cooperate in recoveries, especially since losses are often generated through unauthorized use by parties known to the cardholder.

Merchants can avoid unauthorized charges in two ways. First, they can take measures to ensure that customers are engaged in authorized transactions. For instance, they can check signatures on credit card slips with those on the back of cards or obtain security codes for long-distance credit card transactions. Second, they can avoid fraudulent transactions that either they or their employees initiate with customer information. These measures all require costly creation of policies about the conditions in which credit cards will be accepted and employee use of credit card information, and costly monitoring of the policies that have been adopted. Merchants have incentives to avoid these costs by minimizing security measures, even though they are well positioned to take them and their implementation generates net benefits to the network. One would expect the bilateral contracts between merchants and acquirers and between acquirers and network operators to counter these self-interested incentives.

Indeed, the rules that govern the relationship between network operators and merchants that are entitled to accept cards induce merchants to incur the relevant fraud-minimizing costs by a series of fees and rules. Acquirers are charged additional fees if the merchants with whom they contract meet or exceed specified chargeback activity thresholds. These fees increase with the amount of chargebacks assessed against merchants, and can exceed $100,000 per month. The effect is to induce acquirers to take advantage of their position to monitor fraudulent activity by merchants. Additional penalties are assessed if the acquirer fails to identify high-risk merchants for whom it serves as acquirer or if the acquirer fails to notify the network of suspected or confirmed loss or theft of transaction information. In addition, the network operating rules allow penalties to be imposed on acquirers whose merchants receive inappropriate interchange fees. Finally, the network operating rules attempt to reduce the risk of use of cardholder information to effect unauthorized transactions by prohibiting merchants from retaining customer data after the authorization of a transaction.

Consistent with the predictions, contracts between the acquirer and the merchant then impose obligations on the merchant to take measures that minimize the risk that the acquirer will itself become subject to penalties designated in the operating rules. For instance, processing agreements will include a warranty from the merchant to the acquirer to the effect that each sales record presented for processing is genuine and arises out of a bona fide sale of merchandise or services.[5] Similarly, the merchant also agrees that it will not present for processing any sales record that did not originate as a result of a transaction between a cardholder and the merchant. The agreement also imposes ultimate liability for any chargebacks on the merchant, and defines a chargeback as including (i) a transaction for which an authorization was required but not obtained, (ii) non-delivery of goods or services, (iii) a dispute by the cardholder or the sale or of his or her signature, or (iv) the cardholder denies making the purchase in a long-distance transaction.

The effect of the chain of contract clauses is to induce each party to the credit card transaction to exploit its advantage in minimizing unauthorized use of credit cards. Even those participants who are not parties to a bilateral contract between other participants will benefit from the allocation to the extent that it reduces overall fraud costs and thus enhances the value of the network. Contract design in practice follows this theory.

---

5 See, e.g., *Friedman* v *24 Hour Fitness USA, Inc*, 2009 WL 2711956 (CD Cal).

### *Contractual Networks and Contract Interpretation*

The contracts that govern the relationships among participants in a credit card network are necessarily incomplete. Given the incomplete nature of all contracts, the parties to a contract may disagree on how the written contract assigns a risk as to which there is no explicit allocation. For instance, relatively vague admonitions to behave in 'good faith' or to exercise 'best efforts' will necessarily require interpretation to determine the specific conduct required of at least one of the parties when a contingency that has not been explicitly provided for materializes. Alternatively, a contract within the network will be incomplete in that it fails to address a contingency that materializes while the contract is in effect. For instance, technological developments may cause breakdowns the risk of which were not allocated in the original negotiations. When this occurs, the contract will have to be interpreted to determine how to allocate the unanticipated risk.

When a dispute over the unallocated risk arises, a variety of tools become available to interpret the meaning of the contract. Among the interpretive tools that neoclassical contract law recognizes in these situations is the relational context in which the parties to the contract transact. In some situations, particularly those characterized by long-term agreements in which there are opportunities for holdup, the relational nature of the contract has been invoked to urge courts to fill gaps – both those that result from ambiguity and those that result from materialization of unprovided-for contingencies – by considering the extent to which an underlying motivation for the contract, or for the choice of language in the contract, was to signal an intent to cooperate when contingencies that were not contractually specified materialized. The underlying justification for this relational approach is that the parties presumably entered into their relationship in order to maximize the joint product made available through their relationship and thus increase the surplus available for division between them.

There is a fundamental difficulty, however, with the idea that courts can successfully imply relational duties in bilateral contracts among sophisticated commercial parties. Commercial parties routinely aim to structure their relation to economize on the expected costs of contracting (to them). Their strategies for doing so are a central theme in contemporary contracts scholarship.[6] Typically, these economizing strategies turn on the balance in contract design between broad standards of performance and precise, bright line rules specifying exactly the action the party must take. All else equal, it is harder, and therefore more costly, to verify application of a broad standard than application of a more precise contract term or rule. This is because in verifying a standard, the court first must determine an operative 'proxy' against which to measure a party's performance: what observable (range of) outcomes should count in determining whether (a range of) unobservable behaviour is reasonable? The evidentiary proxies a court selects in

6 See R.E. Scott and G.G. Triantis, 'Anticipating Litigation in Contract Design' 115 *Yale Law Journal* 814 (2006).

applying a standard inevitably will be a noisier signal of a party's performance than either the parties' direct observation of their actual actions or determination of the conformity of an act to a rule specifying an action.[7]

Parties thus delegate proxy choice to the courts through the language of the contractual standard and its combination with the precise rules in the contract. In some cases, the parties might rely exclusively on precise rules and forgo standards. In hindsight, a court may be tempted in these cases (perhaps with the encouragement of one of the parties) to see gaps between the discrete rules and therefore to read into the contract implied relational duties, such as best efforts or commercial reasonableness. Yet commercial parties can include standards in their contract at relatively low cost, and they enjoy superior knowledge of the context of their contractual relationship to determine the optimal allocation of proxy choice. Consequently, the courts are wise to interpret the absence of vague standards in commercial contracts as instructions from the parties to abstain from proxy choice and to limit their construction to the precise terms of the contract.

Notwithstanding the injunction for courts to be cautious in imposing relational duties, the unique collective action problems posed by contractual networks suggest the possibility of using the relational idea to extend the reach of explicit duties of cooperation that are part of a bilateral contract between some (but not all) of the network participants. Because all participants in the network do not necessarily contract with each other, participants who enter into bilateral contracts with other participants do not necessarily reach explicit understandings about what obligations, if any, are owed to other (non-contract-party) participants within the network. The normative claim in this chapter is that the objective of the network structure could be used to resolve claims about the scope of these obligations when parties' actions influence the value of the network positively or negatively, but the parties have not, due to high transaction costs, reduced their obligations towards other participants to an explicit contract.

Given that the function of a network is to increase the surplus available for division among participants, contracts that implement the network presumably would require cooperation when doing so enhances the value of the network. Thus, an interpretive rule that induces cooperation in these situations does for the parties what they otherwise would have provided for themselves had transaction costs not impeded explicit agreement. The participants, however, would not

7 Idem. To illustrate the point in text, assume the parties wish to pair particular future contingencies to corresponding performance obligations, i.e., when X occurs, the promisor must pay $Y. The parties can define X in several different ways. X may be a rule, i.e., a relatively specific fact, such as the delivery of a widget with a specified weight. Here the party's only delegate to the court the determination of what evidence is sufficient to satisfy X and trigger the promisor's payment obligation. Alternatively, X can be a standard, such as the delivery of a widget in excellent condition. Here the court must determine not only what evidence is sufficient to establish the weight of the widget, but also the degree to which weight is relevant to the determination of whether the widget satisfies the standard.

necessarily induce cooperation with respect to measures that did not increase the value of the network, or over which participants had agreed to compete. Where applicable, however, the objective of enhancing network value where contracts are interdependent assumes contractual intent to cooperate even with non-party network participants who are adversely affected by the failure of one of the parties' behaviour. This chapter argues, therefore, that principles for interpreting contracts that implement networks should recognize and enforce legal obligations to cooperate with other network participants when doing so will enhance the network's value. Those principles should not, however, necessarily recognize legal obligations towards non-parties when the value of the network is not implicated.

*Third-Party Beneficiary Theory as a Means of Enhancing Network Value*

Even if one accepts the proposition that participants in a network intend *ex ante* to cooperate where doing so enhances the network's value, it is necessary to identify some doctrinal hook on which courts may rely to implement that objective. To be clear, this chapter is not suggesting that courts create a novel, generalized duty to cooperate unmoored from traditional concepts of contract law. Rather, a preliminary analysis suggests only that the obligations that arise within networks are simply a variation on well-accepted third-party beneficiary principles that grant enforceable rights to non-parties to contracts. The 'hornbook' conditions under which non-parties can assert rights under a contract looks primarily to the intent of the parties. Thus, the Restatement (2d) of Contracts provides that a promise in a contract creates an enforceable duty running from the promisor to an 'intended beneficiary',[8] and defines the quoted term as including a beneficiary of a promise if recognition of a right to performance in that beneficiary is appropriate to effectuate the intention of the parties and 'the circumstances indicate that the promisee intends to give the beneficiary the benefit of the promised performance'.[9] That language is not a model of precision, but neither is it vacuous. It suggests that the benefit of a promise runs to non-parties (1) whom the parties understand will rely on it, and (2) whom the parties prefer to rely on it, presumably because the parties themselves receive some reciprocal benefit from that reliance. It is plausible that a pertinent, if not quintessential, example for application of the doctrine involves a situation in which participants have created a network in order to exploit the advantages of that organizational form over more complete multiparty contracts, but one participant strategically acts in a manner that will save it disproportionate costs by imposing greater risks on other participants.

The contours of that situation can be explored by reconsidering the credit card network. Given the large number of cardholders, issuers, acquirers, and merchants, it is unrealistic to expect that all parties would be able to enjoy contractual privity with one another. Transaction costs, therefore, impede global agreement among

8 Restatement (2d) § 304.

9 Idem. § 302.

all parties. Nevertheless, it is plausible that the actions of one set of parties could create risks for others with whom they have not explicitly entered into contracts. If that action were to create net harm to the contractual network, then one would anticipate that, but for the transaction costs involved, the parties would have contracted to place the risk on the party who is creating the net harm. Under these circumstances, arguably the bilateral contracts that do exist should be interpreted to confer entitlements on non-parties.

A test of this theory has arisen in recent litigation involving liability of participants in the credit card network when hackers break into the computer system of a merchant and steal personal information concerning cardholders that the merchant retained contrary to its contractual obligations. As noted above, network operator rules provide that once a transaction has been authorized, a merchant must not store or retain the cardholder information. The operating rules require the acquirer to ensure that merchants with whom they contract comply with the operating regulations, including the regulations prohibiting retention of cardholder information. That information can be used by the hackers to facilitate unauthorized transactions in the name of the cardholders. Although cardholders will not be liable for unauthorized transactions, they may have to incur significant time and expense demonstrating that the transactions are unauthorized. They also face substantial risks to their credit ratings until they are able to demonstrate that they are not responsible for the transactions. In order to minimize these risks, cardholders whose information is stolen will typically cancel their credit card accounts and receive new credit cards from the issuer. Both the costs of cancelling and replacing cards and the costs of unauthorized transactions that cannot be billed to the cardholder may ultimately fall on the issuer. In order to obtain reimbursement for these expenses, issuers have brought actions against merchants and their acquirers for retaining the personal information of cardholders. But, of course, issuers do not have any contractual agreement with merchants or their acquirers. Instead, they have bilateral agreements with cardholders and with the network operators. As a result, issuers have sought recovery of their costs under theories that transform them into beneficiaries of bilateral contracts between other participants.

The results of the litigation have been quite varied, notwithstanding that much of it has arisen out of the same incident, involving a single merchant. Most courts have exhibited significant scepticism towards inferring any intent to benefit non-party participants. In *Banknorth, NA* v *BJ's Wholesale Club*,[10] the court held that the issuer was not a third-party beneficiary of contract between the merchant and its acquiring bank because that agreement expressly excluded any intent to confer third-party beneficiary on any other person. The court reached a similar result in *CUMIS Insurance Society, Inc* v *BJ's Wholesale Club*.[11] There, an insurer of issuers who suffered losses from replacing customers' cards asserted

10 442 FSupp2d 206 (MD Pa 2006).

11 2008 WL 2345865 (Mass Super).

third-party beneficiary status. The court again concluded that plaintiffs were not 'intended third-party beneficiaries' of these contracts in light, *inter alia*, of the fact that the contracts specifically disavowed any such intention. In that litigation, representatives of both Visa and MasterCard stated at depositions that the primary purpose of the regulations is to protect the integrity of the payment system as a whole. Rather than interpret that testimony as evidence of the intent of all parties to enhance the value of the network, the court used those statements to conclude that the issuers were 'incidental', not 'intended' beneficiaries.

Another court reached a somewhat middle ground on an issuer's claims. In *Regions Bank* v *BJ's Wholesale Club, Inc*,[12] the court denied the issuer the status of a third-party beneficiary, but denied the defendants' motion to dismiss claims based on negligence, equitable subordination, and indemnification. The issuer also failed to establish grounds for recovery in *Sovereign Bank* v *BJ's Wholesale Club, Inc*.[13] There, the bank asserted that the acquirer was liable to it under a theory of promissory estoppel. The court, however, rejected the notion that one who had not transacted directly with the claimant could bear liability under a promissory estoppel theory, because the element of reliance could not be satisfied in the absence of a prior relationship. Instead, the court concluded that 'most promissory-estoppel cases deal with parties that have had direct contact with one another and a course of negotiations that might have led one of them, reasonably or unreasonably, to believe it could act upon the representations of the other'. The court reached this conclusion, notwithstanding that the issuer framed its claim in a manner reminiscent of the interdependence of participants in a network. The issuer argued:

> To survive, the Visa network requires parties unknown to each other to make promises to each other and rely on the promises of others. Because there are so many parties involved in the Visa network, it would be impracticable (if not impossible) for each party to specifically contract with each other party in the network. But this does not mean that Members do not reasonably rely on other Members in the network to do what they promised to do: abide by the Operating Regulations. In fact, within the Visa network, because the Members are virtually unknown to each other, the need to rely on each other is even greater than if an actual contract existed. For example, when Sovereign places the Cardholder Information on the magnetic stripe for its customers' use of the card within the Visa network, Sovereign is reasonably relying on the fact that Merchants like BJ's will not store and retain that confidential information and Members like Fifth Third will make sure Merchants like BJ's are not storing and retaining that information.

The court, however, turned the issuer's assertion on its head. It concluded that the issuer could not have joined the network out of reliance on acquirers, the

12 2006 WL 2841358 (SD Fla).
13 427 FSupp2d 526 (MD Pa 2006).

identities of which were unknown to it. That conclusion, of course, misses the point that the very reason to organize a network is the capacity of that organizational form to enhance value to all participants by creating a relationship among parties who cannot easily transact with, and who may well be unknown to each other.

Finally, the court in *Sovereign Bank* v *BJ's Wholesale Club, Inc*,[14] concluded that the issuer is not a third-party beneficiary of contract between merchant and acquirer, and dismissed the action with respect to the merchant. The contract between the merchant and its acquirer expressly provided that 'This agreement is for the benefit of, and may be enforced only by, Bank and Merchant and their respective successors and permitted transferees and assignees, and is not for the benefit of, and may not be enforced by, any third party'.

Nevertheless, some courts, including the highest federal court to address the issue, have been more receptive to the third-party beneficiary argument. In *Sovereign Bank* v *BJ's Wholesale Club, Inc*,[15] the issuer claimed that it could recover from the merchant and acquirer for defendants' failure to comply with security provisions of contracts between defendants and Visa. Trial court concluded that the issuer did not qualify as intended beneficiary of contract between the acquirer and Visa. That court interpreted the relevant contract as evincing an intent to benefit the Visa system as a whole, but not individual participants in the system. Issuers were, as the Massachusetts court had concluded in *CUMIS*, merely incidental beneficiaries.

The appellate court reversed. It concluded that there was some evidence that Visa intended the benefit of an acquirer's promise to ensure privacy of information would be shared with issuers. The court did not conclude that the necessary intent to benefit had been demonstrated, but it did hold that there existed a genuine issue of material fact on that issue. One other district court adhered to similar reasoning in refusing to dismiss the issuer's claims for recovery. In *Banknorth, NA* v *BJ's Wholesale Club*,[16] an issuer of credit cards claimed losses due to replacement of a customer's card from the merchant victimized by hackers and its acquirer. The issuer contended that it was a beneficiary of the contract between the merchant and the acquiring bank and between each defendant and Visa. The court stated that third-party beneficiary status depends on the intent of parties to the express contract. The court concluded that the plaintiff's claim could not be dismissed because a fact issue existed as to whether those parties intended to make the issuer a third-party beneficiary of the merchant's and bank's contracts with the network operator.

Our theory entails that these latter courts, which have indicated greater willingness to entertain the third-party beneficiary argument, are acting more consistently with the intent of the parties. The protection of cardholder information certainly is intended to benefit the cardholders themselves. But presumably the reason for inserting clauses that implement the obligation into agreements between the network operators and acquirers, and between acquirers and merchants, is out

14 395 FSupp2d 183 (MD Pa 2005).
15 533 F3d 162 (3d Cir 2008).
16 394 FSupp2d 283 (D Me 2005).

of recognition that (1) merchant failure to protect that information will diminish the value of the network as cardholders become more reluctant to use payment systems that subject them to the costs of identity theft; (2) merchants have self-interested incentives not to incur the costs related to protection of that information; and (3) acquirers and merchants are well positioned to take measures that serve the interests of issuers and cardholders, so that contractual clauses that induce those parties to exploit their advantage can enhance the value of the complete network. If the purpose of the clause is to maximize the joint value of all participants, then allowing non-party participants to enforce the contract would appear to be implicit in the understanding that induced formation of the network in the first instance.

Indeed, in the absence of allowing issuers rights under the bilateral contracts to which it is not a party, it is by no means clear how the obligation to protect cardholder information would be enforced. Cardholders would seem to be the natural enforcer, though they, too, are non-parties to the relevant agreement. But even if they were awarded rights under the contract, the fact that they receive new cards and have no liability for unauthorized charges suggests that they have insufficient damages to induce them to seek legal redress. (Moreover, in those few cases, typically class actions, in which cardholders do seek redress, they have been rebuffed.) Acquirers will suffer few losses if they are able to impose chargebacks for unauthorized charges. They will incur only the administrative costs of executing the chargebacks. Issuers, who ultimately absorb much of the losses related to the theft of cardholder information – replacing cards for cardholders – appear to be the parties with sufficient incentive to seek redress against those who violated their contractual obligations. It would be somewhat odd to impose a commitment on participants in the network and then deprive them of the ability to obtain redress from the only party with a sufficient incentive to enforce it. Instead, it seems more plausible to conclude that the issuer would have bargained for the enforcement right if it had been in direct privity with the acquirer or the merchant. Implying such a right within the network, therefore, appears to provide for the parties what they would have provided for themselves, but for transactions costs.

### *Objections*

There are two significant objections to the claim for extending third-party beneficiary liability. First, recall that this argument is based on contractual intent. The underlying assumption is that participants form a network to maximize the joint value of their relationship. As a result, courts that impose obligations of cooperation among participants to achieve that objective are simply enforcing the intent of the parties. But if that is the parties' intent, why don't they include explicit third-party beneficiary clauses in favour of non-party participants?

Of course, it is always difficult to infer the contractual intent behind an excluded clause. Did the parties fail to consider it, or did they affirmatively reject it? In this case, the absence of an express grant of third-party beneficiary status could reflect an explicit decision by rational parties. Recall that the theory does not entail that non-party participants should be considered third-party beneficiaries with respect to all elements of the bilateral contracts that constitute the network. Instead, it proposes that the interests of non-party participants be considered only with respect to those obligations that enhance the value of the network. No such status is implicated with respect to clauses that are intended to instantiate the competitive elements of a contract or of clauses that do not otherwise maximize the joint value of the network. It could, however, be difficult to specify in advance which obligations are intended to fall into which category, or what the specific cooperative act might consist of. For instance, prior to widespread hacking into merchant databases, it is not clear that parties would have thought to require action that minimized the practice or its effect on network participants. Thus, even parties who intend to confer rights on participants in order to induce cooperation in joint maximizing situations could prefer to leave the analysis for *ex post* application by courts rather than include a broad third-party beneficiary clause that courts might misinterpret to confer broader rights on non-parties than was intended. The issue is whether there will be more judicial error if a third-party beneficiary clause is included or excluded, and reasonable parties could conclude that error would be greater in the former.

Second, recall that some of the cases mentioned above were decided on the grounds that the bilateral agreements explicitly excluded any intent to confer rights on third parties. If we claim to be vindicating the intent of the parties, aren't we required to respect those explicit clauses? The answer here may be 'yes', but with less effect on the overall theory than might initially seem apparent. The clauses on which courts relied to exclude third-party rights all involved agreements between merchants and their acquirers. It is plausible that they were included to avoid actions by cardholders, rather than by issuers. In this regard, it is notable that the Visa Operating Regulations contain clauses that appear to make just that distinction. Those Regulations recite that:

> The *Visa Operating Regulations* consist of the *Visa International and Regional Operating Regulations*, and govern the relationship between Visa and its Members. The *Visa Operating Regulations* do not constitute a third-party beneficiary contract as to any entity or person, nor do they constitute a contract, promise or representation, or confer any rights, privileges, or claims of any kind, as to any third parties.

The term 'members', however, includes both issuers and acquirers. Thus, an issuer who seeks to enforce an acquirer's obligations under the operating regulations is not acting as an explicitly excluded third-party beneficiary. If an issuer can require acquirers to comply with their obligations under those regulations, and if acquirers can then recover from defalcating merchants under the bilateral agreement between those parties, then the network-enhancing value of the relationship can be achieved even without conferring third-party rights on issuers with respect to the merchant agreement. It is sufficient if issuers are able to recover against acquirers who fail to monitor compliance by merchants with their obligations to protect cardholder information. Hence, third-party beneficiary theory becomes superfluous in that limited context, but tells us little about the desirability of applying the theory in other contexts.

## Conclusion

Contractual networks allow participants to create relationships within which parties can commit to cooperate when doing so maximizes their joint value. As a matter of contract design, therefore, one would expect to see clauses that mandate cooperation to effect joint maximization either by reducing parties' incentives to act in a self-interested manner that diminishes the value of the network or by solving a coordination problem. An examination of bilateral contracts within the credit card network bears out that prediction. But transactions costs complicate the ability to include all participants within a single contract. That transactional difficulty, however, should not be allowed to defeat the ultimate, value-enhancing function of the network. Instead, those charged with interpretation of contracts should take the presence and purpose of the network into account in determining the reach of explicit obligations and should vindicate the intent of all participants by imposing cooperative obligations under the same circumstances in which parties would have required them if explicit contract had been available.[17]

17 I am grateful to Robert Scott for substantial input in reviewing this chapter.

Chapter 4

# The Lion, the Fox and the Workplace: Fundamental Rights and the Politics of Long-Term Contractual Relationships

Chantal Mak

## Introduction

In long-term contractual relationships between parties holding structurally unequal bargaining positions, fundamental rights may serve as a safeguard against the exploitation of the weaker contract party. An example is the application of the right to a free choice of profession in cases concerning exclusivity or non-competition clauses that forbid employees to work for competing companies. A judge may avoid or adapt such a clause in case it sets too far-reaching restrictions on the employee's freedom to choose in which field to work. Another example is the restriction of the employee's freedom of expression through the inclusion of duties of confidentiality in the contract. Again, fundamental rights argumentation may induce a court to intervene when the clause limits the weaker contracting party's autonomy to too great an extent.

This chapter analyses the political role of fundamental rights in case law concerning long-term contractual relationships between parties holding unequal bargaining positions. The central question is what can be the added value of argumentation based on these rights in respect to pure private law reasoning for the resolution of disputes arising from the contract. In order to answer this question, a comparative legal-political analysis is made of representative cases regarding non-competition clauses in German, Dutch and Italian (employment) contract law. The results of this analysis may define starting points for a further harmonization of the regulation of long-term contracts on the European level.

The chapter is structured as follows. First, an evaluation will be made of the role of the judge in regard to the answering of legal-political questions underlying disputes in long-term contractual relationships (second section). Emphasis will lie on the theoretical view on adjudication. Second, the role of fundamental rights in the adjudication process will be assessed (third section). In particular, it will be investigated how the application of these rights to contractual disputes affects the manner in which judges frame their decisions. Finally, some conclusions will be drawn on the potential impact of fundamental rights on further harmonization in the field of long-term contractual relationships in the EU (fourth section).

## The Judge and the Politics of Long-Term Contractual Relationships

### *Introduction*

Although long-term contracts, such as those concerning employment and tenancy, are usually governed by extensive sets of legislative provisions, the application of these rules regularly requires a judicial assessment of the case at hand. While many legal systems, for instance, have rules on non-competition clauses (e.g. § 90a of the German *Handelsgesetzbuch*; Article 7:653 of the Dutch *Burgerlijk Wetboek*), the extent to which these provisions regulate these clauses in detail differs considerably. As will be seen in the section below, the judiciary in various European countries continues to have considerable influence on the determination of the validity of such clauses in specific cases. The question is how the (long-term) relationship between the judge and the legislator should be perceived in these situations. To what extent should the courts have discretion to formulate restrictions on parties' contractual arrangements of their long-term (employment) relationship? In this context, it is particularly interesting to consider the specific characteristics of long-term contracts as compared to spot contracts, such as many contracts regarding the sale of goods. The question arises as to how the fact that a case concerns a long-term contractual relationship affects the judge's reasoning.

In the following, the legal-political role of the judiciary, with a focus on its relation to the legislature, will be sketched against the background of two different views on adjudication. These concern, respectively, the work of Ronald Dworkin and that of Duncan Kennedy on the topic.[1] This chapter does not aspire to give a comprehensive overview of their standpoints, nor to present fully and elaborately a theory of adjudication. Rather, the ambition is to gain some insights into the manner in which judges are engaged in the solution of questions of a legal-political nature or so-called 'hard cases', in which a rule-solution is not yet available. This will form the starting point for the further analysis of fundamental rights application in contract cases. At the end of this section, therefore, the views of the aforementioned American legal scholars are translated to the European setting, in order to establish the extent to which European judges in civil cases may, in theory, influence the legal-political course taken for the regulation of long-term contracts.

1 For a more elaborate presentation of the controversy between Dworkin's and Kennedy's views on adjudication, see also C. Mak, *Fundamental Rights in European Contract Law. A Comparison of the Impact of Fundamental Rights on Contractual Relationships in Germany, the Netherlands, Italy and England* (Kluwer Law International, Alphen a/d Rijn 2008) in particular Chapter 4.

## *A Matter of Principle*[2]

In legal theory, a distinction is sometimes made between Lions and Foxes.[3] Lions would be those legal scholars who build their theories around the internal analysis of decision making, starting from the presumption that cases in principle are decided in a deductive mode. Judges are assumed to seek a justifiable answer for the disputes before them, an answer that 'fits' with legal materials and values and serves the consistency and coherence of the legal system in question.[4] From the Lions' perspective, the law thus has some degree of predictability and certainty. A Lion seeks to construct his kingdom of theories on this basis. A renowned representative of this group of legal scholars is Ronald Dworkin, who built an impressive theory of adjudication, a central concept of which is the 'right answer' that can be found in all disputes, including 'hard cases'.[5]

Dworkin's thesis assumes that judicial decisions enforce existing political rights. Accordingly, judicial decisions in civil cases 'characteristically are and should be generated by principle, not policy'.[6] Arguments of policy and of principle, according to his theory, can both justify political decisions, but their aims differ: while policy arguments show that the political decision advances or protects some collective goal of the community as a whole, arguments of principle justify a decision by showing that it respects or secures some individual or group right.[7]

In Dworkin's theory, arguments of policy, dissimilar to arguments of principle, lack the democratic legitimacy required for making decisions concerning a community (judges are often not elected). Moreover, they allow a judge to retroactively impose a new duty on the losing party in a case, which implies a punishment (e.g. the recognition of a contractual duty of care of a patient towards

2 This section and the next draws on parts of the book mentioned in the previous footnote.

3 A.-J. Kwak, 'Over leeuwen en vossen (review of W. Lucy, *Understanding and Explaining Adjudication* [Oxford University Press, Oxford 1999])' (2003) *Tijdschrift voor Rechtsfilosofie en Rechtstheorie* 55, commenting on Lucy's distinction between 'orthodox' and 'heretical' accounts of adjudication.

4 W. Lucy, *Understanding and Explaining Adjudication* (Oxford University Press, Oxford 1999) 1–6.

5 See, for instance, R. Dworkin, *Taking Rights Seriously* (Duckworth, London 1977; fourth impression with a Reply to Critics, Duckworth, London 1984) in particular 81 *et seq.*

6 Dworkin, n 5 above, 84. For a comment on Dworkin's theory of principles of law, see for instance R. Alexy, 'Zum Begriff des Rechtsprinzips' (1979) *Rechtstheorie*, Beiheft 1, 59–87.

7 Dworkin, n 5 above, 82. In an earlier chapter of the same book, Dworkin defined a policy as the kind of standard that sets out a goal to be reached, generally an improvement in some economic, political, or social feature of the community. A principle, on the other hand, he defined as a standard that is to be observed, not because it will advance or secure an economic, political or social situation deemed desirable, but because it is a requirement of justice or fairness or some other dimension of morality. Dworkin, n 5 above, 22. In the more elaborate description on 82 *et seq.* he analysed the distinction in more detail.

a doctor, resulting in a duty to co-operate in a blood test to establish the risk of HIV infection[8]). Principles would not have such drawbacks, since they focus on individual or group rights (e.g. the doctor's right to health), and thus do not require the detailed consideration of all demands of a community. Furthermore, a principle would justify imposing a duty on the losing party, since this duty is understood as preceding the relevant legislation: it existed already, even though it was not laid down in so many words in the relevant provisions of law.[9] Therefore, principles rather than policy should be applied when deciding cases in which no existing rules are available.

Still, this leaves the problem of how to establish what legal principles require in 'hard cases', in which no clear rule of law is available. In order to solve this question, Dworkin has invented Hercules, 'a lawyer of superhuman skill, learning, patience, and acumen'.[10] By means of using his extraordinary skills Hercules is capable of discovering a coherent set of principles about justice, fairness and procedural due process. He then follows these principles to solve new legal questions in 'hard cases'.[11] Moreover, as Dworkin stresses, Hercules does not base his judgments on his personal political convictions, but on his sense of what the community's morality provides.[12]

### *A Critique of Adjudication*

Dworkin's work, as well as that of other 'builders', has been criticized by the Foxes in legal theory. The metaphor of the Fox refers to the fact that scholars belonging to this group tend to deconstruct rather than build, like a Fox coming out of its hole to do damage to the Lion's kingdom. These scholars, contrary to the Lions, tend to take an external perspective on law, attempting to deconstruct classical legal theories.[13] The Foxes accept that adjudication, to a certain degree, takes place within the law and that judges try to make their choices on the basis of arguments of 'fit' and coherence. However, they admit that these choices are not in principle capable of justification.[14] There are thus no 'right answers', but rather the judge has a choice among many possible answers in each case. An important argument for this is that judicial law-making cannot be considered

8 See the Dutch Supreme Court's decision *HR* 12 December 2003, *NJ* 2004, 117 (*HIV-test II; dentist case*). The case concerned a dental surgeon who cut his fingers while treating a patient belonging to a population group with a heightened risk of HIV infection. He then asked the patient to undergo a blood test in order to determine whether there had been a risk of transmission of the virus.

9 Dworkin, n 5 above, 83–4.

10 Dworkin, n 5 above, 105. See also R. Dworkin, *Law's Empire* (Belknap Press, Cambridge/Massachusetts 1986) 239.

11 Dworkin, n 5 above, 105–6.

12 Dworkin, n 5 above, 128–9. See also Dworkin, n 10 above, 176 *et seq.*

13 Lucy, n 4 above, 7–15.

14 Lucy, n 4 above, 10–11.

politically and morally neutral, but rather has been and is used for the realization of ideological projects. Since the 1970s, this argument has been elaborated by the American Critical Legal Studies movement, which sought to 'trash' conservative legal theory in order to reveal that adjudication was used as an instrument for the realization of conservative, right-wing ideals.[15] Thus, the Foxes sought to make room for the pursuit of more left-wing ideals of justice. One of the most influential members of this movement is Duncan Kennedy, whose *Critique of Adjudication*[16] uses both internal and external analysis of law in order to demonstrate the role of ideology in judicial law-making.[17]

Kennedy criticizes Dworkin's theory of adjudication for not offering a realistic perspective on judicial reasoning:

> It seems implausible, to say the least, that an interpretation of adjudication that simply excludes consequentialist or social-welfare-oriented policy argument altogether from the repertoire of legitimate judicial behavior can 'fit' the practice. I think a reason why many practitioners find Dworkin unconvincing is that as a matter of fact American judges constantly deploy arguments that look exactly like the ones he claims they generally avoid.[18]

In Kennedy's opinion, arguments of principle cannot be said to be less receptive to judicial ideology than arguments of policy, as Dworkin claimed. Therefore, according to Kennedy, it is unlikely that rights and principle-based legal reasoning will always result in more democratic decision making and legal certainty than policy-based adjudication.

This 'critique of adjudication' is based on the role of rights (derived from principles) in case law. According to Kennedy, (constitutional) rights in the traditional discourse are seen as 'mediators' in two dichotomies: they 'mediate' between factual and value judgments,[19] as well as between law and politics.[20]

---

15 On this movement, R. Mangabeira Unger, *The Critical Legal Studies Movement* (Harvard University Press, Cambridge/Massachusetts 1986).

16 D. Kennedy, *A Critique of Adjudication {fin de siècle}* (Harvard University Press, Cambridge/Massachusetts 1997).

17 The fact that Kennedy now also uses more conventional methods of legal analysis does not seem to imply that the contradiction between Lions and Foxes is losing its sharpness. Although the methods (external or internal analysis) of both groups may sometimes converge, their ideological engagement still signifies a profound difference of opinion. Kennedy's propensity to resort to leftish, deconstructive theory places him with the Foxes, even though he may sometimes apply the internal analysis that characterizes the Lions' work. Compare Kwak, n 3 above, 62.

18 Kennedy, n 16 above, 125.

19 Kennedy, n 16 above, 305. See also D. Kennedy, 'The Critique of Rights in Critical Legal Studies', in W. Brown and J.E. Halley (eds), *Left Legalism/Left Critique* (Duke University Press, Durham 2002) 184 *et seq*.

20 Kennedy, n 16 above, 308, 310.

While facts are usually considered to be objective, values are deemed subjective. Starting from this assumption, a basic distinction can be made between rights and other kinds of normative arguments:

> The point of an appeal to a right, the reason for making it, is that it *can't be reduced* to a mere 'value judgment' that one outcome is better than another. Yet it is possible to make rights arguments about matters that fall outside the domain commonly understood as factual, that is, about political or policy questions of how the government ought to act. In other words, rights are mediators between the domain of pure value judgments and the domain of factual judgments.[21]

'Mediation' in this context means that rights reasoning has characteristics of both sides of the dichotomy: references to rights argument makes it possible to defend that an outcome (value judgment) is better than the alternatives. It suggests a certain neutrality of law-making, aspiring to make policy decisions in the light of a more 'objective' argumentation.

The use of rights arguments for justifying choices does not, however, necessarily imply legal-political objectivity. This is confirmed by the idea of rights mediating in the dichotomy of law and politics: on the one hand, the constitutional rights argument is legal, since it is based on one of the enacted rules of the legal system; on the other hand, it is normative or political, since it has the form of an assertion about the translation of a pre-existing, 'outside' right into law.[22] Although the application of rights argument may result in a certain 'closure' of apparent objectivity of the interpretation of a rule, the mediating of rights between the two aforementioned dichotomies thus bears the risk of ideology affecting adjudication.[23]

As for Hercules, even he does not seem to be completely imperceptive to ideological influence. In Kennedy's opinion 'he is actually a left liberal, as close as you can get in terms of outcomes to a radical', given the fact that the 'right answers' he finds in the examples that Dworkin discussed in general are on the left liberal side of the (American) political spectrum.[24]

---

21 Kennedy, n 16 above, 305.

22 Kennedy, n 16 above, 308. He defines an 'outside right' as 'something that a person has even if the legal order doesn't recognize it and even if 'exercising' it is illegal.' Examples of abstract, outside rights that have been codified in the German, Dutch and Italian Constitutions are: the right of free speech (art 5 *GG*; art 7 *Gw*; art 21 *Costituzione*) and the right to enjoy one's property (art 42 *Costituzione*; art 1 of the 1st Protocol to the European Convention on Human Rights).

23 Kennedy, n 16 above, 319–20.

24 Kennedy, n 16 above, 127–8.

### *The Political Role of the Judge in European Contract Law*

To what extent can Dworkin's rights thesis and Kennedy's critique be translated to the adjudication of European cases concerning disputes in (long-term) contractual relationships? In the remaining part of this chapter it will be argued that the current tendency of applying fundamental rights in these types of cases raises questions that are similar to the ones that have just been described for the US legal system in many European countries. In particular, the alignment of contract law rules with fundamental rights in case law challenges the distinction between the public and the private sphere. It introduces considerations of public policy in relations between private parties, thus assigning judges the difficult task of explicitly determining to what extent parties to a contract should take the public interest into account in their contractual relationship. Here, the question arises as to what extent European judges[25] have discretion to pursue goals of public interest in contract law adjudication.

Furthermore, it may be asked to what extent the long-term character of, for instance, employment contracts influences the manner in which fundamental rights argumentation is integrated into legal reasoning. Dworkin's legal theory seems to apply equally to all 'hard cases', irrespective of whether they concern spot contracts or long-term contracts. Fundamental rights, however, originate from the long-term relationship between the state and its citizens. Therefore, the question arises whether the specific features of long-term contracts, reflecting an analogy with the state–citizen relationship, make them more vulnerable to Kennedy's critique. That is, are they more susceptible to fundamental rights argumentation and legal-political considerations than spot contracts or short-term contracts?

Answering these questions seems to require an analysis based on a combination of the theoretical views on adjudication of both the aforementioned Lions and Foxes in legal theory. In the following section the role of fundamental rights in the regulation of long-term contractual relationships in Europe will be explored on the basis of the example of non-competition clauses in employment contracts.

## Fundamental Rights and the Regulation of Long-Term Contractual Relationships

### *Introduction*

Long-term contractual relationships, such as those concerning employment, are often characterized by a certain inequality of bargaining power of the parties. This inequality may affect the interaction between the parties at several stages. In the

25 This chapter focuses on the case law of the domestic courts of several EU Member States: Germany, the Netherlands and Italy. The choice of legal systems is based on the analysis presented in the book mentioned in n 1 above.

first place, it may have an effect on the drafting and conclusion of the contract, during which the stronger party might seek to almost unilaterally establish the terms and conditions of the agreement (in general to its own benefit, e.g. a very extensive non-competition clause or a confidentiality clause in an employment contract). In the second place, a difference in bargaining power may affect the way in which disputes between the parties are handled. (How should a clause regarding, for instance, a duty of care of the employer be interpreted? And under which circumstances may contractual penalties be mitigated? In which cases should party autonomy be respected and in which cases is a judge allowed to intervene and redress the imbalance between the parties?) Finally, the consequences of inequality of the parties may even extend beyond the contract as it may prevent the weaker party from concluding a new contract with a competitor (again, the example of the non-competition clause).

In the following, it is submitted that the judicial consideration of the imbalance of power between parties to a long-term contract engages two opposing political stakes in contract law, namely those of autonomy and solidarity. On the basis of the example of the non-competition clause in employment contracts it will be illustrated how European judges approach the policy questions underlying disputes in these types of contractual relationships. The analysis of these cases, it is argued, can further explain the value of fundamental rights for the adjudication of long-term contracts.

### *Contract Law Between Autonomy and Solidarity*

While contract law in most European countries is perceived as revolving around the principle of freedom of contract, a new paradigm has gained importance in recent years, namely that of solidarity. Legal scholars have submitted that solidarity between contract parties should be considered to be of equal relevance as the autonomy of parties to arrange their interrelations in the manner they wish.[26]

The analysis of European contract law in terms of autonomy and solidarity is indebted to Duncan Kennedy's concept of a continuum on which rule-solutions in contract law can be depicted as placing relatively more emphasis on the ideal

---

26 M.W. Hesselink, 'The Principles of European Contract Law: Some Choices Made by the Lando Commission', in *Principles of European Contract Law* (preliminary reports Vereniging voor Burgerlijk Recht) (Kluwer, Deventer 2001) 48; B. Lurger, 'The "Social" Side of Contract Law and the New Principle of Regard and Fairness', in A.S. Hartkamp, M. Veldman and others (eds), *Towards a European Civil Code* (Ars Aequi Libri/Kluwer Law International, Nijmegen/The Hague 2004) 273–95; E.H. Hondius, 'De zwakke partij in het contractenrecht; over de verandering van paradigmata van het privaatrecht', in T. Hartlief and C.J.J.M. Stolker (eds), *Contractvrijheid* (Kluwer, Deventer 1999) 387; B. van Zelst, *The Politics of European Sales Law* (Kluwer Law International, Alphen a/d Rijn 2008). See also Mak, n 1 above, Chapter 4.

of autonomy or that of solidarity.[27] Autonomy here refers to self-reliance and the fact that parties may pursue their own interests in the contractual relationships they engage in. It should not be confused with pure egotism, however, since the rights of other, equally self-interested parties should be respected. Solidarity, on the other hand, requires parties to share and make sacrifices on behalf of their contract partners. It does, nevertheless, not add up to complete selflessness, since a certain margin remains within which parties are free to ignore the consequences of their actions on the welfare of others.[28] The distinction thus is one of gradations: a rule-solution in a contractual dispute (e.g. declaring the nullity of a contract clause that seriously endangers the balance between the parties) can be said to emphasize solidarity to a greater extent than an alternative solution (e.g. upholding a clause, because parties in principle have freely agreed to its inclusion in the contract).[29]

In the European context, 'solidarity' is often[30] interpreted in terms of weaker party protection.[31] From this point of view, the stronger contracting party has to actively take into account the other party's interests so as to restore the contractual balance. This should enable the weaker party to freely contribute to the contractual relationship. In cases in which the weaker party's autonomy is limited, judicial intervention might be needed to induce the stronger party to comply with the requirements of solidarity. As will be further elaborated below, this can imply the making of policy choices in contract law adjudication.

In light of the theoretical framework presented in the previous section, it may be assumed that fundamental rights relate to this tension between autonomy and solidarity in European contract law. They can be thought of as mediating between the rules of contract law and the political choices reflected in these rules. They might make clear the legal-political stakes in 'hard cases' and, thus, the range of policy choices available.

Long-term contractual relationships between unequal parties offer an interesting test case for the validity of these hypotheses. Unlike most spot contracts, they combine certain typical features that recall the relationship between citizens and the state and may therefore inspire the application of fundamental rights: they govern a longer period of time, in which it is in the interest of both parties to maintain a relationship of trust; they are characterized by an imbalance of power between the contracting parties; and they often concern basic needs, such as employment and housing. It is not said that fundamental rights may never be applied in cases concerning spot contracts between unequal parties (e.g. consumer sales). However, it may be submitted that long-term contractual relationships show

27 D. Kennedy, 'The Political Stakes in "Merely Technical" Issues of Contract Law' (2002) *European Review of Private Law* 7–28.

28 Kennedy, n 27 above, and the same author, 'Form and Substance in Private Law Adjudication' (1976) *Harvard Law Review* 1685–1778.

29 See Mak, n 1 above, Chapter 6 for further examples.

30 Though not exclusively; see, for instance, Lurger, n 26 above.

31 Mak, n 1 above, 201–6, with further references.

a greater homogeneity and that, accordingly, it might be easier to provide a general explanation for the role of fundamental rights in the regulation of these contracts.

### *Adjudicating Long-Term Contracts: The Example of the Non-Competition Clause*

The case law of various European legal systems on long-term contracts can be analysed in terms of autonomy and solidarity. An illustrative example is the case of non-competition clauses in employment contracts, which limit the employee's possibilities of continuing to work in the same sector after the termination of the contract. Usually, these clauses stipulate certain conditions regarding the territorial scope and duration of the obligation not to work for a competitor of the former employer. The question is, however, what are the boundaries of party autonomy in this context. In particular, legislators and judges have struggled with the question of when to intervene in order to protect the employee's free choice of profession and possibilities for making a living.

The *Handelsvertreter* judgment[32] of the German Constitutional Court, the *Bundesverfassungsgericht*, shows how fundamental rights argumentation may justify a restriction of party autonomy. The case concerned a commercial agent (*Handelsvertreter*) whose contract with a wine trading company contained a non-competition clause that effectively prohibited him from working for any competing company within German territory for a period of two years. Moreover, since the termination of the contract was based on the commercial agent's own actions (he started working for a competitor during the agency agreement with his first principal), the principal did not have to pay him any compensation during the two-year period during which the non-competition clause would have effect.[33] The *Bundesverfassungsgericht* ruled that upholding this extensive clause, as the courts in civil cases had done, implied an inacceptable limitation of the commercial agent's free choice of profession (safeguarded by Article 12(1) of the *Grundgesetz*), since it effectively endangered the basis of his existence (*Existenzgrundlage*). The fact that the agent had in principle agreed to the non-competition clause did not change this judgment. In fact, the court considered that it was the duty of the courts in civil cases to make sure that these types of contract clauses complied with the values protected by the Constitution. They had to ensure that the almost unilateral

32 BVerfG 7 February 1990, *BVerfGE* 81, 242. The considerations of the court are of importance not only for commercial agency contracts, but also for non-competition agreements in employment contracts, which show similar dynamics.

33 In accordance with § 90a(2) *HGB* as it was worded at the time the events of the case took place. At the moment the Constitutional Court handed down its judgment the law had already been changed so as to provide compensation for commercial agents in similar circumstances.

imposition of contract terms by a party holding a stronger bargaining position did not harm the weaker party's constitutionally safeguarded interests.[34]

In other European countries, cases have arisen that show similarities to the *Handelsvertreter* judgment. The Italian *Corte di Cassazione*, for instance, considered that a part-time salary may not be sufficient to provide for the free and dignified existence of an employee's family (protected by Article 36 of the *Costituzione*).[35] The employee should therefore be allowed to work for another company during the time that was not covered by her part-time contract.[36] Furthermore, in light of constitutional provisions (Articles 4 and 35 *Cost*) the *Corte di Cassazione* held that an employer could not unilaterally determine whether or not to invoke a non-competition clause after the termination of the employment contract, thus seeking to avoid having to pay the related compensation.[37]

In the Netherlands, the courts have occasionally reverted to the constitutionally protected free choice of profession (Article 19(3) of the *Grondwet*) when adjudicating the compliance of non-competition clauses with the relevant provisions of the Civil Code (in particular Article 7:653(2) *BW*). In some cases, the focus is almost identical to that of the German Constitutional Court in the *Handelsvertreter* judgment, namely on the possibilities for the employee to provide for his or her means of existence by using the skills and experience s/he has acquired.[38]

A distinctive feature of the legal reasoning that the German, Italian and Dutch courts developed in these cases indeed seems to be the consideration of factors going beyond the specific case. Apart from seeking a solution for the case at hand, the judges appear to have taken into account the wider implications of their judgments for the protection of weaker parties in long-term contractual relationships.[39] This brings us back to the question of how to define the role of fundamental rights in European contract law adjudication.

---

34 Similar considerations lay at the basis of the *Bundesverfassungsgericht*'s judgment of 19 October 1993, *BVerfGE* 89, 214 (*Bürgschaft*).

35 *Cass civ* 26 October 2001, no 13329, *Dir e giustizia* 2001, fasc 41, 51, with a comment by Cardellicchio.

36 A similar judgment was delivered by the French *Cour de Cassation* on 11 July 2000, *JCP* 2000.IV.2556 (*Mme Marchal* v *Pimouguet*). On these judgments, see also C. Perfumi and C. Mak, 'The Impact of Fundamental Rights on the Content of Contracts. Determining Limits to Freedom of Contract in Family and Employment Relations', in G. Brüggemeier, A. Colombi Ciacchi and G. Comandé (eds), *Fundamental Rights and Private Law in the European Union. II. Comparative Analysis of Selected Case Patterns* (Cambridge University Press, Cambridge forthcoming).

37 *Cass civ* 13 June 2003, no 9491, *Dir e pratica lav* 2003, 2644.

38 See the opinion of the Advocate-General in *HR* 4 April 2003, *JAR* 2003, 107, with reference to *Hof Amsterdam* 21 May 1992, *KG* 1993, 14.

39 See further Mak, n 1 above, 235–42.

*The Political Role of Fundamental Rights in European Contract Law*

A legal-political analysis of the European cases on non-competition clauses in which fundamental rights were applied seems to support Duncan Kennedy's view on adjudication that was described earlier[40] rather than to follow Ronald Dworkin's theory of judicial decision making.[41] While the courts have stressed the importance of safeguarding fundamental rights also in private law (in line with Dworkin's rights thesis), their elaboration of the question as to what extent this may interfere with party autonomy involves the explicit consideration of policy issues. In several cases, such as the German *Handelsvertreter* example, the outcome signifies a shift on the legal-political spectrum (as defined by Kennedy's continuum) – from a strong emphasis on autonomy (upholding non-competition clauses, even if they posed serious limitations to the weaker party's basis of existence) towards a reinforcement of solidarity between the parties (redressing the imbalance between the parties by declaring void certain contract clauses).

The approach taken by the courts in these cases shows little similarity to Dworkin's Herculean ideal of legal reasoning. Although it may be contended that the courts seek to comply with a community's views on the regulation of long-term contractual relationships, this does not seem to unambiguously direct them to 'one right answer' for the case at hand. In the example of the extensive non-competition clause, for instance, more than one rule-solution presents itself: upholding the clause, upholding it in combination with compensation to the employee, or declaring the clause void. A proponent of Dworkin's rights thesis may submit that only one of these can be considered the 'right answer' to the case and that it is the judge's (Hercules') task to develop a political theory of principles that indicates which solution best fits the system. It is this author's opinion, however, that the cases discussed here rather seem to confirm the impact of legal-political views or ideology on the choice of a rule-solution. The courts make their choices among several solutions, or 'right answers', against the background of a combined consideration of the individual's rights (principle) and the public interest (policy). This approach cannot be considered free from legal-political influences that determine the balance between ideals of autonomy and solidarity in contract law.

The added value of fundamental rights argumentation in comparison to traditional judicial reasoning in contract cases appears to lie in the fact that it explicitly defines the (potential) political influences on the decision-making process. It raises awareness of the policy questions underlying 'hard cases' and of the extent to which judges can effectively influence the policy that will be pursued in these and later cases.

40 Second section (The judge and the politics of long-term contractual relationships) above.

41 Described in second section above.

An explanation for the occurrence of this type of judicial reasoning in cases concerning long-term contracts may be found in the characteristics that these types of contracts have in common. As said earlier, long-term contracts between structurally unequal parties often concern basic needs of private individuals, such as the possibility to make a living (employment), the availability of housing (tenancy) and the access to public services such as water and electricity (services). These types of contracts thus affect the extent to which private individuals are able to live in circumstances respectful of human dignity and to freely develop their personalities. Contract law has a direct impact on the protection of these fundamental, constitutionally protected values.[42] In disputes arising from the contracts it is up to the judges to rebalance the private interests and public values that are at stake. Given the background to the contractual relationships, it does not seem surprising that especially in these cases judges reach back to fundamental rights in order to guide the balancing process. This does not exclude a similar application of fundamental rights to spot contracts and short-term contracts, but it does support the case for taking into account the legal-political backdrop to disputes between stronger and weaker parties in long-term contractual relationships.

## Concluding Remarks

In the previous sections, an analysis has been made of the manner in which fundamental rights affect judicial reasoning in disputes concerning long-term (employment) contracts. The comparison of case law concerning non-competition clauses shows considerable similarities between German, Italian and Dutch contract law adjudication. Taking inspiration from the work of Dworkin and Kennedy, it has therefore been submitted that similar legal-political considerations affect the outcome of cases in this field: Should the autonomy of the contracting parties be respected by upholding a clause or should the judge intervene to protect the weaker party (usually the employee) against the consequences of the non-competition clause? Fundamental rights play an important role in judicial reasoning on this question, since they place the contractual dispute against a broader legal-political background. Thus, these rights may be said to have an added value in comparison to pure private law reasoning. They induce judges to explicitly look into the policy effects their judgments may have on the further development of regulation regarding long-term contracts between unequal parties.

As a suggestion for further research in this field, it may therefore be argued that the study of relevant contract cases in light of fundamental rights can prove worthwhile for defining common questions of policy in the law concerning long-

42 Compare H. Collins, *The European Civil Code. The Way Forward* (Cambridge University Press, Cambridge 2008) 102–8.

term contracts in Europe. The comparison of the manner in which these policy issues are handled may even provide inspiration for a further harmonization of contract law in this field.[43]

43 On the possible role of fundamental rights for the harmonization of general contract law, see C. Mak, 'Harmonising Effects of Fundamental Rights in European Contract Law' (2007) *Erasmus Law Review*, available at http://www.erasmuslawreview.nl/past_issues/Volume01/harmonising_effects.

# PART III
# Network of Contracts

# Chapter 5
# 'And if I by Beelzebub Cast out Devils, …': An Essay on the Diabolics of Network Failure

Gunther Teubner

## Limits of the Network Society

Hierarchy failure, market failure, yes – but network failure? We have lived through painful experiences of hierarchy failure. One of the great innovations of organizational society was to invent the hierarchy of decision making. The invention achieved tremendous gains in consistency of decisions, their security and impact. Yet, it came at a price. Concentrating external contacts to the pinnacle of the organization dangerously restricts the information flow between the organization and its environment; the consequences of this restriction are so severe that they cannot be remedied by informal contacts on the organization's base. The top of the organization lost sight of its environment; the organization tenaciously held on to its bureaucratic and rigid, internally produced constructions of its 'outside' and its observance of fixed strategies.[1]

The law carried a considerable degree of joint responsibility for this hierarchy failure. With certain rigidity, the public law of the 'organization society' had supported and immunized the hierarchical coordination mechanisms of immobile large scale organizations against change (Ladeur, 1992, 177). Comparable developments had marked private law in a number of areas: the examples of collective labour law, corporate law and tort law illustrate the way in which the law had been fuelling the internal hierarchization and the external concentration towards the organization top. Organizational law, both public and private, must be seen as a major culprit in the production of hierarchy failure (Teubner, 2011, 135ff.).

The last 30 years have seen a network revolution that resulted in a thorough erosion of organizational hierarchies in both the private and the public sector. A dramatic decentralization of decision making took place. This was achieved by a high degree of operational autonomy which the newly emerging network organizations granted to their nodal points. Decentrally organized company groups,

1 Brun et al., 2005. The text simplifies the success story of networks and focuses only on hierarchy failure. A parallel story would be that of market failure as a trigger for network building. See, in addition, Teubner, 2011, 96f., 135ff.

administrative agencies, inter-organizational networks as well as global networks of regulatory agencies now all share a formidably high level of environmental openness and adaptability. It is de-hierarchization that enabled the organization to multiply the observations of its environment, to increase its variety, to move the organization 'closer to life', as well as to augment its responsiveness and flexibility (Littman and Jansen, 2000, 110). In these successful alternative forms of coordination, planning no longer occurs centrally. Instead, different network nodes are able to observe different environments while being internally able to communicate the results of these observations and to concretize different steps of the decision-making process one by one (Luhmann, 2000, 211). Today, heterarchical networks are dominating hierarchical organizations to such a high degree that the world society can safely be referred to as a network society.

Yet, in the background, the diabolics of network failure are lurking. The decentralization caused the devil of hierarchy to exit the organizational body, aching and groaning. The uncertainties connected with the hierarchy's environment were successfully exorcised and made way for an intensive exchange of multiple network nodes with their environments. In spite of these attempts, however, the smell of sulphur will not pass, because the devil was cast out only with the help of Beelzebub, substituting one threatening uncertainty for another. Whereas the devil represented uncertainty with regard to the environment, the name Beelzebub represents a no less threatening uncertainty regarding the inner coordination of the net's autonomized nodal points.

Now, following a first phase of euphoric reactions, the practical practice of networks is documented by a host of reports attesting to their confusing over-complexity. The reasons for failures are manifold: overwhelming environment information, coordination blockades, severe interface problems, permanent decision conflicts, asymmetric power relations, opportunistic behaviour of nodes and centre, as well as negative externalities of net activities (Boehme-Nessler, 2008, 534; Hirsch-Kreinsen, 2002, 118; Weyer, 2000, 25; Messner, 1997, 56). While networks are considered to respond rather successfully to the contradictory challenges of the market environment, it is now their internal structure that gives rise to nagging problems: 'On the one hand, corporate networks aim at an enlarged and intensified economization of corporate activities, on the other, however, they endanger their functional and existential foundations, in particular the stability necessary for the relations among the network partners' (Hirsch-Kreinsen, 2002, 118). Networks tend to aggravate those very problems they simultaneously work to resolve. Like other modern institutions, networks mobilize internal self-destructive dynamics. While it is true that they are able to translate product-related contradictions in their environment internally into tension-laden, yet sustainable expectations, they reinforce their internal self-destructive potential by setting free internal tensions that result from their hybrid form and from internal conflicts of trust. Once you add outside pressures on speed, flexibility, cost cuts and competitiveness to this mix, network partners will begin to act opportunistically. At this point, network failure seemingly becomes inevitable. We have little reason to downplay the potential damage both for the inside of the network and for its third parties. The well-known phenomenon of 'organized irresponsibility' has found a prominent successor in 'reticular irresponsibility'.

Here again, the law is not innocent. It is a co-producer of network failure, as it fails to mitigate the threats of the new uncertainties. With regard to hierarchies, the law had notably reinforced hierarchy failure by dutifully supporting the centralization of decision making. With regard to networks, the law seems to play a different role: treating networks with great resistance against something so 'alien' helps to facilitate network failure. Lawyers tend to dismiss networks as merely 'one of numerous new term creations of the more recent legal debate that lay an unfounded claim to novelty'.[2] A recently published volume of essays shows how public lawyers, when asked to develop a legal doctrine for networks, approach the network category with, indeed, great fear and apprehension.[3] Only two authors succeed in this regard, while the rest indulge in dark metaphors. Similarly, in private law, antitrust law tends to illegalize cooperative forms of networks, in the name of freedom of competition, which goes far beyond what would have been necessary. Here, the law attaches the stain of anti-competitive behaviour to many forms of cooperation among otherwise independent corporate actors, which either inadequately increases the autonomy of nodal points or again reinforces hierarchization.[4] We find a rigid limitation of conceptual choices in both contract and corporate law, where we are asked to opt for either contract or organization – *tertium non datur*. A new comparative study of different European legal systems concludes: 'Both the multilateral and the linked models face serious limitations under current contract law, more in some legal systems than in others' and opts for a European regulatory regime for contractual networks called 'Principles of European Contractual Networks' (Cafaggi, 2008, 40, 43). Although private law is supposed to support private autonomy, it comes empty-handed when asked to provide for an organizational framework to deal with networks. Corporate networks have by now assumed a solid place in regulated markets, ranging from energy to telecommunications markets, from bank networks to transport and air traffic networks. But the law's answer exhausts itself in the concept of bilateral contracts.[5] Still, it gets worse: in recent conflicts arising over the passing-on of network advantages among members of a franchise chain, it would have been adequate to redistribute kick-back payments that the franchisor had kept secret from its franchisees. However, both private law doctrine and the courts refuse

2 Möllers, 2005, 285. For an overview of the reception of network concepts in public law: Nowrot, 2007, 15. See also, Luhmann, 2000, 207.

3 Boysen et al., 2007. Also, Möllers (2005, 295) views the network concept as legally fruitless, but turns this fruitlessness into a positive.

4 Only rarely is antitrust law criticized from this perspective: Ensthaler and Gesmann-Nuissl, 2000, 2269.

5 From a comparative law perspective, Cafaggi, 2008, 52. Some legal systems, however, are more advanced than others.

stubbornly to develop new connexionist concepts for the emerging patterns of action, attribution and liability, which would form an appropriate remedy against the networks' chronic internal coordination weaknesses.[6] Even the *avant-garde* among legal scholars that celebrate the socio-economic accomplishments of networks, and invent finely crafted legal concepts of networks and network typologies, fail to account for their deep-running difficulties in coordination. While the legal concept of 'basis of contract' (*Geschäftsgrundlage*, developed by case law and subsequently codified in § 313 of the German Civil Code, *Bürgerliches Gesetzbuch* – BGB), never designed to address network connections, is drawn upon to establish some few connections between isolated bilateral relations,[7] the doctrine of network contracts resists any direct acknowledgement of reticular responsibility for new liability rules. There would simply be no need! (Wellenhofer, 2009, 119; Bayreuther, 2001, 399; Rohe, 1998, 418). One is almost tempted to pen the second volume to a provocative book, to be entitled 'The Private Law Against Society'.[8]

## Opportunity Structure of Networks and Law's Conceptual Readiness

In the face of network failure the present legal doctrine offers a false alternative by asking us to choose between a return to hierarchy and a move forward to decentralization. The result is a sterile oscillation between two equally unattractive poles: on the one hand the failure of environmental compatibility and that of internal coordination on the other. Devil or Beelzebub? Yet, there is no reason to despair. Waiting already in the background is another exorcist – should one call him Lucifer? – who promises another form of exorcism, this time targeting network failure. Without a detour via the top of the organization, the new bringer of light suggests drastically increasing internal irritability. In order to overcome network failure this approach aims at developing organizational forms and responsibility rules for networks that will hold on to the advantages of the decentralized organization of nodes, while decisively strengthening their mutual coordination (Kulms, 2000, 186, 227). This will drastically reduce the privity principle for all those contracts connected by the network. Furthermore, it will introduce different legal rules for multilateral contracts with regard to their formation, their validity,

6 Decisions of the German Federal Court of Justice (Bundesgerichtshof), 20 May 2003 ('Apollo-Optik: Pflicht des Franchisegebers zur Weitergabe von Differenzrabatten an Franchisenehmer', *Betriebsberater*, 43: 2254) and 22 February 2006 ('Hertz', *Betriebsberater* 46: 1071). Different, however, is the decision of the German Federal Cartel Office (Bundeskartellamt), 8 May 2006 ('Praktiker Baumärkte GmbH', B9 – 149/04). Pursuing the previous line of argument, again: Decision of the Higher Regional Court Düsseldorf (Oberlandesgericht Düsseldorf), 13 December 2006 ('Praktiker', *Betriebsberater*, 47: 738).

7 Network contracts: Rohe, 1998; 'Basis of contract': Grundmann, 2008, 232; Grundmann, 2007, 742.

8 The first volume is entitled 'The State Against Society': Ladeur, 2006.

their defaults, and their termination. In addition, it will facilitate quasi-corporate governance structures in multilateral contracts, identifying the legal conditions under which contractual networks will have to be treated as collective actors. Finally, it will increase individual and collective liability for faulty coordination vis-à-vis suppliers and buyers (Cafaggi, 2008, 6).

Social scientists, indeed, display a certain optimism when it comes to casting out Beelzebub himself (Windeler, 2001, 336; Sydow, 1999, 299; Lemley and McGowan, 1998, 198; Gerum et al., 1998, 267). With a Luciferian gesture they hint at the inner potential of networks to transform external contradictions into merely internal tensions and to deal with these tensions productively through mutual observations of nodes – and all of this without resorting to central-hierarchical organizations. They insist, however, that this would only be possible if there were sufficient support from the outside: 'an institutional environment where fiduciary relationships can arise and also a high level of trust that can allow the development of shared innovative knowledge' (Cafaggi, 2008, 3). The primary candidates who could give this support are organizational culture, governmental economic policies, economic associations, and management consultancies; but, also the law is to play a role. The question for law is:[9] Which norms can contribute to setting free from its blockades the integration potential which exists in what Niklas Luhmann (1990, 165) calls the 'heterarchical, connexionistic and network-like combination of communications'? Which remedies does the law hold in stock with regard to the Achilles heel of networks, namely their inner coordination weakness? What needs to be uncovered here is a latent correspondence relation between social norms and law. It would be the mandate of a 'social epistemology of law' in order to provide for a 'management of coherence between legal and extra-legal rule-boundedness' of networks (Augsberg and Ladeur, 2008, 164). This programme has been formulated as the research agenda of a double institutional analysis, as it was developed by Philip Selznick (1992, 229). Pursuing an institutional analysis of networks, the ensuing question is: Where can the 'opportunity structure', the social potential for an increasingly non-hierarchical coordination within the net, be found? Pursuing an institutional analysis of the law, the question would be: is there a 'conceptual readiness' of the law which would enable it to set this potential free by facilitative rules? This agenda is close to a normative programme of a 'network adequate law', which has already been pursued in internet governance, media networks and virtual auctions (Vesting, 2004, 247).

Which, now, are the components of networks that, by working against the centrifugal tendencies of networks, are able to support their internal coordination? And, by which doctrinal constructs could the law respond and stabilize these components? In spite of the strong scepticism among lawyers who maintain that the term network does not lend itself to legal doctrinal use, this should reveal

9 Viellechner (2007, 43) poses the question for public law and provides preliminary answers.

a correspondence between social structures and legal rules that is capable of addressing network failure.

### *Integration Potential I: 'Spontaneous Orders' – Local Contacts, Overarching Binding Connections*

We do not have Hayek's spontaneous orders, which are able to generate distributed knowledge on the basis of market-competitive acts without central planning, in mind. Here, we are not concerned with competitive markets, but instead with cooperative relations beyond the misleading alternative of contract vs. organization. Networks are spontaneous orders *sui generis*, whose cooperative relations are in fact not dispersing but concentrating the sought knowledge (Heldt, 2009, 144; Teubner, 2011, 162ff.; Gordon, 1994). Net relations create commitments and social bonds out of cooperative actions which connect recursively with each other. Those social ties form the glue that holds networks together – the strength of weak ties (Granovetter, 1973) – and work effectively against the centrifugal tendencies of autonomized profit centres – as long as these ties are sufficiently supported by social and legal institutions.

But, does the law have the conceptual readiness to institutionalize such binding arrangements? This is indeed problematic for the dominant contract paradigm. Since the modern rational binding institutions, consensual contract and hierarchical organization have emerged as winners, casting the spell of illegality, precisely as anti-competitive, clientelistic or even corrupt (in addition, see, Deakin, 2009, 58), over old binding forms.

Yet, private law has undergone a set of promising developments towards the bindingness of networks without contract that one should forcefully pursue. The point of departure is Rudolf von Jhering's good old *culpa in contrahendo* that served to establish, in particular cases, legal bonds precisely without a contract, without a promise, without an act of consensus, but merely on the basis of social coordination. This was achieved with the help of a 'pre-contractual obligation' caused by the 'coming contract' (Jhering, 1861). In the meantime we can, however, observe a considerable expansion of *culpa in contrahendo* that was originally thought to apply only to simple, bilateral relations. The concept has been constructively abused by applying it to multilateral networks without contract. So far, this development has largely gone unnoticed. Comparing different lines of case law that would otherwise evolve in relative ignorance from each other, we can observe rather exotic legal regimes whereby the merely social network relations between several bilateral contracts have served as the ground on which to establish greater degrees of liability. The cases in question here include the so-called prospect liability in grey security markets (*Prospekthaftung*), trustee liability in complex transactions (*Sachwalterhaftung*) and, in parallel fashion to these constellations even if not built directly on the concept of the *culpa in contrahendo*, the third party liability of experts (*Expertendritthaftung*), bank liability in transfer chains (Überweisungsketten) as well as connected contracts in a great variety of contexts

(*Vertragsverbindungen*).[10] Networks have also found their way into the European arena: the rescindment of a contract will have an impact on all those contracts connected to it, even if the agreement among the parties sought to rule out the connection (Acquis Group, 2007, 186). All these isolated legal institutes share the feature that they create legally binding obligations among several mutually connected actors, although their basis is not a specific agreement but merely the factual behaviour through social contact.

The very vagueness, however, of the term 'social contact' which is supposed to create legally binding obligations has proven to be the greatest obstacle in the development of network adequate rules. Obviously, not every social contact can be assumed to be able to create those connexionist social ties or even the legally binding obligations that we are interested in here (Cf. Säcker and Rixecker, 2007, § 311, no. 68). The same is true for the category of 'trust', which is too vague to guide the transition from social ties to legal obligations. It is at this point that the sociological network theory can provide some helpful suggestions: typical net connections can only be assumed when the double condition is met, namely first that the emerging social relation depends on expectations of generalizable reciprocity and, secondly, that the entry into the larger network occurs on the basis of local, bilateral contacts.[11] This condition of 'and-so-forth' of generalizable reciprocity connections, modelled after the idea of *amici degli amici degli amici*, is the prerequisite for the construction of modern, multilateral non-contractual transaction sequences that private lawyers at first tended to equip only with duties to protect, before eventually moving to recognize them as grounds for core obligations, by allowing for compensatory claims when such core obligations had been defaulted on. Following the 2002 reform of the German law of obligations, the newly created § 311 III BGB establishes a contractual obligation without contract, the new § 358 III BGB stipulates spontaneously connected contracts and, finally, § 676b III and § 676e BGB allow for a piercing of the veil in a transfer chain which makes the intermediate bank liable. These rules can altogether be seen as legislative traces of recognizing networks without contract. They represent a subsequent step in a long-term evolution during which judges had begun looking for adequate responses to the pressure of socio-economic developments. The task now is to continue on this avenue and to integrate other types of transactions, such as sponsorship contracts, prospectus contracts, project related expertise contracts, project contracts, engineering contracts, transportation nets, banking networks and credit card systems, into such an emerging law of networks. All these examples still need to be belaboured in a discussion that has hitherto limited itself to financed

10 On the present stage of development, Säcker and Rixecker, 2007, § 311 no. 185 (Prospectus liability); § 311, no. 244 (Trustee); § 328, no. 150 (Expert third party liability); § 328, no. 157 (Bank transfer); § 358 no. 3 (Contract connections).

11 On generalised reciprocity: Stegbauer, 2002, 79; Gouldner (1960, 176) speaks of the 'starting mechanism'. On iterative network building, Bommes and Tacke, 2007, 14; Stichweh, 2000.

sales, franchising, just-in-time and virtual enterprises (in detail, Teubner, 2011, 179ff.). For the time being, however, private law doctrine remains cautious: even the most daring networkers in this field hold a particular legal regime for networks to be 'decisionist', and regard it to be either 'in conflict with existing law' or, at best, to be 'visionary' (Grundmann, 2008, 228; 2007, 724). And we know what happens to visionaries.

### *Integration Potential II: 'Small Worlds' – Dualism of Strict and Loose Coupling*

Sociologists have identified a further peculiarity of networks that deserves the law's attention. The most important advantages of networks do not come to bear merely on connections between individuals. What it takes are connections between social relations: dyads, contract relations, organizations, epistemic communities, functional systems (Buchanan, 2002; Watts, 1999). It is only the duality of dense clusters and loose connections among them that brings about the well-known network intelligence, because the duality itself acts as the competitive unit which combines the clout of organized special units and their coordination. Networks as 'highly improbable reproduction relations of heterogeneous elements' are characterized by the unlikelihood of closed systems opening towards each other (Baecker, 2002, 14). Particular examples of such networks, whose success depends on the simultaneity of strict internal and loose external couplings, are connected contracts, European comitologies as networks of national bureaucracies, inter-organizational networks, networks of epistemic communities and networks of research institutions, firms, and public administrative agencies (Everson and Joerges, 2006). A recent study aptly refers to such cases as 'semi-spontaneous orders', because the foundation of the spontaneous networks lies, paradoxically, in the constructivist orders resting on rational planning abhorred by Hayek – relational contract and formal organization (Heldt, 2009).

This dualism is the reason why Viellechner (2007, 43) can claim that the vague notion of network can be used as a legal term only when it is realized as a connection of bilateral contracts – a connection of formal organizations. The law will have to take this dualism of strong and weak connections into account, in more than one way.

A first impact of the dualism goes to the legal formation of network connections: Are there strict requirements necessary for the conclusion of a multilateral contract among all the participants? Or are only minimal requirements sufficient to render the factual connections between contracts legally binding? Some scholars try to construct a 'network contract' and base it on the traditional law of agency with mutual authorizations between all participants. When a new member enters the network, he is supposed to strike a multilateral agreement with all the other members who in their turn are supposed to have given their authorization in advance. This somewhat monstrous construct disregards the social peculiarities of networks and therefore imposes greatly exaggerated requirements on the legal formation of networks.[12] Other scholars ask for an additional 'coupling agreement', or for a complete multilateral contract, or for a multilateral *synallagma*.[13] They commit the same mistake. The unfortunate case law regarding 'junk real property' has been insensitive to interconnections between the participants of the project. More specifically, the courts raised the requirements for cooperation between the financing bank, the financial advisers and the operators of the real estate to such a high degree that made it easy for banks to avoid responsibility for their scandalous financial practices.[14]

Moreover, the dualism of strict and loose couplings makes it necessary to distinguish different types of legal obligations within the network. Mutual performance obligations within the bilateral contracts must be exactly specified; obligations to cooperate and information on their interconnectedness can be unspecified. This distinction is well known from the field of relational contracts and can be transposed into networks. By contrast, the allocation of risk and of compensation duties between network partners creates novel problems. Being situated in the loosely coupled domain of interconnections, these are implied obligations with an initially unspecified and context-sensitive character. Nonetheless, the Federal Court of Justice, in its opinions mentioned before,[15] applied the strict standards for express contractual obligations to them. In a franchise relation the court requires that a franchisor's obligation to transfer a benefit to the franchisees needs to be expressly laid down in the standard terms, e.g. as duty to support. However, when a firm changes its standard terms and abolishes, or even excludes, these duties to support, the court gets cold feet. It refuses to identify an implied duty to transfer these benefits in the structure of the franchise relation itself. Scholars, of course, applaud. Only the Federal Cartel Office applies parallel structural reasoning from competition law and establishes a duty of transfer.[16]

Finally, the small worlds with their dualism of strict and loose coupling turn up for the question whether the law should stipulate a genuine network purpose that is legally binding for the participants (see Teubner, 2011, 120ff., with further references). The doctrine wants to avoid having to qualify networks as corporate

12 Afterwards, all kinds of fictions are necessary to alleviate the absurd consequences; e.g. Rohe, 1998, 85, 176, 356.

13 Coupling contract: Schluep, 2003, 304; multilateral contract: Vollkommer, 1973, 711; trilateral synallagma: Heermann, 2009, 106.

14 See the brilliant criticism by Kiesow, 2005.

15 Decisions of the German Federal Court of Justice, 20 May 2003 ('Apollo-Optik: Pflicht des Franchisegebers zur Weitergabe von Differenzrabatten an Franchisenehmer', *Betriebsberater*, 43: 2254) and 22 February 2006 ('Hertz', *Betriebsberater* 46: 1071). For pungent criticism, see Böhner, 2009.

16 Decision of the German Federal Cartel Office (Bundeskartellamt), 8 May 2006 ('Praktiker Baumärkte GmbH', B9 – 149/04). In accordance with the previous jurisprudence, see again, the decision of the Higher Regional Court Düsseldorf, 13 December 2006 ('Praktiker', *Betriebsberater*, 47: 738).

structures, so it gets lost in artificial distinctions between a common purpose of corporate entities and a merely unitary purpose of networks. (If common, how not unitary? And *vice versa.*) Or, the doctrine rejects a legally binding purpose for networks altogether and merely speaks of economic goals. Instead, private law should acknowledge that the oscillation between strict and loose coupling cannot be overcome and produces a specific legal network purpose. Networks are multilateral contracts, and yet they act like formal organizations. In the contractual realm, a self-interested focus on the exchange is legitimate. In the realm of interconnectedness, by contrast, an exclusive orientation towards the common purpose is required. In corporate networks, individual corporations are expected to rigorously pursue their own individual interests and yet to comply with the simultaneous, contradictory requirements of cooperation and pursuit of a common purpose (Kirchner, 2000, 351). This twofold orientation of network participants forces the law to recognize an independent network orientation, exposing the equal coexistence of common and individual orientation in the network. Only such a legal recognition of the network purpose will support the integration of decentralized action within the network.

### *Integration Potential III: Iterativity of Network Decisions*

Here, the smell of sulphur becomes especially penetrating. The result of the exorcism is a specific iterativity of network acts. While network failure is extorted by a Beelzebubian, uncertainty is cast out by a Luciferian. When conditions of hierarchy – collectively binding decisions, centralized competences and hierarchically ordered criteria – fail, the reaction is an increased reciprocal observation of nodes within the network. The authoritative final decision by the collective is replaced with a series of iterative decisions in a multiplicity of observer positions, which mutually reconstruct, attach, influence, constrain, control and provoke each other to innovate, but do not result in one collective decision on substantive norms. Instead of uniformity at the top of the hierarchy, we find recursivity of decisions within the network. Such an observers' network legitimates itself 'through a practice of experimentation, accessible neither for the individuals nor for the state.' (Ladeur, 2000, 82). Now, transparency, reciprocal accessibility, and generalized reciprocity of network nodes are the top priority; participation and deliberation acquire new significance. At the same time, it becomes more and more apparent that Lucifer also obeys the logic of exorcism and merely replaces one uncertainty with another. We will have to return to this point.

From a legal perspective, the network iterativity is relevant in three dimensions. In the temporal dimension, legal acts are serialized. In the substantive dimension, obligations are concretized in light of the specific situation. In the social dimension, net knots reciprocally observe each other. What is especially important here is that legal obligations are temporalized through framework agreements and later step-by-step concretion. The problem of uncertainty is resolved so the obligations are specified over time (Andersen, 2008, 97). At the beginning, nothing is really agreed upon in the framework agreement. The parties merely declare themselves to be bound to their new status. Now they are network participants. The result is the paradox of non-binding obligation, the paradox of valid but not binding legal norms, the paradox of formally binding law without substantive obligations (Goldmann, 2007, 242). Only over time do specific obligations emerge, step by step, against the background of the network's own history. They are aptly called 'second-order contracts'. They stabilize expectations in the expectation that expectations will change (Mouzas, 2009; Andersen, 2008, 97). Every external change, but also every internal net event, changes the expectations, which then create respectively different obligations on the basis of the legally binding network among the parties. Such unspecified obligations that can be specified only after a certain period of time were not unknown in classical contract law, but only as secondary obligations opposed to the primary obligation that was expressly defined at the contractual conclusion. In contrast to this, primary obligations are defined by their type of deferred determination, in the network.

Substantively, the arrangement is of remarkably experimental nature. Vagueness and generality, at the first stage, are followed by an experimental learning process towards iterative substantive concretization, on the second stage. The iterativity of decisions is characterized by multiple perspectives of the nodes which produce a 'collective inquiry' as a 'differential order which has no unity, no centre, no beginning, but is nothing but the provisional result of experimenting with self-produced constraints' (Ladeur, 2000, 167). The network partners are legally obliged not to a certain conduct or to clearly defined goals but instead to an experimental situation. The network binds them neither to reliable conditional programmes nor to purposive programmes for which they would have to choose means depending on the situation, but instead to experimental programmes void of substantive content and defined only by the multiplicity of perspectives.

And in its social dimension, iterativity transforms the one binding collective decision – either the central decision, or the conclusion of contract that binds all participants – into a multitude of individual nodes' decisions and their reciprocal-recursive observation. Here, a practice of coordinating different organizational units, familiar from organization theory, is taken to the extreme: uncertainty is absorbed through reciprocal acceptance of decisions by decentralized entities. This absorption of uncertainty is characterized by a peculiar rule-exception relation. The rule: Decentralized entities accept the decisions of other decentralized entities without reappraising their premises, and build their own consecutive decisions on these decisions without further ado. The exception: They can question or even deviate from the prior decision only as a consequence from a specific burden of information and justification. In its principle, this decision modus is also known from hierarchical situations, as exceptional revocation. The difference is the 'directive correlation', the way in which the decision's dependence is directed both horizontally and hierarchically upwards (Luhmann, 2000, 207). It is reminiscent of the principle of 'default deference' in a non-hierarchical court system, in which neither binding precedent nor a merely persuasive force of well-founded arguments govern, but instead the principle that the decisions taken by the other court are binding, and the exception of sharp requirements for the justification of overruling (Alford, 2003, 792).

Again, it is obvious how this way of dealing with uncertainty creates new uncertainty. Lucifer rears his head. Yet, he compensates quite well the internal weakness of coordination. 'That part of that power which would the evil ever do' like Mephistopheles from Goethe's Faust, must finally do the good. Indeed, new legal rules are inserted into the networks to compensate for the compensation. The duty to renegotiate thrives because it is made exactly for such a temporal iteration (see Säcker and Rixecker, 2007, § 241, no. 60). Through proceduralization, it manages to defuse the paradox of non-binding obligation by the mere lapse of time. Opportunistic behaviour that could be expected is countered with the threat of judicial control of duties to negotiate in good faith. Even stronger is the effect of downstream contractual governance mechanisms, expert assessment procedures internal to the network, arbitration and other dispute resolution mechanisms. Here, the interaction between the three dimensions is particularly obvious. Network obligations simply cannot be formulated *ex ante*. Only the iteration of both a multitude of external events and a multitude of internal decisions make it possible to define the specific obligations for each individual participant. If necessary, they can be determined *ex post* by conflict resolution institutions internal to the network or, in the worst case, by courts. Note, the real effect is not the concrete regulation of an individual issue *ex post* by an arbitrator or a court, but the institutional arrangement of iterativity itself, which creates, step by step, legally binding expectations for the concrete situation. These consolidated expectations, not the legal sanction in the individual case, are used by the law to strengthen the potential for coordination within the network.

### *Integration Potential IV: Collective Orientation Without a Collective*

Whether networks take on a collective character is a highly controversial debate among social scientists. Do the networks themselves operate as collective actors or is it only the network nodes? Positions range from simple multipolar connectivity between the nodes to a full personification of the network organization.[17] That should not encourage the law to make juridical persons out of networks. And yet one of the most important potentials for integration seems to hide in a legally supported collectivization of networks which, however, remain at the same time highly individualistic. Thus, it is necessary to uncover the *sui generis* collectivity of networks, if it is supposed to counteract the centrifugal tendencies.

17 Against their collective nature: Tacke, 2000, 317; Kämper and Schmidt, 1999, 219. In favour of their collective nature: Castells, 2000, 381; Sydow and Windeler, 1998, 265. Luhmann (2000, 408) distinguishes various situations in which networks take on a collective character.

Recently, Ladeur (2009) highlighted a peculiarity of networks, which has almost disappeared from sociological and economic theorizing. He spoke of the 'character of the network as a trans-subjective evolutionary structure'. Contrary to what is often said, the connectivity of all with all is not what is crucial – this is too static. What counts is the dynamic process of permanent changes driven by many nodes at the same time, which unavoidably but unpredictably have an effect on the whole. The trans-subjective collective potential lies in this dynamic. It forces us to destroy the usual connection between collective action capacity and the unity of representation. The metaphor of the 'many-headed Hydra', where unity of action comes not from a single centre of will-formation but is produced by a multiplicity of simultaneous decisions, makes it clear where the peculiarity of the network collectivity lies (Teubner, 1993b). In fact, there are networks that are able to act independently as a whole: joint ventures, franchising systems, just-in-time networks.[18] In such cases, the network acts as a collective actor in the political system, in the economy and in other social contexts. Internal and external processes of social attribution create an independent unity of action – but not as a single actor. Instead, they create a 'poly-corporate actor', an until now unfamiliar social organization (Bälz, 1974). Without a centre, without leadership, without a unified management, and without one single authorized representation, the network acts exclusively through its many individual nodes, which do not cease to be collective actors themselves. They operate simultaneously in their own name and in the name of the network. They produce – and this is decisive for our enquiry for internal coordination – collective commitments for the whole network, with each individual action (Teubner, 1993b, 208). This burdens the nodes with enormous responsibility and forces them to take into account not only their own interest but that of the collective in each calculation and decision. These are the social effects of network commitments, which need to be reinforced by legal rules. In such a confusing fragmentation of the collective decision into many single node decisions and in their reverse connections to the whole, one finds the potential for integration. However – possibly due to its strange fragmentation – this has not adequately been taken up by the law.

Here, to operate with the traditional full-fledged juridical person would be counter-productive. This is the categorical mistake of the many doctrinal efforts that try to capture networks with concepts of corporate law (for sources, see Teubner, 2011, 133, n 82 and n 84). To be appropriate for networks, the law would have to develop more subtle, and in particular, ambivalent, concepts of collectivity. That begins already with 'net interest' – an independent legal concept that characterizes the collective interest of the network (Cafaggi, 2008, 7), which is different from the concept of 'interest of the corporation'. Amstutz has developed

18 The sheer richness of variety is impressive. It ranges from simple connecting structures (via) to networking processes (via) to networks as social systems with their own boundaries and own till now recursive usable history to networks as collective actors. Cf. Luhmann, 2000, 408.

a law of contract collisions for these contractual networks, which contain meta-rules for conflicts between bilateral contracts, the vanishing point of which is the 'functional capability' of the contractual network (Amstutz, 2009, 334). This concept should not be misunderstood as instrumental. Instead, the formula of a 'trans-subjective evolutionary structure' indicates a direction. The law should not reduce the interest of the network to a goal–means relationship; nor should it compare it to the interest in continued existence without highlighting the ability to change, the ability to learn and the ability to evolve of the total constellation. Here one can connect with the law of corporate groups, which supports the autonomy of the subsidiaries in relation to the central company (Kropff and Semler, 2000, § 308, no. 101). But we need to go beyond a merely instrumental autonomy that binds the nodes to the profit interest of the total company. Rather, it is reflexive autonomy that should be established (Teubner, 2009, 28). It exists when all network nodes independently reflect on the precarious relationship between their environmental effects (in the broadest sense) and their function in the whole network. Reflexive autonomy plays a decisive role in particular in research networks between governmental actors, economic enterprises and academic institutions (Abegg, 2009, 273). Law will support reflexive autonomy if it imposes a legal duty on the nodes to take into account the functioning of the network as a whole and if it imposes a complementary duty to respect the nodes' autonomy over the centre.

Similar ambivalences should be taken into account by the political regulation of networks. How can one regulate from the outside a 'trans-subjective evolutionary dynamic' if there is no unitary object of regulation that the regulatory actor can grab hold of with command and control, with incentives or with indirect steering? Partisans of the so-called nodal governance approach suggest that the regulation agency, instead of trying to influence the whole network in vain, should concentrate on the individual nodes (Burris et al., 2005). Instead, a Beelzebub–Lucifer strategy seems more appropriate: regulation of networks by networks of regulation. For international networks this means that one national node of the international regulatory network is always responsible for controlling its national counterpart in the regulated network, and that connections on the regulation level should control the connections on the level of action (Slaughter, 2001). Similar proposals have also been made for control of networks by civil society institutions. NGO networks and stakeholder communities will only be able to develop control pressure if they simultaneously build countervailing power to every local node and to the centre of action.[19]

If one finally approaches the collectivity of networks in its core meaning, then the legal controversies become sharper. Here, tough liability regimes for the network as a whole come into play. On the one hand, liability norms need to protect the network as such from damaging actions by its members or by third parties. On the other hand, liability regimes need to react to negative externalities

19 For networked NGOs, Keck and Sikkink, 1998. For networked stakeholder communities, Cohen and Sabel, 2006.

of the network itself. Up to now, legal doctrine, however, blocks this and limits liability to claims originating in bilateral contractual relations (Rohe, 1998, 439, 444; Schimansky, 2003, 117).

Yet, the logic of the network demands that network members who are not tied together by means of bilateral contracts are liable to each other, particularly where they violate the collective interest of the network. At this point, the co-responsibility of private law for network failure becomes evident. Where internal coordination disasters are not sanctioned by rules of liability, the law counteracts the coordination potential latent in the network instead of realizing it. Free-riding as well as standard-lowering in franchising and in supply chains are the dubious constellations. So far only a minority of scholars has developed liability rules for network members that are not bound to each other by a bilateral contract (Heldt, 2009, 150; Lange, 2001, 188; Larenz and Wolf, 1997, 470; Teubner, 1993a, 232; Teubner, 2011, 225). Others adapt the construction of an *actio pro socio* to networks, which allows for them to compensate harm to the reputation of the whole network done by individual members (Heldt, 2008, 224; Cafaggi, 2008, 12, 44; Teubner, 2011, 231). Complementary to this, Wolf developed a liability regime for the protection of networks from damages by third parties. If the operation capability of a network is reduced through damaging the operation of one network node, then the violator is liable also for the additional cost of the damage to the network itself that is felt by other nodes (Wolf, 2009; Cafaggi, 2008, 44).

The resistance against a liability regime becomes strongest in the reverse case, where external liability would be needed to fight against the often criticized reticular irresponsibility. A spectre floats around – the spectre of collective liability. Should the failure of an individual member be the responsibility of the other members, who cannot be blamed for this singular misbehaviour, or even be the responsibility of the totality? But this is only a ghost. In reality, a decentralized collective liability is concerned – a decentralized and at the same time selective responsibility within the network configuration, which answers internal disasters of coordination with an effective threat of sanctions. This is somewhat similar to the long recognized responsibility for violations of organizational duties within hierarchical organizations. 'Interface liability' is the network suitable solution, which reacts to internal coordination failure with liability norms that create several responsibilities for the network nodes involved. French case-law introduced the concept of '*non-divisibilité*' of an '*ensemble des contrats*', which excludes an exit option for network members, even where it is explicitly provided for contractually.[20] Nonetheless, such a collectively distributed responsibility is still a taboo, to which a coalition of lawyers – who consider networks to be judicially irrelevant – and modern network lawyers – who choose to see only the opportunities and not the risks of networks – cling (Bayreuther, 2001, 399; Schimansky, 2003, 125; Grundmann, 2007, 718 (with modifications)). The missing liability for negative

20 E.g. Cass. Civ. April 4 2006 *Répertoire du Notariat Defrénois* 2006, 1194.

externalities is therefore the other major hindrance, and as a consequence private law is co-responsible for the failure of networks.

## Coping with Uncertainty: Reduction, Transformation or Intensification?

If legal arrangements aim to realize the latent integration potential of networks, they should correct reticular irresponsibilities through an effective liability regime and strengthen the fragile coordination mechanisms of networks by imposing appropriate obligations. But there are doubts connected with each of the four potentials for integration discussed. Does Lucifer not simply act like Beelzebub – he who drives out Satan successfully but then takes his place? If that is true, what can be said in general about the diabolics of network failure? No doubt, the connectivity of networks in a decentralized world – the very *symbolon* of networking – is strengthened when the law, with appropriate norms, supports their inner coordination and responsibility. However, the price that is regularly paid is a new dynamic of separation – a new *diabolon* of networking – as we have seen, either through the difference between binding and non-binding effects of factual conduct, or through the divide between contractual sphere and network sphere, or through the division between contractual frame and later concretization, or through the distinction between individual and collective orientation, or through the difference between competition and cooperation.

Lucifer brings light into the darkness of the uncertainty, which is typical for the inner coordination in networks and makes integration possible in spite of high decentralization. But Lucifer, just like Beelzebub before him – who bestowed upon us network failure instead of hierarchical failure – only removes one threatening uncertainty in order to create a new one. Should that be the productive way of dealing with uncertainty: not to reduce uncertainty but to transform and possibly even to intensify it? In medicine this is known as a change of symptom: just as one pain is soothed, a new pain pops up in another place in the body. Apparently, in respect to the changes in the uncertainty of networks, we are on the trail of a general problematic of how to deal with uncertainty: 'If absorption of uncertainty is a process of decision, this means that the process should also take into account the prospect of future decisions and by doing so regenerate the uncertainty that it removes' (Luhmann, 2000, 187). But if uncertainty is not abolished but only regenerated then one could leave it as it is. How would it help the network if it won integration at the expense of damage to its orientation?

The point seems to be that we cannot avoid switching from one devilry to another; however, one devil is not the same as the other. Beelzebub is different from Satan, and Lucifer is different from Beelzebub. And possibly in the future, Lucifer will be driven out by another devil with similar but other hellish qualities. What is decisive are the small differences in the order of demons, from Adramelech via Mammon to Thammuz. There is one question that should be answered whenever one drives out one uncertainty with another. Does the difference in uncertainty make a difference?

Let us go back to our four remedies for network failure and ask this question each time.

*Remedy # 1: Interface Liability*

This liability regime battles, quite successfully, the network-typical uncertainty which emerges at interfaces between nodes, by forcing neighbouring nodes to coordinate their activities. It imposes liability for coordination failure on all those potentially involved in the activity, which is at stake. But as usual, the old uncertainty is replaced by a new one: Which criteria will serve to limit the number of liable nodes? Is this particularly problematic in large scale networks? If so, then this is indeed an unfortunate situation. However, in comparison, the new uncertainty seems rather controllable because it is possible, with hindsight, to determine with sufficient precision the number of responsible actors, if one takes into account the specifics of the concrete situation. In particular, if one applies the criterion: Who is involved in the project at hand – by the realization of which damages arise and which differentiates itself from other network activities – one can avoid an unjust collective responsibility of a too large number of participants or of the whole network (for a detailed analysis, see Teubner, 2003).

*Remedy # 2: Implied Duties of Care*

The network failure which is triggered by centrifugal tendencies in the de-central style of decision, can be corrected by imposing implied duties of care that network nodes owe to each other and to the whole in particular fields. Immediately, however, a new uncertainty on the kind and the extent of such duties arises. Here the difference between contractual sphere and integrated sphere in the network may provide the criterion limiting the catalogue of duties, which in its turn produces new, yet again legally solvable, uncertainties.

*Remedy # 3: Insurance Regime*

If one reacts to negative network externalities with the liability rule of distributed collective liability, one may reduce new uncertainties – as has already been suggested – by imposing a duty of the net centre to insure the members, the costs of which can be calculated with the fees (Emerson, 1992, 667, n 274, 668, 670; King, 2005, 460). Our method of comparative diabolics would make this apparent.

*Remedy # 4: Non-divisibilité*

If the law learns the double strategy for opening up spaces of autonomy and, after a slow learning process, determining via prohibitions the borders of autonomy

(Wiethölter, 2005, 76), then it will generously permit many forms of network contracts. In particular cases this will block the exit option with the 'sword of fire' of the '*non-divisibilité*', that is, it will not allow powerful network participants to withdraw from their network responsibility by means of standard contracts. In that case, a new uncertainty opens up again, namely to distinguish situations of *divisibilité* from situations of *non-divisibilité*. Here, too, the chances of concretizing the *non-divisibilité* in an incremental process of legal decisions seem more attractive than the uncertainty of leaving the limits of exit to private autonomy.

A 'philosophy' of dealing with uncertainty – if it becomes part of legal culture – will care for such distinctions. What is needed is a second-order observation of uncertainty absorption. What does the new uncertainty, which has taken the place of the old one, look like in detail? Comparative diabolics would recommend: do not rigidly reduce uncertainty. Rather, try to arrange the exorcism of the devil in such a way that is possessed only by two other ghosts: the increase of internal irritability and the goal-orientated shift to controllable variables.

And it seems that to increase internal irritability is, in the end, more important than to control the new uncertainty. Without a doubt it is important to change the one uncertainty into the other, to shift it from the market to the organization, from the organization to the network, and from the network to the law, etc, in order to reach decisional advantages. But what is really needed is to maintain, to renew and to intensify the inherent network uncertainty. Why? Because network uncertainty possesses a provocative power. In their nodal points networks create the valuable potential of observing the world from diverging perspectives and of transforming the multiple perspectives into the decision chain. 'A poly-perspectivism replaces the traditional rationalist model which is obsessed by uniformity' (Augsberg, 2007, 485). What counts is not only the diabolic/angelic role of networks to regenerate one uncertainty after another, but their plurality of deviating positions of observation. Inter-systemic networks indeed dispose of a 'social epistemology' because they institutionalize different perspectives by their plurality of autonomous nodes. And if they are able to link these perspectives to a consistent chain of decision, then they systematically provoke the riches of the power of judgment, the role of which is realized in the undecidable collision of incompatible worlds of meanings, which nevertheless needs to be decided.[21] Should this be the hidden agenda of a 'network appropriate law'– a gentle compulsion towards the power of judgment?

## References

Abegg, A., 2009. 'Legislation and Self-Regulation of Hybrid Networks at the Intersection between Governmental Administration and Economic Self-

21 As is known, Immanuel Kant localizes judgment neither in the area of understanding, nor in practical reason, but characterizes it as a 'means of connecting the two parts of philosophy in a whole', Kant, 2007, 12.

Organization' in Amstutz, M. and G. Teubner (eds) *Contractual Networks: Legal Issues of Multilateral Cooperation* (Hart Publishing, Oxford, UK) pp. 255–90.

Acquis Group, 2007. *Principles of the Existing EC Contract Law – Contract I.* (Sellier European Law Publishers, München, Germany).

Andersen, N. A., 2008. *Partnerships: Machines of Possibility* (Policy Press, Bristol, UK).

Alford, R. P., 2003. 'Federal Courts, International Tribunals, and the Continuum of Deference' *Virginia Journal of International Law*, 43: 675–796.

Amstutz, M., 2009. 'The Constitution of Contractual Networks, in Contractual Networks: Legal Issues of Multilateral Cooperation' in Amstutz, M. and G. Teubner (eds) *Contractual Networks: Legal Issues of Multilateral Cooperation* (Hart Publishing, Oxford, UK) pp. 309–46.

Augsberg, I., 2007. 'Das Gespinst des Rechts: Zur Relevanz von Netzwerkmodellen im juristischen Diskurs' *Rechtstheorie*, 38: 479–93.

Augsberg, I. and K.-H. Ladeur, 2008. *Die Funktion der Menschenwürde im Verfassungsstaat: Humangenetik – Neurowissenschaft – Medien* (Mohr Siebeck Verlag, Tübingen, Germany).

Baecker, D., 2002. *Organisation und Gesellschaft* (Universität Witten/Herdecke, Witten/Herdecke, Germany).

Bälz, U., 1974. 'Einheit und Vielheit in Konzern' in Baur, F., J. Esser, F. Kübler and E. Steindorff (eds) *Festschrift für Ludwig Raiser* (Mohr Siebeck Verlag, Tübingen, Germany).

Bayreuther, F., 2001. *Wirtschaftlich-existentiell abhängige Unternehmen im Konzern-, Kartell- und Arbeitsrecht* (Duncker & Humblot, Berlin, Germany).

Boehme-Nessler, V., 2008. *Unscharfes Recht: Überlegungen zur Relativierung des Rechts in der digitalisierten Welt* (Duncker & Humblot, Berlin, Germany).

Böhner, R., 2009. 'Profit Sharing within the Network: Duty to Transfer Network Benefits' in Amstutz, M. and G. Teubner (eds) *Contractual Networks: Legal Issues of Multilateral Cooperation* (Hart Publishing, Oxford, UK) pp. 153–83.

Bommes, M. and V. Tacke, 2007. 'Netzwerke in der Gesellschaft der Gesellschaft. Funktionen und Folgen einer doppelten Begriffsverwendung' *Soziale Systeme*, 13: 9–20.

Boysen, S., C. Franzius, T. Herbst, M. Kötter, A. Krentz, K. v. Lewinski, F. Meinel, J. Nolte and S. Schönrock (eds), 2007. *Netzwerke* (Nomos Verlag, Baden-Baden, Germany).

Brun, M. E., Mastronardi, P. and K. Schedler, 2005. *Hierarchie und Netzwerke* (Haupt Verlag, Bern, Switzerland).

Buchanan, M., 2002. *Nexus: Small Worlds and the Groundbreaking Science of Networks* (W. W. Norton & Company, New York, USA).

Burris, S., Drahos, P. and C. Shearing, 2005. 'Nodal Governance' *Australian Journal of Legal Philosophy*, 30: 30–58.

Cafaggi, F., 2008. 'Contractual Networks and the Small Business Act: Towards European Principles?' 2008/15 EUI Working Paper LAW.

Castells, M., 2000. *The Rise of the Network Society* (Blackwell Publishing, Oxford, UK).

Cohen, J. and C. Sabel, 2006. 'Norms and Global Institutions' Available at: http://www.princeton.edu/~pcglobal/conferences/normative/papers/Session4_Cohen_Sabel.pdf. Accessed 23 November 2009.

Deakin, S., 2009. 'The Return of the Guild? Network Relations in Historical Perspective' in Amstutz, M. and G. Teubner (eds) *Contractual Networks: Legal Issues of Multilateral Cooperation* (Hart Publishing, Oxford, UK) pp. 53–73.

Emerson, R. W., 1992. 'Franchisors' Liability When Franchisees Are Apparent Agents' *Hofstra Law Review*, 20: 609–85.

Ensthaler, J. and D. Gesmann-Nuissl, 2000. 'Virtuelle Unternehmen in der Praxis: Eine Herausforderung für das Zivil-, Gesellschafts- und Kartellrecht' *Betriebs-Berater*, 55: 2265–71.

Everson, M. and C. Joerges, 2006. 'Re-Conceptualising Europeanisation as a Public Law of Collisions: Comitology, Agencies and an Interactive Public Adjudication' in Hofmann, H. and A. Türk (eds) *EU Administrative Governance* (Edward Elgar Publishing, Cheltenham, UK) pp. 512–40.

Gerum, E., W. Achenbach and F. Opelt, 1998. 'Zur Regulierung der Binnenbeziehungen von Unternehmensnetzwerken: Ein Problemaufriss' *Zeitschrift Führung und Organisation*, 67: 266–70.

Goldmann, M., 2007. 'Der Widerspenstigen Zähmung, oder: Netzwerke dogmatisch gedacht' in Boysen, S., C. Franzius, T. Herbst, M. Kötter, A. Krentz, K. v. Lewinski, F. Meinel, J. Nolte and S. Schönrock (eds) *Netzwerke* (Nomos, Baden-Baden, Germany) pp. 225–46.

Gordon, R. (1994). 'Hayek and Cooter on Custom and Reason' *Southwestern University Law Review*, 23: 453–60.

Gouldner, A. W., 1960. 'The Norm of Reciprocity: A Preliminary Statement' *American Sociological Review*, 25: 161–78.

Granovetter, M. S., 1973. 'The Strength of Weak Ties' *American Journal of Sociology*, 78: 1360–80.

Grundmann, S., 2007. 'Die Dogmatik der Vertragsnetze' *Archiv für die civilistische Praxis*, 207: 718–67.

— 2008. 'Vertragsnetz und Wegfall der Geschäftsgrundlage' in Aderhold, L., Grunewald, B. and D. Klingberg (eds) *Festschrift für Harm Peter Westermann* (Schmidt Verlag, Köln, Germany) pp. 227–44.

Heermann, P. W., 2009. 'The Status of Multilateral Synallagma in the Law of Connected Contracts' in Amstutz, M. and G. Teubner (eds) *Contractual Networks: Legal Issues of Multilateral Cooperation* (Hart Publishing, Oxford, UK) pp. 103–18.

Heldt, C., 2008. 'Baukooperation und Franchising als multilaterale Sonderverbindung: Vertragsnetzwerke – Parallelschuldverhältnisse – Personengesellschaften' (Dissertation, Frankfurt, Germany).

Heldt, C., 2009. 'International Relations and Semi-spontaneous Order: The Case of Franchising and Construction Contracts' in Amstutz, M. and G. Teubner (eds) *Contractual Networks: Legal Issues of Multilateral Cooperation* (Hart Publishing, Oxford, UK) pp. 137–52.

Hirsch-Kreinsen, H., 2002. 'Unternehmensnetzwerke – revisited' *Zeitschrift für Soziologie*, 31: 106–24.

Jhering, R. v., 1861. 'Culpa in contrahendo oder Schadensersatz bei nichtigen oder nicht zur Perfection gelangten Verträgen' *Jahrbücher für die Dogmatik des heutigen römischen und deutschen Privatrechts*, 4: 1–112.

Kämper, E. and J.F.K. Schmidt, 1999. 'Netzwerke als strukturelle Kopplung' in Weyer, J. (ed.), *Soziale Netzwerke* (Oldenbourg Wissenschaftsverlag, München, Germany) pp. 211–35.

Kant, I., 1790, reissued 2007. *Critique of Judgement* (Oxford University Press, Oxford, UK).

Keck, M. E. and K. Sikkink, 1998. *Activists Beyond Borders* (Cornell University Press, Ithaca, USA).

Kiesow, R. M., 2005. *Kredite in der Risikogesellschaft* (Berliner Wissenschaftsverlag, Berlin, Germany).

King, J. H. Jr., 2005. 'Limiting the Vicarious Liability of Franchisors for the Torts of Their Franchisees' *Washington and Lee Law Review*, 62: 417–85.

Kirchner, C., 2000. 'Horizontale japanische Unternehmensgruppen (keiretsu) im deutschen Konzernrecht' in Baums, T., K. J. Hopt and N. Horn (eds) Liber Amicorum Richard M. Buxbaum. Kluwer, London, UK, pp. 339–62.

Kropff, B. and J. Semler (eds), 2000. *Münchener Kommentar zum Aktiengesetz* (2nd edition Beck, München, Germany).

Kulms, R., 2000. *Schuldrechtliche Organisationsverträge in der Unternehmens-kooperation* (Nomos, Baden-Baden, Germany).

Ladeur, K.-H., 1992. *Postmoderne Rechtstheorie: Selbstreferenz – Selbstorganisation – Prozeduralisierung* (Duncker & Humblot, Berlin, Germany).

— 2000. *Negative Freiheitsrechte und gesellschaftliche Selbstorganisation* (Mohr Siebeck Verlag, Tübingen, Germany).

— 2006. *Der Staat gegen die Gesellschaft: Zur Verteidigung der Rationalität der 'Privatrechtsgesellschaft'* (Mohr Siebeck Verlag, Tübingen, Germany).

— 2009. 'Was leistet der Netzwerkbegriff für die Verwaltungswissenschaft?' in V. Mehde, U. Ramsauer and M. Seckelmann (eds) *Staat, Verwaltung, Information* (Duncker & Humblot, Berlin) pp.639–58.

Lange, K. W., 2001. 'Virtuelle Unternehmen' in Noack, U. and G. Spindler (eds) *Unternehmensrecht und Internet: Neue Medien im Aktien-, Börsen-, Steuer- und Arbeitsrecht* (Beck, München, Germany) pp. 169–97.

Larenz, K. and M. Wolf, 1997. *Allgemeiner Teil des Bürgerlichen Rechts* (Beck, München, Germany).

Lemley, M. A. and D. McGowan, 1998. 'Legal Implications of Network Economic Effects' *California Law Review*, 86: 479–611.

Littmann, P. and S. A. Jansen, 2000. *Oszillodox: Virtualisierung – die permanente Neuerfindung der Organisation* (Klett, Stuttgart, Germany).

Luhmann, N., 1990. 'The State of the Political System' in Niklas Luhmann, *Essays on Self-Reference* (Columbia University Press, New York, USA) pp. 165–74.
— 2000. *Organisation und Entscheidung* (Westdeutscher Verlag, Opladen, Germany).
Messner, D., 1997. 'Netzwerktheorien: Die Suche nach Ursachen und Auswegen aus der Krise staatlicher Steuerungsfähigkeit' in Altvater, E., A. Brunnengräber, M. Haake and H. Walk (eds) *Vernetzt und Verstrickt. Nicht-Regierungs-Organisationen als gesellschaftliche Produktivkraft* (Verlag Westfälisches Dampfboot, Münster, Germany) pp. 26–64.
Mouzas, S. and D. Ford, 2009. 'The Constitution of Networks' *Industrial Marketing Management* 38: 495–503.
Möllers, C., 2005. 'Netzwerk als Kategorie des Organisationsrechts: Zur juristischen Beschreibung dezentraler Steuerung' in Oebbecke, J. (ed.) *Nicht-normative Steuerung in dezentralen Systemen* (Steiner Verlag, Stuttgart, Germany) pp. 285–302.
Nowrot, K. 2007. *Netzwerke im transnationalen Wirtschaftsrecht und Rechtsdogmatik* (Universität Halle-Wittenberg, Halle-Wittenberg, Germany).
Rohe, M., 1998. *Netzverträge: Rechtsprobleme komplexer Vertragsverbindungen* (Mohr Siebeck Verlag, Tübingen, Germany).
Säcker, F. J. and R. Rixecker (eds), 2007. *Münchener Kommentar zum Bürgerlichen Gesetzbuch* (5th edition, Beck, München, Germany).
Selznick, P., 1992. *The Moral Commonwealth: Social Theory and the Promise of Community* (University of California Press, Berkeley, USA).
Schimansky, A., 2003. *Der Franchisevertrag nach deutschem und niederländischem Recht unter besonderer Berücksichtigung seines Netzcharakters und der Ansprüche bei Vertragsbeendigung* (Mohr Siebeck Verlag, Tübingen, Germany).
Schluep, W., 2003. 'Zusammengesetzte Verträge: Vertragsverbindung oder Vertragsverwirrung' in Honsell, H., W. Portmann, R. Zäch and D. Zobl (eds) *Festschrift für Heinz Rey* (Schulthess, Zürich, Switzerland) pp. 285–306.
Slaughter, A.-M., 2001. 'The Accountability of Government Networks' *Indiana Journal of Global Legal Studies*, 8: 347–67.
Stegbauer, C., 2002. *Reziprozität: Einführung in soziale Formen der Gegenseitigkeit* (Westdeutscher Verlag, Wiesbaden, Germany).
Stichweh, R., 2000. 'Adresse und Lokalisierung in einem globalen Kommunikationssystem' in Stichweh, R., *Die Weltgesellschaft: Soziologische Analysen* (Suhrkamp, Frankfurt, Germany) pp. 220–31.
Sydow, J., 1999. 'Management von Netzwerkorganisationen: Zum Stand der Forschung' in Sydow, J. (ed.) *Management von Netzwerkorganisationen* (Westdeutscher Verlag, Wiesbaden, Frankfurt) pp. 279–314.
Sydow, J. and A. Windeler, 1998. 'Organizing and Evaluating Interfirm Networks' *Organization Science* Special Issue, 9: 265–84.
Tacke, V., 2000. 'Netzwerk und Adresse' *Soziale Systeme*, 6: 291–320.

Teubner, G., 1993a. 'Piercing the Contractual Veil: The Social Responsibility of Contractual Networks' in Wilhelmson, T. (ed.) *Critical Contract Law* (Dartmouth Publishing, Aldershot, UK) pp. 211–38.

— 1993b. 'The Many-Headed Hydra: Networks as Higher-Order Collective Actors' in McCahery, J., Picciotto, S. and C. Scott (eds) *Corporate Control and Accountability* (Clarendon Press, Oxford, UK) pp. 41–60.

— 2003. 'Expertise as Social Institution: Internalising Third Parties into the Contract' in Campbell, D., H. Collins and J. Wightman (eds) *Implicit Dimensions of Contract Discrete, Relational and Network Contracts* (Hart Publishing, Oxford, UK) pp. 333–63.

— 2009. 'Coincidentia Oppositorum: Hybrid Networks Beyond Contract and Organisation' in Amstutz, M. and G. Teubner (eds) *Contractual Networks: Legal Issues of Multilateral Cooperation* (Hart Publishing, Oxford) pp. 3–30.

— 2011. *Networks as Connected Contracts*, with an Introduction by Hugh Collins (Hart, Oxford).

Vesting, T., 2004. 'The Network Economy as a Challenge to Create New Public Law (beyond the State)' in Ladeur, K.-H. (ed.) *Public Governance in the Age of Globalization* (Ashgate Publishing, Aldershot, UK) pp. 247–88.

Viellechner, L., 2007. 'Können Netzwerke die Demokratie ersetzen? Zur Legitimation der Regelbildung im Globalisierungsprozess' in Boysen, S., C. Franzius, T. Herbst, M. Kötter, A. Krentz, K. v. Lewinski, F. Meinel, J. Nolte and S. Schönrock (eds) *Netzwerke* (Nomos Verlag, Baden-Baden, Germany) pp. 36–57.

Vollkommer, M., 1973. 'Der Schutz des Käufers beim B-Geschäft des "finanzierten Abzahlungskaufs"' in Paulus, G. (ed.) *Festschrift für Karl Larenz* (Beck, München, Germany) pp. 703–16.

Watts, D., 1999. *Small Worlds: The Dynamics of Networks between Order and Randomness* (Princeton University Press, Princeton, USA).

Wellenhofer, M., 2009. 'Third Party Effects of Bilateral Contracts within the Network' in Amstutz, M. and G. Teubner (eds) *Conctractual Networks: Legal Issues of Multilateral Cooperation* (Hart Publishing, Oxford, UK) pp. 119–36.

Weyer, J., 2000. 'Zum Stand der Netzwerkforschung in den Sozialwissenschaften' in Weyer, J. (ed.) *Soziale Netzwerke: Konzepte und Methoden der sozialwissenschaftlichenNetzwerkforschung*(OldenbourgWissenschaftsverlag, München, Germany) pp. 1–34.

Windeler, A., 2001. *Unternehmungsnetzwerke: Konstitution und Strukturation* (Westdeutscher Verlag, Wiesbaden, Germany).

Wiethölter, R., 2005. 'Justifications of a Law of Society' in Perez, O. and G. Teubner (eds) *Paradoxes and Inconsistencies in the Law* (Hart Publishing, Oxford, UK) pp. 65–77.

Wolf, M., 2009. 'The Protection of Contractual Networks Against Interference by Third Parties' in Amstutz, M. and G. Teubner (eds) *Contractual Networks: Legal Issues of Multilateral Cooperation* (Hart Publishing, Oxford, UK) pp. 225–40.

Chapter 6

# Contracts with Network Effects: Is the Time Now Right?

Roger Brownsword[1]

## Introduction

For some time, the English law of contract has been undergoing a quiet transformation: the idea that (subject to exceptions for minors, and the like) the general law of contract applies to all transactions, irrespective of the identity, status, or standing of the parties, no longer governs. Nowadays, it is trite that consumers and their transactions are to be distinguished from business people and their contracts.[2] However, this is by no means the full story. First, the law that applies to consumer transactions is part of a regulatory package that is driven by ideas of a flourishing (and increasingly online) consumer marketplace in Europe. The law continues to set standards for these transactions, harmonizing the responsibilities of suppliers and the remedies available to purchasers. However, the doctrinal features of this segment of the law are chosen purely for their instrumental value relative to the guiding regulatory objectives.[3] Second, it is a corollary of this first point that transactional rights and responsibilities in the consumer marketplace are no longer voluntarily assumed by the parties in the way that, according to classical thinking, we understand the obligations of

1 Earlier versions of this chapter were presented at the annual SECOLA conference, 'From Exchange to Cooperation – Networks and Long-Term Relationships in European Contract Law', Florence, June 5 and 6, 2009, and at a seminar organized by the Singapore Academy of Law, Supreme Court of Singapore, July 6, 2009. The author is grateful to those who participated at these meetings for their questions and comments. Needless to say, the usual disclaimers apply.

2 It is a recurrent theme, for example, in the UK government's response to the proposed Regulation on a Common European Sales Law: see, Ministry of Justice and BIS, *A Common European Sales Law for the European Union – A proposal for a Regulation from the European Commission: The Government Response* (2012).

3 Generally, see Hugh Collins, *Regulating Contracts* (Oxford: Oxford University Press, 1999); and, more particularly, see Roger Brownsword, 'Regulating Transactions: Good Faith and Fair Dealing' in Geraint Howells and Reiner Schulze (eds), *Modernising and Harmonising Consumer Contract Law* (Munich: Sellier, 2009) 87.

contract to be engaged.[4] Participants in the consumer marketplace simply take up their positions as regulatees – whether as suppliers or purchasers, the parties have a status, with routine rights and responsibilities, as dictated by the regulatory regime. Thirdly, inspired by a new 'contextualism',[5] operating in conjunction with a reinvigorated commercial realism,[6] the commercial law of contract sets default standards for business transactions but tries very hard to respect the moves made by business contractors to self-regulate their affairs (even to the point of tracking the *implicit* expectations of such parties). In this sense, the commercial law of contract is increasingly responsive to business practice and is less concerned with standard-setting than with standard-reflecting. Finally, the overarching purpose of contract law is understood to be to protect the reasonable expectations of honest parties.[7] In the *consumer* marketplace, expectations are reasonable only insofar as they are in line with the terms of the regulatory regime (which is supposed to embody a reasonable balance between the interests of suppliers and purchasers); but, in *commercial* dealing, expectations can be judged to be reasonable relative to several reference points – notably, the background rules of the general law, the express terms of contracts, the implicit practice of the particular sector, or the implicit signals given by one's co-contractor.[8]

In the wake of these changes, it is arguable that English law might now become more receptive to ideas that it has traditionally opposed or ignored. Most obviously, English law, having already accepted a minimal idea of good faith in relation to the exercise of contractual discretion,[9] might now expand the requirements of fair dealing by reference to the particular (and, potentially, variable) contextual

4 See Roger Brownsword, 'The Theoretical Foundations of European Private Law: A Time to Stand and Stare' in Roger Brownsword, Hans Micklitz, Leone Niglia, and Steven Weatherill (eds), *The Foundations of European Private Law* (Oxford: Hart, 2011) 159.

5 The root cases on contextualism are *Mannai Investments Co Ltd v Eagle Star Life Assurance Co Ltd* [1997] 3 All ER 352 and *Investors Compensation Scheme Ltd v West Bromwich Building Society*[1998] 1 All ER 98; but, these cases need to be read in conjunction with perhaps the most critical precedent, *Transfield Shipping Inc v Mercator Shipping Inc* [2008] UKHL 48.

6 This is exemplified in *Rainy Sky v Kookmin Bank* [2011] UKSC 50, as well as *RTS Flexible Systems Limited v Molkerei Alois Müller Gmbh and Co (UK Production)* [2010] UKSC 14, where (at paras 58, 62, and 86–87) Lord Clarke rejects the Court of Appeal's view that there was 'no contract' between the parties as making no commercial sense.

7 Seminally, see Johan Steyn, 'Contract Law: Fulfilling the Reasonable Expectations of Honest Men' (1997) 113 *Law Quarterly Review* 433; and Roger Brownsword, *Contract Law: Themes for the Twenty-First Century* (Oxford: Oxford University Press, 2006).

8 See Roger Brownsword, 'After *Investors*: Interpretation, Expectation and the Implicit Dimension of the "New Contextualism"' in David Campbell, Hugh Collins, and John Wightman (eds), *The Implicit Dimensions of Contract* (Oxford, Hart, 2003) 103.

9 See, e.g. T. Daintith, 'Contractual Discretion and Administrative Discretion: A Unified Analysis' (2005) 68 MLR 554 and R. Hooley, 'Controlling Contractual Discretion' (2013) CLJ (forthcoming).

features of the case – indeed, in just the way that Leggatt J recently put it in *Yam Seng Pte Limited* v *International Trade Corporation Limited*:[10]

> What good faith requires is sensitive to context. That includes the core value of honesty … In some contractual contexts the relevant background expectations may extend further to an expectation that the parties will share information relevant to the performance of the contract …[11]

Applying this understanding of good faith, Leggatt J held that the defendant suppliers of Manchester United fragrances committed repudiatory breaches by, inter alia, being less than honest with the distributor claimants about the prices being set for Singaporean domestic retail outlets (as against duty-free outlets) when, in the context, it was clear that it was vital that the information given was honest and reliable.

In this chapter, a less obvious, and much less-debated, possibility is considered. This is the idea that contract law might now be receptive to the idea of 'network contracts' or 'contracts with network effects' – ideas that have been floated in the academic literature but that have not yet been taken up in mainstream contractual thinking.[12] There are many reasons for being attracted by the idea that there should be an explicit doctrinal coding for networks – for example, that such a coding would develop the shape of contract thinking in a way that brings it more closely into alignment with networking forms of economic organization and business practice; that it would present the opportunity to specify distinctive and desired legal effects – particularly effects that tend towards the heightening of cooperative contractual obligations and the recognition of connected third-party interests; that it would facilitate a more appropriate framing of questions concerning the fairness

10 [2013] EWHC 111 (QB).

11 Ibid., paras 141–142. Leggatt J went on to suggest that 'the traditional English hostility towards a doctrine of good faith in the performance of contracts, to the extent that it still persists, is misplaced' (para 153).

12 See, e.g. John N. Adams and Roger Brownsword, 'Privity and the Concept of a Network Contract' (1990) 10 *Legal Studies* 12; John N. Adams and Roger Brownsword, *Key Issues in Contract* (London: Butterworths, 1995) Ch. 5; and John N. Adams, Deryck Beyleveld, and Roger Brownsword, 'Privity of Contract – the Benefits and the Burdens of Law Reform' (1997) 60 MLR 238. Recently, there has been a small explosion of the contractual networks literature, including: Fabrizio Cafaggi, 'Contractual Networks and the Small Business Act: Towards European Principles?' (2008) 4 *European Review of Contract Law* 493; Fabrizio Cafaggi (ed.), *Contractual Networks, Inter-Firm Cooperation and Economic Growth* (Cheltenham: Edward Elgar, 2011); Marc Amstutz and Gunther Teubner (eds), *Networks: Legal Issues of Multilateral Cooperation* (Oxford: Hart, 2009); Gunther Teubner, "'And if I by Beelzebub Cast Out Devils,…': An Essay on the Diabolics of Network Failure" (2009) 10 *German Law Journal* 395; and Gunther Teubner, *Networks as Connected Contracts* (Oxford: Hart, 2011) (translated by Michelle Everson, and with an exceptionally helpful introduction by Hugh Collins).

of exclusion and limitation clauses in connected contracts;[13] and that, by releasing courts from the shackles of classical contract thinking, doctrinal recognition of networks would reduce the artificiality (and increase the transparency) of judicial reasoning.

Although it is in the sphere of commercial contracting that we see the clearest examples of networked business practices, we can consider the possible doctrinal reception of networks across the full span of contract law. In the light of the transformation of English contract law, it will be appreciated that the prospects for network contracts hinge on two rather different questions: first, whether, in *consumer* transactions, they assist the regulatory purposes; and, secondly, whether, in *commercial* transactions, they are in line with the practice-based reasonable expectations of the parties.

We can proceed by focusing on three illustrative cases: first, a competition between private contractors of the kind litigated in the case of *Clarke* v *Earl of Dunraven: The Satanita*[14] (where there were potentially some difficulties in constructing or inferring contractual relationships between the competitors); second, as a representative consumer case, *OFT* v *Lloyds TSB Bank plc* [15] (in which the House of Lords held that the protection given to credit card holders by section 75(1) of the Consumer Credit Act 1974 extends to more complex modern credit networks as well as to transactions made with overseas suppliers); and, third, *New Zealand Shipping Company Ltd* v *A M Satterthwaite & Co Ltd: The Eurymedon*[16] which we can treat as a representative commercial case, in this instance involving the carriage of goods by sea, but it could equally well be an example from franchising or construction (where the commercial purpose will be effected through a hub-and-spoke arrangement or a cluster of connected contracts). By reflecting on these cases, we can make a dual assessment: first, whether there is an unbridgeable gap between the current law and a body of law that employs ideas of network contracts and network effects; and, second, whether there is any prospect of these network ideas being adopted by English law.

The chapter is in four principal parts. First, the three illustrative cases are outlined; and, then, in the second, third, and fourth parts, we can consider the possibility of networks being recognized in relation to, respectively, consumer, commercial, and purely private contracts.

---

13 See, e.g. R. Brownsword, 'Network Contracts Revisited', in Amstutz and Teubner (eds), n 12 above, 31.

14 [1897] AC 59.

15 [2007] UKHL 48.

16 [1975] AC 154.

## Three Illustrative Cases

In its classical form, the English law of contract assumes that the standard marketplace deal is a discrete spot transaction: A and B make their exchange; there is neither context nor continuity. This assumption militates against taking into account any relational elements in the dealings between the parties – which, in turn, can make it difficult to draw on the background to read cooperative obligations into the particular transaction.[17] It also militates against locating the particular transaction in a context of connected contracts that, as a set, reflect and articulate the underlying (commercial) purpose of the deals. Nevertheless, there are occasions when the courts, even without a jurisprudence of network contracts, are able to declare what are, in as many words, network effects. In this section, we can introduce three such instances of implicit network thinking.

### *Clarke* v *Dunraven*

Somewhat surprisingly, *Clarke* v *Dunraven* is a case that has a place in the classical canon of contract law. Far from being a convenient illustration of the coming together of offer and acceptance to form an agreement between the parties, it is a case in which commentators struggle to find an account of offer and acceptance that smoothly fits the facts. If *Clarke* v *Dunraven* has a point to prove, it is not entirely clear what that point is.

Briefly, the facts of the case were that the Mudhook Yacht Club organized a regatta on the Clyde. While the competitors were manoeuvring their yachts to get into position for the start of the 50-mile race for the Muir Memorial Challenge Cup, there was a collision: one yacht, the *Satanita*, ran into and sank another, the *Valkyrie*. The question was whether the owner of the *Satanita* should pay to Lord Dunraven, who was the owner of the *Valkyrie*, the limited damages set by the Merchant Shipping Act Amendment Act 1862 or 'all damages' as provided for by the competition rules. Although each entrant had signed a letter to the club secretary agreeing to be bound by the competition rules, there was no explicit and direct contractual relationship (incorporating the competition rules) between the competitors themselves.

At first instance, Bruce J. held that, even if there was a contract between the competitors, it was not so express as to override the statutory limitation. However, this decision was reversed by the Court of Appeal, the owner of the *Satanita* being held liable for 'all damages'; and the view of the Court of Appeal was duly upheld by the House of Lords. According to Lord Esher MR (in the Court of Appeal),

17 Compare R. Brownsword, 'Suisse Atlantique', in P. Mitchell and C. Mitchell (eds), *Landmark Cases in the Law of Contract* (Oxford: Hart, 2008) 299. Even where the court is sensitized to the relational dealing between the parties, there still might be a reluctance to embrace a cooperative ethic: see, e.g. *Baird Textile Holdings Ltd* v *Marks and Spencer plc* [2001] EWCA Civ 274.

it was a condition of entering the race that each yacht owner 'must enter into an obligation with the owners of the yachts who are competing, which they at the same time enter into similarly with you…'.[18] The puzzle, however, is quite how the competitors entered into contractual relationships with one another. To fit these facts into the classical contractual matrix, we need to ask who was offering what and when, and then we should ask how and when the offer was accepted.

The best traditional account of the contracting process as between the competitors runs along the following lines. The first entrant [A], when agreeing with the club to be bound by the competition rules, made an offer to each and every subsequent entrant to be bound by the competition rules in return for those subsequent entrants also agreeing to be so bound. The second entrant [B], when agreeing with the club to be bound by the competition rules, (i) made an offer to each and every subsequent entrant to be bound by the competition rules in return for those subsequent entrants also agreeing to be so bound, and (ii) accepted the offer made by the first entrant [A]. The third entrant [C], when agreeing with the club to be bound by the competition rules, (i) made an offer to each and every subsequent entrant to be bound by the competition rules in return for those subsequent entrants also agreeing to be so bound, (ii) accepted the offer made by the first entrant [A], and (iii) accepted the offer made by the second entrant [B], and so on.[19] For pragmatists, this is the only sensible view, but, for contract purists, this analysis stretches to breaking point the classical understanding of contractual formation, the main problem being that the entrants are being treated not only as offerors (in relation to fellow competitors) when they had no awareness that they were acting in this role but also (the first entrant apart) as acceptors of offers of which they were unaware.[20]

If the common law jurisprudence had featured the idea of a contractual network, it would have been simplicity itself to have treated the complex as constituting a network, one of the effects of which was that the competitors could enforce the

18 [1895] P 248, 255.

19 Compare Teubner, '"And if I by Beelzebub Cast Out Devils,…": An Essay on the Diabolics of Network Failure' (2009) 10 *German Law Journal* 395, 404–405: Some scholars try to construct a 'network contract' and base it on the traditional law of agency with mutual authorizations between all participants. When a new member enters the network, he is supposed to strike a multilateral agreement with all the other members who in their turn are supposed to have given their authorization in advance. This somewhat monstrous construct disregards the social peculiarities of networks and therefore imposes greatly exaggerated requirements on the legal formation of networks.

20 To this day, even in the most modern of texts, the puzzle persists. See, e.g. A. Burrows, *A Casebook on Contract* (Oxford: Hart, 2007) 56: It is unclear whether the judges thought that the contract was formed when sending in an entry for the race or when the yachts began to race. On either view, how could the (bilateral) contract between each yacht-owner be analysed in terms of offer and acceptance? Apart from problems over acceptance in ignorance of an offer, it would seem to require one to say, absurdly, that each yacht-owner was at the same time making an offer to the others and accepting their offers.

competition rules directly against one another. Moreover, such a characterization might have been defended equally well by saying either that there is a general rule that competitions are to be treated as having third-party network effects unless the organizers clearly signal otherwise (in effect, opting out from the default rules), or that competitions are to be treated as having such network effects where the organizers clearly signal that this is their intention (in effect, opting in).[21]

Granted, in *Clarke* v *Dunraven*, the nature of the particular competition rule at issue might give one reason to pause, for this was a rule that increased the obligations that otherwise applied in the case of collisions at sea. Even if a general rule licensing competitors to hold one another to the competition rules is plausible, it is not so obvious that the general rule should also endorse intensified responsibilities in competitions. Rather, the reason why the competitors raced under these conditions of heightened obligation was because the competition organizers had so stipulated. In other words, without over-elaborating the analysis, we might treat the third-party network effects as a feature of the default rules for competitions without also treating the heightened obligation in this way – competitors who wanted to race on such terms would need to signal this explicitly.[22]

### *OFT* v *Lloyds TSB*

Under the provisions of section 75(1) of the Consumer Credit Act 1974, a creditor who is party to a debtor-creditor-supplier agreement is jointly and severally liable with the supplier for the latter's misrepresentation or breach of contract in relation to a transaction (with the creditor) that is financed by the credit arrangement.[23] In 1974, consumer use of credit cards was (by today's standards) at a relatively low level, it was largely domestic, and it was all offline. With the increasing use of credit cards to support consumer transactions, and particularly with the development and growth of online shopping, the question for the courts in *OFT* v *Lloyds TSB* was whether the protections in section 75(1) applied where a UK consumer, using a credit card issued by a UK card issuer, dealt with a foreign supplier. Even though a protective scheme with application to foreign suppliers would expose UK card issuers to some 29 million suppliers worldwide, and even though the credit infrastructure no longer maps on to the tripartite debtor-creditor-

21 Compare the forthright approach by Rigby LJ [1895] P 248, 262: It appears to me that all that is necessary to constitute a contract between the yacht owners is to bring home to each of them the knowledge that the race is to be run under the Yacht Racing Association rules, and that they deliberately enter for the race upon those terms.

22 Whether or not this was the competitors' intention was the principal point that was argued on the final appeal to the House of Lords.

23 Section 75(3) of the Act disapplies the protection afforded by section 75(1), inter alia, where the cash price is under £100 or over £30,000.

supplier template of the 1970s, the House of Lords ruled that section 75(1) so applied.[24]

The changing nature of the credit infrastructure is described by Lord Mance in the following way:

> Large-scale consolidation has led to card issuers becoming members of one of the two main international credit card networks, VISA and MasterCard. Under the rules of these networks, certain card issuers are authorised to act as 'merchant acquirers'... They contract with suppliers ... to process all such supply transactions made with cards of the relevant network ... Suppliers do not become members of the network, but contract with merchant acquirers to honour the cards of the network ... Where the merchant acquirer is itself the issuer of the card used in a particular transaction, the transaction is tripartite ... But in the more common (and in the case of a foreign transaction inevitable) case of use of a card issued by a card issuer other than the merchant acquirer who acquired the particular supplier, the network operates as a clearing system, through which the merchant acquirer is reimbursed by the card issuer ...[25]

At all levels, however, the courts were clear that the fact that 1970s-style three-party networks have been overtaken by four-party networks, did not derail the legislative intention that consumers should be given the protection envisaged by section 75(1).[26]

We should not overstate the significance of the court talking the talk of networks. Credit card arrangements are networked – such is the economic reality – but it does not follow that there is a special doctrinal coding for networks. In the *OFT* v *Lloyds TSB* case, the fact that networks are involved is not seen as legally significant; it is simply a matter of whether the legislative purposes encompass credit card-supported transactions with foreign suppliers.

### *The Eurymedon*

The factual background in *The Eurymedon* was a familiar one. Stated simply, A (the owner of goods) contracted with B (a carrier) for the carriage of the goods from Liverpool to Wellington, and B contracted with C (stevedores) to unload the goods when they arrived in Wellington. As a result of C's carelessness, the goods were damaged and A sued C for compensation. By way of defence, C relied on various exemptions and limitations of liability that were written into the carriage contract (the contract between A and B). If, at that time, English law had not

24 Seemingly, even with such a large exposure, the value of credit card transactions with foreign suppliers is less than 10 percent of that of domestic transactions. See [2007] UKHL 48, para 23.

25 [2007] UKHL 48, para 23.

26 Ibid., para 24.

operated with a doctrine of privity of contract, there would have been no difficulty in allowing C, who was clearly an intended beneficiary of the relevant contractual provisions, to plead this defence. However, with privity standing between C and the protective clauses, the Privy Council needed to find a contractual connection between A and C.

Introducing the majority's opinion, Lord Wilberforce famously remarked that commercial deals (including the complex of contracts at issue) are often put together in ways that do not correspond particularly well to the classical model:

> The whole contract is of a commercial character, involving service on one side, rates of payment on the other, and qualifying stipulations as to both. The relations of all parties to each other are commercial relations entered into for business reasons of ultimate profit. To describe one set of promises in this context as gratuitous, or *nudum pactum*, seems paradoxical and is *prima facie* implausible. It is only the precise analysis of this complex of relations into the classical offer and acceptance, with identifiable consideration, that seems to present difficulty, but this same difficulty exists in many situations of daily life, eg sales at auction; supermarket purchases; boarding an omnibus; purchasing a train ticket; tenders for the supply of goods; offers of rewards; acceptance by post; warranties of authority by agents; manufacturers' guarantees; gratuitous bailments; bankers' commercial credits. These are all examples which show that English law, having committed itself to a rather technical and schematic doctrine of contract, in application takes a practical approach, often at the cost of forcing the facts to fit uneasily into the marked slots of offer, acceptance and consideration.[27]

Having signalled that a practical approach was to be taken, how were the facts to be forced into the appropriate slots? According to Lord Wilberforce:

> There is possibly more than one way of analysing this business transaction into the necessary components; that which their Lordships would accept is to say that the bill of lading brought into existence a bargain initially unilateral but capable of becoming mutual, between the shippers and the stevedore, made through the carrier as agent. This became a full contract when the stevedore performed services by discharging the goods. The performance of these services for the benefit of the shipper was the consideration for the agreement by the shipper that the stevedore should have the benefit of the exemptions and limitations contained in the bill of lading.[28]

27 [1975] AC 154, 167.
28 Ibid.

The artificiality of this analysis did not go unnoticed by the minority members of the judicial panel,[29] nor has it gone unnoticed by contract commentators.[30] Rather like the analysis in *Clarke* v *Dunraven*, we have (in *The Eurymedon*) B acting as agent of A to transmit an offer by A to C, in circumstances where A did not know that it was making such an offer and where C, in performing its work for B, did not realize that, at the same time, it was accepting an offer made by A. Nevertheless, as in *Clarke* v *Dunraven*, where the practical sense of the arrangements gives a clear steer, the purity of the classical law of contract has to yield to pragmatism.

If the Privy Council had been able to tap into a jurisprudence of network contracts, it might have been much easier to allow C to plead the defence. One view would be that, where commercial contracts are connected by a common purpose[31] and fit a common pattern (as in carriage or construction), then they should be treated as a network unless there is a clear contrary intention – and that one of the network effects is to license third-party claims and defences within the network.[32] Alternatively, one might want to rest the argument on the intentions of the contractors – in which case, we would be looking for signals from the contractors that they intend to adopt a network (with standard network effects) or that they at least intend to adopt some particular network effect.

## The Possible Reception of Networks: Consumer Contracts

Bearing in mind the transformation of the English law of contract, we can start by considering the possible reception of networks and of particular network effects in the sphere of consumer contracting. This can be taken in two stages: first, an amplification of the introductory remarks to the effect that, following the bifurcation between consumer and commercial transactions, the former are now subject to a European regulatory regime, and second, a revisiting of cases such as *OFT* v *Lloyds TSB* in this light.

29 Viscount Dilhorne and Lord Simon.

30 See, e.g. Burrows, n 20 above, 480. Having outlined the reasoning of the majority, Burrows asks: 'Was the reasoning artificial in (i) regarding the unloading of the goods as consideration for the exclusion of liability and (ii) treating the carriers as agents for the stevedores in receiving the offer of a unilateral contract?'

31 Compare Teubner, n 19 above, 406; and C. Heldt, 'Internal Relations and Semi-Spontaneous Order: The Case of Franchising and Construction Contracts', in Amstutz and Teubner (eds), n 12 above, 137.

32 Compare Lord Wilberforce's even bolder approach in *Port Jackson Stevedoring Pty Ltd* v *Salmond & Spraggon (Australia) Pty Ltd: The New York Star* [1981] 1 WLR 138.

### *The Nature of the Modern Regulation of Consumer Transactions*

For some time, it has been clear that the general law of contract has crafted a special set of rules to cover consumer transactions – for example, this is a sector that is distinguished by a high level of control over allegedly unfair terms and unfair commercial practices,[33] by a high threshold for the incorporation of terms,[34] by an unquestioned (and non-excludable) right of rejection where goods are not of satisfactory quality or reasonably fit for purpose,[35] and by the recognition of consumer surplus in making awards of damages.[36] When we say that the modern law has retreated somewhat from the classical principles of freedom and sanctity of contract, it is in relation to consumer contracts that we find the clearest evidence of such a retreat. However, with the systematic programme of single market consumer protection that has emanated from Brussels, it is time to move on from the concession that the law of consumer contracts represents a set of exceptions to the general law of contract. The idea of the bifurcation of contract law no longer does justice to the actuality.

In this author's view, we should now replace the idea that consumer transactions in Europe are covered by a special division of the law of contract with the idea that the consumer marketplace, and the transactions made therein, represents a particular regulated zone. In short, we should view consumer transactions as a class of regulated transactions. This new (regulatory) paradigm might not sound so very different, but it reflects two fundamental shifts in our thinking.

The first shift is to appreciate that, as with any regulatory enterprise, our evaluations need to start with the purposes that either are being pursued or that should be pursued by regulators. If transactions in the consumer marketplace are to be regulated, the question is: for what purpose is the regulation introduced, that is, what are regulators trying to achieve – or, to be more critical, what purposes should regulators pursue? It is only then that we can consider whether particular regulatory initiatives and interventions are fit for purpose. In other words, it is no longer relevant to ask how well some modification to consumer law fits with the general law of contract; rather, we need to focus on whether we are trying to do the right thing in relation to consumer transactions and whether our interventions are

33 See the Directive on Unfair Terms in Consumer Contracts 1993/13/EC and the Unfair Commercial Practices Directive 2005/29 EC.

34 In English law, the best example from a clutch of cases is *Thornton* v *Shoe Lane Parking Ltd* [1971] 2 QB 163.

35 In English law, see section 14 of the Sale of Goods Act 1979, reinforced by section 6(2) of the Unfair Contract Terms Act 1977.

36 Seminally, see *Jarvis* v *Swan's Tours Ltd* [1973] QB 233 and case 168/00 *Simone Leitner* v *TUI Deutschland* [2002] ECR-I-2631.

effective.[37] It is not coherence with the general law of contract that now controls: it is coherence with the (actual or the critically justified) regulatory objectives.

The second shift is to assess the appropriateness of some legal change by locating it in the broader landscape of the regulatory environment. Not only is this a matter about which the author has written at length elsewhere, it is also less pressing for present purposes,[38] so will not be rehearsed again here. Suffice it to say that regulators have many strategies available for the channelling of conduct.[39] Law in general, and contract law in particular, is just one mode of regulation. In some regulatory environments law is critical, in others it is not; as the evolution of eBay illustrates, the relative importance of law can change over time.[40]

Once we start viewing transactions in the European consumer marketplace through a regulatory lens, it becomes apparent that regulators are seeking to put consumers in a position where they are able to make free and informed choices, and where they have the confidence to deal in any part of the single market, but without this amounting to a wholly unacceptable burden on business (especially on small businesses). As the European Commission explains in its proposal for a Regulation on a Common European Sales Law,[41] the economic benefits of cross-border trade are not being fully realized; 'the majority of European consumers shop only domestically'[42]; and, even with e-commerce options, 'when consumers try to place orders with a business from another Member State, they are often faced with the business practice of refusal to sell which is often due to differences in [national] contract law'.[43] Accordingly,

> The overall *objective* of the proposal is to improve the establishment and functioning of the internal market by facilitating the expansion of cross-border trade for business and cross-border purchases for consumers.[44]

---

37 For a comparable case, consider the limited regulatory effectiveness of European law in relation to the use of consumer data (e.g., by supermarkets who operate loyalty card schemes): see EC Health and Consumers Directorate-General, *Data Collection, Targeting and Profiling of Consumers for Commercial Purposes in Online Environments* (Brussels, 05.03.2009, SANCO/B2/GA/SR/GR), 23–24.

38 See, n 3 above and, in general, R. Brownsword and H. Somsen, 'Law, Innovation, and Technology: Before We Fast Forward – A Forum for Debate' (2009) 1 *Law, Innovation and Technology* 1, and R. Brownsword and M. Goodwin, *Law and the Technologies of the Twenty-First Century* (Cambridge: Cambridge University Press, 2012) Ch.2.

39 Seminally, see L. Lessig, *Code and Other Laws of Cyberspace* (New York: Basic Books, 1999) ch 7; and L. Lessig, 'The Law of the Horse: What Cyberlaw Might Teach' (1999) 113 *Harvard Law Review* 501, 507–514.

40 See, e.g. the discussion in J. Goldsmith and T. Wu, *Who Controls the Internet?* (Oxford: OUP, 2006).

41 COM(2011) 635 final, Brussels, 11.10.2011.

42 Ibid., at 3.

43 Ibid., at 4.

44 Ibid.

Such is the regulatory vision in Europe.[45] Given this perspective, if it is proposed that networks or network effects should be taken up in the regulation of consumer transactions, the only question is whether giving consumers third-party rights, or increasing the obligations of suppliers, or the like, is in line with the current regulatory objectives. Or, if we are to challenge the prevailing regulatory purposes, the question is whether such innovation would assist whatever objectives we think that regulators should be pursuing.[46]

### *Networks and OFT* v *Lloyds TSB*

In the light of the above, what would we now make of the issues arising in *OFT* v *Lloyds TSB*? To put network thinking to the test, imagine that section 75(1) had never been enacted. Imagine, then, a case such as *David Boyack* v *The Royal Bank of Scotland*[47] – a case alluded to by Lord Hope in the *Lloyds TSB* case – where Mr Boyack, having used a credit card (issued by RBS) to buy a clock in Dubai, now alleged that the contract was induced by misrepresentations made by the seller, and contended that RBS (qua card issuer) should be treated as jointly and severally liable for the supplier's misrepresentation. Without the support of section 75(1), Mr Boyack would need to claim (i) that, for the purposes of the law of contract, debtor-creditor-supplier arrangements (whether three or four-party schemes) should be treated as networks and (ii) that one of the network effects is to increase the responsibility of credit card issuers in relation to their card holders, specifically by securing the rights of card holders arising from any card-facilitated sale.

Given that much of European thinking about the consumer marketplace is now highly 'regulatory' in its approach, we can take it that the fate of Mr Boyack's claim would hinge on whether the doctrinal adoption of networks or network effects would assist the regulatory objectives. Clearly, it would not help Mr Boyack that he purchased a clock in *Dubai*; let us suppose that, instead, the purchase was from a seller in *Paris*. Now, with the right ingredients to engage the attention of European regulators, we might test out the utility of networks. For example, would it advance the regulatory objectives if consumers like Mr Boyack were to be given (networked) third-party rights, or if they enjoyed enhanced rights against

---

45 Where regulators have less interest in encouraging consumers to cross borders, and where consumers themselves are perfectly happy to shop at home, the shift from contract to regulation might be less marked (such might be the case, for example, in countries such as Singapore).

46 Compare G.-P. Calliess, 'Fitness Clubs: Consumer Protection between Contract and Association', in Amstutz and Teubner (eds), n 12 above, 241. Whilst we might think it appropriate for regulators to shield consumers against terms that are truly unfair and unreasonable, Calliess argues that regulators and judges also need to be sensitive to holding consumers to their obligations as members of clubs.

47 At the time of *OFT* v *Lloyds TSB*, pending in the Sheriff Court at Kirkcaldy: see [2007] UKHL 48, paras 10–11 (Lord Hope).

credit card issuers or retail suppliers?[48] Other things being equal, such enhanced protection would surely promote consumer confidence in credit card transactions (and in markets, such as e-commerce, where credit card payments are the norm) and this would not overburden the card companies (who are adept at shifting risks to retailers and whose business model is to charge their costs to card holders who do not clear their accounts each month). If, however, this meant that the costs were then shifted by the large card companies to SME suppliers, this might require further adjustment so that the risk was distributed fairly.[49]

Moving beyond the *OFT* v *Lloyds TSB* case, there are a number of possible network effects that we might want to consider in relation to consumer transactions. For example, what if consumers were able (as in product liability claims) to leapfrog over their immediate suppliers (say, where those suppliers had gone out of business) to pursue a claim for breach of contract against an upstream producer (particularly where the supply chain was strongly integrated);[50] or why not afford consumers who use debit cards or cheques to make their purchases the same kind of protection that obtains under section 75(1); or should there be other kinds of heightened obligation to be assumed by suppliers into the consumer marketplace (always bearing in mind that the voluntary assumption of such obligations by top-end retailers might be a feature of the regulatory environment), and so on? Each proposal invites careful consideration relative to the regulatory purposes and, if a network effect would seem to assist those purposes, then (but only then) should it be adopted.

### *Taking Stock*

Recalling our focal questions, is there an unbridgeable gap between the current law of consumer contracts and a network-enabled version of the law, and if not, is it likely that networks will be doctrinally recognized in this section of the law? In

48 A question, indeed, raised by Hector MacQueen in 'Europeanisation of Contract Law and the Proposed Common European Sales Law' in Larry DiMatteo et al. (eds), *Commercial Contract Law: Transatlantic Perspectives* (Cambridge: Cambridge University Press, 2012) 529.

49 Compare Roger Brownsword and John MacGowan, 'Credit Card Fraud' 147 *New Law Journal* (1997) 1806 (Response by Susan Ward at 148 NLJ (1998) 7–8; and Reply to Susan Ward at 148 NLJ (1998) 133); and Roger Brownsword, 'Judicial Revision of Abusive Contractual Terms: Credit Card Fraud and Charge-Back Clauses' *Revista de Direito Bancário*, Special Edition, (Proceedings of the First International Symposium of Banking Law: *Banking Law and the Globalization of the Financial System*, Sao Paulo, Brazil, 1998) 668.

50 For such an example, see the decision of the Karlsruhe Court of Appeals, OLG Karlsruhe NZV 1989, 434, where it was held that the consumer purchaser of a car was not restricted to a claim against the now insolvent car dealer but, instead, could sue the Japanese importer (as the central node within the distribution system). See Gunther Teubner, *Networks as Connected Contracts* (Oxford: Hart, 2011) 78 *et seq*.

some parts of consumer law, particularly that dealing with the credit infrastructure for transactions, networks are already doctrinally recognized and consumers enjoy the benefits of heightened protection. Here, there is no gap to be bridged. However, this is relatively unusual. Typically, consumers are not transacting as members of a network; if anything, they are dealing with networks. Rather than being insiders, consumers tend to be outsiders relative to networks. It follows that consumers do not generally have practice-based network expectations. Nevertheless, regulators might see fit, from time to time, to bridge this gap by adopting network-like effects where this facilitates the regulatory purposes.

## The Possible Reception of Networks: Commercial Contracts

If the prospects for the adoption of networks in consumer contracts hinges on their compatibility with the general regulatory purposes, then the prospects for their recognition in commercial contract law hinge much more on the interlocking of the modern 'contextualist' approach and the prevalence of networked business organizations.

In this part of the chapter, we can take the discussion forward in four stages. First, our introductory remarks concerning the transformation of the commercial law of contract are elaborated somewhat. Second, we consider the possibility of networked thinking in cases like *The Eurymedon* where a number of commercial contracts are connected. Third, entering the first of two cautions, a question about the dynamic (or evolving) development of networks is identified. And fourth, entering the second caution, some reflections are offered on the vulnerability of some smaller network players.

### *The Transformation of the Commercial Law of Contract*

In a number of seminal cases, most famously in *Investors Compensation Scheme Ltd* v *West Bromwich Building Society*,[51] the House of Lords (led, in particular, by Lords Hoffmann and Steyn) has transformed the way that commercial contracts should be interpreted. Famously, in the *Investors Compensation* case, Lord Hoffmann declared that, in relation to commercial contracts, 'contextual' interpretation should be preferred to an abstracted 'literalism'. Text, so to speak, has been replaced by context (or by text in context); as one commentator has put it, contextualism 'is rapidly becoming the bible for the courts in contract interpretation disputes'.[52]

Whereas literalism treats the words of a contractual agreement as having an abstracted life, or meaning, of their own (any context to be supplied being

51 [1998] 1 All ER 98.

52 D.W. McLauchlan, 'The New Law of Contract Interpretation' (2000) 19 *New Zealand University Law Review* 147.

minimal), the fundamental feature of contextualism is that it seeks out the meaning that fits best with the context. In *Mannai Investments Co Ltd* v *Eagle Star Life Assurance Co Ltd*,[53] where Lord Hoffmann prefigured the key aspects of his approach in *Investors*, he sketched his understanding of the relevance of context as follows:

> The meaning of words, as they would appear in a dictionary, and the effect of their syntactical arrangement, as it would appear in a grammar, is part of the material which we use to understand a speaker's utterance. But it is only a part; another part is our knowledge of the background against which the utterance was made. It is that background which enables us, not only to choose the intended meaning when a word has more than one dictionary meaning but also ... to understand a speaker's meaning, often without ambiguity, when he has used the wrong words.[54]

Context, thus, plays an important corrective part in the process of interpretation. Hence, in *Mannai* itself, where a tenant purported to give notice to determine leases on 12 January 1995, when (to comply strictly with the terms of the leases) the tenant should have specified 13 January 1995, it mattered little why this mistake had been made. The critical point, as the majority ruled in *Mannai*, was that the landlord, receiving the notice, would have realized, *in this particular context*, that the tenant was intending to give notice in accordance with the terms of the lease and that a slip had been made in specifying 12 January rather than 13 January.

Similarly, in *Total Gas Marketing Ltd* v *Arco British Ltd*,[55] Lord Steyn (who, along with Lord Hoffmann has been the principal author of the new contextualism) summarized the key idea in the following way: '[questions of interpretation] must be considered in the light of the contractual language, the contractual scheme, the commercial context and the reasonable expectations of the parties.'[56]

Applying this approach in one of the leading recent cases, *Rainy Sky* v *Kookmin Bank*,[57] the UK Supreme Court decided that, regardless of how the shipbuilding contracts (that were at the root of the dispute) might be read under a literal approach, the context demanded that the performance bonds taken out for the benefit of the buyers must be interpreted as covering the risk of the shipbuilders' insolvency. Or, to put this in other words, the context supported the proposition that the buyers had an honest and reasonable expectation that the performance bonds covered them

53 [1997] 3 All ER 352.

54 Ibid., 376.

55 [1998] 2 Lloyd's Rep 209.

56 Ibid., 221. For his own part, Lord Steyn was particularly adept at applying such thinking to questions of implied terms: see, e.g. *Mosvolds Rederi A/S* v *Food Corpn of India* [1986] 2 Lloyd's Rep 68; and *Equitable Life Assurance Society* v *Hyman* [2000] 3 All ER 961.

57 [2011] UKSC 50.

against the most obvious commercial risk that they were taking (given the advance payments to which they were committed), namely the risk of the shipbuilders' insolvency.

Although Lord Hoffmann, in company with a unanimous House of Lords, has confirmed that the 'context', for the purposes of interpreting a commercial contract, does not include the pre-contractual negotiations,[58] all the indications are that contextualism itself does not stop at interpretation. Thus, shortly before his retirement, in *Attorney General of Belize* v *Belize Telecom Limited*,[59] Lord Hoffmann took the opportunity to explain how contextualism entails some revision of the traditional approach to implied terms. In the *Belize* case, relying on *Investors Compensation*, Lord Hoffmann explained that the implicit meaning of an instrument is that 'which the instrument would convey to a reasonable person having all the background knowledge which would reasonably be available to the audience to whom the instrument is addressed…'.[60] According to Lord Hoffmann:

> It follows that in every case in which it is said that some provision ought to be implied in an instrument, the question for the court is whether such a provision would spell out in express words what the instrument, read against the relevant background, would reasonably be understood to mean.[61]

Moreover, the several stock litmus tests for implication – such as whether the implication goes 'without saying', or is 'necessary to give business efficacy to the contract', or would be self-evident to the officious bystander, and so on – must be read as articulations of the general test, namely whether the proposed implied term would be an expression of 'what the instrument, read as a whole against the relevant background, would reasonably be understood to mean'.[62] While this does not speak directly to networks, it does signify that, where the working practice of contractors assumes more than minimal cooperation, this will be reflected in the terms that are implied.

However, the most radical implications of contextualism become apparent in the period-defining case of *Transfield Shipping Inc* v *Mercator Shipping Inc*.[63] There, the charterers of a single-deck bulk carrier were in breach of contract by being some nine days late in redelivering the vessel to the owners. As a result of this late redelivery, the owners were put in a difficult position in relation to a new fixture of the vessel that had been agreed with another charterer. In order to retain

58 See *Chartbrook Limited* v *Persimmon Homes Limited* [2009] UKHL 38, affirming the view in *Prenn* v *Simmonds* [1971] 1 WLR 1381 where Lord Wilberforce, a proto-typical contextualist, ruled that pre-contractual negotiations are inadmissible.

59 [2009] UKPC 11.

60 Ibid., para 16.

61 Ibid., para 21.

62 Ibid.

63 [2008] UKHL 48.

this fixture, the owners agreed to reduce the daily rate by $8,000. The question was whether the owners were entitled to recover the loss of $8,000 per day for the duration of the new charter (a sum of $1,364,584.37) or merely the difference between the market rate and the charter rate for the nine days' late redelivery (a sum of $158,301.17). The majority of the arbitrators and the lower appeal courts held that the owners were entitled to the higher amount: their reasoning was that the charterers must have known that the owners were likely to arrange a new onward charter, that market rates fluctuate, and that late delivery might reduce the profitability of the onward charter (i.e. the forward fixture). However, the House held unanimously (albeit with some hesitation) that the owners were restricted to the lesser sum.

According to Baroness Hale, the issue presented by the appeal 'could be an examination question'. Moreover, in response to the question,

> [t]here is no obviously right answer: two very experienced commercial judges have reached one answer, your lordships have reached another. There is no obviously just answer: the charterer's default undoubtedly caused the owner's loss, but a loss for which no-one has ever had to pay before. The examiners would surely have given first class marks to all the judges who have answered the question so far.[64]

Reflecting on the answers given by her colleagues, Baroness Hale identified two lines of reasoning in support of the lower sum.

One line of reasoning focuses on whether the particular type of loss was within the reasonable contemplation of the charterers. Following this line of thinking, the charterers 'would expect that the owner would be able to find a use for his ship even if it was returned late. It was only because of the unusual volatility of the market at that particular time that this particular loss was suffered. It is one thing to say … that missing dates for a subsequent fixture was within the parties' contemplation as "not unlikely". It is another thing to say that the "extremely volatile" conditions which brought about this particular loss were "not unlikely".'[65]

The alternative line of reasoning 'is that one must ask, not only whether the parties must be taken to have had this *type of loss* within their contemplation when the contract was made, but also whether they must be taken to have had *liability for this type of loss* within their contemplation then. In other words, is the charterer to be taken to have undertaken legal responsibility for this type of loss?'[66]

It is Lord Hoffmann who most clearly favours the alternative line of reasoning, but that is only half the story. The more important aspect of Lord Hoffmann's approach is the way in which he proposes that it should be determined whether a

64 Ibid., para 89.
65 Ibid., para 91.
66 Ibid., para 92.

contract breaker has assumed responsibility for a particular type of loss. In a key section of his speech, Lord Hoffmann says:

> The case therefore raises a fundamental point of principle in the law of contractual damages: is the rule that a party may recover losses which were foreseeable ('not unlikely') an external rule of law, imposed upon the parties to every contract in default of express provision to the contrary, or is it a prima facie assumption about what the parties may be taken to have intended, no doubt applicable in the great majority of cases but capable of rebuttal in cases in which the context, surrounding circumstances or general understanding in the relevant market shows that a party would not reasonably have been regarded as assuming responsibility for such losses?[67]

Drawing a parallel with his own favoured contextual approach to the interpretation of contracts, Lord Hoffmann prefers the latter view. And, applying such a view, Lord Hoffmann finds that, relative to background market expectations in the shipping sector, 'it is clear that [the parties] would have considered losses arising from the loss of the following fixture a type or kind of loss for which the charterer was not assuming responsibility.'[68]

*Transfield,* thus, offers an important insight into the role of the modern law of contract. Contextualism is a particular expression of dynamic market-individualism,[69] and dynamic market-individualism is the expression of private governance in a larger co-regulatory regime. Stated simply, what this signifies is that the state sets certain public interest limits on the freedom of commercial contractors, but that, within the (considerable) area of freedom left to them, such contractors may order their transactions as they wish. Where contractors do not signal their intentions, the law of contract offers a stock of default rules that can be applied. However, where it is either clear from the context, or the most reasonable interpretation of that context, that the contractors proceeded on the basis of certain rules, those rules (rather than the default rules of contract law) should be applied.

### *Network Effects and The Eurymedon*

In the absence of any obvious reasons for public interest restriction on networks, the trajectory of the modern law seems to be towards making it easy for contractors to opt for networks and network effects.[70] In other words, once any required public

---

67 Ibid., para 9.

68 Ibid., para 23.

69 See R. Brownsword, *Contract Law: Themes for the Twenty-First Century* (Oxford: Oxford University Press, 2006) ch 7.

70 Compare, too, the discussion in *OFT* v *Lloyds TSB Bank plc* [2007] UKHL 48, para 36, concerning the variety of network provisions that might be adopted by the commercial parties.

interest restrictions have been put in place, there are reasons for expecting the regulatory approach to be one of facilitating the full range of private governance options. How might this be articulated?

One view is that where commercial contracts are connected by a common purpose[71] and fit a common pattern (as in franchising, carriage, or construction), then they should be treated as a network unless there is a clear contrary intention – and that one of the network effects is to license third-party claims and defences within the network. However, the transformed modern law invites a less radical response. Quite simply, this is that the law should reflect the reasonable expectations of commercial contractors – in which case, we would be looking for signals from the contractors that they intend to adopt a network (with standard network effects) or that they at least intend to adopt some particular network effect, or simply that there are implicit network-related customs and practices in the sector.

Taking the latter approach, the legal regime would have three layers. First, networks and network effects should not be permitted (or, at any rate, their activities should be restricted) where this would be contrary to the public interest – for example, if networks were seen as having unacceptable anti-competitive effects, or unacceptable inefficiencies, or as being productive of unacceptable externalities, and so on. Second, once any public interest concerns have been dealt with, in the area where the contractors are free to privately order their dealings, the default setting has to be determined. Broadly speaking, that setting will be either for or against networks. Quite why the default setting should be tilted one way or the other merits regulatory attention (although this might be less important for commercial dealing, where the parties are legally advised, than for purely private dealing where the parties might be unaware that there is a default or that it can be switched). For the sake of illustration, let us suppose that the default is against network effects – as it would be in the classical English law of contract where the defaults are for privity of contract and adversarial dealing. Thirdly, with the default set against networks, it needs to be determined how the contractors may switch the default. Explicit signalling by the contracting parties is the clearest option, but a legal regime might also allow for implicit signalling – in the language of *Transfield Shipping*, this would be to draw on the context (sectoral or relational) in which the parties dealt – and this is where, in practice, there are likely to be interpretive difficulties and controversial applications.

Revisiting the majority's pragmatic approach in *The Eurymedon*, had Lord Wilberforce talked the talk of networks and contexts, he would have said that the parties involved in carriage of goods by sea operate on the assumption that the liability of the parties who handle the goods is limited and that the parties

71 Compare Gunther Teubner, '"And if I by Beelzebub Cast Out Devils,...": An Essay on the Diabolics of Network Failure' (2009) 10 *German Law Journal* 395, at 406; and Cordula Heldt, 'Internal Relations and Semi-Spontaneous Order: The Case of Franchising and Construction Contracts' in Marc Amstutz and Gunther Teubner (eds), *Networks: Legal Issues of Multilateral Contracts* (Oxford: Hart, 2009) 137.

cover themselves with appropriate levels of insurance. Such an operational practice presupposes that the contracts have certain network effects (in relation to third-party claims and defences). Unless there is some public interest reason for restricting the parties' freedom to govern their dealings in this way, they should be permitted to do so. In other words, even if privity rules obtained as defaults, after *Transfield Shipping* we would say that the Hoffmann override applied and that network effects should be recognized.

What would we say about heightened obligations in commercial networks such as franchise schemes? For example, what would we say about a case such as Apollo (Optik)[72] where a number of German courts were faced with fixing the extent of the franchisor's responsibility to pass on to franchisees the benefit of discounts negotiated by the former with suppliers to the network. The Federal High Court eventually ruled in favour of the claimant franchisees, holding that multilateral connectivity within the franchise may create an obligation to pass on advantages to members of the network. Given the current state of English law, this might be a case in which there is an argument for building such cooperative principles into the default rules for this class of contracts (a development that might be assisted by a less hostile view of good faith and fair dealing). But, irrespective of this, if the express intention of the parties or if the implicit practice of franchising discloses a contextually supported reasonable expectation of cooperative benefit-sharing, this kind of network effect should be applied (possibly by way of interpretation or through an implied term). Moreover, if rigid and dogmatic doctrinal barriers stand in the way of what are perceived, in network settings, to be commercially sensible results, there will be pressure from the new realists for change.

### *Network Dynamics*

Contractual obligation is at its purest where the parties freely and explicitly agree to deal in accordance with certain framework rules. Transactions that are negotiated in accordance with the framework rules are binding because this is the effect of agreeing to such rules. If the parties have the option of adopting network effects as part of their framework understanding (as part of their private governance structure), then they self-regulate for such effects, and it is clear why networks then rule and why their requirements are a matter of obligation.

The parties may signal their agreement to deal on a basis that includes network effects either by expressly adopting a governance structure that has the desired effects or by simply participating in a practice that is understood by all participants to have such effects – when we join in a game of soccer, we do not need to reaffirm that we are playing in accordance with the official rules of association football, and so it is with transactions, where the practice is clearly established. However, this presupposes (to borrow from soccer) a set-piece view of transactions, when the actuality is that transactional practices (just like the game of soccer) can be

72 Discussed at length by Teubner, n 12, ch 4.

much more fluid with shifting patterns and practices. Accordingly – and this is the essence of this first cautionary remark – to do justice to networks, we must be careful not to stick too rigidly to the classical view of set-piece dealing.

What this means is that we must also allow for the possibility that network effects arise other than by regulatory prescription or express contractual promise, and that they can arise not only implicitly but also by virtue of an evolving practice (and the expectations generated by practice). The dynamics of networks are such that, as Gunther Teubner has put it, there is 'the expectation that expectations will change'.[73] Hence, what starts out as a non-networked transaction might develop some network characteristics as the relationship between the parties grows. In this way, networks can arise both 'implicitly' and 'dynamically'. This, admittedly, is a proposition that favours doctrinal flexibility over certainty; we know that there will be different interpretations as to whether a transactional practice or a particular trading relationship has evolved to a point that takes it over the threshold for a network. Nevertheless, so long as we are trying to track the practice-based expectations of contractors, there will always be grey areas where, no matter how the legal characterization goes, there will be scope for disagreement.

*Big Businesses, Small Businesses, and Shopping Malls*

Under a co-regulated arrangement, commercial contractors are free to punch their weight. Rather obviously – and this is the second cautionary remark – it follows that more powerful contractors may, and often will, strike hard bargains with less powerful contractors. Provided that the public interest has been secured, we might simply shrug our shoulders and conclude that this is the nature of the market. Unless we are to switch to a stronger regulatory approach, as with consumers, small business contractors face a tough time. There is every reason to suppose that asymmetries of power will be exploited within networks just as without them.[74]

Consider a hypothetical shopping mall development. The developer lets a large unit to a major national retailer knowing that this will attract both customers and small businesses. However, the terms on which small businesses are brought into the shopping mall does them no favours. If the large retailer pulls out, the small businesses will be stranded. Is there anything in the idea of a network – particularly the idea that, in a network, the members share both the benefits and the burdens of their collective endeavours – that might assist them?[75]

---

73 Teubner, n 19 above, 407. Teubner adds (ibid.): Such unspecified obligations that can be specified only after a certain period of time were not unknown in classical contract law, but only as secondary obligations opposed to the primary obligation that was expressly defined at the contractual conclusion. In the network, by contrast, primary obligations are defined by this type of deferred determination.

74 In general, compare Teubner, n 12 above.

75 On benefit sharing, see R. Böhner, 'Asset-Sharing in Franchise Networks: The Obligation to Pass on Network Benefits', in Amstutz and Teubner (eds), n 12 above, 153.

If we start in the spirit of co-regulation, we must make sure that the contracts made at the mall development are consistent with any relevant public interest considerations. One consideration might be the importance of the mall flourishing; it is no good for anyone if the mall is blighted by the withdrawal of a major anchor retailer. Another consideration might be the importance of securing the confidence of small business people. But, how are these desiderata to be translated into legal principles?

If the public interest is sufficiently compelling, it might be reflected in the terms of the regulatory authorization for the mall. Failing this, let us suppose that the developer and the major retailer are acutely aware of the considerations just identified. Accordingly, acting in a public-spirited way, they freely adopt network effects for the development and its contracts that respond to these concerns. Clearly, though, for the most part, this assumption is too good to be true and, in the absence of such enlightened contractors, the burden of responsibility will lie with the *ex ante* prescriptions of regulators or the *ex post* rulings of courts.

If we think that regulators should be prescriptive in their protection of the interests of small business retailers, what do we think they should prescribe? Quite possibly, there might be some general protection for small businesses as part of the larger regulatory project to develop a pan-European consumer marketplace; signals of this kind are evident in the proposed Regulation on a Common European Sales Law.[76] However, this would not fit the shopping mall case. Here, if regulators prescribe a network effect that ties in the major retailer, even when trading conditions are bad, this is likely to discourage investment by such retailers (who will see the risk as being loaded too heavily on their side) and, even if a tie-in is part of the deal, there might be difficulties in enforcing it.[77] Perhaps a more promising effect would be along the lines that major retailers should not make economic decisions without taking account of the stakeholding interests of smaller retailers. This is not a particularly demanding requirement, but, where the default ethic is entirely one of short-term self-interest, it at least nudges doctrine towards a more cooperative approach.[78] A further possibility is to protect the smaller retailers by offering them the option, where a major retailer pulls out of the mall, of pulling out themselves, or of renegotiating the terms of their contracts with the developers.[79]

If all else fails, we might turn, *ex post*, to the courts. Relying on standards of good faith and fair dealing, and exercising some control over unconscionable

76 See COM/2011/0635 final. For discussion, see Hector L. MacQueen, 'Europeanisation of Contract Law and the Proposed Common European Sales Law' in Larry DiMatteo et al. (eds), *Commercial Contract Law: Transatlantic Perspectives* (Cambridge: Cambridge University Press, 2012) 529.

77 Compare *Co-operative Insurance Society Ltd* v *Argyll Stores (Holdings) Ltd* [1998] AC 1.

78 Compare Böhner, n 75 above.

79 The author is indebted to his colleague John Phillips for this latter suggestion.

conduct, the courts might be able to deal with individual instances of unfair exposure. It must be conceded, however, that this, if not exactly an admission of regulatory defeat, is something of a last resort.

These cautionary comments should not be misunderstood. They do not speak against recognizing networks and network effects and, other things being equal, they do not speak against giving effect to practice-based reasonable expectations. However, if practice over-exposes vulnerable small businesses, regulators might need to step in, either by reducing the scope for private ordering relative to a more protective expression of the public interest, or by specifying equalizing conditions for the negotiation of the framework governance conditions of the network.

### *Taking Stock*

Is there an unbridgeable gap between the English commercial law of contract and a network-enabled version of the law? Clearly, there is not. Equipped with contextualist and realist approaches and guided by reasonable expectations, English law seems to be in a position to recognize and enforce whatever network-like effects comport with business practice. In other words, although the law has not announced that it now recognizes networks and network effects, it seems that the reception of these ideas is already history. Whether it would make any practical difference if networks were explicitly embedded in contract doctrine is a matter for further reflection, but on the face of it, most of the work has already been done.

## The Possible Reception of Networks: Private Contracts

Appeal court litigation of purely private transactions is relatively unusual. Nevertheless, it was transactions of this class – witness, cases such as *Tweddle* v *Atkinson*[80] and *Beswick* v *Beswick*[81] – that were the focus for the relaxation of the privity rules in the Contracts (Rights of Third Parties) Act 1999. We should not assume, therefore, that disputes such as that in *Clarke* v *Dunraven* are wholly exceptional. Even so, private transactions are not one of the more obvious targets for regulators and, certainly, they are not on the radar in the way that consumer transactions are.

Insofar as there is a background co-regulatory plan for purely private transactions, it probably mirrors that of commercial contracts. Accordingly, there will be some public interest regulatory restriction – for example, with regard to purely domestic agreements, surrogacy contracts, pre-nuptial agreements, and so on.[82] Such restrictions apart, the regulatory purpose will be to let the parties order

80 (1861) 1 B & S 393.

81 [1968] AC 58.

82 For a recent instance, see *MacLeod* v *MacLeod* [2008] UKPC 64. And, see Teubner, n 19 above, 415 (concerning the possible blocking of an exit option for powerful

their transactions in their own way. Hence, if competitors such as those in *Clarke* v *Dunraven* wish to adjust the usual liability rules, public policy permitting, they should be free to do so. And, if they wish the rules to be enforceable horizontally as between the competitors, they should be free to do this too.

However, in the absence of legal advice, private transactors are unlikely to be aware of the full range of their legal options. And, we might assume that, in general, disputes between private transactors will need to be adjudicated by reference to the default rules. If this is correct, and if the default rules are not network sensitive (as they conspicuously were not, so long as privity ruled), when they should be, regulators need to give this some attention. In this light, what should we make of the two key changes made by the Contracts (Rights of Third Parties) Act, 1999? First, for that class of transactions where the contracting parties intend to confer a benefit on a third party, the legislative default position seems to be that the third party has a right of enforcement; in other words, the default is set for this particular network effect. The default may be switched, however, where the parties expressly so signal or where the circumstances (for which, perhaps, we should read context) indicate that no right of enforcement is contemplated. Secondly, in all other cases, including where the contract is simply of benefit to a third party, the default remains against network effects. Again, though, the default may be switched but only where the parties expressly signal that they are conferring a third-party right of enforcement.

Where the default rules are not appropriate, there is the question of whether judges might have a discretionary override to bring in network effects. While an unpredictable judicial discretion is not ideal, in this class of case, it probably can be tolerated.

Taking stock, we can see that, in some respects, private contractors are akin to consumers in the sense that they are not typically members of networks. The competition cases are not typical. This means that there will be no general practice-based expectation that private transactions will have network effects. Moreover, the legislative relaxation of the privity restrictions for simple third-party beneficiary cases will mean that network thinking is not needed to resolve the injustice otherwise felt in the older cases. However, unlike consumers, private contractors are not subject to a policy-driven regulatory scheme. Accordingly, where network constellations are found (albeit exceptionally), there is no reason why the regulation of private transactions should not follow that of commercial transactions and protect the on-the-ground expectations of private contractors.

## Conclusion

Although this chapter deals with private law, it has a heavy emphasis on 'regulation', and it proceeds in a somewhat tortuous way through consumer,

---

parties who wish to withdraw from their network responsibilities).

commercial and purely private transactions. What are the principal conclusions with regard to network contracts and network effects? Are these ideas that English law, as now transformed, is likely to embrace or reject?

First, in relation to consumer transactions, the utility and appropriateness of networks will be judged entirely by reference to larger European regulatory objectives. If we accept the current regulatory objectives, the question is whether networks cohere with and assist the realization of those objectives. If we reject current regulatory objectives, we need to defend a different set of objectives and then assess the utility and appropriateness of networks relative to those revised regulatory objectives. In both cases, the question needs to be pursued with an awareness of the significance of legal provisions in the larger regulatory environment.

Second, in relation to commercial transactions, provided that networks or network effects are compatible with public interest considerations, the way seems to be clear for their reception. Quite simply, where the general rules are simply defaults, and where express intention, context, and practice displace the defaults, the law is now geared to recognize networks and network effects wherever this is in line with the parties' reasonable contextualized expectations.

Third, with regard to purely private contracting (where explicit adoption of network effects is less likely to occur), the basic outlook is again co-regulatory. It might be more important here (than in commercial contracts) to attend to the default rules. Generally, though, we can entrust judges with a residual discretion to declare a group of contracts as having network effects where this is necessary in order to give effect to the implicit reasonable expectations of the parties.

Finally, there is plenty of unfinished business – for example, concerning the network protections that might be applied for the benefit of small businesses, the extent to which network effects might be incorporated into the default rules for commercial and for purely private transactions, how widely the effects of a network apply (the question of who has standing for network purposes),[83] the external liability of networked parties, and how courts should respond where regulators have not given a clear steer as to their objectives in relation to consumer transactions. Before we can tackle this agenda, however, there needs to be a double revision to the general appreciation of contract law: first, we need to take on board the reality that many of the transactions that the law seeks to address are networked, that the discrete exchange of the classical law has been eclipsed by more complex and shifting forms of dealing, and second, we need to grapple with the thought that the regulatory environment of which the law of contract is just one part is itself complex, dynamic, and networked – in short, that the regulation of networks is to be effected by a network of regulation.[84]

83 This is a question that should be clarified by regulators who provide for networks or by the lead contracting parties where they adopt networks as a feature of their private ordering.

84 Compare Teubner, n 19 above, 411.

# Chapter 7
# Networks of Contracts and Competition Law

Michael Martinek[1]

## Introduction

### *Contracts and Competition*

The movement from exchange to cooperation and the significance of networks and long-term relationships in the law of contracts[2] can hardly be justly appreciated without taking into account the law of competition. Contracts are, after all, the legal instrument to perform and stimulate competition.[3] Competition takes place and gains shape by negotiating and concluding contracts, and also, of course, by terminating contracts to pave the way for new negotiations and conclusions of new contracts. The more contracts are negotiated, concluded and terminated, the more vivid the competition. Once a contract has been concluded, competition is reduced and partly over for a while, since the contracting parties are bound and saturated, their former competitors on either side have lost this race and have to turn their

---

1 This is the extended version of a paper which was presented to the Conference of the Society of European Contract Law (SECOLA) at Florence, Italy, on June 5/6, 2009, about Networks and Long-Term-Relationships in European Contract Law.

2 For the emergence of contractual network relations in the law cf. the contributions in M. Amstutz and G. Teubner (eds), *Networks: Legal Issues of Multilateral Co-operation* (Oxford: Hart Publishing, 2009), and in M. Amstutz (ed.), *Die vernetzte Wirtschaft – Netzwerke als Rechtsproblem* (Zurich: Schulthess, 2004); G. Teubner, *Networks as Connected Contracts. With an Introduction by Hugh Collins* (Oxford, Hart, 2011); D. Campbell, H. Collins and J. Wightman (eds), *Implicit Dimensions of Contract: Discrete, Relational and Network Contracts* (Oxford: Hart Publishing, 2003); for the basics see I.R. Macneil, 'The Many Futures of Contracts' 47 *Southern California Law Review* (1974) 691 *et seq.*; I.R. Macneil, 'Contracts: Adjustment of Long-Term Economic Relations under Classical, Neoclassical and Relational Contract Law' 72 *Northwestern University Law Review* (1978) 854 *et seq.*; I.R. Macneil, *The New Contract Law* (New Haven/London: Yale University Press, 1979); M. Castells, *The Rise of the Network Society* (Oxford: Blackwell, 2000); K.W. Lange, *Das Recht der Netzwerke – Moderne Formen der Zusammenarbeit in Produktion und Vertrieb* (Heidelberg: Recht und Wirtschaft, 1998).

3 See M. Martinek, 'Contract law theory in the social welfare state of Germany – developments and dangers' (2007) *TSAR - Tydskrif vir die suid-afrikaanse reg / Journal of South African Law* 1–18; M. Martinek, 'Vertragliche Schuldverhältnisse', in D. Willoweit (ed.), *Rechtswissenschaft und Rechtsliteratur im 20. Jahrhundert* (Munich: Beck, 2007) 141–179.

attention on different races with different possible partners. As far as long-term contracts are at stake, which provide not only for one discrete exchange, but for a long-standing cooperation and for a framework for future exchanges between the same parties, competition can be noticeably quenched by the establishment of a quasi-monopolistic relationship between these two parties which hereby exclude all other possible future partners from any chance to successfully compete. A long-term contract tends to be adverse to competition. Even more so, extensive networks of long-term contracts in a particular market tend to be adverse and harmful to competition. It comes as no surprise, therefore, that networks of long-term contracts are of special interest for the law of competition.

### *Distribution Contracts as a Paradigm for Networks*

This is particularly true with regard to distribution contracts, i.e. vertical systems of long-term contracts between a producer or wholesaler as the supplier on the one side and a number of dealers as distributors of goods and services on the other side.[4] The distributors can be commercial sale agents, commission agents, authorized dealers or franchised dealers. Distribution contracts have always been the focus of contract lawyers when discussing the problems of long-term contractual agreements, of relational contracts and of networks of contracts. They also serve very well as the main paradigm for the impact of networks of long-term contracts on market and on competition and for the reaction of the law of competition.[5]

4 For the foundations of the law of distribution see M. Martinek, in M. Martinek, F.J. Semler, S. Habermeier and E. Flohr (eds), *Handbuch des Vertriebsrechts* (3rd edn, Munich: Beck, 2010) 1–137; R. Baldi, *Distributorship, Franchising, Agency* (Deventer: Kluwer Law and Taxation Publishing, 1987).

5 See the contributions in Amstutz and Teubner (eds), n 2 above; C. Ott, 'Contract Network in Distribution Systems' 151 *JITE – Journal of Institutional and Theoretical Economics* (1995) 212–17; L. Müller-Hagedorn, 'The Variety of Distribution Systems' 151 *JITE – Journal of Institutional and Theoretical Economics* (1995) 186–202; E. Schanze, 'Symbiotic Contracts: Exploring Long-Term Agency Structures Between Contract and Cooperation', in C. Joerges (ed.), *Franchising and the Law, Theoretical and Comparative Approaches in Europe and the United States* (Baden-Baden: Nomos, 1991) 67–103; E. Schanze, 'Symbiotic Arrangements' 149 *JITE – Journal of Institutional and Theoretical Economics* (1993) 691–7; H.P. Schwintowski, *Alleinvertriebssysteme.* Ökonomische Funktionen – wettbewerbliche Grenzen (Baden-Baden: Nomos, 1992); J.E. de Cockborne, 'Franchising and the European Competition Law', in Joerges (ed.), ibid., 281–314; C. Joerges, 'Contract and Status in Franchising Law', in Joerges (ed.), ibid., 11–66; M. Martinek, *Franchising: Grundlagen der zivil- und wettbewerbsrechtlichen Behandlung der vertraglichen Gruppenkooperation beim Absatz von Waren und Dienstleistungen* (Heidelberg: von Decker, 1987); M. Rohe, *Netzverträge: Rechtsprobleme komplexer Vertragsverbindungen* (Tübingen: Mohr Siebeck, 1998).

## Vertical Integration and Vertical Group Cooperation

### *Historical Background*

The economies on the levels of distribution of goods and services in the Western world (and also meanwhile of the Eastern hemisphere) are covered and overrun nowadays by networks of distribution contracts.[6] Marketing channels are to a high extent organized by means of vertical systems of contracts. In general (and all future descriptions and statements are meant here 'in general'), this ensues from the successful attempts and efforts of industrial enterprises on the production level to employ formerly independent dealers to serve producers' marketing interests and to bind them to their strategies to sell their goods to consumers. By means of distribution contracts the dealers become instrumental for the marketing objectives of the producers. The dealers who formerly possessed the pride and self-esteem to act as independent advocates for consumers' demands have been transformed into contracted dealers identifying their interest, to a fair degree, with the ideas and strategies of their suppliers to jointly compete for, or to 'exploit' consumers. The earlier classical model of distribution of goods, still in existence between the two world wars, was characterized by a relatively clear functional separation between the levels of production, wholesale and retail business. Dealers reacted to consumers' demands and were free and independent to conclude contracts accordingly with suppliers of their choice; they were legally and economically independent. Under the influence of the marketing philosophy, however, in the European countries particularly since the sixties and seventies, producers became more and more aware of the importance and exigency to 'pre-sell' their goods, i.e. to create and to foster, first of all, a demand for their goods and to fully control marketing channels and distribution levels. This development, commonly called the vertical downstream integration of distribution systems,[7] aimed at the planning, organizing and controlling of as many distributive activities as possible.

---

6 G. Bogaert and U. Lohmann (eds), *Commercial Agency and Distrubution Agreements: Law and Practice in the Member States* (3rd edn, The Hague: Kluwer Law International, 2000); Martinek, Semler, Habermeier and Flohr (eds), n 4 above; Baldi, n 4 above; F. Bortolotti and G. Bondanini, *Il contratto di agenzia commerciale* (Padova: CEDAM, 2003); Principles of European Law – Study Group on a European Civil Code (M.W. Hesselink, J.W. Rutgers, O. Bueno Diaz, M. Scotton and M. Veldman), *Commercial Agency, Franchise and Distribution Contracts* (Munich: Sellier, 2006).

7 Cf. R. Lademann, *Machtverteilung zwischen Industrie und Handel* (Göttingen: GHS, 1988); M. Martinek, 'Vertriebsrecht und vertikale Integration in der BGH-Rechtsprechung', in A. Heldrich / K.J. Hopt (eds), *50 Jahre Bundesgerichtshof*, vol II (Munich: Beck, 2000) 101 *et seq.*; W. Irrgang (ed.), *Vertikales Marketing im Wandel* (Munich: Vahlen, 1993); D. Ahlert (ed.), *Vertragliche Vertriebssysteme zwischen Industrie und Handel* (Wiesbaden: Gabler, 1981); M. Laurent, *Vertikale Kooperationen zwischen Industrie und Handel – Neue Typen und Strategien zur Effizienzsteigerung im Absatzkanal* (Frankfurt/M: Deutscher Fachverlag, 1996); A. Sölter, *Kooperative Absatzwirtschaft –*

In establishing networks of long-term distribution contracts with selected dealers the producers relied on their market dominance and assumed the leadership for the marketing of their goods. The dealers, by and large, turned out to be willing and prepared to subordinate their interests and activities under the leadership of the suppliers, because of the many advantages they gained from a long-standing cooperation. Often enough, they preferred to operate a 'sheltered enterprise'.

### *Horizontal and Vertical Group Cooperation*

The establishment of networks of distribution contracts entailed new forms of cooperation which are commonly called vertical group cooperation as opposed to horizontal group cooperation. Horizontal groups, for example, voluntary chains or cooperative groups among retailers had already been in existence for more than a century; they were, at the beginning, defensively oriented and were designed to build up market power on the demand side to profit from economics of large scale buying by rebates, kick-backs and the like. Horizontal group cooperation is organized in corporations or partnerships; horizontal groups of distributors are companies which try to counterbalance the bargaining power of industrial enterprises.[8] A vertical group, however, consists of a system of long-term distribution contracts, the centre of which is the supplier and/or producer. This system is 'fan-shaped' or 'pyramid-shaped' with the supplier and/or producer being the hub of the system and the centre of a more or less autocratically organized administration. It is a vertical system or vertical network of contracts, because one partner, namely the supplier (mostly a producer belonging to the commodity industries), is positioned on a higher step of the different levels of the economy, whereas his many distributors and contracting partners (mostly belonging to the retail business) are situated on a lower step closer to the consumers' level. Unlike in a horizontal group there are no, or no important, links between the different distributors. In a vertical group the inter-organizational management is run by the centre of the system unilaterally. The supplier and/or producer entertain isolated bilateral relationships with each of his contracting distributors, and the different parallel contracts basically show the same content.

---

*Grundlagen, Erfordernisse und Möglichkeiten der Zusammenarbeit zwischen Industrie und Handel* (Cologne: Heymanns, 1971).

8 G. Olesch, *Die Einkaufsverbände des Einzelhandels – Typologie und Dokumentation* (Frankfurt/M: Deutscher Fachverlag, 1980); F. Kutscher-Puis, *Die Verbundgruppen des Handels und ihre Anschlussverträge* (Baden-Baden: Nomos, 2006); A. Geiger, *Europäische Verbundgruppen im EU-Kartellrecht* (Baden-Baden: Nomos, 2001); F. Markmann and G. Olesch, 'Franchisesysteme und Verbundgruppen – Ein Vergleich von Struktur und Strategie', in D. Ahlert (ed.), *Handbuch Franchising & Cooperation* (Neuwied: Luchterhand, 2001) 107 *et seq.*; R. Purtschert, 'Einkaufsgenossenschaften des Handels' 52 *Zeitschrift für das gesamte Genossenschaftswesen* 2002, 271 *et seq.*; G. Schulte, *Kartellrechtliche Fragen der Verbundgruppen* (Wiesbaden: DG-Verlag, 2000).

*Characteristic Features of Vertical Group Cooperation*

Among the most characteristic features of vertical groups, the very high degree or intensity of cooperation must be emphasized.[9] This means that not only the conditions of the future sales of goods, but a variety of circumstances and activities are being regulated in the contracts like the presentation of the goods, the modalities of approaching the consumers, questions of advertisement, the training of the distributors' staff members and so on. Of course, the intensity of cooperation depends on the particular type of distribution contract in question. Contracts with authorized dealers show a lower degree of cooperation, whereas franchise contracts are characterized by a multiplicity of provisions subjecting practically all entrepreneurial activities to the contractual agreement. Franchise contracts provide for what is called 'total cooperation'. A corollary of this high intensity of cooperation is the consciousness among all the group members that they belong to a unit and strive for the success of the same product. The members of the network are not acting autonomously, but in concerted efforts. They all know that their success depends on the system and thereby on each individual member. The failure of one partner has detrimental effects on the image of the entire distribution system. Another feature of vertical groups is the high degree of adaptability of marketing activities to the changing needs and demands of the market. Depending on the channel administration of the hub of the system, the vertical distribution group allows for a strategy of quick response to the challenges of the day, in that an improved variation of the product, a new business administration idea or an innovative pre- or after-sales service can be enforced easily and swiftly upon all the network members. Vertical groups are highly flexible. In addition, the consumers perceive a vertical group as an entrepreneurial unit and often enough consider the members of the network to be just branches of the same enterprise. This is particularly true with franchise systems, because the different franchised outlets show the same uniform appearance which the consumer regards as a guarantee for the same standard of service and for the same quality of the product.[10]

---

9 H. Köhler, 'Individualwettbewerb und Gruppenwettbewerb' 146 *Zeitschrift für das gesamte Handels- und Wirtschaftsrecht* 1982, 580 *et seq.*; B. Tietz, *Der Gruppenwettbewerb als Element der Wettbewerbspolitik – Das Beispiel der Automobilwirtschaft* (Cologne: Heymanns, 1981); B. Tietz and G. Mathieu, *Das Kontraktmarketing als Kooperationsmodell* (Cologne: Heymanns, 1979); V. Beuthin, 'Das Franchising im Gruppenwettbewerb des Handels' *Betriebs-Berater* 1993, 77 *et seq.*; H. Meffert (ed.), *Marketing im Wandel* (Wiesbaden: Gabler, 1980); N. Gahrens, *Die Ökonomisierung der Warendistribution durch zwischenbetriebliche Kooperationen* (Göttingen: Schwartz, 1990).

10 Cf J.N. Adams, K.V. Pritchard Jones and J.J.B. Hickey, *Franchising: Practice an Precedents in Business Format Franchising* (5th edn, Edinburgh: Tottel Publishing, 2004); B. Tietz, *Handbuch Franchising – Zukunftsstrategien für die Marktbearbeitung* (2nd edn, Landsberg/Lech: Verlag Moderne Industrie, 1991); Tietz and Mathieu, n 9 above; E. Flohr, *Der Franchisevertrag – Formularhandbuch* (2nd edn, Munich: Beck, 2001); P. Giesler and J. Nauschütt, *Franchiserecht* (Neuwied: Luchterhand, 2002); B.C. Haager,

It has often been described that the formation of vertical groups modifies the structure of competition in a market. As long as there are no networks of long-term contracts and no vertical distribution systems in existence, competition takes place in the anarchical way of 'man against man', enterprise against enterprise. In the absence of distribution systems the individual distributors of a particular product and of concurring products compete against each other. Universal distribution entails universal and individual competition. The formation of networks and systems, however, produces groups of distributors with parallel and homogeneous interests in the success of their product. By means of marketing channel administration and by shaping the distribution contracts carefully, the supplier intentionally aims at a reduction of competition among the members of this particular network. The intra-brand competition among the distributors of the same brand will be decreased by the establishment and administration of a vertical group. However, the competition between the different brands, the inter-brand competition between different, but concurring products, will be intensified at the same time, because it is now the vertical groups that fight against each other to sell the product of their system. Instead of the individual distributors, now the groups of distributors compete against each other. It is well established, therefore, that the formation of vertical groups, i.e. the introduction of networks of distribution contracts in a market, remarkably modifies the structure of competition: it changes the anarchical, universal and individual competition into a more orderly, more structured group competition with reduced intra-brand competition and with increased inter-brand competition.

## Vertical Restraints of Trade as Elements of Distribution Networks

### *Exclusive Dealing, Territorial Restrictions, Customer Restrictions, Tying Agreements and the Like in Distribution Contracts*

Distribution contracts of a particular network are always standard form contracts for the entire system: one network, one standard form contract. Concerning the rights and duties of the partners of a distribution contract the competition lawyer is mainly interested in those clauses which directly or indirectly unfold an effect to the competitiveness of the pertinent market and hereby concern the workability of competition. These clauses are regarded as vertical restraints of trade which bind the partners to prescribed activities and harmonized behaviour and which the supplier, when designing the distribution contracts for his network, sets in

---

'Die Entwicklung des Franchiserechts in den Jahren 1999, 2000 und 2001', *Neue Juristische Wochenschrift* 2002, 1463–74; M. Martinek, *Moderne Vertragstypen vol II: Franchising, Know-How-Verträge, Management- und Consultingverträge* (Munich: Beck, 1992); K. Metzlaff (ed.), *Praxishandbuch Franchising* (Munich: Beck, 2003).

motion to push through his marketing objectives.[11] In fact, a variety of vertical restraints of trade can be distinguished and put in a systematic order.[12] They are all elements available for the design and shape of the distribution contracts in a particular network, and hardly conceivable is any network of distribution contracts without a certain number of vertical restraints of trade.

Examples are manifold: restrictions on the retail price, when selling the product to the customers of the distributor, are perhaps the most prominent example. They appear in many forms, such as minimum price clauses or maximum price clauses or even clauses fixing prices firmly and absolutely. By means of supply restraints – another example – the distributor is obliged to buy products of a certain quality and/or quantity only from his partner or from 'approved' suppliers – approved by the partner, that is. They also appear in different forms. Sometimes the distributor is also permitted to buy certain qualities and/or quantities from external, unapproved suppliers; sometimes he is bound exclusively to his one supplier only, which is the case in so-called requirement contracts, full line performance contracts or exclusive dealing agreements. The distributor is foreclosed from any activity promoting the sale of concurring products and is forced to concentrate solely on the sale of the one supplier's goods. Territorial restrictions – the next example – impose on the distributor the duty to abstain from promotion activities outside the area allocated to him. Most distribution systems operate a zoning scheme allotting certain geographical areas to selected distributors. Again different forms and intensities of relative or absolute territorial restrictions can be distinguished – starting out with rather harmless agreements on an area of primary responsibility for the distributor, ending up with closed or even airtight territorial restrictions flanked by profit pass-over clauses; the latter demand a distributor to renounce the benefit of a business transaction by passing over his gain (partly or fully) to the neighbour member of the network whose exclusive territory has been violated. Also, location clauses or one-place-business clauses, by which the distributor is confined to a certain location of his enterprise, must be mentioned in this context. Similar in effect to territorial restrictions are customer restriction clauses which bar the distributor from access to certain types of customers (like public institutions, other retailers or special types of companies which the producer may reserve for his own direct business activities). Tying arrangements or tie-in restrictions aim at

11 Cf. T. Kapp, *Wettbewerbsbeschränkung durch vertikale Vertriebsbindungen?* (Baden-Baden: Nomos, 1984); F. Rittner, *Die Ausschließlichkeitsbindungen in dogmatischer und rechtspolitischer Betrachtung* (Düsseldorf: Verlag Handelsblatt, 1957); E. Sundhoff, 'Über vertikale Absatzbindungen', in *Festschrift für Seyffert* (Cologne: Westdeutscher Verlag, 1968) 479 *et seq.*

12 Cf. D. Ahlert, *Distributionspolitik* (Stuttgart: Fischer, 1985) 43 *et seq.*; C.J. Meier, *Der selektive Vertrieb im EWG-Kartellrecht* vol 1 and 2 (Diessenhofen: Rüegger, 1979) 192 *et seq.*; O. Sandrock, *Grundbegriffe des Gesetzes gegen Wettbewerbsbeschränkungen* (Munich: Beck, 1968) 31 *et seq.*; R. Krasser, *Der Schutz von Preis- und Vertriebsbindungen gegenüber Außenseitern* (Cologne: Heymanns, 1972).

the promotion of certain products which the distributor does not like so much (tied products), since he can only obtain products he does like (tying products), if he buys the tied products as well. The distributor gets what he wants only if he also takes what he does not want.

### *Anti-Competitive Effects of Vertical Restraints*

*The ambiguity issue* It is not so easy for competition law to deal appropriately with vertical restraints of law.[13] Their effects in the market and their impact on competition cannot always easily and clearly be determined and appraised. Exceptions are perhaps price fixings, i.e. clauses on retail price maintenance. If a producer and/or suppliers attempt to prescribe absolutely fixed prices in the distribution contracts which the distributors are then obliged to impose on their consumers, the vertical restraints of the entire network have the same effect as a horizontal price cartel agreement between the distributors as members of this network. Vertical price fixing can reduce the price competition to zero with regard to the product distributed in the network. Since pricing is the most important competition parameter, those clauses are commonly seen as pernicious per se.

On the other hand, some types of vertical restrictions can possibly be regarded as useful for and beneficial to competition.[14] This is often demonstrated by the so-called free-rider-paradigm with regard to territorial restrictions.[15] This can be shortly described as follows: in cases where a distribution system would not provide for any territorial or customer restrictions at all, but leave it to the members of the network to deal with any consumers wherever possible, the special efforts of a certain distributor to promote the sale of the product by the rendition of a particular service would not be honoured. The reason for this is that the rendition of a particular service (let's say in the form of elaborate advice, of knowledgeable consultation, of innovative advertisement or of a time-consuming demonstration

13 Cf W. Veelken, 'Vertriebssysteme unter besonderer Berücksichtigung des deutschen und europäischen Wettbewerbsrechts' 89 *Zeitschrift für vergleichende Rechtswissenschaft* (1990) 358 *et seq.*; Meier, n 12 above; D. Ahlert, 'Die Bedeutung Vertraglicher Vertriebssysteme für den freien Wettbewerb und die Funktionsfähigkeit von Märkten' *Wettbewerb in Recht und Praxis* 1987, 215 *et seq.*; B. Glasow, *Vertikale Preisbindung, Wettbewerbstheorie und Wettbewerbsrecht in den USA, Deutschland und Europa* (Frankfurt/M: Lang, 1999); Th. Pawlikowski, *Selektive Vertriebssysteme* (Frankfurt/M: Lang, 1983).

14 U. Loewenheim, *Warenzeichen und Wettbewerbsbeschränkung* (Bad Homburg: Athenäum-Verlag, 1970) 99 *et seq.*; H. Grossekettler, 'Die gesamtwirtschaftliche Problematik Vertraglicher Vertriebssysteme', in Ahlert (ed.), n 7 above, 255 *et seq.*; H. Grossekettler, 'Die volkswirtschaftliche Problematik von Vertriebskooperationen. Zur wettbewerbspolitischen Beurteilung von Vertriebsbindungs-, Alleinvertriebs-, Vertragshändler- und Franchisesystemen' 28 *Zeitschrift für das gesamte Genossenschaftswesen* (1978) 325 *et seq.*; Martinek, n 5 above, 468 *et seq.*

15 See e.g. Kapp, n 11 above, 49 *et seq.*; Martinek, n 5 above, 439 *et seq.*

of the product) is costly and leads to an increase of the price for the product. The consumers would, therefore, tend to benefit from the particular rendition of services of the eager distributor, but would abstain from buying the product from him, go over to the less eager neighbour distributor, who relinquishes any service efforts, thus can sell the same product at a lower price and essentially enjoys a 'free ride', benefiting from the eager distributor's efforts. The less eager distributor exploits the eager distributor. The remuneration for the special efforts of a distributor is wrongly allocated to the distributor who abstains from the efforts. Eventually, all distributors would be best advised to renounce all special marketing efforts and just place the plain product on the shelf. No doubt, this would be highly detrimental for the consumers who would be confronted, at the end of the day, only with discount retail shops selling the naked commodities without any service. This mechanism, at least in theory, demonstrates that, by means of territorial restrictions, the special sales promotion efforts employed by a distributor can more likely be honoured, because the benefit of the sale can be reserved for and allocated to him. This demonstrates that vertical restrictions of trade can also have a pro-competitive effect.

In general, it can hardly be denied that networks of contracts and vertical distribution groups can have immense rationalizing effects, and can lead to an orderly supply to consumers at remarkably reduced costs as compared with universal, 'anarchical' distribution. Consumers can benefit to a high degree from better market transparency, from lower transportation costs, from improved warranty services and so on.

*Effects of market foreclosure* With regard to exclusive dealing agreements it has already been mentioned that the parties of the distribution contract enter into a long-term relationship and establish a quasi-monopolistic connection between them which excludes all other possible partners from business.[16] This means that the competitors of the producer and/or supplier are barred from entering into a contractual relationship with the distributor already belonging to a distribution system. The distributor is bound by the exclusive dealing agreement with his one and only partner and is no longer open for other supply contracts with other possible partners on the level of his supplier. This also means that potential competitors of the distributor in a particular area cannot successfully apply for admission to the system, because the supplier is obliged to supply his goods exclusively to his chosen contracting partner and to reject all demands by concurring distributors in this area where the distribution business is reserved for the members of the network. It is clearly visible that long-term distribution contracts partly eliminate both contracting partners on both levels of the economy from the interplay of

16 M. Martinek and S. Habermeier, in Martinek, Semler, Habermeier and Flohr (eds), n 4 above, 640 *et seq.*; Köhler, n 9 above, 580 *et seq.*; Sölter, n 7 above; Tietz, n 9 above; B. Tietz and G. Mathieu, *Das Franchising als Kooperationsmodell für den mittelständischen Groß- und Einzelhandel* (Cologne: Heymanns, 1979).

market powers. The more long-term contracts come into existence and the more networks of contracts are established, the more difficulties arise for the competing producers and/or suppliers to find suitable distributors on the lower level and to gain access to the consumers through the distributors as gate-keepers. Accordingly, the more long-term contracts come into existence and the more networks of contracts are established, the more impediments have to be surmounted for the distributors to find suitable suppliers and to obtain the desired goods for their retail distribution to the consumers. The downstream marketing channels for the producers are being obstructed and suffocated; the upstream supply resources are being cut off and made unattainable for the distributors. This market foreclosure effect is intensified by an increase of long-term contracts and of networks and vertical groups. On the distribution level the number of concurring enterprises is reduced and the degree of homogeneous competition parameters is enhanced, which can result in each distributor assuming a monopoly position for a particular product in a particular area. The dangers of a lack of dynamics and flexibility in the market are obvious. Competition can become disarranged, crippled and crusted. The dangers loom larger and larger the more producers and the more dealers enter into a long-term relationship within a network of contracts and become members of a vertical group. Admittedly, up to a certain quantity and density of networks of contracts the rationalizing effects, which have been discerned in vertical groups, can prevail over the market foreclosure effects. Vertical restraints obviously become dangerous, however, if a multitude of networks of contracts employing vertical restraint clauses cover and coin the market. It must be added, of course, that here as always in competition law the determination of the relevant market with regard to the territory and to interchangeable and concurring products decides over everything.

The ambiguity of vertical restraints in networks of distribution contracts can also be demonstrated with regard to the previously mentioned phenomenon that vertical groups tend to *de*crease the *intra*-brand or product-internal competition, whereas they *in*crease the *inter*-brand or product-external competition. This mechanism can be welcomed or at least be taken into account as long as a relatively high degree of inter-brand competition, i.e. group competition, takes place in the market. The advantages which the rationalizing effects of networks of contracts show for the consumer and which the enhanced intensity of inter-brand group competition brings about can easily compensate for or even prevail over the disadvantages of a reduced intra-brand competition among the members of a particular network, as long as a relatively high degree of inter-brand competition occurs. This, of course, depends mainly on the number of players in the market on the production level. As long as we find a broad oligopoly on the production level with intensely competing producers of concurring products, the decrease of intra-brand competition can be neglected. If concurring brands of different origins are subject to a workable competition, one does not need to care so much about competition among distributors of the same brand. The mitigation of intra-brand competition can hardly produce serious detrimental effects for the consumers who are easily able to satisfy their demand by the acquisition of substitute products from different producers and their distributors. If, however, the intensity of inter-brand competition slows down and slackens, e.g. because of a reduced number of producers forming a narrow oligopoly, it can become an inexorable necessity to procure a high degree of intra-brand competition and to hereby prevent the exploitation of the consumers through high-priced products.

## Distribution Networks and EU Competition Law

### *The Block Exemption Regulation for Vertical Agreements*

Distribution contracts which are able to noticeably impair the trade between EU member states are prohibited by the competition provision of Article 101 sec 1 of the Treaty on the Functioning of the European Union (TFEU – Lisbon Reform Treaty; formerly Article 81 sec 1).[17] The ruling idea of this provision is that vertical restraints of trade (as well as horizontal cartel agreements and concerted actions) are, as a matter of principle, null and void. According to the principle of legal exemptions, however, agreements containing vertical restraints of trade are generally permitted, if they are covered by a so-called block exemption regulation or if they comply with the pre-requisites of Article 101 sec 3. The European Commission has issued a block exemption regulation 2790/99 of December 22, 1999, which entered fully into force on January 1, 2001 and which covers all vertical restraints of trade in all types of distribution contracts except those of the automobile industry.[18] This so-called umbrella block exemption regulation replaced a number of formerly existing block exemption regulations for different types of vertical restraints.[19] For the distribution of cars a special block exemption regulation is still in existence which takes into account the particular circumstances in this field of distribution. Also, agreements on technology transfer involving

17 Cf. S. Habermeier, in Martinek, Semler, Habermeier and Flohr (eds), n 4 above, 179 *et seq.* and Martinek and Habermeier, n 16 above, 643 *et seq.*

18 Commission Regulation (EC) No 2790/1999 of 22 December 1999 on the application of Article 81(3) of the Treaty to Categories of vertical agreements and concerted practices, *OJEC* L 336/21; now – very similar – Commission Regulation (EU) No 330/2010 of 20 April 2010 on the application of Article 101(3) of the Treaty on the Functioning of the European Union to categories of vertical agreements and concerted practices, *OJ EU* 2010L 102/1.

19 T. Ackermann, 'Die neuen EG-Wettbewerbsregeln für vertikale Beschränkungen' *Zeitschrift für europäisches Wirtschaftsrecht* 1999, 741 *et seq.*; F. Bayreuther, 'Die Reform der EG-Wettbewerbspolitik gegenüber vertikalen Wettbewerbsbeschränkungen' *Europäisches Wirtschafts- und Steuerrecht* 2000, 106; R. Bechtold, 'EG-Gruppenfreiste llungsverordnungen – eine Zwischenbilanz' *Europäisches Wirtschafts- und Steuerrecht* 2001, 49; V. Behr, 'Die Behandlung von Vertikalvereinbarungen nach der 7. GWB-Novelle' *Wirtschaft und Wettbewerb* 2004, 259.

patents or know-how licensing agreements are dealt with in a special block exemption regulation.

The umbrella block exemption regulation 2790/99 or vertical block exemption regulation (VBER) – like its successor – covers all fields of commerce and includes the distribution of goods as well as the rendition of services on all levels of the economy. It is applicable to all kinds of vertical restraints to competition (a revised version of the VBER is presently on its way). In contrast to its predecessors the umbrella block exemption regulation does not expressly enlist all restrictive contractual clauses which are permitted, but describes certain restraints of trade which definitely exclude an exemption from the prohibition and thus are forbidden.

It is noteworthy in our context that the vertical block exemption regulation (2790/1999 and 330/2010) provides for an exemption from the general prohibition of restraints of competition, only if the supplier or the buyer has a market share of less than 30 per cent. This threshold is based on the opinion that the advantages of vertical restrictions in networks of distribution contract, namely the increase of economic efficiency, prevail over the detrimental effects to competition (namely the decrease of intra-brand competition among the distributors) only up to the limit of 30 per cent market share. In cases of exceeding market shares, this presumption cannot be maintained. At this point for the competition lawyer the notion of networks of contracts already comes into play. Up to the limit of 30 per cent market share, networks of distribution contracts can be established to penetrate the market, if the contractual provisions comply with the vertical block exemption regulation. Beyond this limit the question of permissibility must be scrutinized on the grounds of Article 101 sec 3.

The European Commission has also published so-called guidelines for vertical restraints of trade which serve as an additional and an important source of law for competition law practitioners, especially for corporate lawyers drafting distribution contracts.[20] The guidelines contain helpful explanations, hints and examples for the interpretation and application of the vertical block exemption regulation.[21] Although the vertical guidelines are by no means binding for the national courts, nor for the Court of Justice of the European Union, the Commission, however, strictly adheres to the guidelines which have a self-binding effect on European competition administration.

20 Commission Notice, Guidelines on Vertical Restraints (2000/C 291/01).

21 M. Hughes, C. Foss and K. Ross, 'The Economic Assessment of Vertical Restraints under U.K. and E.C. Competition Law' *European Competition Law Review* (2001) 421; S. Bishop and D. Ridyard, 'E.C. Vertical Restraint Guidelines – Effects Based or Per se Policy?' *European Competition Law Review* (2002) 35; L. Pepperkorn, 'E.C. Vertical Restraint Guidelines – Effects Based or Per se Policy?' *European Competition Law Review* (2002) 38; A. Griffith, 'A Glorification of de minimis – The Regulation on Vertical Agreements' *European Competition Law Review* (2000) 241; F. Rittner, 'Die neuen Guidelines für Vertikalvereinbarungen' *Wirtschaft und Wettbewerb* 2000, 831; F.J. Semler and M. Bauer, 'Die neue EU-Gruppenfreistellungsverordnung für vertikale Wettbewerbsbeschränkungen – Folgen für die Rechtspraxis' *Der Betrieb* 2000, 193.

The provisions of the vertical block exemption regulation are highly detailed and sophisticated and try to deal with all the common types of vertical restraints of trade which marketing experts and legal practitioners have developed to shape networks of distribution contracts. The regulation tries to balance out the advantageous and the detrimental effects which vertical restraints of trade can exert to competition. It hereby attempts to cope with the ambiguity of vertical restraints.

Article 4 of the regulation (2790/1999 and 330/2010) enlists certain types of hard core restrictions which are deemed to be pernicious per se and therefore cannot be at all exempted. This is the catalogue of definitely forbidden 'black clauses'. A black clause in a distribution contract makes the entire contract null and void according to the principle of all-or-nothing. Hard core restrictions are, first of all, resale price fixing clauses. This refers not only to the fixing of the price for the good or service, but also to rebates, transportation costs and other price constitutive elements. Among the hard core restrictions, certain types of territorial restrictions and customer restrictions are also mentioned in Article 4. However, restrictions to active sales promotion outside the territory allotted to a dealer can be permitted, whereas passive sales activities, i.e. sales to customers coming from outside the allotted territory or area of responsibility, cannot be restricted.

Article 5 of the vertical block exemption regulation (2790/1999 and 330/2010) contains a catalogue of so-called 'red clauses' which, under the rule of reason, can be individually exempted from the prohibition. Red clauses are, for instance, contractual provisions about distribution activities for concurring goods during the performance of the contract or clauses on post-contractual restrictions of competition.

### *The Impact of Competition Law on the Content of Distribution Contracts*

Since the umbrella block exemption regulation does not enlist – as its predecessors did – all vertical restraint clauses which are exempted from the prohibition and thus are permitted, but describes only the clauses which exclude an exemption, it leaves ample room for parties in drafting their distribution contracts. The former block exemption regulations exerted a so-called strait-jacket effect, because they invited the contracting parties to copy exactly the clauses enumerated in the block exemption regulations and hereby impeded the competition in the field of innovative contractual provisions. Vertical restraint clauses which were not listed in the catalogue of permitted clauses had to be exempted by means of an individual application for exemption according to Article 101 sec 3, former Article 81 sec 3. This grievance has now been abolished for the sake of contractual freedom.

In fact it is fair to say that the current European competition law on vertical restraints of trade leaves the freedom of contract and the freedom to organize a distribution system widely untouched. Vertical restraints of trade which are necessary for the efficiency of the distribution system are tolerated. Apart from the few black clauses on price restrictions which are deemed to be detrimental per se, it is the rule of reason that governs EU competition law in the field of vertical restraints. Only misuse is prohibited. It is beyond doubt, though, that the contract lawyer has to be fully aware of the impact of competition law on the content of distribution law. We are dealing here, in the realm of networks of long-term distribution contracts, with a field of law in which EU competition law, particularly the vertical block exemption regulation, matters enormously. The contract lawyer must also be a competition lawyer to fulfil his task of designing and organizing an efficient and legally permitted distribution system by a network of contracts. This state of the art exemplifies that long-term contractual relationships and networks of contracts are by no means a matter for contract law only.

## Distribution Networks and Competitive Anti-Discrimination Law

### *Basic Content of Competitive Anti-Discrimination Law and Applicability on Distribution Contracts*

Attention can now be focused on another issue where competition law looms large in the field of networks of long-term distribution contracts. Not so much on the European Union level, but in many national competition laws of member states, and decidedly so in Germany, provisions against unjustified or undue discrimination play a major role.[22] Enterprises with a certain market power or even market dominance are subject to special control of their performance in the market. Since they, because of their powerful market position, are not fully and sufficiently controlled by market mechanism and concurring enterprises, it is the law that imposes particular performance-related requirements on them and demands a certain behaviour from them in the market, as if there were a scene of workable competition. Particularly powerful or dominant enterprises are not permitted to treat their business partners on the supply side upstream or on the demand side downstream unequally without a justifying reason. This rule, as provided for in Article 20 of the German Antitrust law, for instance, also applies in many cases to the producer and/or supplier which has created and entertains a distribution system by a network of long-term contracts with a multitude of dealers. The powerful supplier is then bound to observe the competitive anti-discrimination law. The market power which subjects the head of a distribution system to this rule depends by no means only on its share in the relevant market. A powerful market position qualifying an enterprise as addressee of the anti-discrimination rule can also be constituted by the very nature of the distribution network itself. It is well established that small and medium sized distributors, for instance, franchised dealers, whose businesses totally depend on the continuous cooperation with the franchisor, are protected by the competitive anti-discrimination law, since the distribution system centre assumes a powerful market position face to face with their dealers who are in an inferior position of business-related dependence. Moreover, even

22 Martinek, n 5 above, 598 *et seq.*; Martinek and Habermeier, n 16 above, 650 *et seq.*; W. Epp, *Franchising und Kartellrecht* (Cologne: Heymanns, 1995) 185 *et seq.*

in simply structured supply relationships a dealer can be dependent on the regular and continuous delivery of certain products which the consumers expect the dealer to offer on his shelves. A dealer of 'American Whiskeys', for example, can hardly survive without the leading brands 'Jim Beam' and 'Jack Daniels' on his shelves, and a shop named 'Japanese Notebooks' must either offer Toshiba or Sony computers, if not both brands. This type of product-related market power can also qualify the head of a distribution network as addressee of the anti-discrimination rule.

*Protection of Network Insiders – The Termination and Non-Renewal Issue*

In the above cases the competitive anti-discrimination rule aims, first, at the protection of network insiders, i.e. the dealers who entertain long-term distribution contracts with their supplier. They cannot be treated unequally without a justifying reason. This is the situation where competition law has a direct influence on contract law. A supplier who wants to terminate the contractual relationship with a particular member of his distribution network, or intends to abstain from a renewal of the contract for another term, is required and indeed, legally compelled, to justify his decision and give good reasons, otherwise his course of action would be considered a violation of the anti-discrimination rule. The contract lawyer has to consider, therefore, competition law rules setting limits to the freedom to terminate a long-term contract.

*Protection of Network Outsiders – The Business Denial and Network Admission Issue*

Second, the competitive anti-discrimination rule can also serve as a protection of network outsiders, i.e. dealers who so far had no access to the distribution network and were foreclosed from the supply with the products of the distribution system. They can, under certain conditions, sue the supplier to abandon his strategy of business denial, to provide for access to the goods, and even sometimes for admission to the network of the distribution contracts. In this field of discriminatory business denial and discriminatory exclusion from admission to the distribution network, competition law can even compel the supplier to conclude a distribution contract with a dealer. In this context the contract lawyer has to consider competition law rules setting limits even to the freedom to refrain from the conclusion of a contract.

## Conclusion

*Summary*

As has been shown, long-term contractual relationships and networks of contracts are by no means a matter for contract law only. The longer a contractual relationship lasts and the more contracts of the same kind penetrate the market, the more questions of competition law arise and have to be taken into account. The duration of a contract, i.e. its relational character, as well as the multitude of contracts of the same kind, i.e. their network character, calls for competition law to be considered and to be included in a comprehensive and complete normative appraisal of this type of contractual cooperation. Admittedly, this statement is trivial, but it is simply true. This is not confined to the paradigm of distribution contracts. To almost the same degree, competition influences the contractual law view in the field of just-in-time agreements between assemblers and suppliers on the production level.[23] To a lesser degree, it refers also to networks of long-term contracts of financial leasing. And systems of factoring contracts as well as networks of credit card agreements are governed to a fair extent by rules of competition law.

### *'Network' as a Decidedly Legal Concept of Competition Law*

The term 'network' relating to long-term contracts is not just a sociological and descriptive term. It decidedly denotes a legal concept of competition law, at least a legal concept in a wider sense.[24] It does not, or perhaps not yet, constitute a legal concept in the sense of a precisely defined term with clear factual presuppositions and clear legal consequences. However, it already constitutes for the competition lawyer a notion which turns out to be inevitable for the normative appraisal of competitive practices and particularly of vertical restraints of trade. As we have seen, the network approach in competition law also exerts a remarkable influence on contractual law issues. The reason is simply that contracts are the legal media to organize competition. This can pave the way to develop the network approach towards a legal concept even in a narrower sense. This leads us to the somewhat capricious suggestion that we should perhaps rename our society SECOLA: Society of European Contract and Competition Law.

23 M. Wellenhofer-Klein, *Zulieferverträge im Privat- und Wirtschaftsrecht* (Munich: Beck, 1999); F. Graf von Westphalen and C.-O. Bauer, *Just-in-Time-Lieferungen und Qualitätssicherungsvereinbarungen* (Cologne: Recht Wirtschaft Steuern, 1993); B. Steckler, *Die rechtlichen Risiken der Just-in-Time-Produktion* (Stuttgart: Boorberg, 1996).

24 For the term 'network' denoting a future legal concept cf. J.N. Druey, 'Organisationsnetzwerke: Die "schwebende" Rechtsform', in Amstutz (ed.), n 2 above, 123–49, 148; R.M. Buxbaum, 'Is "Network" a Legal Concept?' 149 *JITE - Journal of Institutional and Theoretical Economics* (1993) 698–705; M. Eisenberg, 'Why there is no Law of Relational Contracts' 94 *Northwestern University Law Review* (2000) 805 *et seq.*

# PART IV
# Knowledge Exchange in Long-Term Contractual Cooperation

# Chapter 8
# Good Faith Related Duties of Disclosure and a View on Franchising

Massimo Bianca

### The Problem of a General Duty of Disclosure Arising from the Good Faith Principle

The first question about duties of disclosure concerns whether there is a common, general rule under European national laws. It would seem that there is not. On the basis of the good faith principle, in continental European countries, duties of disclosure are generally acknowledged. The extension of this acknowledgement, however, is disputed and a general duty of disclosure is not easy to find.[1] However, duties of disclosure have, more or less by way of an extension, been found in a principle which is already present in European contract law. Indeed, the principle of good faith is present in the Directive 1993/13/EC on unfair terms in consumer contracts. According to Article 31, a contractual term shall be regarded as unfair if, contrary to the requirement of good faith, it causes a significant imbalance in the parties' positions to the detriment of the consumer.[2]

Good faith also occurs in the Unidroit Principles of International Commercial Contracts. These state that each party must act in accordance with good faith and fair dealing in international trade (Article 1.7). 'Good faith and fair dealing', it explains, 'may be considered to be one of the fundamental ideas underlying the Principles'. A similar provision is contained in the Lando Principles of European Contract Law (Article 1.106: in exercising his rights and performing his duties each party must act in accordance with good faith and fair dealing). Good faith is also mentioned in the Gandolfi Code Européen des Contrats, which contains an article dealing with 'obligation of good faith' (Article 6). Finally, the Draft Frame

---

1 Even in Germany, the land of Treu und Glaube, according to H. Grigoleit, *Vorverträgliche Informationshaftung*: *Vorsatzdogma, Rechtsfolgen, Schranken* (Munich: Beck, 1997), a general rule to disclose information does not exist.

2 See G.A. Benacchio, 'La buona fede nel diritto comunitario', in L. Garofalo (ed.), *Il ruolo della buona fede oggettiva nell'esperienza giuridica storica e contemporanea, Atti del Convegno internazionale di studio in onore di Alberto Burdese* (Padova: Cedam, 2003) I 189, who recalls other mentions of good faith in other Directives.

of Reference asserts that a person who is engaged in negotiations has a duty to negotiate in accordance with good faith and fair dealing (3.201[3]).

In spite of these favourable signs the good faith principle has raised many objections, particularly from those eminent scholars who would have it that this principle is strange to English law.

One of the difficulties in accepting the principle is apparent in the lack of a sure, common notion of good faith. This difficulty has been pointed out in a paper produced by the British Government at the London SECOLA Convention of 2002. According to the paper, the government was seriously apprehensive about the introduction of the good faith principle, which could raise serious problems, as it is extremely difficult to find an agreement among the member States about the notion of fairness. There are, the paper insists, different notions of fairness depending on different legal systems and traditions. On the other hand, a vague formula would lead to uncertainties in business trading owing to the different notions of good faith assumed by the national courts.[4]

The concern expressed by this paper finds a close parallel in the criticism of many Common Law scholars based primarily on the uncertainty of the concept of good faith. Eminent academics offer no fewer than three different meanings of the good faith principle, giving grounds to doubts about the introduction of such a principle in European law.[5] No fewer functions have been attributed to good faith

3 According to J. Smits, 'Toward a Multi-Layered Contract Law for Europe', in S. Grundmann and J. Stuyck (eds), *An Academic Green Paper on European Contract Law* (The Hague: Kluwer Law International, 2002) 393, various meanings of good faith are also detectable inside the member States owing to the various cultural and ethnic compounds resulting from the immigration phenomenon, so that 'fairness nowadays is a pluralistic concept'. About the different meanings of good faith in the European legal system, see also S. Patti, 'Significato del principio di buona fede e clausole vessatorie: uno sguardo all'Europa', in Garofalo, n 2 above, III 62.

4 H. Collins, *The Law of Contract* (3rd edn, London: Butterworth, 1997) 251, who sees fairness as one of the main contractual concepts, gives three notions of it: 'first, in cases involving the fairness of the price, the criterion is likely to be connected to the market price. Secondly, for challenges to ancillary terms, we discover a combination of the ideas of balance of advantage and conformity to reasonable expectations. Thirdly, in connection with subsequent events which arguably render the contract unfair in its application, the comparison lies with the original balance of advantage at the time when the contract was formed'. Three other meanings of good faith related to performance of the contract are signalled, also by A. Farnsworth, *The Concept of Good Faith in American Law* (Roma: Centro di studi e ricerche di diritto comparato e straniero, 1993) 3.

5 M.H. Whincup, *Contract Law and Practice* (The Hague: Kluwer Law International, 2001) 69, 130: 'It is one of English law's most remarkable characteristics, and one most clearly distinguishing it from its continental and even American counterparts, that it has neither an express requirement of good faith in contracts generally, nor … any principle of common law by which such a general duty be implied'. Whincup, however, concedes that 'this situation may be changing' and that 'a limited good faith obligation has been imported into English law under European Union influence, in the form of the Unfair

in civil law countries, adding perplexities about the role the good faith principle should play in future European Private law.[6]

## In Search of a Specific Meaning of Good Faith in European Community Provisions

The old negative attitude toward good faith in Common Law countries – also expressed in terms of superfluity[7] or neutrality[8] – seems to be changing,[9] if not

Terms in Consumer Contracts Regulations 1999'. On the (divergent) interpretations of the Directive fairness test in United Kingdom and Italy, see P. Nebbia, *Unfair Contract Terms in European Law* (Oxford and Portland/Oregon: Hart, 2007) 143. On the impact of the Directive on the English system, see also L.A. Deflorian, 'L'interazione del diritto inglese con il diritto comunitario: l'esempio della Direttiva sulle clausole abusive nei contratti con i consumatori ed il principio di buona fede' *Rivista di diritto civile* 2002, I 451.

6 See the essay by M.W. Hesselink, 'The Concept of Good Faith', in A. Hartkamp et al. (eds), *Towards a European Civil Code* (3rd edn, Nijmegen: Kluwer, 2004) 471, who recalls the interpretation, supplementation and correcting role ascribed to good faith in conformity of the model of the Papinian definition of ius praetorium (libro secundo definitionum, in D. 1.1.7.1: ius praetorium est, quod praetors introduerunt adiuvandi vel supplendi vel corrigendi iuris civilis gratia propter utilitatem publicam) transposed in the Wieacker's tripartition of good faith functions (F. Wieacker, *Zur rechtstheoretischen Präzisierung des § 242 BGB* [Tübingen: Mohr, 1956]). These functions – in Hessenlink's view – correspond to the tasks of the judge and render good faith a completely open norm, that is 'no norm at all', as it reveals itself as broad as the autonomy of the judges in the application of the law. In this respect 'good faith does not differ much from what English lawyers have experienced with equity'.

7 Instead of trying to introduce a 'general ethical imperative' it is better to find the solutions already offered by the positive law: M. Bridge, 'Good Faith in Commercial Contracts', in R. Brownsword, N. Hird and G. Howells (eds), *Good Faith in Contract. Concept and Context* (Aldershot: Dartmouth, 1999) 131. Observes A. de Vita, 'Buona fede e Common law, attrazione non fatale nella storia del contratto', in Garofalo, n 2 above, I 484: it is rooted in the persuasion that the good faith principle is superfluous in a system 'dotato da tempo di strumenti idonei a far rispettare ai cittadini regole di "fairness, reasonableness and honesty" nell'esercizio della propria autonomia contrattuale'.

8 The 'neutral' position, is portrayed and criticized by R. Brownsword, 'Positive, Negative, Neutral: the Reception of Good Faith in English Law', in Brownsword, Hird and Howells (eds), n 7 above, 21.

9 Having overcome the contestations phase, the good faith notion 'has now become so entrenched in the American legal vocabulary that it is difficult to imagine life, without it': J. Nehf, 'Bad Faith Breach of Contract in Consumer Transactions', in Brownsword, Hird and Howells (eds), n 7 above, 137. In English law J.F. O'Connor, *Good Faith in English Law* (Aldershot: Dartmouth, 1999) 100, points out the operative aspect of good faith referred to in the prevailing community standards.

being rejected outright.[10] In fact, as has been observed above, the good faith principle has already been introduced into European law through the regulation concerning consumer contracts – and in the field of consumer contracts fairness is already a legal concept present in English law (see the 1973 Fair Trading Act and the 1999 Unfair Terms in Consumer Contracts Regulations[11]). It therefore seems necessary to examine the *acquis communautaire* in order to find out what specific notion of good faith is meant in European Community provisions.

The above mentioned 1993 Directive does not give a definition of good faith,[12] but from one of its recitals (the 16th) we apprehend that the seller or supplier must deal with the consumer in a fair and just way taking into account his legitimate interests: 'Whereas the requirement of good faith may be satisfied by the seller or supplier where he deals fairly and equitably with the other party whose legitimate interests he has to take into account'.

This formula – that we find similarly in the continental and English law literature[13] – draws attention to its two elements, 'taking into account' and

10 R. Brownsword, 'Two Concepts of Good Faith' *Journal of Contract Law* 1994, 197: 'English contract law urgently needs an explicit doctrine of good faith to enable it to deal more openly, more rationally, with the many manifestations of bad faith encountered in commercial contracting'. See also A. Mason, 'Contract, Good Faith and Equitable Standards in Fair Dealing' *Law Quarterly Review* 2000, 94: 'recognition of good faith and fair dealing concepts would bring greater coherence and unity to the varied array of principles which are presently available in the area of contract performance'.

11 Nor is a definition given by the Draft Common Frame of Reference. The necessity to make clear what the inclusion in the CFR of general principles such as good faith does mean, is underlined by H. Beale, 'The Future of Common Frame of Reference' *European Review of Contract Law* 2007, 264.

12 Brownsword, n 10 above, 49: 'each party must respect the legitimate interests of the other contracting party (as defined by a co-operative ideal of contracting)'; D. Friedmann, 'Good Faith and Remedies for Breach of Contract', in J. Beatson and D. Friedmann (eds), *Good Faith and Fault in Contract Law* (Oxford: Clarendon, 1995) 400: the contracting party must not behave in a way that 'greatly exceeds that required for the protection of one's legitimate interest or for its legitimate exploitation, where such conduct leads to a disproportionate loss to another party'.

13 On the notion of legitimate interests see H.-W. Micklitz, 'Legitime Erwartungen als Gerechtigkeitsprinzip des europäischen Privatrechts', in L. Krämer, H.-W. Micklitz and K. Tonner (eds), *Law and Diffuse Interests in the European Legal Order, Liber amicorum Norbert Reich* (Baden-Baden: Nomos, 1997) 245, who points out that 'wirkliche Beachtung hat "Treue und Glauben" erst mit der Verabschiedung der Richtlinie 93/13, über missbräuchliche Vertragsklauseln gefunden'. About the 'reasonable expectations' of the parties preserved by the contextual good faith, see J. Wightman, 'Good Faith and Pluralism in the Law of Contract', in Brownsword, Hird and Howells (eds), n 7 above, 41: 'The contextual meaning of good faith derives the content of good faith from the reasonable expectations of the parties. These expectations are based on norms which are widely observed in their contracting community'. According to the Hungarian Civil Code (s 205) – as referred to by N. Reich, 'Transformation of Contract Law and Civil Justice in the new

'legitimate interests'. Legitimate may be envisaged as the interests acknowledged as worthy of protection in the law but also in a broader sense as the reasonably relevant interests.[14] 'Taking into account' indicates a significant difference of good faith duty compared to the contractual obligations, where the debtor's interest is subordinated to the creditor's interest and the obligation has to be fulfilled as far as is possible. Taking into account, instead, means a reasonable respect of the other party's interests as long as it does not substantially impair his own legitimate interests. This notion of good faith principle implies cooperation duties in the performance of the contract and fairness duties in the formation of the contract (procedural fairness).

As provided by the quoted Directive, fairness implies not taking advantage of a stronger contractual position, and not imposing unreasonable conditions to the detriment of the counterpart. How far this duty may be transplanted in the general context of the European contract is an open problem. The problem concerns the control of the content of contracts, and ultimately the relevance of contractual justice in a free market system.[15]

Leaving aside an examination of all the other pre-contractual duties based on good faith,[16] let us have a look at fairness with regard to duty of information. Fairness in the formation of contract implies taking into account the legitimate interests of the counterpart to receive proper information concerning the contract.[17]

---

Member Countries: the Example of the Baltic States, Hungary and Poland', in F. Cafaggi (ed.), *The Institutional Framework of European Private Law* (Oxford: University Press, 2006) 298 – the parties have to cooperate when concluding a contract and take care of the *justified* interests of the other side.

14 M. Mekki and M. Kloepfer-Pelèse, 'Good Faith and Fair Dealing in the DCFR' *European Review of Contract Law* 2008, 338, recall the introduction of the Draft where it is said that 'general clauses like good faith also serve the overarching aim of justice' and add that 'numerous provisions of the DCFR can be regarded as an instrument of justice'.

The possible link of the good faith principle with constitutional values of the European Member States is indicated by A. Colombi Ciacchi, 'The Constitutionalization of European Contract Law: Judicial Convergence and Social Justice' *European Review of Contract Law* 2006, 167, who quotes a decision of the Cassazione (20 April 1994, n 3775, *Giustizia civile* 1994, I 2169), according to which the contractual freedom to unilaterally determine the price of the goods (in that case, mineral water) can be limited by the principle of good faith and fair dealing, to be interpreted in the light of the duty of solidarity under art 2 Italian Constitution.

15 An aspect of information duties concerns the remedies granted to the parties. In this regard V. Roppo, 'L'informazione precontrattuale: spunti di diritto italiano, e prospettive di diritto europeo' 2004, 761, refutes that the problem of remedies is the 'crucial problem' in the regulation of legal information duties.

16 It does not seem that giving information is different from disclosing information. Anyway, see T. Wilhelmsson and C. Twigg-Flesner, 'Pre-contractual Information Duties in the Acquis Communautaire' *European Review of Contract Law* 2006, 447.

17 B. Nicholas, in D. Harris and D. Tallon (eds), *Contract Law Today, Anglo-French Comparisons* (Oxford: Clarendon Press, 1989) 167, and R. Goode, *The Concept of Good*

But here the good faith principle encounters the main objection. This objection is that the principle would compel the contracting parties to give information about factors affecting the value which the deal has for them, i.e. questions of their market chances.

In this context, English scholars quote a passage from Cicero's *De officiis* (3.12), where Cicero describes the imaginary case of the wheat merchant who had the chance to sell his wheat in Rhodes at a very high price due to a famine which was afflicting the island. But the merchant knew that several loads of wheat had been shipped from Alexandria. Should the merchant reveal to the Rhodian customers that the wheat price would drop soon to a normal level and it would be better to wait? For Cicero the answer is a positive one, because – he says – according to natural law (precisely: secundum natura) nobody should take advantage of the other's ignorance.[18]

The English scholars see in Cicero's answer a solution corresponding to the good faith principle ruling in civil law. They point out that in a similar case an English merchant is not obliged to reveal the imminent fall of the price of his goods. These English scholars also refer to similar cases, in order to underline the deep differences between English law and continental codes with regard to good faith and duty of disclosure.

## Need to Determine the Extent of Fairness Related Duty of Disclosure

Exposing the 'classical English position' it has been said that the English system and the French one (i.e. the system of a civil code law country) diverge quite widely in regard to the existence of a general obligation of disclosure.[19] The wideness of this alleged divergence requires verification in the light of a more precise notion of good faith and a more precise extent of the connected duties of disclosure.

---

*Faith in English Law* (Roma: Centro di studi e ricerche di diritto comparato e straniero, 1992) 10 (though in problematic terms).

18 On this passage see L. Solidoro Maruotti, *Gli obblighi di informazione a carico del venditore. Origini storiche e prospettive attuali* (Napoli: Satura, 2007) 20.

19 Nicholas, n 17 above, 187: 'That the two systems diverge quite widely in regard to the existence of a general obligation of disclosure is beyond question'. The divergence of the two systems is also closely examined by P. Legrand Jr, 'Pre-contractual Disclosure and Information: English and French Law Compared' *Oxford Journal of Legal Studies* 1986, 322, who sums up the characters of French law 'as positive (there is an obligation of information), solidarist (a party must share certain knowledge with his co-contractor), and concrete (the status of the parties is what chiefly matters)', while 'English common law remains more negative (one cannot deceive or misrepresent), individualist (every party must acquire the necessary knowledge for himself), and abstract (every party is deemed to have the same ability to see to his interest)'. See also the recent essay by S. van Erp, 'The Pre-contractual Stage', in Hartkamp et al. (eds), n 6 above, 363, who refers to the dispute among Common Law academics about the good faith principle.

If we go back to Cicero's question we can say that the answer is negative not only under English law, but also under civil law, notwithstanding the good faith principle. Good faith does not require information concerning the market chances or economic soundness. In a free market system a contracting party has an appreciable interest in drawing advantage from his contracting ability and from the favourable circumstances of the market. Each party entering into the affair runs the risk of its economic inconvenience. But if the good faith principle does not compel one party to inform the other about the market chances or economic soundness, what kind of information, then, is one party obliged to give to the other party?

The varieties of meanings that may be attached to duties of information[20] require an examination of the extent of these duties beyond the vague terms of a general acknowledgement.[21]

As a preliminary, it may be observed that information asymmetries linked with an unequal contracting power of the parties can give way to market failures and justify the enactment of more or less pervasive mandatory rules.[22] In the absence of mandatory rules a problem of good faith related duties of disclosure occurs only when the information asymmetry – occasional or inherent in the parties' positions – concerns the goods and services that are the subject of the contract and elements relevant for its conclusion.

Proceeding with regard to the elements relevant to the conclusion of the contract, we may first recognize that each party must inform the other about the causes that

20 The variety of the purposes pursued by information is pointed out by Wilhelmsson and Twigg-Flesner, n 16 above, 441: 'one may distinguish at least five main purposes of information' (duty to protect the real consent of the party, to provide equipment for rational market behaviour, and so on).

21 The importance of information in modern contract law is stressed by S. Grundmann, 'The Structure of the DCFR – Which Approach for Today's Contract Law?' *European Review of Contract Law* 2008, 238, who, looking critically at the Draft provisions on information, rightly observes that 'if really the informational basis is as important as submitted here, what could have been expected is a more thorough endeavour than transcribing the *acquis* and adding a general clause which does not really add a lot'. Grundmann points out that a regime on formation of contract is changed by modern phenomena such as publicity, aggressive marketing techniques, etc'.

22 P. Sirena, 'L'integrazione del diritto dei consumatori nella disciplina generale del contratto' *Rivista di diritto civile* 2004, I 805, notes that, while market failures also give grounds to legislative interventions in business relations, the indiscriminate removal of every information asymmetry in business-to-business contracts could result in a collective prejudice. On this point S. Grundmann, 'La struttura europea dei contratti' *Rivista di diritto civile* 2002, I 395, notes that with a certain generalization it is possible to say that taking advantage of information asymmetry is the main incentive to create valuable economic information. S. Grundmann, 'L'autonomia privata nel mercato interno: le regole d'informazione come strumento' *Europa e diritto privato* 2001, 276, points out that problems arise only from information asymmetries which a party is not able to remove or whose removal exacts prohibitive costs: only these information asymmetries lead to a market failure and ask for a rebalancing of the parties' positions.

render the contract void or ineffective. A specific provision in that sense is dictated by the Italian civil code (Article 1338). But even without a specific provision such duty takes place according to good faith as every party has a legitimate interest to enter into a valid and effective contract and to be informed about causes of voiding or ineffectiveness that the other party knows or should know.

With regard to duties of disclosure we must distinguish between goods and services. A broad duty of disclosure is here provided by the Draft Common Frame of Reference. This mentions the business's duty to disclose information about goods and services (3.101) and duties specific to the business's marketing goods or services to consumers. The information comprises the main characteristics of the goods or services, the identity and address, if relevant, of the business, and so on (3–102).[23] This provides such material information as the average consumer needs in the given context to make an informed decision whether to conclude a contract.

However, outside the consumer contracts field, it does not seem correct to envisage a general duty to provide information about the characteristics of the goods or the services. While it is in the interest of the seller or the supplier to stress the qualities of the goods or the services, their reticence should not entail any liability unless in the case of fraudulent silence.[24]

The seller or the supplier, instead, must surely disclose the latent defects of the goods or the services and not give false information about their qualities. Failure to disclose latent defects and assumption of false qualities concern the content of the contract and may lead to remedies for non-conformity of the goods or the services to the contract. The seller and the supplier must also inform of any potential for harm in the goods or the services. Risk of harm or danger may lead to remedies for non-conformity of the contract (lack of safety qualities of the goods) or to tort liabilities.

Failure of duty to disclose assumes a specific importance when, though the goods or the services do conform with the contract, the legitimate expectations of the party have not been taken into account. The problem here is to find out if it is possible to acknowledge legitimate expectations which do not enter into the content of the contract. What if, for instance, the customer lets the seller know the specific purpose he is buying the goods for? According to the Directive on sale of consumer goods (1999, 44, EC) the seller has to deliver goods fit for the particular

23 To provide consumers with information about products and services is a central element of European consumer policy: G. Howells, 'Consumer Concepts for a European Code?', in R. Schulze (ed.), *New Features in Contract Law* (Munich: Sellier, 2007) 119.

24 On the 'misleading omission' provision (art 7(1)) contained in the Unfair Commercial Practices Directive (2005/29), see H. Collins, 'The Unfair Commercial Practices Directive' *European Review of Contract Law* 2005, 433. See also the critical remarks of F. Gomez, 'The Unfair Commercial Practices Directive: a Law and Economics Perspective' *European Review of Contract Law* 2006, 23, who among others, stresses the often overlooked problems of information overload.

purpose the buyer has made known to the seller and which the seller has accepted (Article $2^2$ b).

When the seller has not promised that special fitness of the goods, there is no breach of contract, but by selling the goods he has not taken into account the buyer's expectation, which is legitimate, because the buyer who informs the seller of the purpose for which he is buying the goods can reasonably expect that the goods are fit for that purpose. According to Italian law, in this case, the buyer is entitled to receive goods fit for the specific purpose even if the seller has not expressly promised that fitness. If – according to the Directive – we exclude that in this case the lack of specific fitness is a breach of contract, we must admit that the seller has violated the duty of good faith. More generally, we must admit that if a party informs the other about the purpose for which he intends to acquire the goods or the services, the seller or the supplier must let him know that the goods or the services are not fit for that purpose. A duty of disclosure concerning the lack of fitness of the negotiated goods and services does not endanger the certainty of contracts because the duty is related to what the customer publicly declared as his goal or concrete planned use.

The reticence of English scholars on this point is not so sure. In a case referred by Nicholas, a customer had ordered an electrical system for a certain purpose, but the system resulted in not being fit for that purpose. Nicholas does not doubt that the customer should have been informed of the unsuitability of the system.[25]

The good faith principle, instead, does not go so far as to enforce warning the counterpart about future events related to the goods or the services. A cheaper price asked by other sellers, a new technology that is expected to render the service obsolete and so on, these fall within the risks that affect the convenience of the affair and are therefore outside the good faith disclosure duty.

Leaving the convenience of the affair outside the duty of disclosure is one absolute condition of coexistence of this duty with the canons of a system based on freedom of contract and freedom of competition.[26] In short, good faith requires the party to disclose causes for invalidity of the contract, defects of goods or services, the absence or presence of attributes which render the goods or services non-compliant with the legitimate expectations of the other party. It does not require the disclosure of elements concerning the economic convenience of the affair.[27]

---

25 Provided a gap between English law and other European legal systems exists, it would be necessary to verify how wide this gap is, comparing the courts practices. In this regard the comparative approach is carried out by R. Zimmermann and S. Whittaker (eds), *Good Faith in European Contract Law* (Cambridge: University Press, 2000).

26 According to B. Lurger, 'The Future of European Contract Law between Freedom of Contract, Social Justice and Market Rationality' *European Review of Contract Law* 2005, 442, it is still unclear as to the position of EU law, and where to draw the line between the conflicting principles of contractual freedom and regard and fairness.

27 V. De Lorenzi, 'Correttezza e diligenza precontrattuale: il problema economico' *Rivista di diritto civile* 1999, I 675, correctly writes: 'fairness does not impose an unlimited

It can be acknowledged, in these terms, that good faith related duties of disclosure do not jeopardize the free market system.[28] In fact, they leave the parties free to determine the content of the contracts and let each one exploit their knowledge of the favourable chances of the market. On the other hand they meet a primary need of a free market system. A free market system, indeed, needs primarily reliable contractual relations and reliability is firstly ensured when the contracts rely on the informed consent of the parties.

## Franchise as a Benchmark of Duties of Disclosure Required in Information Asymmetry Relations: The Unidroit Model

The problem of duty of disclosure claims particular attention in the field of long-term contracts, where the parties need to know which factors may affect the future development of their relationship in order to value the affair properly. In this respect franchising is an interesting benchmark. Although franchising is not a consumer contract, it offers a typical situation of information asymmetry.

This example, born out of the growing area of distribution contracts, has taken shape in models worked out in deontological guides,[29] in standard forms and schemes elaborated by international bodies,[30] and in legislative regulation enacted by some States.[31] These models present a core of similar patterns and striking characteristics, dealing mainly with the disclosure aspects of the transaction.

The most complete model, that approved by Unidroit, has been presented as the 'Unidroit Model Franchise Disclosure' (enacted 25 February 2002). The preamble of the document points out the need for state legislators to consider 'whether prospective investors are more likely to protect themselves against fraud

---

disclosure duty ... it does not concern circumstances inessential to the contract ... the market trend, the convenience of the affair, the own speculative aims'.

28 B. Fages, 'Pre-contractual Duties in the Draft Common Frame of Reference – What Relevance of the Negotiation of Commercial Contracts?' *European Review of Contract Law* 2008, 304, criticizes the provisions of the Draft concerning a general disclosure duty affirming that 'it is a pity that certain pre-contractual duties take a priority over the freedom of negotiation which, in commercial transactions, is and will remain predominant. Liberty first, duties second'. But – he admits – 'the duty of good faith is of great importance in business practice ... it does not play against but in favour of legal security and economic efficiency of contracts'.

See also the critical remarks of Legrand, n 19 above, 342.

29 See the codes of ethics edited by the European Franchising Association and the Associazione Italiana del Franchising (reported by M. Cian, *Nuove leggi civili commentate* 2004, 1183).

30 See, for instance, the *Model International Franchising Contracts* edited by the International Chamber of Commerce. See also the guidelines and the standard form set out by J. Pratt, *Franchising. Law and Practice* (London: Sweet & Maxwell, 1991) 9.001.

31 See, for instance, the Spanish Real decreto 2485/1998, of 13 November 1998.

if they have access to truthful, important information in advance of their assent to any franchise agreement; whether the nation's economic and social interests are best served by legally requiring a balance of information between the parties to a franchise agreement'.

The Unidroit model is the most exhaustive and can be taken as a reference point in the examination of the kind of information that parties may be requested to give and of how far the duties of disclosure can be extended when a business-to-business contract presents an imbalanced position regarding parties' information, analogous to the imbalanced position which characterizes consumer contracts.

The Unidroit model shows a set of items of information concerning the content of the contract, such as the terms and conditions of the renewal of the franchise, the extent of exclusive rights to be granted, the initial franchise fee, and so on (Article 6.2). Other rules require the description of the franchisor's intellectual property to be licensed to the franchisee and the categories of goods or services that the franchisee has to purchase or lease (Article 6.1).

In every transaction it is in the parties' interest to specify the rights arising from the contract, but they need only determine the substantial points of the affair. The Unidroit document, instead, imposes a detailed specification of all the aspects of the franchise agreement and requires the franchisor to inform (in a disclosure document) the prospective franchisee about the content of the contract in advance.

A second broad set of items of information concerns elements related to the contract but not intended to enter into its content. These items include the professional experience of the franchisor and his affiliates, any criminal convictions and civil actions against the franchisor and his affiliates involving franchises or businesses or relating to fraud, misrepresentation, etc, any bankruptcy proceedings, the number of franchisees and company-owned outlets of the franchisor, and so on.[32] Furthermore, the franchisor must inform the prospective franchisee about the state of the general and local market of the products or services that are the subject of the contract (Article 6.1).

The information required by the Unidroit model generally exceeds the range of information that, according to the good faith principle, has to be given in commercial transactions. But even with respect to franchising the Unidroit model goes too far in asking the franchisor to inform the franchisee about the state and the prospects of the general and local market. This information is directly related to evaluations of market chances which should fall into the realm of responsibility of each contracting party.

32 In case of a subfranchise (authorized by a master franchise) the subfranchisor's disclosure duties also concern the franchisor and the masterfranchise (art 6.3).

## Italian Franchise Law

Italian franchise law[33] follows the Unidroit model requiring the franchisor to deliver in advance the text of the contract and a list of elements related to the contract (data concerning the franchisor, description of the trademarks, etc) (Article 4). No mention is made, instead, about duty of information concerning the state and prospects of the market.

Apart from the specific items included in the disclosure lists, Italian law provides a basis for the franchisor's pre-contractual duty to give every piece of information that the prospective franchisee thinks necessary or useful regarding the contract.[34] The prospective franchisee must give any piece of news concerning the affair even if the counterpart does not make a specific request (Article $6^3$). Also, in this case, as it seems, the duty of information depends on a request by the other party, though not expressly formulated. A different opinion, on this point,[35] leads to the unreasonable result that it renders the position of the weaker party more burdensome than that of the stronger party.

The franchisor's duty of disclosure, relating to the goods and the services that are the subject of the contract, deals with what is necessary to value their entity, nature and usefulness. Furthermore, it should involve those aspects and circumstances that affect the duration of the contract as the expected end of the production of the goods. The franchisee, indeed, is entitled to know how long he may profitably avail himself of the franchisor's goods. This is because this contract requires a minimum duration in order to let the franchisee recover the investment cost. This legitimate expectation of the franchisee is well expressed in Italian franchise law, which requires the franchisor to guarantee a contract length sufficient for the franchisee to amortize the investment (at least three years).

The special duties of information imposed on the franchisor or vice versa regarding only items indirectly related to the contract, such as previous bankruptcy proceedings, do not take place outside that contract and do not seem susceptible to generalization, as they would excessively burden the commercial trade.

The imposition of a duty of disclosure regarding the economic convenience of the affair would more openly conflict with commercial practice. Even in the presence of an information asymmetry each party has to autonomously value

---

33 Legge sull'affiliazione commerciale, n 128, 6 May 2004.

34 According to G. Zuddas, *Somministrazione, concessione di vendita, franchising* (Torino: Ciappichelli, 2003) 309, the franchisor could not refrain from illustrating the possible developments of the financial-economic situation. Likewise, A. Frignani, *Il franchising* (Torino: Ciappichelli, 1999) 63.

35 According to A. Di Biase, 'La violazione degli obblighi di disclosure nel contratto di franchising e l'abuso di dipendenza economica' *Europa e diritto privato* 2007, 812, the prospective franchisee should give any useful information, regardless (a prescindere) of requests from the franchisor.

the economic risks of the transaction, according to a fundamental rule of the free market.

## Remedies in the Unidroit Model

A duty of disclosure implies a correlating right of the other party to be informed. A right calls for a sort of protection in law, a convenient remedy in case of its infringement. The Unidroit model grants remedies of damages and termination. According to this model the franchisee may terminate the franchise agreement and claim damages when the franchisor has not delivered the disclosure document at least 14 days before the signing of the contract, and in cases of misrepresentation or omission of a material fact (Article 8.1).

The model excludes termination when it appears to be a *disproportionate* remedy. Termination may be seen as a disproportionate remedy when the missing disclosure document would have probably not influenced the franchisee's decision to enter into the contract. The same idea is expressed by the disposition which provides the franchisee's right to terminate only in cases of misrepresentations and omissions concerning *material* facts. According to the Unidroit definition (Article 2), material fact refers to information that can reasonably be expected to have a *significant* effect on the franchisee's decision to acquire the franchise.

## Remedies Under Italian Law

Italian franchise law has not followed the Unidroit model in providing a right to termination. A lone rule establishes that in cases of false information the party may void the contract in accordance with the civil code disposition regarding fraud in the formation of the contract (Article 1439), plus damages (Article 8).

In the absence of a special provision, the mere lack of information may entitle the franchisee to void the contract in cases of fraudulent silence or a fundamental mistake.[36] Under the general rules of contract, it is instead questionable to envisage the voiding of the franchise agreement as a straight effect of duty of disclosure violations.[37]

According to the Italian civil code, voiding occurs when the contract is contrary to a mandatory rule (Article $1418^1$).[38] Violation of the duties of disclosure imposed

36 See art 1428 of the Italian civil code on the 'errore essenziale'. European Contract Law Principles specifically provide the fundamental mistake 'caused by information given by the other party' (art 4.103).

37 The only remedy of damages is envisaged by D. Valentino, *Obblighi di informazione, contenuto e forma negoziale* (Napoli, 1999) 242.

38 On the interpretation problem arising from this disposition about 'virtual' voidness see M. Rabitti, *Contratto illecito e norma penale* (Milano: Giuffrè, 1999) 49.

on the franchisor amounts to a mandatory rule violation. But the Cassazione denies that the violation of disclosure duties invalidates the contract. The Cassazione, indeed, holds firm the distinction between behaviour rules, involving only pre-contractual liabilities, and rules concerning the validity of the contract.[39] This distinction is not so clearly defined, considering the 'contamination' of behaviour and validity rules introduced by several European and national dispositions.[40] Besides, one must take into account the possible understanding of duties of disclosure rules as forbidding a contract with a not previously informed party.[41] However, it is difficult to admit the voiding of the franchise agreement in cases concerning lack of information.[42]

39 See Cassazione, Sezioni Unite, 19 December 2007, n 26724, *Nuova giurisprudenza civile* 2008, I 432, with comment by U. Salanitro, and in *Danno e responsabilità*, 2008, 525, with comment by Roppo and Bonaccorsi. On this *sentenza* see, ia, D. Achille, 'Contratto d'intermediazione finanziaria e violazione degli obblighi d'informazione: tra nullità del contratto e responsabilità dell'intermediario' *Rivista trimestrale di diritto e procedura civile* 2008, 1451, and M. Maugeri, 'Pratiche commerciali scorrette e disciplina generale dei contratti', in A. Genovese (ed.), *I decreti legislativi sulle pratiche commerciali scorrette. Attuazione e impatto sistematico della Direttiva* 2005/29/CE (Padova: Cedam, 2008) 273. On the open problem whether good faith and other behaviour duties may affect the validity of the contract, see, among several authors, F.D. Busnelli, 'Note in tema di buona fede ed equità' *Rivista di diritto civile* 2001, I 537; L. Bigliazzi Geri, 'Buona fede nel diritto civile', in R. Sacco (ed.), *Digesto delle discipline privatistiche, Sezione civile*, II (Torino: Utet Giuridica, 1988) 170; G. D'Amico, 'Regole di validità e regole di comportamento nella formazione del contratto' *Rivista di diritto civile* 2002, I 37; De Lorenzi, n 27 above, 581. Among the last contributors see also A. Gnani, 'Contrarietà a buona fede e invalidità del contratto: spunti ricostruttivi' *Rivista di diritto civile* 2009, II 435.

40 See V. Scalisi, 'Il diritto europeo dei rimedi: invalidità e inefficacia' *Rivista di diritto civile* 2007, I 843, and E. Pellecchia, *Scelte contrattuali e informazioni personali* (Torino: Ciappichelli, 2005) 175.

41 On the problem of the remedies available in cases of duty of disclosure violations, moving from the field of investment financial contracts, see G. Alpa, 'Gli obblighi informatiie precontrattuali nei contratti di investimento finanziario. Per l'armonizzazione dei modelli regolatori e per l'uniformazione delle regole di diritto comune' *Contratto e impresa* 2008, 889.

42 The authors are generally contrary to or do not take into account the hypothesis of the voiding remedy: see L. Guerrini, 'Sulla violazione degli obblighi di informazione in materia di affiliazione commerciale' *Contratto e impresa* 2005, 1263; F. Toschi Vespasiani, 'Prime note di commento alla l 6 maggio 2004, n 129, recante norme per la disciplina del contratto di affiliazione commerciale o franchising' *Studium iuris* 2004, 1350. In order not to leave the franchisee's rights without defence, Cian, n 29 above, 1171, looks out for a possible granting to the franchisee of the cooling-off period even after the conclusion of the contract. The need to *invent* proper solutions in favour of the franchisee in underlined by G. Magri, 'Precetti e sanzioni nella nuova disciplina dell'affiliazione commerciale' *Giurisprudenza italiana* 2006, 2214.

The franchisee's right to repudiate an agreement based on uninformed consent appears reasonable as a remedy, and in tune with the protection of franchisee policy. But Italian franchise law precludes this interpretation as it endows the franchisee with the right to obtain from the court the annulment of the contract in cases of fraudulent false information (Article 8).[43] On the grounds of the coherence canon this provision excludes that the mere lack or inexactness of information should involve *ex se* the radical voiding of the franchise agreement.

Leaving aside the problem of the kind of answers that the category of asymmetric contracts awaits in future European contract law,[44] it may be noted that specific grounds for voiding the franchise can be the abuse of economic dependence. The abuse of economic dependence is forbidden by the Italian industrial subcontracting law, which declares the voiding of the contract or the clause through which that abuse is realized.[45] The rule is expressed in general terms,[46] legitimating the opinion that considers it a rule governing the transactions where a party has the control of the contract.[47]

An abuse of a dominant position may surely be envisaged in the franchisor's behaviour.[48] But an economically dominant position does not simply mean the possession of more knowledge. It means, rather, the economic power to dictate the contract conditions.[49] The abuse of the franchisor's position, therefore, does not consist in taking advantage of an information superiority but in imposing

43 V. Roppo, 'L'informazione precontrattuale', in P. Sirena (ed.), *Il diritto europeo dei contratti d'impresa. Autonomia negoziale dei privati e regolazione del mercato* (Milano: Giuffrè, 2005) 147, criticises Italian franchise law, as the only disposition concerning remedies is a mere recall of an article of the civil code (art 1439).

44 See V. Roppo, 'From Consumer Contracts to Asymmetric Contracts: a Trend in European Contract Law?' *European Review of Contract Law* 2009, 304.

45 Art $9^3$, law n 192, 18 June 1998. On the problem of the application range of the disposition see, ao, E. Navarretta, 'I contratti d'impresa e il principio di buona fede', in Sirena (ed.), n 43 above, 518.

46 Art $9^1$: E' vietato l'abuso da parte di una o più imprese dello stato di dipendenza economica nel quale si trova, nei suoi o nei riguardi di una impresa cliente o fornitrice.

47 On the submitting of a franchise to subcontracting law, see L. Delli Priscoli, *Franchising e tutela dell'affiliato* (Milano: Giuffrè, 2000) 125, and Di Biase, n 35 above, 826.

48 On the possible franchisor's abuses, see Delli Priscoli, n 47 above, 40, 117; F. Macario, 'L'abuso dell'autonoma negoziale nei contratti tra imprenditori', in Sirena (ed.), n 47 above, 227; B. Goodwin, 'Franchising in the economy: the franchise agreement as a security under securities acts, including 10 b-5 considerations', *Il Diritto negli scambi internazionali* 1969, 215.

49 On the notion of abuse of economic dependence see, ao, L. Delli Priscoli, 'L'abuso di dipendenza economica nella nuova legge sulla subfornitura, rapporti con la disciplina delle clausole abusive e con la legge antitrust' *Giurisprudenza commerciale* 1998, I 833; S. Pagliantini, 'L'abuso di dipendenza economica', in G. Vettori (ed.), *Squilibrio e usura nei contratti* (Padova: Cedam, 2002) 455; F. Prosperi, *Il contratto di subfornitura e l'abuso di dipendenza economica* (Napoli: Edizioni Scientifiche Italiane, 2002) 267; A. Barba, in V. Cuffaro (ed.), *La subfornitura nelle attività produttive* (Napoli, 1998) 297.

unfavourable conditions on the franchisee:[50] that is to say, we are dealing here with the different matter of the abusiveness of the contract (51).[51]

50 The principle concerning abuse of economic dependence requires the party not to take advantage of its strong position in determining the content of the contract: F. Prosperi, 'Subfornitura industriale, abuso di dipendenza economica e tutela del contraente debole: i nuovi orizzonti della buona fede contrattuale' *Rassegna di diritto civile* 1999, 669.

51 E. Gabrielli, 'Sulla nozione di consumatore' *Rivista trimestrale di diritto e procedura civile* 2003, 1170, observes that the informative contractual weakness, which claims the protection of the 'profane' party, is to be distinguished from contractual economic weakness: the contractual economic weakness that we can find in some business contracts, as in subcontracting relations, requires other remedies than disclosure duties.

# Chapter 9
# Trade Secrets vs Skill and Knowledge

Aurea Suñol

## Introduction

Rational exploitation of secret information and the maximization of the competitive advantage it provides to the owner requires sharing it with other owners. This is especially the case in employment relationships, where employees acquire knowledge of many trade secrets belonging to their employer in their capacity as employees. But this is also the case in other contractual relationships, such as licensing, where contract partners have access to a great deal of secret information about a process or product. This is the case too for contracting partners in collaborative arrangements (hereinafter 'other contract partners'): suppliers who must receive secret specifications given by the customer on a regular basis; and, of course, commercial agents, franchisees and other links in the down-side distribution chain.

As we shall see, the majority of legal systems impose obligations on all the above mentioned parties to maintain the secrecy of the information received or otherwise acquired through their position either during their contract or after the contract has expired. Closely related to such obligation, legal systems ban and sanction misappropriation of trade secrets, which include disclosure or use of trade secrets acquired under circumstances giving rise a duty to maintain its secrecy or limit its use without the express or implied consent of the holder. At the international level the most important legal text concerning trade secrets protection is the international Agreement on Trade-Related Aspects of Intellectual Property Rights (hereinafter, TRIPS). This is signed by, among others, the European Community and the Member States of the EU. For the first time, it specifically establishes, in its Article 39, a minimum standard of protection for the so-called 'undisclosed information', that is to say, trade secrets.

However, every employee and other party in collaborative arrangements with an entrepreneur possesses a personal stock of knowledge and ability (the so-called, '*skill and knowledge*'), which they are free to use after the termination of the contract. The main problem here is, of course, how to draw the line between the ordinary stock of acquired knowledge and skill, which contract partners are free to use after the termination of the contract, and the principal's trade secrets, which they are forbidden from using, for their own purposes after the contract expires. Moreover, may those people be prevented, under a specific circumstance, from misusing certain information gained during the contract that qualifies as trade secrets?

This chapter aims at answering this set of questions and it is structured as follows: after briefly presenting the policies underlying trade secret protection, I will examine the basic components of the notion of trade secrets in the second section. Then, in the third section, I will analyze the criteria by which a duty to maintain secrecy or to limit its use, either during the contract or after the contract expires, arises when employees and other contract parties acquire trade secrets (see fourth section on duty of confidentiality and collaborative arrangements). In the fourth section, I will present the core analysis of the chapter, the principles that will allow us to identify the information and abilities that should count as part of the 'skill and knowledge'. Following this section, I will consider whether explicit non-competition clauses are a useful and valid instrument to prevent former employees or contract parties from using their 'skill and knowledge'. Finally, the chapter deals with one of the most complex situations related to imminent use or disclosure of the principal's trade secrets by the above parties (see final section).

## Policies Underlying Trade Secret Protection

There is a clear lack of consensus concerning the reasons underlying trade secret protection. Nonetheless, the main lines of reasoning focus on two ideas that have been addressed alternatively or cumulatively. The first idea is based on trade secret protection seeks to impose a minimum standard of best trade practices – which are commonly identified with commercial ethics or morals – as a means to ensure fair competition on the market. The second idea focuses on the need to safeguard trade secret protection as an indispensable driving force for creating new socially worthy information and likewise places emphasis on ensuring that innovative endeavours will not be thwarted by certain actions enabling other parties to gain access to or use confidential information.

It is this author's understanding that the latter idea is precisely the fundamental reason justifying trade secret protection, though not the only reason. Indeed, trade secret protection is an essential means for avoiding sub-optimal investment in R&D. It is also crucial to encourage the creation of information given that the holder is not deprived of the chance to reap the supra-competitive benefits resulting from the outcomes of their own merit or endeavours – regardless of the nature thereof – whereby these are understood to be the holder's own activity rather than actual resources, such as cost or time – which are needed to justify the decision to innovate. At the same time, trade secret protection encourage trade secret holders to devote fewer means to setting up physical security measures to maintain its secrecy. This is so, because, as the costs and potential risks brought about by the acquisition of such secrets increase, at least some potential infringers are discouraged from investing in unlawful acquisition, which in turn means that the holder finds it less necessary to invest in hugely expensive measures to protect such secrets.[1] Accordingly, from this standpoint trade secret protection reduces socially unnecessary costs (brought about by the game of precaution-acquisition) and likewise enables the holder to focus their resources on R&D and the creation of subsequent information.

However, as mentioned at the beginning, for secret information to be shared and used to an optimal extent it is logically necessary for the holder to be able to share it with other parties (employees and managers, external contributors, customers, partners on joint ventures, companies that can finance its implementation, etc) without the worry that those parties will take advantage of or allow third parties to unlawfully take advantage of said information, thus destroying its value. Otherwise, operators will tend to hoard the information and reorganize their business in a less efficient way (for instance, increasing salaries to prevent staff from fleeing, distributing positions so that they are given less information, avoiding subcontracting and outsourcing and ensuring that business tasks are carried out within the company, etc), restricting its transfer to third parties (for instance, by means of licenses, joint ventures) or even preventing its disclosure (for instance, during pre-contractual dealings) and, in short, making it impossible to maximize the benefits brought about by any information. This is the very motive that makes it possible to say that trade secret protection, no matter how paradoxical it may appear, also encourages the circulation of secret information, making the holder more likely to share it with other parties, thereby assuring it is used in a more efficient manner, in economic terms.[2]

## The Basic Components of the Notion of Trade Secrets

Article 39.2 of the TRIPS touches on the definition of a trade secret in mentioning a set of requirements[3] that essentially coincide with those set out in several US

1 See among authors who uphold that legal trade secret protection against (unlawful) acquisition reduces the costs of the precaution/theft game, D.D. Friedman, W.M. Landes and R.A. Posner 'Some Economics of Trade Secret Law' *The Journal of Economic Perspectives* 5 (1991) 67–9, W.M. Landes and R.A. Posner, 'The Economics of Trade Secrecy Law', in idem, *The Economic Structure of Intellectual Property Law* (Cambridge/Mass and London: The Belknap Press of Harvard University Press, 2003) 365–7. In line with the fact that trade secret protection is a good substitute for (ineffective) investment in protection measures the holder of the secret would otherwise adopt, M.A. Lemley, 'The Surprising Virtues of Treating Trade Secrets as IP Rights' (June 2008) *Stanford Law and Economics Olin Working Paper* No 358, available at SSRN: http://ssrn.com/abstract=1155167, 31–2. Along these lines, though following another argument, V. Chiappeta, 'Myth, Chameleon or Intellectual Property Olympian? A Normative Framework Supporting Trade Secret Law' 8 *Georg Mason Law Review* 1999, 109–14.

2 Accordingly, Lemley, *supra* n 2, 3 and 29–35.

3 See art 39.2 TRIPS: 'Natural and legal persons shall have the possibility of preventing information lawfully within their control from being disclosed to, acquired

texts in order for information to qualify as a trade secret.[4] Specifically, these requirements can be summed up as follows: the *first* states that the subject matter involved must be information and, to be precise, business information. The *second* requirement stipulates that this information must be, of course, secret. The *third* stipulation is for the secret knowledge to have a commercial value – i.e. competitive value. And last, the *fourth* requirement is for the holder to have adopted reasonable measures to maintain its secrecy.

Nonetheless, although these legal requirements have gone a long way to clarifying the essential traits of the notion of a trade secret, the essence of it still remains unclear. This is because the definition has been founded on several requirements, the application of which calls for a substantial effort in terms of interpretation. This goes to show that the trade secret, as demonstrated, 'is one of the most elusive concepts',[5] and because of this, one of the most difficult concepts to define. As a result, to be able to give a more specific definition to this notion than the one sketched until now, it is first necessary to give a general overview of the specific meaning of the required elements which, according to Article 39.2 of the TRIPS, information must satisfy to qualify as a trade secret. I will address this goal in the following four sections.

### *Information Related to Business*

As mentioned, the first requirement set out in Article 39.2 of the TRIPS for certain knowledge to be qualified as a trade secret is to be deemed as information and, specifically, information related to business.

---

by, or used by others without their consent in a manner contrary to honest commercial practices so long as such information: (a) is secret in the sense that it is not, as a body or in the precise configuration and assembly of its components, generally known among or readily accessible to persons within the circles that normally deal with the kind of information in question; (b) has commercial value because it is secret; and (c) has been subject to reasonable steps under the circumstances, by the person lawfully in control of the information, to keep it secret'. 'For the purpose of this provision, "a manner contrary to honest commercial practices" shall mean at least practices such as breach of contract, breach of confidence and inducement to breach, and includes the acquisition of undisclosed information by third parties who knew, or were grossly negligent in failing to know, that such practices were involved in the acquisition'.

4 See, § 1(4) *Uniform Trade Secrets Act* (UTSA), 14 ULA 539–40 (Commissioner's Prefatory Note) (1980), a model legislation drafted by the National Conference of Commissioners on Uniform State Laws. Forty-one states have enacted various statutes modelled after the USTA; § 1839(3) of the *Economic Espionage Act*, Publ L n 104–294, 18 USC, 1831–1839 (Supp V 1999), 18 USC, 31 670 (1996), and § 39 of the *Restatement* (*third*) *of Unfair Competition*, American Law Institute Publishers, St Paul, 1995, 407 to 527.

5 See, making this statement, *Lear Siegler Inc* v *Ark-Ell Springs Inc*, 569 F2d 286, 288 (5th Cir 1978).

According to the first premise it is useful to bear in mind that the subjective and intrinsic qualities and skills of a subject (i.e. the ability to carry out a specific activity, manual skills, professional expertise), can not be strictly classified as information and, accordingly, cannot be eligible subject matter for a trade secret, inasmuch as they cannot be formalized and, as such, cannot be conveyed. Moreover, the secret is the very immaterial element (information) and not the tangible medium (textual expressions, tapes, disks, diskettes, sketches, photographs, etc) on which the information is contained; therefore, for it to be protected it does not matter whether or not it is fixed in a tangible medium. Along these lines, from another standpoint, it should be kept in mind that the simple fact of being able to gain access to a trade secret information by no means rules out the possibility that its acquisition and, if applicable, its subsequent disclosure or use, may be deemed unlawful.

According to the second premise, it should be pointed out that any information regarding an element related to the company may be considered a trade secret. This is true whether the information has to do with the technical and production divisions of a company (formulae, manufacturing methods or processes, designs, information regarding the optimization, organization or maintenance of a product, a process or industrial facility, the products themselves as well as the specifications for their manufacture, the results of research or analyses, etc) or whether it concerns the commercial, organizational, financial or other spheres of the company (business, marketing and new product development plans and strategies, information on clients and suppliers and, specifically, their identities, purchasing habits, addresses, prices, information regarding the techniques or ways of organizing business activities, production costs and the calculation thereof, sources of funding, market strategies and studies, business methods, etc).

### *The Secret Nature of Information*

The next requirement for certain information to be deemed a trade secret is of course, as per Article 39.2 of the TRIPS, for it to be secret. Simply stated, the information must not be in the public domain. The confidential status of information is really the basic foundation underpinning the entire trade secret protection system, because its value lies in this element, as this chapter will try to show.

Even so, this aspect, i.e. whether specific information shall be deemed as secret, is not as easy to determine as it would initially appear. Courts and scholars have offered several approaches that illustrate how difficult this task is.

Article 39.2 of the TRIPS lays down two criteria along these lines: firstly, the information must not be generally known; and secondly, it must not be readily available to interested third parties. In our view, this latter criterion is the only pertinent one to determine when an information is indeed secret because the first – requiring that the information not be generally known – brings about two major drawbacks: the *first* is the difficulty in drawing the line, because those who support this approach must back the opinion that information loses its secret nature at an intermediate point which is somewhat blurry and falls between absolute secrecy and the complete opposite, that is for it to be known by all. Needless to say, such a point is difficult to define. The *second* drawback, intimately linked to the first, is that under that criterion the secret nature of knowledge depends on a numerical judgment that is not easy to defend. The reason is simple: the deciding factor along these lines is not for the information to be unfamiliar to a reduced quantity of people, but rather for it to be ignored and, accordingly, of value to someone. There are at least three reasons backing this argument.

Firstly, trade secret protection does not require the information to have merely one holder; rather, as often occurs, it is perfectly feasible for several entrepreneurs to have independently created the same information which, if kept by them in a confidential manner, enables it to be deemed as secret. Secondly, the information which is familiar to most of the interested parties but unknown by some of them has value for its holder with respect to a specific competitor. Furthermore, the advantages an operator can get by keeping information secret do not necessarily stem from hiding it from current competitors (who may also be familiar with it); rather, this advantage may be due to the fact that potential competitors are unaware of such information. Lastly, the secret may relate not so much to the content of the information itself, which may generally be known (for instance, the ingredients used to prepare a specific product), but to the fact that competitors ignore that this information is being used by a specific operator or are unaware of the significance of the vital importance it has for his activities.

Accordingly, it is necessary to reinterpret the first criteria of Article 39.2 of the TRIPS in light of the second and thereby to conclude that specific information will be secret when it is difficult to ascertain[6] and, more specifically, when the circle of (current or potential) interested parties cannot ascertain it using lawful means without investing significant resources in terms of time, effort or cost.[7]

---

6 Among the authors bringing together both rules, J. Cohen and A.S. Gutterman, *Trade Secrets Protection and Exploitation* (Washington DC: The Bureau of National Affairs, Inc, 1998) 90–92, F. Gurry, *Breach of Confidence* (Oxford: Clarendon Press, 1984) 70, J. Dratler and D. Conway-Jones, *Intellectual Property Law: Commercial Creative and Industrial Property* (New York: Law Journal Press, 2004) § 4, 414 and 417, I. Farrando, *El deber de secreto de los administradores de sociedades anónimas y limitadas* (Madrid: Civitas, 2001) 127. Among decisions, *Douglas and others* v *Hello! Ltd and others* (2003) EWCH 786 (Ch), (2003) All ER (D) 209 (Apr), Trib *Verona*, 28 December de1985, *GADI*, 1985, 2011, STS 21-X-2005 (RJ 2005\8274), *Crane Helicopters Services Inc* v *United States* (C Fed Cl 2003), who stated that classifying information as secret shall only be carried out based on the difficulty entailed by discovering it and that this was in actual fact the guideline resorted to by the most contemporary decisions passed in the US.

7 Determining the ease or difficulty entailed by accessing information according to this criterion is a theory that is by and large upheld in the US [see, i.e. Dratler and Conway-Jones, *supra* n 7, R. Callmann, *Trademarks, Unfair Competition and Monopolies* (Louis Altman ed., 4th edn, Deerfield/Ill: Clark Boardman Callaghan cop, 2005) 54, Cohen and Gutterman, *supra* n 7, 92; *Crane Helicopters Services Inc* v *United Status* (C Fed Cl 2003),

*The Competitive Advantage Stemming From the Secret Nature of Information*

The third requirement referred to in Article 39 of the TRIPS when setting out the conditions that a concrete information must fulfill to qualify as a trade secret is for it to have 'commercial value'. As almost unanimously supported by scholars, this must be interpreted as a reference to the need for the secret information to endow its holder with a current or potential competitive advantage.[8]

However, I do think that 'competitive value' must not be conceived as an independent element of the secrecy requirement; in other words, as an added extra element that the specific information must possess in addition to its secret nature. Quite the opposite, as laid down in Article 39.2 of the TRIPS, this value depends on the secret nature itself: the latter is a prerequisite for the former and the former is determined on the basis of the latter.

One excellent example showing that the value of specific information may solely stem from third parties lack of awareness, whereby it does not necessarily have to be tied to the results of its use, or its likelihood to be exploited, is *negative information*. This is information that makes it possible to know whether a specific procedure or method does not work, is not appropriate, is commercially inapt, or is merely ineffective. Indeed, one should have no qualms agreeing that information

---

*Guy Carpenter & Company, Inc* v *Anthony Provenzale*, 2003 US App LEXIS 12001 (5th Cir 2003), *Lucini Italia Co* v *Grappolini*, 2003 US Dist LEXIS 7134 (ND Ill 2003), *DTM Research, LLC* v *AT & T Corp*, 245 F3d 327 (4th Cir 2001)]. Likewise, various authors from other countries have backed this construal. See, among others, Gurry, *supra* n 7, 70, R. Dean, *The Law of Trade Secrets* (Sydney: The Law Book Company Limited, 1990) 114, L. Mansani, 'La nozione di segreto di cui all'art 6 *bis* li' *Il Diritto Industriale* n 3, 2002, 217, S. Di Paola, 'Conocorrenza sleale per l'utilizzo di notizie "segrete": quale avvenire per l'ex-dipendiente?' *Il Foro Italiano* 1993, 3156, O. Weniger, *La Protection des secrets économiques et du savoir-faire (know-how): étude comparative des droits allemand, français et suisse* (Genève: Droz, 1994) 146 and R. Schlosser, *Le contrat de savoir-faire, étude de droit Suisse* (Lausanne: thèse, 1996) 50, Farrando, *supra* n 7, 127.

8 See among scholarly works, J. Pooley, *Trade Secrets* (New York: Law Journal Press, 1997–2009) § 4.05 [1], R.M. Milgrim, *Trade Secrets* (New York: Matthew Bender, 1967–…–2009) § 1. 01 [2], 2–46, 2–47, Cohen and Gutterman, *supra* n 7, 95, P.A. Alces and H.F. See, *The Commercial Law of Intellectual Property* (Boston-New York-London: Little, Brown and Company, 1994) 8, Mansani, *supra* n 8, 218, G. Floridia, 'L'abusiva sottrazione ed utilizzazione dell'altrui segreto aziendale', in P. Auteri et al., *Diritto Industriale, proprietà intellecttuale e concorrenza* (Torino: Giappichelli, 2001) 330–31 and G. Bonelli, 'Tutela del segreto di empresa e oblighi dell'ex dipendiente' *Il Diritto Industriale* n 1, 2002, 73, J. Massaguer, *Comentario a la Ley de Competencia Desleal* (Madrid: Civitas, 1999) 387–389; among the case law, SSAP *Barcelona* 9-V-2008 (JUR 2008\243447), *Barcelona* 28-XI-2005 (JUR 2006\86380), *Barcelona* 26-X-2005 (AC 2006\216), *American Model Home Corp* v *Resource Mortgage Capital Inc*, 1999 US App LEXIS 2849 (4th Cir 1999), *Capital Asset Research Corp* v *Finnegan, Utilase, Inc,* 160 F3d 683 (11th Cir 1998), *AT & T Communications of California Inc* v *Pacific Bell*, *3M* v *Pribyl*, 259 F3d 587 (7th Cir 2001), *Guy Carpenter & Co, Inc* v *Provenzale*, *supra* n 8.

reporting on studies, research or experiments that have failed; information reporting on the ineffectiveness of some sales or advertising campaigns; on the irrelevance of certain data; on the fact that certain marketing plans have failed, etc, lacks all intrinsic use, that is to say, the execution thereof provides no benefit to the holder. However, it is also clear that the trial and error process making it possible to determine precisely 'what we should not do' is costly in terms of time and money. Therefore, the likelihood of it being known by third parties who are unaware of it enables them to save costs associated with its discovery. This is also the case with respect to the possibility of this information being used to create or enrich their methods or procedures, improving thus their competitive position. Hence, given the value that this information possesses, it should be protected and is worthy of protection behind the veil of trade secrecy.[9]

If it is the case, and I do believe so, that the value of information depends on the fact of its secret nature, and thus, on not being readily available to interested parties, it is clear that it is not necessary to call upon any third party (particularly a court) to assess whether this information has an objective competitive value. Trade secret protection should be applied provided that the information is secret whilst meeting the latter requirement in this regard, that is, that the holder has taken reasonable measures under the circumstances to protect its secrecy.

*Reasonable Measures to Maintain its Secrecy*

I do think that any consideration of this latter requirement first requires an acknowledgment of an idea that has been typically overlooked: there are two spheres for secret protection. The first protects the secret nature of information with respect to people to whom the holder has voluntarily disclosed it or people who, in any event, have become aware of it with due consent. The other, the external sphere, involves protecting information from interferences by third parties who are unaware of it: spies and the like. Indeed, both spheres are aimed to same purpose – preventing the information from being disclosed – though while the former tries to prevent direct disclosure by adopting measures immediately intended to require those accessing the information not to disclose it or use it (and therefore, protect its secret nature in a remote manner from acquisition by third parties), the latter sphere seeks to prevent information from being indirectly disclosed by taking precautions aimed at immediately preventing third parties from having access to it.

This distinction carries an enormous significance for two reasons: firstly, it shows us that the measures required to protect secrecy in each of the above spheres must logically be different; and secondly, and more importantly, it shows us that

9 The possibility of protecting negative information as a trade secret is currently the predominant theory upheld in the US. See, for all, Pooley, *supra* n 9, § 4.03 [3], *Metallurgical Ind Inc* v *Fourtek Inc*, 790 F2d 1125 (8th Cir 1986), *Courtesy Temporary Service Inc* v *Leone*, 222 Cal App 3d, 1288, 272 CalRptr 352.

the standard of reasonableness required by Article 39.2 of the TRIPS cannot (and should not) be homogeneous in both cases. As a result, the criteria allowing for the determination of said standard must likewise be distinct.

Indeed, if we examine the scope of both spheres, of protection of the confidential nature of information, we will readily realize that the first sphere is entirely controlled by the holder. The reason is quite simple: it is on the basis of the holder's intentions that the disclosure or assignment of the information takes place. The same is true, with the adoption of any pertinent preventive measures to require those accessing it to keep it confidential. This unique position maintained by the trade secret holder allows us to maintain that the protection standard that must be required in this sphere needs to be more rigid. On the other hand, the second of the spheres of protection which we have distinguished is not entirely under the control of the trade secret holder, since the adoption of measures to prevent alien third parties from gaining access to it does not always depend on the holder's intent. Thus, it would be necessary at this juncture to incorporate factors or criteria that balance and suitably offset both interests and, specifically, that make it possible to conclude that the holder has adopted precautions that are reasonable even if third parties nevertheless manage to gain access to the information, or, on the contrary, that the information has been indirectly disclosed due to the holder's negligence or laxity. In the last instance, this goes to show why the standard of reasonableness in this sphere must be more flexible and the determination thereof will, by and large, depend on the conduct and strategies intended to be promoted, tolerated or prevented by the holder of the secret and the intruder.

Specifically, from this author's point of view, the measures adopted within the *first sphere* should be deemed reasonable when the holder provides the information only on a need to know basis to employees, associates, directors, managers, etc and requires them not to disclose it or use it for any other purpose than that for which they were provided – unless of course there is already a conventional or legal duty causing them to keep the information confidential. Moreover, it is also necessary for them to have been informed about the confidential nature of the specific information that must be kept secret, and some additional protective measures should have been put in place when the relations come to an end.

With regard to the *second sphere* of protection, it is more complicated to determine *ex ante* and generally when these measures intended to preserve the secrecy of the information can be deemed as reasonable. Within the uncertainty surrounding the determination of this matter there lies at least one clear idea: in order to reasonably preserve the secret nature of information *companies do not need to set up impenetrable fortresses*. Another idea is clear as well: the fulfilment of this requirement does not call for the trade secret holder to adopt every conceivable precaution, or extravagant or heroic measures. There is a simple explanation for this: given that one of the main policies underlying trade secret protection is for it to encourage research on, and the creation of, socially valuable information, it would be incoherent to require the economic players to re-divert their means to implementing self-protection measures which, in themselves, generate no value whatsoever. As a result, it is necessary to identify the criterion, which in light of the foregoing, would make it possible to define this minimum level of protection.

The solution to this issue starts with the awareness that the vital function of protective measures in this second sphere – which fits in best with the mentioned policy underlying trade secret protection – does not lie so much in preventing third parties from gaining access to the information (as commonly stated), but rather in warning them that this information is confidential. In line with this informative purpose, I think that the level of protection will suffice when the holder sets up measures which, in light of the nature of the specific information, the size and financial means of the company, and the trade usages in that sector, clearly make it externally known that the information is secret. This can be done either by directly preventing or limiting access to unauthorized individuals, or by clearly highlighting the fact that the information is secret.

*Summary: The Notion of Trade Secret*

In light of all the foregoing, one could synthetically define a trade secret as follows: *all information relating to the company which cannot be readily ascertained by third parties by lawful means without investing substantial means and, information for which the holder has adopted reasonable measures to ensure it remains confidential, both with respect to the individuals to whom it is voluntarily disclosed and to those who are unaware of it.*

## The Duty of Confidentiality of Employees and Other Collaborative Arrangements Concerning Trade Secrets Disclosed on the Basis of the Contract

The majority of scholars and courts in different jurisdictions accept that individuals accessing trade secrets on the basis of a contract, and for a specific purpose, are required to maintain its secrecy due to a duty of good faith, fidelity or loyalty, even if no specific clause or agreement stipulates this. This obligation, unless a specific stipulation states otherwise, does not merely apply for the duration of the respective contract. Quite the opposite, as is acknowledged in most countries, the effects of that obligation, in terms of time, extends beyond termination of the contract for as long as the protected information remains secret. This virtually uniform pattern in comparative law has not occurred by chance; rather, it shows a clear rationale: due to the very nature of the purpose with which revelation is made or, in general, access is provided to or enabled for trade secrets, and on account of obvious requirements of the duty to good faith, the obligation of these subjects to preserve its secrecy must survive after the termination of contract; otherwise, this duty would merely become an easily avoidable formal obligation.

This applies, for instance, to employees for trade secrets belonging to their employer that they have received or otherwise acquired in their capacity as employees.[10] The same can also be stated for other parties in collaborative arrangements with the entrepreneur,[11] whose duty of confidentiality entails both not to disclose secret information, and adopting the measures needed to prevent third parties from gaining access. For instance, this group includes licensees when it comes to secret information entrusted to them for operations relating to the licensed object; suppliers who are enabled access to trade secrets by the holder so they can carry out their directions; external consultants when it comes to secret information they access in order to provide their services for a specific company and even with regard to information they have generated for the company. These cases also include independent contractors, when it comes to secret information they access to perform their duties or information they themselves have produced as part of their duties (for instance, the manufacturer regarding information they have been provided with to produce a specific product); the participants to a

10 See, among scholars and case law upholding that the employee is required to maintain secrecy over trade secrets belonging to his employer he has accessed in his capacity as employee, even following the termination of the contract, in *United Kingdom*, Gurry, *supra* n 7, 198–199, A. Coleman, *Legal Protection of Trade-Secrets* (London: Sweet & Maxwell, 1992) 59, K. Brearley and S. Bloch, *Employment Covenants and Confidential Information: Law, Practice and Technique*, (London-Dublin-Edinburgh: Butterworths, 1993) 60–61, *Alperton Rubber Co* v *Manning* (1917) 86 LJ Ch 377, *Amber Size & Chemical Co Ltd* v *Menzel* (1913) 2 Ch 239, *Archer* v *William* (2003) EWHC 1670 (QB), *Sietech Hearing* v *Digital Hearing & Co* (2003) ECDR 26, *Swan* v *Bereta and others* (2005) EWHC 928 (Ch); in *Spain*, G. Boza, *El deber de sigilo de los representantes de los trabajadores* (Valencia: Tirant Lo Blanch, 1997) 157, M. Nogueira, *El pacto laboral de no competencia postcontractual* (Madrid: Mc Graw Hill, 1998) 132, Massaguer, *supra* n 9, 398–399, SSTS 17-VII-1999 (RJ 1999/5957), 12-V-2008 – Sala de lo Penal – (RJ 2008\3583); in Italy, recently, P. Ichino, 'Tutela della riservatezza, circolazione delle información, obblighi di segreto e di non concorrenza', in idem, *Trattato di Diritto Civile e Commerciale, Il contrato di lavoro,* vol III (Milano: Giuffrè, 2003) 297 and 301 *et seq.*, Bonelli, *supra* n 9, 65, A. Vanzetti and V. Di Cataldo, *Manuale di Diritto Industriale* (4th edn, Milano: Guiffrè, 2003) 105 and 446; in France, M. Malaurie-Vignal, 'La protection des informations privilégiés et du savoir-faire' *Dalloz* 1997, chron, 210. The most extreme example is, beyond doubt, Switzerland given that art 321 to 4 CO expressly ban employees from using or disclosing secrets they accessed during employment relations and determine that this ban is upheld following the end of relations, when required to safeguard the genuine interests of the company (see Weniger, *supra* n 8, 237 *et seq.* US case law and literature also commonly point to this approach (see Milgrim, *supra* n 9, *with case law references,* Lemley, *supra* n 2).

11 See among those that generally point to the fact that this type of contract partner is bound by a duty to confidentiality during the period of application of the contract and subsequent to its termination, in Italy, A. Frignani, 'Segreti d'impresa', *Novissimo Digesto Italiano Apéndice*, vol VII (Torino: UTET, 1980-1987) 21; in Switzerland, Weniger, *supra* n 8, 235–6; in Germany, Weniger, *supra* n 8, 230; and in France and the United Kingdom, although the author understands that it is subject to the application of contractual relations, see Trib Grande inst Limoges, 8 November de 1989, *PIBD*, 1991, III, 704 and Gurry, *supra* n 7, 122 respectively.

joint venture when it comes to secrets they access in relation to said venture;[12] commercial agents whose duty of loyalty and bona fide requires them to preserve the secrecy of the information they received or otherwise acquired through their position at the company or, among many other examples, franchises and other links in the down-side distribution chain.

Even so, it is necessary to point out that, although signing a confidentiality agreement would not be mandatory in these cases, it does have its advantages. These include the fact that it goes a long way to showing that reasonable measures have been adopted to protect the confidential nature of the information.[13] Indeed, as pointed out, for this requirement to be met, it is necessary for the holder to have warned whomever they entrust with the specific information that it is secret in nature, unless the circumstances make it reasonable to infer that it is a trade secret that must be kept as such (i.e. documents containing the information are marked as confidential; in the specific industry it is understood that the type of information is secret; the value of the information and the need for it to remain secret is patent and intuitive for the individuals handling it; the knowledge and experience of the subjects receiving it or the purpose for its disclosure make it unthinkable for any other conclusion to be reached). This is confirmed by many judicial decisions wherein the lack of warning as to the secret nature of certain information that the holder wished to protect was one of the determining factors as to conclude that reasonable measures had not been adopted.[14] Needless to say, since the confidentiality agreement, makes it possible to accurately identify information and therefore warn that it is disclosed, used and developed under confidentiality, is a particularly suitable instrument for reaching this goal. This is probably what has encouraged courts and some scholars to consider them essential or even decisive for the information to be qualified as a trade secret. This is especially the case in circumstances where employers face their former employees[15] in courts.

---

12 See *General Universal System Inc* v *Hal Inc*, 379 F3d 131 (5th Cir 2004), which stated that partners to a joint venture are normally bound by a duty to confidentiality with respect to each other.

13 See the following example among many decisions admitting circumstances in this respect, *Aries Information Sys, Inc* v *Pacific Management Sys Corp*, 366 NW2d 366, 226 USPQ 440, 442–3 (Minn *Ct* App 1985), *Schalk* v *State*, 823 SW2d 633, 638-640, 21 USPQ2d 1838 (Tex Crim App 1991), *cert denied,* 118 L Ed 2d 425 (1992), *Den-Tal-Ez Inc* v *Siemens Capital Corp*, 9 USPQ2d (BNA) 1932, 1942, 1988 WL 252394 (Pa Super Ct 1988).

14 See, among others, SSAP *Barcelona* 19-XI-2007 (JUR 2008\76447), *Barcelona* 13-VII-2005. In this regard, decisions passed in the US are clearer. See *Tubos de Acero de Mexico, SA,* v *American Intern*, 292 F3d 471 (5th Cir 2002), *Telecom America, Inc* v *Oncor Communcations, Inc*, 31 Fed App 809 (A4 (Md), 2002), *Buffets, Inc* v *Klinke*, 73 F3d 965, 969 (9th Cir 1996), *Cruises of Distinction* v *Northstar Cruises Inc* (cit *supra*), *Incase Inc* v *Timex Corp*, 488 F3d 46, 2007 (1st Cir 2007).

15 Along these lines, Cohen and Gutterman, *supra* n 7, 132 and in case law, among many other judicial decisions, *Aries Information Sys, Inc* v *Pacific Management Sys Corp*,

However, this is not the only advantage of confidentiality agreements. They are also useful if one considers that they make it possible to foresee other relevant circumstances for the parties, such as the period for which holding certain information secret will be applicable; the consequences stemming from non-compliance (such as license revocation, liquidated damage clause); a conflict resolution system (e.g. arbitration); choice of jurisdiction; or the procedure that must be followed to obtain authorization to disclose or to use the information covered by the agreement, among other aspects. Lastly, these agreements can similarly prove useful for specifying the lawful means by which secrets can be acquired (i.e. limiting access to reverse engineering to discover it). They are also useful as a supplement to a technology transfer agreement (i.e. a know-how license, patents) and to uphold the validity of a non-compete clause. This is because, unless they can be considered identical, said agreements carry an advantage over the clause inasmuch as there is no need for them to meet the validity requirements of the later (for instance, payment of financial compensation).

## The 'Skill and Knowledge' of Employees and Other Contracting Parties in Collaborative Arrangements with the Entrepreneur

### *Approach*

Since former employees and other contract partners own a duty of confidentiality regarding trade secrets acquired by through their position, it is clear that the disclosure or use of such secrets without the express or implied consent of the holder constitutes an unlawful conduct that is banned by virtually all current European systems.[16] Nonetheless, it should not be overlooked that commonly it is stated that all the above parties may indeed freely use the skills, abilities and certain general knowledge they have built up by lawful means through their position after the contract with the holder had expired.[17] In other words, they can lawfully use what has come to be known as 'skill and knowledge'.

366 NW2d 366, 226 USPQ 440, 442–3 (Minn Ct App 1985), *Schalk* v *State*, 823 SW2d 633, 638–40, 21 USPQ2d 1838 (Tex Crim App 1991), *cert denied*, 118 L Ed 2d 425 (1992), *Den-Tal-Ez Inc* v *Siemens Capital Corp*, 9 USPQ2d (BNA) 1932, 1942, 1988 WL 252394 (Pa Super Ct 1988, *BDT Products Inc* v *Lexmark International, Inc*, 124 Fed App 329 (6th Cir 2005).

16 See, in private law, for instance, in Spain, art 13 Ley de Competencia Desleal; in Italy, arts 98 and 99 del *Il Codice della Propietá Industriale*; in Germany, §§ 17, 18 and 20 UWG; in France, arts 1382 and 1383 Code Civil.

17 See, among European scholarly works, Massaguer, *supra* n 9, 389, Farrando, *supra* n 7, 201 *et seq.*; Frignani, *supra* n 12, 18, F. Massa Felsani, *Contributo all'analisi del Know-How* (Milano: Giufre, 1997) 169, Di Paola, *supra* n 8, 3154; Dean, *supra* n 8, 21–4 and 204 *et seq.*, Gurry, *supra* n 7, 199, Coleman, *supra* n 11, 10, Weniger, *supra* n 8, 150 and 219. In the US *per omnia*, Cohen and Gutterman, *supra* n 7, 194, Pooley, *supra* n 9,

The basis for this recognition lies in the right to work, the free choice when it comes to occupation or trade, and the promotion through work, as well as in freedom of enterprise as recognized in most European legal systems (in Spain it is laid down in Articles 35 and 38 of the Constitution). Also, from a more general standpoint, it is recognized in the free development of personality (in Spain in Article 10.1 of the Constitution). And what seems to be legitimate from the individual standpoint of the subject affected is also called for from a social perspective: society as a whole is keen to foster mobility of employees and professionals, given the social and economic benefits it brings about. It is not surprising that there are studies establishing direct links between this factor on the one hand and economic growth and innovation on the other; accordingly, establishing restrictions on those rigths may harm the public interests.[18]

Nevertheless, when scholars and courts have had to address the complex task of outlining the specific knowledge and personal skills falling into the 'skill and knowledge' of employees and other parties, many of the solutions put forward have been imprecise and variable. Indeed, not all the knowledge gathered by these subjects when providing their services for a specific principal can be deemed as falling within this concept. The purpose of the following lines is to try to establish more precisely which elements fall within the category 'skill and knowledge', providing some criteria that may be useful in this regard and likewise highlighting the weakness of other elements that may ultimately be put forward for identification.

### *Outlining Knowledge and Information included in the 'Skill and Knowledge'*

Before dealing with the criteria that shall enable us to define the elements of 'skill and knowledge', it is pertinent to point out one consideration with regard to the approach to this matter. Most scholars and courts have attempted to deal with the matter by separating knowledge that can qualify as a trade secret from

§ 4, 10, Callmann, *supra* n 8, 88-89, Dratler and Conway-Jones, *supra* n 7, § 4 27. Many judicial decisions have thus warned, see all, SSTS 24-XI-2006 (RJ 2007\262), 8-X-2007 (RJ 2007\6805), Cass (it) 20 March 1991, *Il Foro Italiano*, 1993, 3154), *Faccenda Chicken* v *Flower* (Neil, J), (1987) ch 117, (1986) 1 All ER 617; (1986) 3 WRL 188, *Crowson Fabrics Ltd* v *Rider* (2007) EWHC 2942 (Ch) and, among the abundant US decisions, *Schulenberg* v *Signatrol Inc*, 33 Ill2d 379, 212 NE2d 865 (1965), *Foolmer, Rudzewick & Co PC* v *Kosco*, 420 Mich 394 (Mich 1984), *Utilase Inc* v *Williamson*, 1999 US App LEXIS 22452 (6th Cir 1999), *The Agency Inc* v *Grove* (cit *supra*), *Nike, Inc* v *McCarthy*, 379 F3d 576 (9th Cir 2004), *Q-Tech Labs Pty Ltd* v *Walker* (cit *supra*), *Abetter Trucking Co* v *Arizpe*, 113 SW3d 503 (Tex App Houston 1st Dist 2003), *Glenayre Electronics, Ltd* v *Sandahl*, 830 FSupp 1149 (C D Ill 1993).

18 See, although encompassed within markets having high employment mobility, A. Hyde, *Working in Silicon Valley: Economic and Legal Analysis of a High-Velocity Labor Market* (Armonk: Sharpe, 2003) *passim*.

knowledge forming part of the 'skill and knowledge'. To do so they have provided or resorted to a heterogeneous range of generally successful criteria.

This approach, which indeed entails excluding *ex ante* certain knowledge from the notion of the trade secret, would appear to be difficult to accept without some reservation. In order to realize this we must consider that 'skill and knowledge' can ultimately comprise two kinds of knowledge, the distinction of which is highly important when it comes to addressing them: knowledge that cannot be strictly classified as information or which, even if it is, still lacks a confidential nature, and knowledge that can be considered a trade secret. It is clear that in the case of the former the approach made by courts and scholars seems pertinent; this knowledge is by nature separate from the concept of trade secret and, therefore, from the legal protection thereof, which is logical. However, the same cannot be said of the latter, because if that approach were exact it would require us to leave genuine trade secrets entirely unprotected. The unfounded aspect of this solution is patent; the very positive foundation of the right of former employees and other contract partners to benefit from their 'skill and knowledge' shows its very limits: this right does not cover the acquisition and disclosure by said individuals of trade secrets, because such conduct by no means contributes to their personal and professional performance. Hence it would be incorrect to exclude them *ex ante* from the notion of the trade secret and this is why it is proper to instead exclude their use *ex post* by former employees or other contract partners of a specific principal from trade secret protection.[19] Indeed, given that trade secret protection lasts as long as the information remains secret and, therefore, can go beyond the termination of the contract, it is clear that inasmuch as the trade secret in question forms part of the 'skill and knowledge' of the former employees and other contract partners, this extension may cause restrictive effects on their right to develop their professional career and to choose a job or occupation in line with their qualifications.

In accordance with the considerations outlined above, we will go on to analyse and define the knowledge comprising 'skill and knowledge' from this twofold

---

19 UK case law and scholars have acknowledged that confidential information learnt by employees or other contract partners when carrying out their duties for a specific principal can form part of their 'skill and knowledge' and, accordingly, they can use it freely following the end of the employment relationship with the aforementioned principal. See, among other authors, A. Brooks, '"Fidelity" in the Post-Industrial Age: Developments in Case Law on Employee Disclosure of Confidential Information?' 28 *Monash University Law Review* 2002, 127 *et seq.*, Coleman, *supra* n 11, 10, J. Phillips / A. Firth, *Introduction to Intellectual Property Law* (London-Dublin-Edinburgh: Butterworth, 1995) 269, Dean, *supra* n 8, 22 and 204; and among the case law, the leading case *Faccenda Chicken* v *Flower* ([1984] ICR 589 affirmed by [1986] 3 WLR 288). Even so, there is no shortage of authors from other countries that have accepted this approach, albeit in a more reserved manner, M.J. Feldman, 'Toward a Clearer Standard of Protectable Information: Trade Secrets and the Employment Relationship' 9 *High Tech Law Journal* 1994, 153 and 155 *et seq.*, L. Wheeler, 'Trade Secrets and the Skilled Employee in the Computer Industry' 61 *Washington University Law Quarterly* 1983, 834, Farrando, *supra* n 7, 206.

stance (in other words, knowledge that is not able to constitute a trade secret on the one hand, and secret information on the other). This consideration is made notwithstanding the fact that we may use the criteria handled by scholars and courts, regardless of whether they followed this approach.

*Knowledge and information lacking the status of a trade secret*

*Objective knowledge vs subjective knowledge* For a long time, courts have used the nature of knowledge as a criterion for distinguishing trade secrets from 'skill and knowledge', specifically contrasting objective knowledge – which is likely to constitute a secret – and subjective knowledge (such as skills, aptitude, ability, etc) which on the other hand may freely be used by whoever possesses it, even if it has been acquired or improved due to the performance of their duties.[20]

In this manner, this criterion does not appear to be fully satisfactory because, as we will see, objective knowledge can become subjective inasmuch as it can form part of the 'skill and knowledge' of whoever acquired it when providing their services for a specific principal. Nonetheless, it gives a slight indication of the first idea I wish to highlight which may result in the following commonly shared proposal: the sphere of skills and abilities of a subject (such as talent or the ability to perform a specific task, leadership skills, a specific ability to solve certain problems, skill for concluding business or establishing relations, personal worth or individual credit, aptitude, charisma for drawing in clients, specific sales skills or indeed, among many other examples, mental, manual or management skills) are not covered by trade secret protection, even though they inevitably provide a competitive advantage.[21]

Indeed, quite frequently, the value of information and its ability to be exploited by a specific company is not so dependent on the data in itself, but rather on the skill or ability related to its creation, development and execution as possessed by an individual which, in turn, has been built up thanks to experience and learning acquired while carrying out certain duties for their principal at any given time.

20 This distinction has been typically resorted to in Italian case law (as pointed out by Frignani, *supra* n 12, 18 and F. Scirè, *La concorrenza sleale nella giurisprudenza,* Tomo III (2nd edn, Milano: Giuffrè, 1989) 12, with case law references) and also, although to a more heightened extent, English and Spanish case law (see, respectively *SBJ Stephenson Ltd* v *Mandy* (2000) IRLR 234, *RL Crain Ltd* v *Ashton & Ashton Press Manufacturing Co* (1950) 1 DLR, 601, *Herbert Morris Ltd* v *Saxelby* (1916) 1 AC 688, *Navarra* 10-VI-1998 [EDJ 1998/188823]), and even US case law on some occasions [see, for instance, *Eaton Corp* v *Appliance Valves Corp*, 526 FSupp 1172 (ND Ind 1981), *Atmel Corp* v *Vitesse Semiconductor Corp*, 30 P3d 789 (Colo Ct App 2001), *Pittsburgh Cut Wire Co* v *Sufrin*, 38 A2d 33, 34 (Pa 1994), *Christopher M's Hand Poured Fudge, Inc* v *Hennon,* 699 A2d 1272, 1275 (Pa Super 1997)].

21 See, among many other decisions confirming this idea, SSAP *Tarragona* 10-III-2008, *A Coruña* 21-III-2007 (JUR 2007\237796), *Valencia* 1-IX-1997 (AC 1997\1775), *CA Bologna*, 9 August 1977, 6 *Giur ann dir ind* 1977, 957, Paris, 24 January 1975, PIBD 1975, III, 323, *Coventry First, LLC* v *Ingrassia*, 2005 WL 1625042 (E D Pa 2005).

It is highly likely to give a detailed description in a manual as to how to achieve a specific result from a range of chemical processes, though of course in practice the best outcome would not simply be achieved by following all the guidelines given, but rather by doing things exactly as a skilled person would. Now, in contrast to information that is easily coded and therefore transferable, this type of *tacit knowledge*, considered as skill or aptitude, is solely acquired through experience.[22] It travels with an individual and can be lawfully used no matter how it may compromise the interests of the former principal. This is the case, not only because it forms part of the 'skill and knowledge' possessed by a subject but also especially because inasmuch as it cannot be formalized or guided and it is therefore non-transferable, it cannot strictly be classified as information. Accordingly, it cannot fall within the realm of what is considered a trade secret and thus is not subject to the respective protection.

*General information vs specific information* It is commonly affirmed that with general information on a specific business sphere, deemed as that information which any employee or other contract partner carrying out tasks in a company in a specific industry obtains without the need to provide his services for a particular company, also forms part of an individual's 'skill and knowledge'. Thus, trade secrets are separated from the 'skill and knowledge' by contrasting general information that remains with a subject even when it is learnt through their position or trade, and specific information about a certain company, which, as it may only be gleaned from said company, is likely to be a trade secret.[23]

---

22 On the distinction between explicit or coded and tacit knowledge, M. Polanyi, *Personal Knowledge: Towards a Post-critical Philosophy* (London: Routledge & Kegan Paul, 1958) 69–131. Among scholarly works resorting to this distinction on the context of the trade secret include, R.J. Gilson, 'The Legal Infrastructure of High Technology Industrial Districts: Silicon Valley, Rute 123, and Covenants not to Compete' 74 *New York University Law Review* 1999, 577 n 10, 582 and 597, and in line with said individual, R. Arnow-Richman, 'Bargaining for Loyalty in the Information Age: A Reconsideration of the Role of Substantive Fairness in Enforcing Employee Noncompetes' 80 *Original Law Review* 2001, 1190.

23 See, *Santa Cruz de Tenerife* 21-III-2005 (JUR 2005\103284); Cour d'appel de Paris, 23 enero 1954, *Annales de la propiété industrielle*, 1954, 28 (32), *Westminster Chemical NZ Ltd* v *McKinley & Tasman Machinery & Services Ltd* (1973) 1 NZLR 659, *Hogan Systems, Inc* v *Cybresource*, 158 F3d 319 (5th Cir 1998), *Jacono* v *Invacare Corporation*, 2006 WL 832451 (Ohio App 8 Dist, 2006), *The Agency Inc* v *Grove*, 362 Ill App 3d 206, 839 NE2d 606, 298 Ill Dec 283 (2nd Dist 2005), *Nike Inc* v *McCarthy*, 379 F3d 576 (9th Cir 2004). Among scholars, those that resort to this criterion include, L. Bently and B. Sherman, *Intellectual Property Law* (Oxford: University Press, 2004) 919, Frignani, *supra* n 12, 19, with additional references, Cohen and Gutterman, *supra* n 7, 104–5, Callmann, *supra* n 8, 88, Feldman, *supra* n 20, 175 *et seq.*, Pooley, *supra* n 9, § 4, 10, and R.T. Nimmer, *Information Law* (St Paul: MN, West Group, 2005) § 5, 122.

It is beyond question that general information as it has been defined must be deemed as falling within the experience and knowledge which employees or other contract partners are free to use after their respective contract expires. For instance, this is true of knowledge and general customs in a specific industry, of the general operating and negotiation methods of a company, of the strategy employed to launch new products into the market, of general experience and knowledge on how to operate a specific line of business, of the manner to overcome certain hurdles or analyse productive costs or, in general, of how an individual should carry out their job or duties.

However, one should not be deceived: often this type of information lacks secrecy in nature. Unsurprisingly, it is commonly identified with common or widely known information within a specific sector, industry or activity and therefore readily available to parties seeking to acquire it. This is especially shown by those judicial decisions which support the classification of specific information as general or, on the other hand, as being specific in a given case. Indeed, in the first instance, the underlying reason leading courts to conclude that the information under dispute was not a trade secret lay specifically in the fact that it was commonly known in a specific sector; accordingly, it lacked secrecy in nature.[24] On the other hand, in the second instance, the very reason leads courts to conclude that the information under dispute was to be considered a trade secret, was that it indeed had a confidential nature since it was difficult for interested parties to ascertain it.[25]

As a result, in most cases, in order to disqualify this kind of information from the protection offered under the secrecy system, it would not actually be necessary to maintain that its entire protection would constitute an unfair, undesirable restriction on the mobility of employees and other contracting partners. Nor would it be necessary to weight the various interests at stake, because they are automatically excluded from the notion of the trade secret, as soon as it is verified that they are not secret at all.

*Secret information*

As addressed earlier, the 'skill and knowledge' possessed by employees and other contract partners can also encompass information gained through the

24 See, for instance, *Central Bldg & Cleaning Co Inc* v *Vodnansky*, 406 NE2d 32 (Ill App Ct 1980), *Unisource Worldwide Inc* v *Carrara* 244 FSupp 2d 977 (C D Ill 2003), *Weibold Studio Inc* v *Old World Restorations*, 19 Ohio App 3d 246, 248, 484 NE2d 280, 284 (1985), *Microbiological Res Corp* v *Muna*, 625 P2d 690 (Utah 1981); *Cudahy Co* v *American Labs, Inc*, 313 FSupp 1339 (D Neb 1970), V SSAP *Barcelona* 26-X-2005 (AC 2006\216), *Barcelona* 4-VII-2007 (JUR 2007\285110), *Santa Cruz de Tenerife* 21-III-2005 (JUR 2005\103284).

25 See, for instance, *The Agency, Inc* v *Grove*, 362 Ill App 3d 206, 839 NE2d 606, 298 Ill Dec 283 (2nd Dist 2005), *Sun Dial Corp* v *Rideout*, 16 NJ 252, 257 (1954), *Black, Sivalls & Bryson, Inc* v *Keystone Steel Fabrication, Inc*, 584 F2d 946 (10th Cir 1978).

exercise of their duties for a specific principal which qualifies as a trade secret. Accordingly, it is necessary to clarify the criterion according to which a trade secret must be deemed as falling within the 'skill and knowledge' possessed by these subjects.

*The general criterion for identifying trade secrets comprised in the 'skill and knowledge'* The starting point for our analysis shall concern the acknowledgment of the fact that there is no foolproof, universal method to carry out an identification *a priori* of trade secrets falling within the scope of the 'skill and knowledge' possessed by employees and other contract partners. This matter must stem from a suitable balance of the specific circumstances of each case. Nonetheless, in light of the very basis by which former employees and other contract partners may use their 'skill and knowledge', the following general criteria may be put forward: a trade secret must be deemed as forming part of 'skill and knowledge' when, due to the fact that is intimately tied to experience, ability and other innate knowledge possessed by an individual, the prohibition of its use would either openly hinder the individual in question from carrying out the activity for which they are professionally trained or it would lead to excessive restrictions being placed on the development of their professional and personal capabilities.[26]

Although it is clear that this analysis may only be carried out in a casuistic manner, below we will look into some parameters or criteria that may help us, in an alternate or cumulative fashion, to identify trade secrets which, for this reason, must be deemed as forming part of 'skill and knowledge'.

*Specific criteria (1) Information, the use of which is vital for the regular exercise of a specific occupation or trade.* The most evident criterion suggesting that the trade secret of a specific principal forms part of the professional experience of a former employee or other contract partners. It is the fact that its use is vital or necessary for carrying out, either in another company or one's own company, a similar activity to the one formerly performed.[27] Indeed, it seems that in such cases the employer's interest in protecting secret information from use by former employees or other contracting partners must be forgone in favour of the latter.

---

26 Prior to the commonly known decision made in the *Faccenda Chicken* v *Flower* case (*supra* n 20), UK Courts upheld a similar approach and reasoning (see, with an extensive explanation and legal analysis of this approach which, according to the author's viewpoint is, unquestionably, the right one to address this issue, Brooks, *supra* n 20, 127 *et seq*.

27 Authors pointing out this idea include J. Massaguer, *El contrato de licencia de Know-How* (Barcelona: Librería Bosch, 1989) 56, E. Barbeta, 'Concorrenza dell'ex dipendente- Inidoneità di essa danneggiare l'azienda dell'ex datore di lavoro quan egli non ni risenta una trestrizione delle vendite' *Rivista di diritto industriale* 1965, II, 228–229 and G. Ghidini, *Della concorrenza sleale*, in P. Schlesinger (dir), *Il Codice Civile: Commentario* (Milano: Giuffrè, 1991) 236.

Not to do so would hinder them from obtaining and performing a new position in the industry within which they have built up their entire experience.

From the opposite standpoint, it can be argued that 'skill and knowledge' does not include information that, despite being built up as part of the general stock of knowledge possessed by an individual, is not necessary to carry out the occupation and does not contribute to the individual's personal or professional development. This is true for secret information that is not especially relevant when unrelated to the activity or business of the former principal (such as the fact that a company has undergone major losses in a specific period; the commercial relations of said company had the opportunity to, at any given time, confer with specific suppliers, clients or financial institutions about its pending invoices, the launch date of a new product or the date on which a certain transaction will be carried out, etc). This category may also include information that is not directly associated with the duties the employee or other contract partner in question regularly carried out in their former job or position (for instance, an engineer recruited to develop a specific product who ultimately gains knowledge relating to the clients of the company employing him) or information, the disclosure or use of which may only be detrimental to the principal.

However, the criterion I have just laid down, albeit useful, does not fully address the issue raised, for several reasons. The *first* reason is that it only allows for the identification of the most extreme and, accordingly, extravagant cases, because there would not be many instances in which protection of the trade secret in question would entail fully hindering the subject affected from developing the activity or trade they were carrying out. The *second* is based on the fact that it fails to clarify or provide us with guidelines to determine when the use of information is vital for the regular practice of a specific occupation or trade. As a result, there is a need to identify other factors to help us identify instances when banning the use of a trade secret may prevent the individual affected from carrying out their activity or trade or, even when the ban does not lead to such an effect, when it would entail an unacceptable restriction or limitation on the development of the individual's personal and professional abilities.

*Specific criteria (2) Information that can be retained in the memory or that is remembered naturally* Certain judicial decisions have rightly pointed out that 'requiring an individual who is changing jobs to delete the blackboard on his memory' is impossible.[28] Accordingly, it would seem reasonable to maintain that, following the end of the contract between said individual and the holder of the trade secret, the former may use all knowledge stored in their memory. They may only be prevented from using secret information acquired by appropriating or reproducing the tangible format where it was stored or simply by gathering the

28 See, with this graphic expression, *Peerless Pattern Co* v *Pictorial Review Co*, 147 App Div 715, 132 NYS 37.

information using any other method.[29] According to this approach, the memory factor would constitute a criterion for distinguishing secret information forming part of the 'skill and knowledge' possessed by former employees or other contract partners from information which, on the other hand, would indeed be covered by the legal trade secret protection specifically because it cannot be retained in human memory.

Even so, the robustness of this approach is only apparent. It is unquestionable that availing oneself of, or copying a tangible format incorporating a trade secret or copying its content is, in most cases, shows that it is not comprised within the 'skill and knowledge' of the individual who thus utilizes it. However, it is also just as questionable that the mere fact that a subject is able to retain the information in their memory makes it impossible to conclude the opposite. To realize this, one only needs to observe how easy it is to evade this criterion, given that one only needs to deliberately memorize a trade secret for it to be freely exploited when it is certain that this conduct constitutes an unlawful way of gaining access to trade secrets.[30]

Not surprisingly, it has been attempted to correct this judgment by restricting it to information that a subject retains *naturally* in their memory.[31] What is now affirmed is that at any given time former employees and other contract partners of the principal can freely use secrets they retain naturally; in other words, those secrets that would otherwise be remembered by another individual, for example,

---

29 This stance has been backed by certain decisions in different jurisdictions [see, *Universal Thermosensors Ltd* v *Hibben* (1992) 3 All ER 257, (1992) 1 WLR 840, (1992) FRS 361 and *Crowson Fabrics Ltd* v *Rider* (2007) EWHC 2942 (Ch), SSAP *Barcelona* 9-V-2008, *Madrid* 12-IV-2007– (JUR 2007\313230)] and by certain authors [see, though only with respect to commercial trade secrets, R.S. Hetrick, 'Employee "Head Knowledge" and the Alabama Trade Secrets Act' 47 *Alabama Law Review* 1996, *passim*, M.E. Babirak, 'The Maryland Uniform Trade Secrets Act: A Critical Summary of the Act and Case Law' 31 *University of Baltimore Law Review* 2002, 196].

30 This is recalled by, among others, W.R. Cornish and D. Llewelyn, *Intellectual Property: Patents, Copyright, Trade Marks and Allied Rights* (London: Sweet & Maxwell, 2003) 318, Gurry, *supra* n 7, 69 and 202 and Pooley, *supra* n 9, § 6, 14.

31 A distinction is made between the information a person normally retains in his memory from that memorized, for the purposes of considering the use thereof to be unlawful, by Cornish and Llewelyn, *supra* n 31, 317, and in case law, *Johnson & Bloy* v *Wolstenholme Rick* (1989) FSR 135. Also in the US some authors and judicial decisions uphold this approach [see, M. Goudreau, 'Protecting Ideas and Information in Common Law Canada and Quebec' 8 *Intellectual Property Journal* 1994, 278, *Arnol K Davis & Co Inc* v *Ludemann*, 160 AD2d 614, 559 NYS2d 240, 241 (1st Dist 1990)] and although it is circumscribed to information regarding clients, see A. Cundiff, 'How to Hire Your Competitor's Employee: A Trade Secrets Perspective' *PLI* Order n B0-00HA, 2000, 839–840, G.S. Moohr, 'The Problematic Role of Criminal Law in Regulating Use of Information: the Case of the Economic Espionage Act' 80 *North Carolina Law Review* 2002, 510 and Hetrick, *supra* n 30, 536.

in the same position.[32] Nonetheless, this theory is not entirely convincing because, aside from the obvious evidentiary problems that it entails, it focuses the protection of secret information on one sole aspect: its tangibility or intangibility. This dichotomy is clearly subject to a specific criticism: not all information a subject has gained when performing certain duties and which is remembered precisely because it has been used frequently when carrying out said duties can be excluded from trade secret protection. If examined thoroughly, the greater part of highly valuable secrets – such as specific ingredients of certain chemical components or other sophisticated products – are naturally etched into the mind of whoever works with them, and, nonetheless, there is no doubt that they are covered by trade secret protection. Indeed, this approach, which is solely based on the fact that subjects cannot delete from their memory trade secrets they remember, goes some way to favouring the principle of merit-based competition and overlooks the interest and very foundation underlying the protection of this kind of information. It is important to remember that, in regard to the above, the unrestricted use of such information by the employee or other contract partner would imply its use by the new company or the employee's own company, without bearing the costs of its obtainment or development.

The foregoing considerations lead to the conclusion that the very fact of the former employee or other contract partner retaining in their memory a specific trade secret, even if it has not been deliberately remembered, does not necessarily mean they can lawfully use it following the end of their contract.[33] This by no means signifies that the memory factor lacks all relevance in this regard. It merely means that such criterion, although useful for identifying which information can be retained by an employee or other contract partner and, therefore, is liable to become part of their 'skill and knowledge', does not suffice in order to conclude that it is

32 This is the standpoint which, at least in relation to information on clients, has been imposed by Spanish Courts [see all, SSTS 24-XI-2006 (RJ 2007\262), 8-X-2007 (RJ 2007\6805)]. Also, in the United Kingdom and US, Courts have occasionally resorted to this judgment. See, respectively and for instance, *Universal Thermosensors Ltd* v *Hibben and others* (1992) 3 All ER 257, (1992) 1 WLR 840, (1992) FRS 361, *Frosty Bites Distribution LLC* v *Dippin'Dots Inc*, 2003 US Dist LEXIS 8472 (ND Texas 2003); *Rogerscasey, Inc* v *Nankof*, 2002 WL 2010748 (2th Cir 2002), *Western Med Consultants, Inc* v *Johnson*, 80 F3d 1331, 1337 (9th Cir 1996).

33 Also, it is upheld that this factor is not decisive, according to Pooley, *supra* n 9, § 6, 14, Callmann, *supra* n 8, §14:25, Brearley and Bloch, *supra* n 11, 70, Feldman, *supra* n 20, 176, Gurry, *supra* n 7, 68 and 201. See many particularly representative judicial decisions in this regard concerning information on clients, including *SBJ Stephenson Ltd* v *Mandy*, *supra* n 21, *Cass* (it), de 20 March 1991 *supra* n 18. In the US, as pointed out by Pooley (*supra* n 9, § 6, 14), this is the predominant theory. Just to give some examples, see *Al Minor & Assoc, Inc* v *Martin* (117 Ohio St 3d 58, 2008-Ohio-292), *North Atlantic Instruments Inc* v *Haber*, 188 F3d 38 (2nd Cir 1999), *Allen* v *Johar Inc*, 823 SW2d 824, 827 (881 NE2d 850), *Stampede Tool Warehouse, Inc* v *May*, 272 Ill App 3d 580, 651 NE2d 209 (1st Dist 1995), *Morlife Inc* v *Perry*, 56 Cal App 4th 1514, 66 Cal Rptr 2d 731 (1st Dist 1997).

inextricably intertwined with their professional stock of knowledge and experience. To determine this, it is still necessary to demonstrate that, by preventing the use of this naturally remembered secret information, an inadmissible restriction, veto or limitation would be placed on the former employee or other contract partner from carrying out the activity for which they are professionally qualified or from developing their personal or professional abilities. Of course, this effect does not always take place and is dependent on the specific circumstances, whether the information subject to secrecy is technical, industrial, commercial, financial or organizational in nature, to name but a few examples.

In the case of information associated with the technical and production divisions of a company it is clear that preventing an employee from using a specific secret procedure pertaining to their former employer and to which they had access to during their duties, thereby meaning they remember it, will not affect the development of their professional abilities. In this regard, one only needs to note that it does not prevent them from carrying out the activities concerned for another principal or for themselves using their experience and knowledge obtained in that specific occupation, activity or trade. It merely requires the employee to refrain from using the specific secret procedure from their former employer. This is clearly shown by some US caselaw preventing former employees unlawfully using the industrial secret of the holder, even when only stored in human memory, thereby disregarding the argument that blocking them from being able to exploit it would lead to the aforementioned effect.[34]

The same is true when the trade secret involves commercial and organizational information and, in particular, data on clients or suppliers (IDs, addresses, prices, discounts, etc). In this regard, it is pertinent to emphasize that preventing former employees or other contract parties from using this type of information, which they have come to know as a result of carrying out their duties, does not inherently entail a non-competition ban or an unjustified restriction on their right to carry out a job or set up a company. Quite the opposite, the impact such a ban on using secret information may have on these individuals will usually depend on the specific circumstances, such as the length of the client list; the small or broad range of the circle of potential clients in the specific industry; or, in short, the kind of relations existing between the client and the specific employee or other contract partner. Specifically, this restriction may either operate in a functional manner as a non-compete agreement, for instance, when the range of clients for a specific area is highly limited and dominated by the holder of the secret list or, in the case of an extensive market, when most clients already belong to the former principal. Likewise, requiring employees or other contract partners to not

34 See, for instance, among the most eloquent, *Custom Mfg* v *Rymer*, 1995 US Dist LEXIS 9059 (ND Ill 1995); *Televation Telecommunication Systems, Inc* v *Saindon*, 169 Ill App 3d 8, 522 NE2d 1359 (2nd Dist 1988), *A H Emery Co* v *Marcan Products Corp*, 389 F2d 11, 16 (2nd Cir 1968), *Sperry Rand Corp* v *Rothlein*, 241 F Supp 549, 563, 143 USPQ (BNA) 172 (D Conn 1964).

use knowledge and relations they had with their former principal's customers may be unjustified when, in the specific market or sector of activity, contractual relations linking clients to specific service providers are based on trust due to the individual's abilities, skills, competence, earnestness, and so on. Precisely because in these latter cases clients choose their service providers based on these factors or, if you will, based on personal relations, it must be pointed out that it would not be uncommon for them to follow the specific employee or other contract partner if they decide to leave their former employment, trade or position and set up their own company, or to provide their services for a new employer. Consequently, even if one concluded that the secret list of such clients does not form part of 'skill and knowledge' possessed by employees and other contract partners, it is clear that, inasmuch as the principal has – as indeed he should – informed them of the termination of the relationship, it may be stated that this list has not been exploited and, accordingly, a misappropriation of the trade secret has not occurred.

(a) *Internalized* information. Another criterion making it possible to determine that specific information is so intertwined with the stock of experience and skills possessed by an individual that banning its use in future would unjustifiably restrict the individual from deploying their personal and professional skills, depends on whether the information has been *internalized.* In other words, when an employee or another contract partner who becomes aware of it internalizes it by retaining it in their memory, whereby once learnt it is unavoidably absorbed by their toolkit of skills and knowledge that are inseparable from said individual.

Although it is only feasible to verify this aspect on a case by case basis, it is possible to identify by way of indication some of the instances wherein this internalization of secret information can be affirmed. These include, firstly, cases where the memorization or retention of information requires prior comprehension thereof, plus assimilation and processing (such as an analysis technique, a system for calculating prices, a method enabling a chemical to be produced in a swifter manner, etc), in contrast to those instances where the memorization of information merely entails a simple mechanical process involving the transference of information from the tangible format on which it is stored to the memory of the individual (such as memorizing a list of clients).[35] For instance, it is thereby clear that to learn a specific programming system it is necessary to understand and take on the information beforehand in order to memorize it. Once the individual concerned retains it in their memory, it is mixed and combined with their own schemes and knowledge on the subject, whereby it becomes part of their skills, which their former employer cannot prevent them from using.

Secondly, closely related to the knowledge just set out is the knowledge concerning problems, difficulties and errors suffered or found by the subject in a

35 Also holding this counter-position, see Y. Feldman, 'The Behavioural Foundations of Trade Secrets: Tangibility, Authorship and Legality' (July 6, 2004) *Bar Ilan University Public Law* Working Paper No 1-05, available in SSRN: http://ssrn.com/abstract=562233.

procedure, method, technique, etc, as well as the respective solutions discovered by a process of trial and error or, in general, any kind of negative information learnt while carrying out their duties. Indeed, although this is not a settled issue in case law,[36] it is by no means easy to imagine that, while carrying out the duties that employees or other contract partners have been assigned in a new company or in their own, they can disregard or dispense with the experience they possess, in order to avoid the errors or problems they encountered in the past. Likewise, it is unrealistic to assume – or, indeed, demand – that those parties will avoid using techniques, procedures and methods that did not work or were unsatisfactory or inefficient when carrying out their duties in future employment. As the most basic logic indicates, no one is willing to invest means into something they know only too well will result in failure.

Lastly, this group of cases may also include knowledge which, as often occurs with negative information, is built up through experimentation. One example can help us to better understand this concept. Let us suppose that some employees hired by a specific employer to produce pipes, after many years devoted to the task knows without the need for experimentation which are, by and large, the mixes and proportions of fibre needed to obtain a specific result and such mixes are secret, or let us assume they know the optimal concentration percentage for diluting a specific material and that this is also confidential. Beyond question, if in the future they are recruited by another employer or set up their own company to devote themselves to what they know how to do, working in their field of professional expertise – in other words, manufacturing pipes – they will use this knowledge. Indeed, it would be unreasonable to require them (and in any event illusory) to once again experiment in their new position to try and ascertain the right mix or the pertinent concentration percentage which they already know right away.[37] The reason behind this lies in the fact that in such cases allowing a principal to protect the result of ordinary experience as a trade secret, in a specific sector, would be tantamount to requiring their former employees or other contract partners to 'reinvent the wheel as a price to pay to enter into the market'.[38]

---

36 While some decisions have opted for the theory suggested here [including *FSS Travel and Leisure Systems ltd* v *Johnson and another* (1998) IRLR 382, *SI Handling Sys, Inc* v *Heisley*, 753 F2d 1244 (3rd Cir 1985), *Winston Research Corp* v *Minesota Min & Mfg Co*, 350 F2d 134 (9th Cir 1965)], others have taken the opposing viewpoint [see, *On-Line Technologies, Inc* v *Perkin-Elmer Corp*, 253 FSupp 2d 313 (D Conn 2003), *Courtesy Temporal Serv* v *Camacho*, 22 Cal App 3d 1278 (1 Dist 1990), *Cinebase Software, Inc* v *Media Guaranty Trust, Inc*, 1998 US Dist LEXIS 15007 (ND Cal, 1998), *Novell Inc* v *Timpanogos Research Group Inc*, 46 USPQ2d 1197 (Utah, 1998)].

37 A case such as this is resolved as we suggest, *Balston* v *Headline Filters Ltd* (1987) FSR 330.

38 See, using this expression, *Fleming Sales Co* v *Bailey*, 611 FSupp 507 (ND Ill 185).

(b) The stock of knowledge and experience already possessed by the affected subject. Although it is not a decisive factor in this regard, the stock of knowledge and experience built up by an individual prior to providing their services for a specific principal also plays a vital role in the task of deciding whether the secret information must be considered as falling within the individual's 'skill and knowledge'. Caselaw proves it in the matter.[39] This has also been defended, though from another standpoint, by those who support the idea that the simplicity or difficulty with which one can isolate specific information from other knowledge that is intimately tied to the sphere of skills and abilities of the former employee or other contract partner is an element that respectively tips the balance in favour of protecting the information as a trade secret or, contrariwise, of considering it to be comprised within 'skill and knowledge'.[40] It is clear that taking this element into consideration does not appear to be erroneous at all, in this context. And for a simple reason: the mere fact of preventing an employee or other contract partner who has extensive prior experience in the sector from using the information learnt while carrying out their duties for a specific principal will, more than likely, lead to them being prevented from using and benefiting from this stock of knowledge and experience that has been previously acquired and which, indeed, can lawfully be used. Indeed, there is no great difficulty in accepting that in these cases it is more likely that the knowledge needed to develop a specific product, procedure, strategy, sales method, etc., does not originally stem from the specific secret information an employee or other contract partner obtained in their former position or employment, but rather from their stock of general knowledge built up in the pertinent sector. In relation to the latter idea, it is highly likely that, on account of their high level of training and experience in the sector, these employees or other contract partners are in a position to proceed in the same manner regardless of the particular knowledge they may have gained providing their services for a specific principal. Accordingly, one can say that often determining whether the secret formed part of the 'skill and knowledge' of the individual in question would be a futile task in these cases.

---

39 See SAP *Barcelona* 18-I-2001 (JUR 2001\89259), *Jacono* v *Invacare Corporation*, 2006 Ohio 1596, P8-P9 (8th Dist Ct App 2006), *Dynamics Research Corp* v *Analytic Sciences Corp*, 9 Mass App Ct 254, 400 NE2d 1274, 1282 (1980).

40 This argument has primarily been forwarded by Courts and commentators in the UK. See all judicial decisions, *Printers & Finishers* v *Holloway* (1965) RPC 239, *Faccenda Chicken* v *Flower*, *supra* n 20, and more recently, *Dranez Anstalt and others* v *Hayek and others* (2002) 1 BCLC 693. Among other authors, Cornish and Llewelyn, *supra* n 31, 319, Coleman, *supra* n 11, 12 *et seq.*, and despite pointing out that it is not a definitive criterion, Brearley and Bloch, *supra* n 11. Also in the US, some decisions and scholars have been in favour of encompassing this judgment within the criteria that may be useful for identifying information forming part of the 'skill and knowledge' of employees and other contract partners. See, for instance, *Jacono* v *Invacare Corporation*, *supra* n 40, Nimmer, *supra* n 24, § 5, 123, L.S. Friesen, 'Distinguishing Between an Employee's General Knowledge and Trade Secrets' 23 *Colo Law* 1994, 2124.

(c) Definition and scope of the information to which the duty to secrecy applies. Lastly, one relevant though formal aspect that must be borne in mind when deciding whether banning the use of information affects the development of an individual's personal and professional abilities is whether the specific information the holder wishes to protect has been sufficiently identified and defined.[41] This is closely tied to the protection measures the holder of a secret should adopt.

Indeed, beyond question, the broader and more general the information that must be kept confidential is, the more likely it is that protecting it will severely restrict an individual's genuine right to carry out their occupation or trade. On the other hand, if the information, the use of which is sought to be prevented, is duly circumscribed to a specific portion of a certain technology or other secret information, it may be assumed that the protection thereof will not greatly affect the right of the former employee or the other contract partner to use their knowledge and general experience in the trade or occupation. Hence, it is unsurprising that courts tend to be especially reluctant to grant legal protection for information claimed to be secret when it relates to generalized sets of information[42] or when it has not been identified precisely enough with sufficient detail to enable the former employee or other contract partner to know exactly what information they may freely use and what they may not.[43]

### *Resorting to the Explicit Non-Compete Clauses or Agreements to Prevent the Use of 'Skill and Knowledge'*

In the foregoing sections we have seen how the exploitation by former employees or other contract partners of the skills, aptitudes and information comprising 'skill and knowledge' is not covered by legal trade secret protection. Now it is pertinent to investigate whether there is another means for preventing the former principal from being protected from the competitive advantages stemming from the use of their 'skill and knowledge' by said individuals, which may work for a new principal or for themselves. Along these lines, the main legal instrument available to the former employer is signing a pertinent post-term non-compete clause or agreement, the effectiveness and validity of which in this content varies according to the kind of knowledge affected by it.

When the information whose use is sought to be prevented because it qualifies as a trade secret, resorting to a post-term non-compete agreement entails no

41 Accordingly, Nimmer, *supra* n 24 § 5, 51–52 and 121; with a similar view, Freisen, *supra* n 41, 2123, Weniger, *supra* n 8, 380.

42 See, along these lines, *John Zink Co Ltd* v *Lloyds Bank Ltd* (1975) RPC 385, wherein protection was called for with respect to the technical information set out in 68 documents.

43 As especially pointed out by *Lock International plc* v *Beswich and others* (1989) 3 All ER 373, (1989) 1 WLR 1268, (1989) IRLR 481, *Manor Electronic Ltd and another* v *Dickinson and anothers* (1988) RPC 618 and SAP *Madrid* 12-IV-2007 (JUR 2007\322863).

specific problems. The reason behind this conclusion is that the preservation of the secret asset may constitute a legitimate interest suitable for justifying the validity of the agreement,[44] inasmuch as they satisfy the remaining requirements called for to this end. Indeed, although this kind of information already forms part of the personal and professional stock of experiences possessed by former employees or other contract partners, they are still trade secrets. As a result, the use of said secret by these individuals may pose a major risk to the competitive interests of the company whereby the exclusive benefit falls on the employee or new employer. Therefore, there may be a true legitimate interest, as is required, to support the validity of the agreement. A paradigm to the foregoing would be secret information related to clients (buying habits, profiles, applicable prices, etc), which have been merged with the stock of knowledge and professional experience possessed by the individuals in question. In this regard, it must be observed that the non-compete agreement is set up as a particularly appropriate mechanism for preventing the information from being gathered to the detriment of the former employer and in favour of the employee or their new principal.

On the other hand, from the standpoint of its validity there are many reservations regarding resorting to the non-compete agreement in order to prevent former employees or other contract partners of the principal from being able to benefit from the host of knowledge and information falling within their 'skill and knowledge' and which does not benefit from the status of a trade secret. Given that, in fact, what the non-compete clause seeks to achieve in these cases is merely to prevent individuals from benefiting from the skills, abilities or general information they possess, it does not seem entirely mistaken to maintain that signing a non-compete agreement does not meet a legitimate commercial or industrial interest and, therefore, lacks validity. This is the case whether the interest the principal

44 See, among many others, the authors who generally accept the validity of non-compete agreements when protecting trade secrets, Gurry, *supra* n 7, 210, Arnow-Richman, *supra* n 23, 1176, Coleman, *supra* n 11, 42–43, L.C. Hermle, 'Protecting Trade Secrets in an Era of Increased Information Sharing and Employee Mobility' *BLI Glass-CLE* 2002, 318, Brearley and Bloch, *supra* n 11, 113, Nogueira, *supra* n 11, 87 *et seq.*; and decisions admitting this fact include, *Lasing Linde Ltd* v *Kerr* (1991) 1 All ER 418, (1991) WLR 251, (1991) 428, (1991) IRLR 80. *FSS Travel and Leisure Systems Ltd* v *Johnson and another* (1998) IRLR 382, STSJ *Navarra* 30-IV-2001 (AS 2001\2238), *Comprehensive Technologies Int'l, Inc* v *Software Artisans*, Inc 3 F3d 730, 735–7 (4th Cir 1993), *vacated and dismissed on petition for rehearing*, 1993 US App LEXIS 28601 (4th Cir 1993), *Earthweb Inc* v *Schlack*, 2000 US App LEXIS 11446 (2th Cir 2000), *Unisource Worldwide Inc* v *Carrara*, 244 FSupp 2d 977 (CDIll 2003), *Lucente* v *Int'l Bus Mach Corp*, 310 F3d 243 (2th Cir 2002), *Outsource Intern Inc* v *Barton*, 192 F3d 662 (7th Cir 1999). The authors pointing this out specifically in relation to trade secrets forming part of the 'skill and knowledge' of the employee or other contracting parties in collaborative arrangements with the entrepreneur include Dean, *supra* n 8, 22 and 204, Goudreau, *supra* n 32, 279 and Callmann, *supra* n 8, 112. Among Courts, see *Faccenda Chicken* v *Flower*, *supra* n 20, *Ixora Trading Inc* v *Jones* (1990) 1 FSR 251.

seeks to protect concerns special skills or subjective abilities inherent to the individual concerned (such as their skill, aptitude, mental or manual ability), or whether it concerns general information that is not secret in nature (such as general knowledge in the sector).[45]

## The Inevitable Disclosure of Trade Secrets

Close to, though substantially distinct from the cases we have just examined and which in practice entail major complexities, are instances where a former employee or other contract partner that has a great deal of knowledge about certain trade secrets of the former principal, seeks to work or collaborate with a competitor, takes on the same or similar duties to those they previously carried out, whereby they must make decisions based on knowledge they have of the aforementioned secrets; therefore, they are required to disclose them or inevitably use them when performing the new duties and responsibilities entrusted. Specifically, we are referring to cases where trade secrets which will inevitably be used in the new company cannot be deemed as falling within the individual's 'skill and knowledge' and, accordingly, its use would in any event amount to a misappropriation of trade secrets.[46]

An example may help to clarify this idea. Let us imagine that an employee hired by a specific company to manage the prices and terms and conditions of a bid to a tender, which is secret information, decides to leave the company one

45 See, in the first respect, among others, Brearley and Bloch, *supra* n 11, 114, Goudreau, *supra* n 32, 279 and Nogueira, *supra* n 11, 131. See in the second respect, W.G. Porter and M.C. Griffaton, 'Using Noncompete to Protect Legitimate Business Interest' 69 *Defense Counsel Journal* 2002, 194 *et seq.* and Gurry, *supra* n 7, 211. Indeed, there is no lack of even extreme stances. See T. Robison, 'The Confidence Game: An Approach to the Law about Trade Secrets' *Arizona Law Review* 1983, 347–93, upholding that resorting to this kind of agreement to protect trade secrets must be eliminated because they tend to protect, aside from trade secrets, the general aptitudes and experience of the employee.

46 This has been revealed by many decisions which, when judging a case of this nature, have declared that it is unnecessary to resort to the inevitable disclosure doctrine to maintain the cautionary order in the specific case, given that the breach of the secret, aside from being imminent, had already taken place. See, recently as an example, *Hatfield* v *AutoNation Inc*, 939 So2d 155 (Fla Dist Ct App 2006), that temporarily banned the defendant (the former manager of a dealership of Mercedes-Benz who entered into negotiations to gain a similar position with another car dealership for the same brand that was competing with the former), from disclosing any information about his former principal, as well as from selling, providing or using vehicles or parts thereof as a wholesaler or retailer for a number of months because, prior to leaving his current job, he had taken documents containing secret information on the plaintiff regarding sales transactions at various dealerships, internal programmes, etc, and copied other similar information onto his laptop.

month prior to the deadline and takes on the selfsame duties in another company and, therefore, manages the bid for their new employer for the same tender. It is clear that this secret information does not form part of the stock of skills and knowledge they are free to use. In this respect, one only needs to realize that its use is not entirely necessary for practising the occupation or trade, nor can it be stated, in this author's view, that by preventing the use of such information the individual is unjustifiably limited from carrying out the activity for which they are professionally qualified or from developing their personal or professional abilities. However, it is also clear that they cannot separate this secret information retained in their memory in order to make decisions; therefore, they will inevitably disclose it or use it to carry out their new duties.

As pointed out, the difficulty in these circumstances is not in accepting that in certain situations there are evidences of imminent or threatened misappropriation (unlawful use or disclosure) of the trade secret. Rather, the complexity lies in outlining the content of the remedy, since merely preventing the disclosure or use of the trade secret learnt by the former employee or other contract partner while working for the holder of said secret is scarcely promising in practice, even though it may be flawless from a theoretical point of view. For this reason, in the US some courts and, in turn, some scholars have developed the *inevitable disclosure doctrine* which, generally speaking, makes it possible to temporarily ban, as a preventive measure, the acceptance of duties and responsibilities that are similar or the same as those carried out in a former job, trade or position in another competing company (one's own or of a third party), the performance of which does indeed require the disclosure or exploitation of the trade secrets pertaining to the former principal.[47]

The problems brought about by these instances are not, of course, easy to address. Indeed, the absolute, systematic acceptance of inevitable disclosure doctrine as a mechanism to address these instances may bring about perverse, counterproductive effects for innovation in companies and economic growth in general.[48] However, it is also the case that repudiating this technique categorically

47 See, among the more recent decisions, the leading case, *Pepsico* v *Redmond*, 54 F3d 1262 (7th Cir 1995) and after this case among other decisions applying this doctrine, *La Calhene Inc* v *Spolyar*, 938 FSupp 523 (WD Wis 1996), *Atenia Retirment Servs* v *Hug*, 1997 Conn Sup Lexis 1781, *Merck & Co, Inc* v *Lyon*, 941 FSupp 1443 (MDNC 1996), *Essex Group, Inc* v *Southwire Co*, 501 SE2d 501 (Ga 1998), *Cardinal Freight Carriers, Inc et al* v *JB Hunt Trans Serv Inc*, 337 Ark 143, 987 SW2d 642 (1999), *Procter & Gamble Co* v *Storeham*, 747 NE2d 268 (Ohio Ct App 2002), *Barilla America, Inc* v *Wright et al.*, 2002 WL 31165069 (SD Iowa 2002).

48 See, among other hostile views about this doctrine, L. Koh, 'From Hoops to Hard Drives: an Accession Law Approach to the Inevitable Misappropriation of Trade Secrets' 48 *AMUR* 1998, 284, J.L. Sauling, 'Locating Inevitable Disclosure's Place in Trade Secret Analysis' 100 *Michigan Law Review* 2002, 1195, S.S. Whaley, 'The Inevitable Disaster of Inevitable Disclosure' 67 *University of Cincinnati Law Review* 1999, 836. And specially though in high mobility markets, Hyde, *supra* n 19, *passim*, spec 30–40. Nonetheless, see

would not give rise to more advantageous outcomes either,[49] especially if one considers that proving that a trade secret has been infringed tends to be not easy at all and, damages are very difficult to quantify. Consequently, suitable protection for trade secrets and, accordingly, a boost to the development and dissemination of socially worthy information will take place provided the holder possesses a remedy enabling them to prevent inevitable, unfair use or disclosure.

Accordingly, it is this author's understanding that the most plausible, respectful solution in light of the interests at stake, must be sought from an interim standpoint, which prevents irremediable detriment that the misappropriation of a trade secret can cause to the holder, on the one hand, and which mitigates the restrictive effects that the application of this doctrine may have on employees' mobility on the other. Specifically, I support the notion of allowing application of the inevitable disclosure doctrine in an exceptional manner, in any event, restricting the content of an injunction to merely prohibiting use, during a brief, limited period of time (i.e. until the new product is ultimately released on the market), with respect to the former employee or other contract partner of the holder of the secret when it comes to carrying out their duties or taking on responsibilities in those specific activities, areas, or relating to the lines of products and services that are closely related to the position held with the former employment. In fact, this is the scope of application often granted by US courts for preliminary injunctions issued in application of this doctrine.[50] It should be noted, however, that there is no judicial opinion preventing

---

for some pertinent critiques on the study conducted by Hyde, M. Risch, 'Comments on Trade Secret Sharing in High Velocity Labour Markets' (September 16, 2008) *Employee Rights and Employment Policy Journal* vol 12, 2008. Available at SSRN: http://ssrn.com/abstract=1269039.

49 In favour of its application, W.A. Scott and R.S. Sinder, 'The Inevitable Disclosure Doctrine in Franchise Disputes' 22 *Franchise Law Journal* 2003, 212, D. Pasqualone, 'Intellectual Property: D Trade Secret: 1. Employment Relationships: Globespan v O'Neill' 17 *Berkeley Technology Law Journal* 2002, *passim*, spec, 252 and 266, N. Hamler, 'The Impeding Merger of the Inevitable Disclosure Doctrine and Trade Secrets: Is Trade Secrets Law Headed in the Right Direction?' 25 *The Journal of Corporation Law* 2000, 402, R.M. Halligan, 'Trade Secrets and the Inevitable Disclosure Doctrine' *PLI* Order n G0-011Q, 2002, *passim*, spec, 164, L.K. Stevens, 'Trade Secret and the Inevitable Disclosure' *Tort & Insurance Law Journal* 2001, 927, T.A. Martin, 'The Evolution of Trade Secret Law in Texas: Is It Time to Recognize the Doctrine of Inevitable Disclosure?' *South Texas Law Review* 2001, 1388.

50 See, for instance, *FMC Corp v Varco Int'l Inc*, 677 F2d 500 (5th Cir 1982), where the content of the injunction resulted in a ban from taking on a position that would give rise to an inherent risk of disclosure, notwithstanding the fact that the employee in question could work for his new employer; *Merck & Co, Inc* v *Lyon, supra* n 48, which required the former employee not to deal with certain products competing with those of his former employer; *Allis Chalmers Manufacturing Co* v *Continental Aviation and Engineering Corp*, 255 FSupp 645 (ED Mich 1966), wherein only a ban was passed down for negotiations with certain clients; *Essex Group, Inc* v *Southwire Co, supra* n 48, which limited the ban to a specific division of the competitor. As an example of decisions limiting the sentence

a former employee from providing their services for a competing company regardless of the position they would occupy.[51]

Nonetheless, one could argue that the acceptance of the inevitable disclosure doctrine, in light of the consequences thereof, entails transforming a ban on disclosure or the use of a trade secret into a *de facto* non-compete agreement. Accordingly – so the argument follows – it would become an intolerable retroactive alteration of the terms applicable to the employment relationship.[52] However, according to the manner in which this doctrine has been outlined, it would not appear that it technically serves as a non-competition clause either when it comes to the essence or the effects. In terms of essence, this doctrine is based on the protection of trade secrets and the authority that most lawmakers have granted to courts to prevent misappropriation of such secrets (in Spain see Article 18.2 of the Law on Unfair Competition). The underlying principles are not therefore those governing Contractual Law, but rather those regulating trade secrets misappropriations. In terms of the effects, the inevitable disclosure doctrine does not imply a generalized ban on competing with a former principal. Along these lines, it is necessary to point out that it does not prevent an employee or other contract partners from carrying out a similar job or position even in the same sector, provided they do so in positions not requiring the use of the specific trade secrets or, if you will, provided that, for a certain period of time, the new principal limits their duties and the scope of their responsibility to products and services that do not involve direct competition with those manufactured, marketed and offered by the former principal, to which the employees were devoted in the former employment.

---

to cessation during a specific timeframe, see *Pepsico* v *Redmond, supra* n 48, and *Lumex, Inc* v *Highsmith, supra* n 48, wherein, in both instances the ban was issued for six months.

51 See *La Calhene, Inc* **v** *Spolyar***,** *supra* n 48**,** where the Court deemed that, although the defendants could not work in the competitor's company given that it would lead to exploitation of the secrets held by the former employer, they had extensive work experience in many fields and sales capacity they could use and benefit from by selling other products aside from those of the plaintiff.

52 See, along these lines, J. Edelstein, 'Intellectual Slavery?: The Doctrine of Inevitable Disclosure of Trade Secrets' 26 *Golden Gate University Law Review* 1996, 732, J.O. Harris, 'Note: The Doctrine of Inevitable Disclosure: A Proposal to Balance Employer and Employee Interests' 78 *Washington University Law Quarterly* 2000, 325, Koh, *supra* n 49, 278, M.K. Miller, 'Inevitable Disclosure where Non-Competition Agreement Exists: Additional Guidance Needed' 6 *Boston University Journal of Science & Technology Law* 2000, 31, n 104, S.L. Sheinfeld and M.A. Konkel, 'Protecting Employers Secret and the "Doctrine of Inevitable Disclosure"' *PLI/Lit* 411, 2002, 503, Whaley, *supra* n 49, 836, Gilson, *supra* n 23, 622 and Farrando, *supra* n 7, 207–8. See, in case law, *EarthWeb, Inc* v *Schlack*, 71 FSupp2d 299 (SDNY 1999), *Whyte* v *Shlagee Lock Co*, 1001 Cal App 4th 1443, 125 Cal Rptr 2d 277 (2002), *Zemco Mfg, Inc* v *Navistar Int'l Transportation Corp (cit supra)*, *Lejeune* v *Coin Acceptors Inc* 381 Md 288, 849 A2d 451 (2004) and *L-3 Communications Corp* v *Nelly*, 2005 WL 3304130 (NY Sup 2005).

In this regard also, it is important to dispel the impression that the application of this doctrine shows inconsistent treatment between operators signing non-compete agreements with respect to those that do not.[53] In the former instance, one could say that it is necessary to meet exacting requirements for the agreement to be effective. In the latter, however, one could add that it is merely necessary to prove that infringement of the secret is inevitable. The inevitable disclosure doctrine could therefore be seen as favouring operators who do not establish the pertinent ban on competition and, therefore, discourages others from doing so in future. Nonetheless, it is understood that when considered in this light, this objection does not appear to be highly persuasive. In this regard, it is first necessary to observe that, in contrast to what may be perceived, cases of trade secret infringement based on the inevitable disclosure doctrine are the most difficult ones to win, owing to the demanding requirements to which its application is subject. Indeed, this is shown by the experience in the US, where countless decisions have been made where courts have ended up rejecting the application of this doctrine in the case.[54] Secondly, one must not overlook the fact that, even though it may prove useful for protecting trade secrets when they effectively form part of the 'skill and knowledge' of the individual in question, the non-compete agreement is, generally speaking, not an instrument aimed at preventing disclosure. It is merely necessary to point to the fact that disclosure of the secret does not necessarily entail a breach of a ban on competing. Lastly, by examining the content and effects of these agreements one may soon become aware of the fact that the manner in which they affect competition and have a bearing on the chances of the individual bound by them being able to freely carry out their occupation or trade are greater than when applying the doctrine we are looking into. Accordingly, it seems natural that its effectiveness must not be subject to payment of economic compensation by the former employer. We must not overlook the fact that certain decisions have required this.[55] However,

53 See, along these lines, Whaley, *supra* n 49, 820 *et seq.*

54 This is more so in states that are more likely to protect employees' mobility. See, for instance, *Patio Enclosures, Inc* v *Herbst*, 39 Fed App 964 (6th Cir 2002), *Campbell Soup Co* v *Giles*, F3d 467 (1st Cir 1995), *Tactica Int'l Inc* v *Atlantic Horizon Int'l Inc*, FSupp 2d 586 (SDNY 2001), *Del Monte Fresh Produce Co* v *Dole Food Co, Inc*, 136 FSupp 2d 1271, 1292 (SD Fla 2001), *Barilla America, Inc* v *Wright et al.*, 2002 WL 31165069 (SD Iowa 2002), *Architetext Inc* v *Kikuchi*, 2005 WL 2864244 (Mass Super 2005), *Hoskins Mfg Co* v *PMC Corp*, 47 FSupp 2d 851 (ED Mich 1999), *Jacono* v *Invacare Corporation*, *Bridgestone/Firestone Inc* v *Lockhart*, 5 FSupp 2d 667, 682 (SD Ind 1998), *Doubleclick, Inc* v *Henderson*, 1997 NY Misc LEXIS 577 (Sup Ct NY Co 1997), *Lumex Inc* v *Highsmith*, 919 FSupp 624 (EDNY 1996), *Gov't Tech Serv Inc* v *Intellisys Tech Copr*, 1999 WL 1499541 (Va Cir Ct 1999), *EarthWeb, Inc* v *Schlack*, *supra* n 53, *Bayer Corp* v *Roche Molecular Systems Inc*, 72 FSupp 2d 1111 (ND Cal 1999), *Whyte* v *Shlagee Lock Co*, *supra* n 53, *Lejeune* v *Coin Acceptors Inc*, *supra* n 53.

55 See *Emery Industries, Inc* v *Cottier*, 202 USPQ 829, 836 (SD Ohio 1978), where the employee was granted financial compensation involving averaging his former salary in line

the interesting point is that in the few instances where this has happened, the preliminary injunction issued prevented the former employee completely from working for a particular operator.

with the current one; and along these lines, *Cabot Corp* v *King*, 790 FSupp 153, 156–8 (ND Ohio 1992) WHERE HE WAS GRANTED HALF OF THE FORMER SALARY HE RECEIVED.

# Chapter 10

# Long-Term Relationships, Networks and Exchange of Knowledge in Production and Distribution Contracts

Marco Gobbato

## Introduction

Contracts are mainly designed to allow for exchanges that do not take place instantaneously, envisaging mechanisms for the enforcement of the parties' undertakings.[1] However, contracts can also serve other purposes: for instance, they can divide the risk between the parties and transfer knowledge.[2]

In general, contracts have two main roles when dealing with knowledge: they may be entered into to produce innovation or they may be used to transfer existing knowledge.[3] For example, a contract for the production of an innovative research

---

1 See e.g. Restatement (second) of contracts § 1 (1979): 'A contract is a promise or a set of promises for the breach of which the law gives a remedy, or the performance of which the law in some way recognizes as a duty.' See also R. Scott and G. Triantis, 'Incomplete Contracts and the Theory of Contract Design' 56 *Case Western Reserve Law Review* 187 (2005).

2 For instance, the contract can allocate the risk between the parties. See A. Schwartz and R. Scott, 'Contract Theory and the Limits of Contract Law' 113 *Yale Law Journal* 541 (2003) and, above all, R. Scott, 'Conflict and Cooperation in Long-Term Contracts' 75 (6) *California Law Review* 2005 (1987); C. Gillette, 'Commercial Rationality and the Duty to Adjust Long-Term Contracts' 69 *Minnesota Law Review* 521 (1985); V. Goldberg, 'Price Adjustments in Long-Term Contracts' 1985 *Wisconsin Law Review* 527.

3 When it is not specified, references are to technical knowledge or technical information. The text does not distinguish between knowledge and information. In economics the distinction has not been totally addressed yet. For instance R. Cowan, P. David and D. Foray, 'The Explicit Economics of Knowledge and Tacitness' 9 (2) *Industrial and Corporate Change* 211 (2000) p. 221 refer that 'following the seminal work of Arrow and Nelson, an entire generation of economists treated scientific and technological knowledge as "information"'. At 216 the authors define information as 'a message containing structured data, the receipt of which causes some action by the recipient agent, without implying that the nature of that action is determined solely and uniquely by the message itself.' See also Y. Benkler, 'The Wealth of Networks', 2006, available at http://www.benkler.org. At 313 a distinction between the two is provided: 'I use "information" ... to refer to raw data, scientific reports of the output of scientific discovery, news, and factual reports. I use

project falls within the first category of contracts, whereas a patent licence falls within the second category.

Technological knowledge may be transferred through the assignment or licence of intellectual property rights. In this case, knowledge is the main subject matter of the agreement. Yet, the transfer of knowledge may not be the main subject matter of the agreement and, rather, be functional thereto. The latter kind of transfer can be found especially when firms collaborate to produce or distribute goods or services. This is the case, for example, for a subcontract where the contractor provides the subcontractor with the information the latter needs to produce the good or to perform the service that is the main subject matter of the contract.

In these cases, the contract also transfers knowledge that is not covered by intellectual property rights. This chapter examines the distinct features of knowledge transfer between 'propertizable' and 'non-propertizable' knowledge and within the latter between transfer of explicit and tacit knowledge.

The transfer of non-proprietary knowledge implies higher costs than the transfer of proprietary knowledge. When knowledge is propertized, property remedies are often associated to contractual remedies. When knowledge is not propertized mainly contractual remedies are available. This reduces the protection of the producer and the transferor, thereby decreasing his incentives to enter into the contract in the first place. Thus, the contract may offer the transferee of knowledge a weak, albeit effective (up to a certain extent), protection through special agreements, such as trade secrets agreements, exclusive dealing arrangements and covenants not to compete. Indeed, these agreements, albeit in different ways, limit the use that one or both contractual parties may make of the information provided by the other party, thus fostering such transfer.

We will deal with the contractual transfer of knowledge and with the ways in which contract law can foster the circulation of knowledge in bilateral contracts for the production and distribution of goods and services as well as in inter-firm contractual networks.

Knowledge is transferred differently in bilateral contracts and inter-firm networks. As this chapter will try to explain, the value of knowledge in contractual networks is higher than its corresponding value in market exchanges. The role of systems that foster the circulation of knowledge within the network, while limiting it outside the network, may increase the efficiency of the network as an organizational system for the transfer of knowledge.

The second section of this chapter will focus on the many purposes that contracts may serve when dealing with knowledge distinguishing between production and transfer. The third section illustrates the devices that may be used by contractual parties to transfer knowledge. The fourth section focuses on the

"knowledge" to refer to the set of cultural practices and capacities necessary for processing the information into either new statements in the information exchange, or more important in our context, for practical use of the information in appropriate ways to produce more desirable actions or outcomes from action.'

transfer of knowledge in contracts for the production and distribution of goods and services. The fifth section discusses the transfer of knowledge in inter-firm networks. The sixth section examines up to what extent knowledge transferred contractually may be protected by the law on unfair competition and by contract law. The last section concludes.

## Contracts for Producing Innovation and for Transferring Knowledge

### *Contracts for the Production of Innovation*

Firms rarely possess all the resources necessary to innovate. Thus, they often carry out the research activity in collaboration with one or many other firms.[4]

In the case of bilateral contracting, the production of knowledge usually concerns the carrying out of a research activity by both parties or by one party in return for good consideration provided by the other. The results of the research work should lead to a new development or, in any event, should take the shape of an activity that pursues an innovative result.

Innovation is also produced when research is conducted jointly by different firms. In this case, a multilateral agreement is used, whereby two or more firms regulate their different involvement in the performance of scientific or technical research to have access to its ensuing results.[5] The collective arrangements for production of knowledge provide means for technical coordination, and also regulate the access to tangible and intangible resources.[6]

---

4 See P. David and D. Foray, 'Economic Fundamentals of the Knowledge Society' 1 (1) *Policy Futures in Education – An e-Journal, Special Issue* (2003) 8; E. Rullani, *Economia della conoscenza: creatività e valore nel capitalismo delle reti* (Roma: Carocci, 2004) 285; W. Powell, 'Neither Market nor Hierarchies: Network Forms of Organization', in L. Cummings and B. Staw (eds), *Research in Organizational Behaviour* (Greenwich: JAI Press, 1990) 295 *et seq.*

5 See the EC Regulation 1906/2006 of 18 December 2006 in GUCE of 30 December 2006 L 391/1 which requires the setting up of consortium agreements for the participation of undertakings, universities and research centres in projects under the Seventh Framework Programme, where the parties are required to internally organize the research and exploitation and use of intellectual property. See M. Cassier and D. Foray, 'Public Knowledge, Private Property, and the Economics of High-tech Consortia' 11 (2) *Economics of Innovation and New Technology* 123 (2002). For the Italian doctrine, see E. Caruso, 'Ricerca tecnologica, trasferimento delle innovazioni e società consortili miste' *Rivista di Diritto Industriale* 1983, I, 412 *et seq*; G. Aghina, 'I contratti di ricerca' *Rivista di Diritto Industriale* 1995, I, 281 *et seq.*; L. De Angelis, 'L'associazione a fini di ricerca scientifica: forme giuridiche' *Rivista di Diritto Civile* 1993, I, 591 *et seq.*

6 See D. Foray and W. Steinmueller, 'On the Economics of R&D and Technological Collaborations: Insights and Results from Project Colline' 12 (1) *Economics of Innovation and New Technology* 77 (2003); Cassier and Foray, n 5 above.

The most critical issue that contracts must usually deal with is the assignment of the right to own and use the so-produced invention.[7] In fact, the allocation of such rights has an impact on the incentive to innovate. The link between the allocation of rights and the incentives to enter the contract is even stronger in case of specific investments by the parties. In these cases, the rights should be allocated to the firm that has the most invested in the project.[8] However, different allocation schemes may be envisaged by the contract and the agreements between the parties.[9]

Among the many kinds of allocation available, the parties may resort to the 'inventorship' paradigm, whereby intellectual property rights are vested in the party that produces the invention.[10] This kind of allocation reduces the incentive to participate in the research activity where the production of innovation is the result

7 See A. Grandori and M. Furlotti, 'Facio ut Facias: Associational Contracts for Innovation', 2007, available at http://papers.ssrn.com/sol3/papers.cfm?abstract_id=985077; G. Moore, 'Joint venture and strategic alliances: ownership of developed intellectual property: issues and approaches', in Practising Law Institute Patents, Copyrights, Trademarks, and Literary Property Course Handbook Series PLI Order No 18794 January-February, 2009, Lexis Nexis database.

8 See P. Aghion and J. Tirole, 'The management of innovation' 109 *Quarterly Journal of Economics* 1185, (1994). As the specific investments are neither observable nor verifiable, the authors demonstrate that the ideal allocation of title to the results of innovation is determined by the kind of specific investments made by the parties involved in the relationship. For an application of this theory, J. Windsperger, 'The structure of ownership rights in franchising: an incomplete contracting view' 13 *European Journal of Law and Economics* 129 *et seq.* (2002). On the general theory of ownership rights, see O. Hart and J. Moore, 'Property Rights and the Nature of the Firm' 98 *Journal of Political Economy* 1119 *et seq.* (1990).

9 In the Italian legal system the allocation of the rights over an innovation is affected by whether the inventor is an employee or the innovation arises within a contract among firms (out of an employment contract). In the latter case (which we pay attention to) usually parties can decide autonomously how to allocate the rights over intangible assets. See F. Ronconi, 'Attribuzione e circolazione dei diritti di proprietà intellettuale sui risultati della ricerca scientifica pubblica: i margini dell'autonomia', in R. Caso (ed.), *Ricerca scientifica pubblica, trasferimento tecnologico e proprietà intellettuale* (Bologna: Il Mulino, 2005) 181 *et seq.*; A. Vanzetti and V. Di Cataldo, *Manuale di Diritto Industriale* (Milano: Giuffrè, 2003) 382.

10 Research and development agreements are diffuse on the subject of joint property over innovation produced by collaboration. See considering 11 of Commission Regulation (EC) No 2659/2000 of 29 November 2000 on the application of Article 81(3) of the Treaty to categories of research and development agreements: 'The joint exploitation of results can be considered as the natural consequence of joint research and development. It can take different forms such as manufacture, the exploitation of intellectual property rights that substantially contribute to technical or economic progress, or the marketing of new products.'

of a common development, since the rights thereto are shared by all the firms and none of them can be deemed its exclusive owner.[11]

In order to redress this potential reduction of the incentive to participate in research projects, rights may be allocated according to the subject matter of innovation, regardless of the investor that develops it. For example, where one investor is involved in a research project carried out by several investors and one firm produces an innovative result disconnected from its own activity but connected to another investor involved in the project, the right to the innovative result pertains to the firm interested in the latter. Quite clearly, this system of allocation is ideal only where the activities of the participants in the project strongly complement each other. Moreover, the effectiveness of this system is guaranteed only where the result of research work is highly unpredictable, so that no undertaking can possibly foresee whether innovation will be produced and in what ambit. If this were not the case, no firm would be prompted to invest in an invention that would then go to another competitor.

Mixed rules may be used in several cases, so that the allocation of an invention to a party may go hand in hand with its obligation to grant an exclusive or non-exclusive licence to the other party/ies.[12]

Lastly, contracts for the production of innovation may also imply the transfer of existing knowledge held by one or more parties. In these cases, such contracts describe the information held by the contract partner. They indicate the main obligations for the transfer of knowledge as well as the scientific methods, processes, analyses and activities to be performed.

These contracts also include trade secret clauses concerning the invention produced, which usually regard substantial information, as well as the obligation not to perform research works in similar fields for a certain period of time after contractual termination.

### *Contracts for the Transfer of Knowledge*

Unlike contracts for the production of an invention, contracts for the transfer of knowledge concern existing knowledge.

First of all, it should be underlined that knowledge may be transferred not only by contract. Knowledge may circulate in other ways, even by merely distributing goods or services on the market which other firms may have access to through reverse engineering.[13]

---

11 See Moore, n 7 above. See also, Foray and Steinmueller, n 6 above and Cassier and Foray, n 5 above.

12 In collective agreements for production of innovation high levels of institutional creativity with regard to rules for sharing and appropriating knowledge are observed. See Foray and Steinmueller, n 6 above, 89.

13 See P. Samuelson and S. Scotchmer, 'The Law and Economics of Reverse Engineering' 111 *Yale Law Journal* 1574 (2002). See, also, in the US, *Linko, Inc* v *Fujitsu, Ltd*, 230 F Supp

We need to separate contracts whose main subject matter is the transfer of knowledge from those where such transfer is functional to a different activity that is the subject matter of the contract.

A second and correlated distinction concerns transfer of propertized knowledge versus transfer of 'non-propertizable' knowledge and within the latter between explicit and tacit knowledge.

Knowledge is a peculiar good since it has no physical extension. As pointed out in the economics literature, the holder of economically relevant information is seldom able to exploit it adequately. In fact, it has 'no rivals' and can be easily transferred. While its production cost is quite significant, its duplication cost is nearly zero.

This has quite different implications according to the kind of transfer involved: where knowledge is transferred, the lack of protection through an intellectual property right may make its assignment very difficult. In fact, failing any protection as to the information that is assigned, the potential buyer ignores the content of such information and thus cannot evaluate it and decide on the price it is willing to buy it for; however, when he discovers its content, he will not be willing to pay the other party, since, in concrete terms, such information will already be held thereby.[14]

Firstly this section briefly addresses the transfer of proprietary knowledge and the focus on the transfer of non-proprietary knowledge by distinguishing between explicit and tacit.

*Transfer of proprietary knowledge* The assignment and licence of patents or know-how are the contractual forms that are most frequently used for the sole purpose of transferring knowledge.[15] They may assign the right on a definitive basis or license it on an exclusive or non-exclusive basis.

The transfer of knowledge is functional to other activities that represent the main subject matter of a contract in cases of contracts for production and distribution of goods and services. For example, in cases of subcontracting, the contractor requires

2d 492; 2002 US Dist Lexis 20860. The court found that the information the plaintiff claimed was a trade secret was actually not afforded trade secret protection. The product was computer software architecture, which could not remain secret once it was marketed, and therefore not rise to the level of a trade secret as a matter of law.

14 See K. Arrow, 'Economic Welfare and the Allocation of Resources for Inventions', in R. Nelson (ed.), *The Rate and Direction of Inventive Activity* (Princeton: Princeton University Press, 1962) 609 *et seq.*; see also S. Winter, 'The Logic of Appropriability: From Schumpeter to Arrow to Teece' 35 *Research Policy* 2006, 1100 *et seq.* and S. Scotchmer, 'Innovation and Incentives' *MIT Press* 2004, 31 *et seq.*

15 Italian law does not expressly regulate contracts for the transfer of knowledge. Apart from publishing contracts and representation and execution contracts, there is no specific regulation of these kinds of contract. M. Granieri, G. Colangelo and F. De Michelis, *Introduzione ai contratti per il trasferimento di tecnologia: profili contrattuali e diritto della concorrenza* (Bari: Cacucci, 2009).

the subcontractor to produce a given good or service according to the instructions given thereto.[16] When speaking of distribution, the most significant example is that of a franchising agreement, where the transfer of knowledge from the franchisor to the franchisee is functional to the promotion and sale of products.[17] In these cases, the contractual relationship concerns the production or distribution of a good or service, though the licence of a party's intellectual property rights is necessary to the other party's performance.

Contracts that transfer knowledge may give rise to very complex forms of collaboration, which are especially frequent when the contract regulates a long-lasting activity.[18] In particular, this phenomenon now seems to be typical of the post-Fordism, where the reduction of vertical integration has led to unprecedented forms of interaction where the contract plays a key role.[19] This change has also been promoted by the spreading of ICTs.[20]

---

16 See Commission notice of 18 December 1978 concerning its assessment of certain subcontracting agreements in relation to art 81(1) of the EEC Treaty, art 1: '"the contractor", whether or not in consequence of a prior order from a third party, entrusts another, called "the subcontractor", with the manufacture of goods, the supply of services or the performance of work under the contractor's instructions, to be provided to the contractor or performed on his behalf'. See also Law no 192/1998 that regulates subcontracts in the field of production, whereby the subcontractor's production is 'in compliance with executive projects, technical and technological knowledge, models or prototypes supplied by the contractor' (art 1).

17 See DCFR, 2009, IV E – 4:101 concerning franchising contracts in which 'one party (the franchisor) grants the other party (the franchisee), in exchange for remuneration, the right to conduct a business (franchise business) within the franchisor's network for the purposes of supplying certain products on the franchisee's behalf and in the franchisee's name, and under which the franchisee has the right and the obligation to use the franchisor's tradename or trademark or other intellectual property rights, know-how and business method.'

18 Such agreements are not similar to market transactions: 'Where buyer and seller accept no obligation with respect to their future conduct, however loose and implicit the obligation might be, then cooperation does not take place and we can refer to a pure market transaction.' See B. Richardson, 'The Organisation of Industry' 82 *The Economic Journal* 883 (1972) part 886.

19 See, on the importance of the reduction of vertical integrations and of the increase in trade flows, R. Feenstra, 'Integration of Trade and Disintegration of Production' 12 (4) *Journal of Economic Perspectives* 31 (1998). For a reconstruction of the debate on inter-firm collaborations, R. Gilson, C. Sabel and R. Scott, 'Contracting for Innovation: Vertical Disintegration and Inter-firm Collaboration' 109 (3) *Columbia Law Review* 431 (2009); C. Sabel, 'A real-time revolution in routines', in P. Adler and C. Heckscher, *The firm as a collaborative community* (Oxford: Oxford University Press, 2006) 106 *et seq.*; S. Helper, J. Macduffie and C. Sabel, 'Pragmatic Collaborations: Advancing Knowledge while Controlling Opportunism' 3 *Industrial and Corporate Change* 482 (2000).

20 See G. Dosi, A. Gambardella, M. Grazzi and L. Orsenigo, 'Technological Revolutions and the Evolution of Industrial Structures: Assessing the Impact of New Technologies upon the Size and Boundaries of Firms' 3 (1) *Capitalism and Society* Article 6, 2008; see also the suggestions included in R. Langlois, 'Comment on "Technological Revolutions and the

In these cases, firms transfer knowledge protected by intellectual property rights; yet, knowledge that does not enjoy this protection may also be transferred, even tacitly.[21] Moreover, the firms' collaboration may take place in a very uncertain environment,[22] which requires the parties to continuously redefine their interaction while constantly monitoring each other.[23]

The focus here is on the case where the holder of knowledge does not wish to sell it, rather to assign to the counterpart the right of exploiting it by putting it at the other party's disposal for given purposes laid down in the contract and thus for a specific period of time. The holder is exposed to the further risk that the other party may disclose the information to third parties, thus reducing its market value. Let us think about the contractor who reveals to the subcontractor the technological information needed to manufacture a good and the latter then passes it on to a competitor of the contractor. The market disclosure of information rapidly annuls its value.

The intellectual property system reduces the cost of drafting contracts since it becomes easier to identify the information being assigned as this is described in the intellectual property right. Let us think about the information that is identified in a patent through its filing process. Intellectual property rights also define the rights of the patent holder in the knowledge transferred and provide for *erga omnes* protection in case of infringement. Therefore, when dealing with technological

---

Evolution of Industrial Structures" (by Giovanni Dosi, Alfonso Gambardella, Marco Grazzi, and Luigi Orsenigo)' 3 (2) *Capitalism and Society* Article 7 (2008).

21 Indeed, codified knowledge may be described in different kinds of support, including instructions. For instance, codified knowledge may be identified, that is described quite clearly, in codes or instructions. Tacit knowledge, instead, is not codified in that it is embedded in people or institutions. Tacit knowledge, … embraces not only knowledge that cannot be codified but also knowledge that has not been codified for various reasons. See P. Cohendet and W. Steinmueller, 'The Codification of Knowledge: a Conceptual and Empirical Exploration' 9(2) *Industrial and Corporate Change* 195 *et seq.* (2000) in part 198. Some economists have recently engaged a debate over the nature of tacit and codified knowledge trying to address whether all knowledge is not codified because of costs or whether it is actually impossible to codify a part of knowledge because of its tacit nature. See Cowan, David and Foray, n 3 above, 211 *et seq*. See also M. Polanyi, *Personal Knowledge: Towards a Post-Critical Philosophy* (New York: Harper and Row, 1962); for knowledge embedded in institutions see R. Nelson and S. Winter, *An Evolutionary Theory of Economic Change* (Cambridge: Harvard University Press, 1982).

22 The uncertainty stems from the fact that 'the future states of those relationships cannot be predicted probabilistically'. See Gilson, Sabel and Scott, n 19 above, part 433.

23 See, Gilson, Sabel and Scott, n 19 above, part 440: 'Collaboration with groups of key technology suppliers, involving continuing mutual adjustment and exchange of quintessentially proprietary knowledge, becomes the norm' and also 447 where it is said that the interaction process fosters the codification of tacit knowledge. See also M. Jennejohn, 'Collaboration, Innovation, and Contract Design' Columbia Law and Economics Working Paper No 319 (2007), http://ssrn.com/paper=1014420.

knowledge, the role of patents affects positively arm's-length transactions, while weak rights call for different governance settings.[24]

*Transfer of non-proprietary knowledge* If the knowledge transferred is not protected by an IPR, the cost of transfer increases.[25] For non-proprietary knowledge it may be very costly to specify the knowledge to be transferred and the precise actions that each party should take with regard to the knowledge transferred. The circumstance that it is difficult to specify the economic value and the uses of knowledge explains why contracts are incomplete.

Different forms of protection are envisaged for non-proprietary knowledge.[26] However, contractual devices can also play the role of increasing safeguards on misuses or misappropriations.[27]

---

24 The 'transactional' role of IPRs makes it possible for technological inputs to be supplied by separate firms contributing to the viability for the firms to stand alone. See A. Arora and R. Merges, 'Specialized Supply Firms, Property Rights and Firm Boundaries' 13 (3) *Industrial and Corporate Change* 451 *et seq.* (2004) part 452; empirical evidence are provided in B. Anand and T. Khanna, 'The Structure of Licensing Contracts' 48 (1) *Journal of Industrial Economics* 103 *et seq.* (2000). See also J. Oxley, 'Institutional Environment and the Mechanisms of Governance: The impact of intellectual property protection on the structure of inter-firm alliances' 38 *Journal of Economic Behavior and Organization 283 et seq.* (1999). See also F. Denozza, 'Licenze di brevetto e circolazione delle tecniche, Giuffrè, Milano, 1979, 96 ss.; Guglielmetti, La gestione di affari e la riversione degli utili' *Annali italiani del diritto d'autore, della cultura e dello spettacolo*, vol 1, 2000, 174 *et seq.*

25 See C. Bessy and E. Brousseau, 'Technology Licensing Contracts: Features and Diversities' 18 *International Review of Law and Economics* 451 *et seq.* (1998); C. Bessy, E. Brousseau and S. Saussier, 'The Diversity of Technology Licensing Agreements', 2002, available at http://www.brousseau.info/.

26 We may consider the case of confidential information. The majority of European national legislation does not acknowledge trade secrets as the object of IPRs proper protection. See G. Ghidini and V. Falce, 'Upgrading Trade Secrets as IPRs: a Recent Breakthrough in Italian IP Law' 2 *Il diritto d'autore* 2008, 117 *et seq.* In the common law regime trade secrets are considered a sort of intellectual property. However the issue is not totally addressed. See R. Epstein, 'Trade Secrets and Private Property: Their Constitutional Protection', 2003, http://papers.ssrn.com/sol3/papers.cfm?abstract_id=421340; A. Mossoff, 'What is Property? Putting the Pieces Back Together' 45 *Arizona Law Review* 371 (2003). The TRIP agreements do not use the word 'property'; rather, they refer to the holders of undisclosed information as those who have 'information lawfully within their control' (art 39.1). Therefore, the circumstance that undisclosed information is considered within the scope of intellectual property does not imply the existence of a property right; rather, it means that the protection afforded to undisclosed information (that is unfair competition) falls within the scope of the protection granted to intellectual property in a wide sense, including unfair competition. See C. Correa, *Trade Related Aspects of Intellectual Property Rights. A Commentary on the TRIPS Agreement* (Oxford: Oxford University Press, 2008) 366 *et seq.*

27 See Bessy and Brousseau, n 25 above.

The party that holds the information to be transferred for the fulfilment of the characteristic performance of the contract may not have an incentive to transfer it or may have no option but to take costly measures to protect itself against the risk of the other party stealing such information. Contract law can thus (i) impose obligations either on the transferor or (ii) on the party that exploits the information up to the extent of the activity that is regulated by the contract.

The first case may take the shape of collaboration obligations concerning knowledge, which are collateral to the performance of the main obligation.[28] These obligations are usually not included in the contract; rather, they are the result of an interpretative process that is grounded on general clauses such as good faith.[29]

We will mainly deal with the second case. Within their contractual relationship, parties can face two different risks:

a. the risk that the transferee will use the transferred knowledge beyond what is contractually allowed.
b. the risk she will transfer the knowledge without the transferor's consent to a third party.

As we are going to illustrate, contractual safeguards may be deployed to reduce both risks.

## Knowledge and Contractual Devices: The Management of Risk Connected to Knowledge Transfer

### *Trade Secret Agreements*

As stated above, the highest risk implied in the transfer of non-proprietary knowledge is the other party's use thereof in dealing with third parties, thus

28 See principles included in the DCFR, 2009, IV A – 1:101 (Contracts covered) '(1) This Part of Book IV applies to contracts for the sale of goods and associated consumer guarantees. (2) It applies with appropriate adaptations to … (c) contracts for the sale of other forms of incorporeal property, including rights to the performance of obligations, industrial and intellectual property rights and other transferable rights.'

29 See S. Grundmann, 'The structure of the DCFR – Which Approach for Today's Contract Law?' 3 *European Review of Contract Law* 225 (2008) 240; B. Fages, 'Pre-contractual Duties in the Draft Common Frame of Reference – What Relevance for the Negotiation of Commercial Contracts?' 3 *European Review of Contract Law* 304 (2008) 308, 314 *et seq.*; M. Mekki and M. Kloepfer-Pelèse, 'Good faith and fair dealing in the DCFR' 3 *European Review of Contract Law* 338 (2008). See also C. Castronovo, *Obblighi di protezione* (Roma: Enciclopedia Giuridica Treccani, 1998) and its references to German legal doctrine.

spreading it throughout the market and reducing its value.[30] The risk is internalized to some extent when knowledge is protected by intellectual property rights.[31]

There arises a problem specifically when knowledge cannot be or is not protected by an intellectual property right.[32] As seen above, the firm that transfers knowledge to another firm may wish the other party not to reveal it to third parties and to use it only for the purposes of contractual performance.

In order to protect the transferor's interest, a first option may be that of executing secrecy agreements which may reduce the risk connected to transferring knowledge from one party to another.[33] This should promote the transfer of knowledge between parties. Quite clearly, a secrecy agreement related to knowledge embodied in an intellectual property right (such as a patent) is meaningless.[34] It may, instead, concern non-proprietary knowledge that is (or is not) complementary to that embodied in the right.

The protection of knowledge through patents or other intellectual property rights is ideal where the goal is to avoid third parties using such knowledge in

30 See B. Nooteboom, 'Learning and Governance in Inter-firm Relations', ERIM, 2004, available at www.erim.eur.nl, 8: 'Between competitors, one needs to consider the trade-off between risks and benefits of knowledge flows. In other relations, one needs to assess the risk that sensitive knowledge spills over indirectly, via partners to competitors.'

31 Property rights can internalize the externalities stemming from the diffusion of knowledge and can provide the owner with strong remedies in the case of infringements of the right. See Demsetz's seminal article: H. Demsetz, 'Toward a Theory of Property Rights' 57 (2) *American Economics Review* 347 (1967). However 'rarely, if ever, do patents confer perfect appropriability'. See D. Teece, 'Profiting from technological innovation: implication for integration, collaboration licensing and public policy' 15 *Research Policy* 285 (1986) 287.

32 See n 25 above.

33 In this respect we should remember that confidentiality agreements are not the only option available to control knowledge or limit its circulation. There are a variety of precautionary steps that have been implemented by trade-secret owners to protect secret information: use of techniques to put employees on notice of the trade-secret status of the matter on which they are working; posting of warning or cautionary signs or use of document legends; restricting visitors; maintaining internal secrecy by dividing the process into steps and separating the various departments working on the several steps; using unnamed or coded ingredients; keeping secret documents under lock; and limiting access to computer materials by use of passwords to prevent unauthorized access and keeping magnetic tapes, flow charts, symbolics and source codes under lock and key when not in use. See, in the US, *Tyson foods, Inc* v *Conagra, Inc, and ConAgra Poultry Co* 349 Ark 469; 79 SW3d 326; 2002 Ark Lexis 391; 18 IER Cas (BNA) 1609. Lexis Nexis database head n 7.

34 On the contrary, the grant of a patent deprives information that is disclosed thereby, and not only the patented information, of the requisite of secrecy. See, in the US, *Arco Industries Corp* c *Chemcast Corp*, 663 F 2nd 435, 443, 208 USPQ 190 6th cir 1980.

their production process or taking advantage thereof. However, this is not always convenient or feasible.[35]

It is worth noting that secret knowledge is not short of protection. In some legal systems, including that in Italy, secret knowledge is viewed as a real intellectual property right. Legislative Decree no 30/2005, which has introduced the Italian Code of Intellectual Property, grants secret information that satisfies given requisites the same protection afforded to an intellectual property right, even if lacking a registered title.[36]

In the TRIPS agreements undisclosed information enjoys the protection granted by the law on unfair competition.[37] Yet, the protection is often granted only

---

35 For instance, in the US but also in other legal systems, in order for knowledge to be patentable it must satisfy the requisites of novelty and non obviousness. Novelty is determined quantitatively, because all that is required is that it be different to the prior art. Obviousness is a qualitative evaluation, which assesses the extent of difference between the invention and the prior art, and whether the difference is sufficient. The non-obviousness standard is used 'to distinguish patent-worthy inventions from routine or slight advances to the prior art that do not require a patent as an incentive'. See L. Bentley and B. Sherman, *Intellectual Property Law* (2nd edn, New York: Oxford University Press, 2004) 470; V. Chilakamarri, 'Structural Nonobviousness: How Inventiveness is Lost in the Discovery' 10 *Virginia Journal of Law & Technology* 7 (2005). R. Eisenberg, 'Obvious to Whom? Evaluating Inventions from the Perspective of PHOSITA' 19 *Berkeley Technology Law Journal* 885 (2004) part 886. Even in Italy trade secret that is not included in the patentable area is not entitled to the protection of an IPR according to art 98 and 99 of d lgs 30/2005, of 10 February 2005. See M. Bertani, 'Proprietà intellettuale e nuove tecniche di appropriazione delle informazioni', in A.A.V.V., *Studi in onore di Gerard Schricker* (Milano: Giuffrè, 2005) 22 *et seq.* part 35.

Note, in a wider perspective concerning the strategy for managing knowledge, it could be true that patents are the gold standard of intellectual property protection but 'that may be true if patents are compared to other formal legal protections, but there are many instances where informal business strategies like secrecy and lead time may protect more strongly.' See Scotchmer, n 14 above, 261.

36 See Ghidini and Falce, n 26 above. In common law systems, the holder of a trade secret is often defined as its 'owner', though this mostly depends on the different recognition of the right of ownership in common law and civil law systems. See Correa, n 26 above.

37 See para 6 on remedies. The TRIPs agreements refer to 'undisclosed information' without defining it. It would appear, therefore, that any secret information or knowledge may be protected. See Correa, n 26 above, 368. Moreover, the terms 'trade secrets' and 'confidential information' have been used somewhat interchangeably by US courts. 'Trade secrets' generally refers to information relating to more technical matters such as secret processes or formulas; and 'confidential information' relates to non-technical matters such as business plans or pricing information. See M. Manson, 'What are trade secrets, and how are they different from confidential information and intellectual property?', in R. Fashler et al. (eds), *Trade Secrets and Confidential Information* (Vancouver: The Continuing Legal Education Society of British Columbia, 2002) 1.1 at 1.1.2.

where the transferor has taken steps to keep knowledge secret,[38] which include both material measures and specific agreements with his own employees or with other firms that are aimed at identifying the shared information and establishing a confidentiality obligation thereon.[39] Hence, secrecy agreements could be one of the conditions precedent to enjoying the law's protection.[40]

In addition, trade secrets and know-how enjoy further protection. Generally speaking however, the protection is fragmented into several disciplines which require non-coincident conditions for accessing the protection. For instance, in Italian legislation, secret information is protected by criminal law.[41] In other cases,

---

38 In the TRIPs, undisclosed information is protected if it (a) is secret in the sense that it is not, as a body or in the precise configuration and assembly of its components, generally known among or readily accessible to persons within the circles that normally deal with the kind of information in question; (b) has commercial value because it is secret; and (c) has been subject to reasonable steps under the circumstances, by the person lawfully in control of the information, to keep it secret (art 39.2). According to the Uniform Trade Secret Act, the secret is protected against misappropriation (and not against unfair competition) if it is information, including a formula, pattern, compilation, program device, method, technique, or process, that: (i) derives independent economic value, actual or potential, from not being generally known to, and not being readily ascertainable by proper means by other persons who can obtain economic value from its disclosure or use, and (ii) is the subject of efforts that are reasonable under the circumstances to maintain its secrecy (see UTSA §1(4)).

39 The courts do not usually grant legal protection where the secrecy agreement does not specify the information which is to be kept secret. See, in Italy, Court of La Spezia, 3 December 2007, n 1409 where the appropriation of a secret related to the drawings of machinery was not deemed unlawful even though a confidentiality clause had been signed, because it was unknown whether such clause also referred to the construction of the disputed part of the machinery. See, for Italian legislation, B. Franchini Stufler, *Il know how e la tutela dei segreti d'impresa* (Torino: Giappichelli, 2009) 105.

In the US, a postemployment confidentiality was simply one measure that could be taken by the company to assure trade-secret protection. However, the failure of a business to protect against the disclosure of information it considers to be secret following employment is critical to the ultimate decision regarding whether the information is in fact a trade secret. See *Cardinal Freight Carriers, Inc v J.B. Hunt Transp Servs, Inc*, 336 Ark 143, 987 SW2d 642 (1999), or in *ConAgra, Inc v Tyson Foods, Inc*, 342 Ark 672, 30 SW3d 725 (2000) (*Tyson I*).

40 Even according to the interpretation given to art 98 and 99 of d lgs no 30/2005, of 10 February 2005 the protection of trade secret due to exclusivity ceases if the secret is communicated to the counterparty without an inclusion of a confidentiality duty. See Bertani, n 35 above, 40.

41 In the Italian legal system, knowledge is protected by art 622 and 623 Criminal Code. The entrepreneur cannot resort to criminal law if the information is not secret, if he fails to take actions that are such as to protect its secrecy, if the other party's actions are not deliberate or if third parties become aware of the secret in a non-abusive way, i.e. lawfully. B. Franchini Stufler, 'Il know how' *Il Diritto Fallimentare e delle Società Commerciale* 2002, I, 1044–6.

specific confidentiality duties are imposed by labour law regulations.[42] However, these kinds of protection are often subject to certain limits.[43]

Moreover, knowledge may not be such as to be open to protection, not even under unfair competition law.[44] Contract law may have the (residual) function of protecting knowledge where this is the subject matter of secrecy agreements, or, as stated above, may play the role of identifying the knowledge in order to make the access to law's protection possible.

It is worth nothing that a secrecy obligation may be recognized, even without an explicit contractual provision on the matter. In particular, this occurs when the courts recognize an implied confidentiality obligation either based on good faith or implied in normal business practice.[45] However, the uncertainty of this recognition

---

42 See, with regard to Italian legislation, art 2105 of the Italian civil code according to which the employee does not have to deal in competition with the employer (neither on his own account nor on behalf of third parties) and he does not have to disclose or use information concerning the organization of the employer or the production methods of the employer's enterprise such as to give a prejudice against the employer.

43 According to art 98 d lgs 30/2005 the information should be secret, it should have an economic value because of secrecy, and has been subject to reasonable steps to keep it secret. Moreover, art 2105 of the Italian civil code is applicable to non-codified information, such as skills, but it is applicable only to secret information which has an economic value for the employer's enterprise. In addition, the employer can sue only the employee (for the case of ex-employee see n 65 below) and only if the enterprise receives a prejudice. Another example is provided by the Italian penal code (art 622 and 623) which protects only the information for which there is an interest to keep it secret. However, the protection is acknowledged only towards specific agents which may access the knowledge only under an authorization given by the holder because of the tasks they carry out within the firm. See also Franchini Stufler, n 39 above, 136 *et seq.*, 166 *et seq.*

The Courts have denied the protection of the law to the holder of information related to the constructive drawings of a machine since such information could be inferred *aliunde* by experts in the field through the so-called reverse engineering process and had not been specifically identified by the secrecy agreements that had been signed. See Court of La Spezia, 3 December 2007, n 1409.

44 The failure of protecting knowledge can follow a lack of requirements included in art 39.2 of TRIPs. But it can be due to other circumstances. For instance, in the Italian legal system knowledge not subjected to the protection of art 99 d lgs 30/2005 is nonetheless protectable under 2598 of the Italian civil code. However, in such a case, the knowledge should be disclosed to competitors which have to be entrepreneurs. It is difficult to satisfy such requirements in contracts for production and distribution of goods and services. For instance in subcontracting it is difficult to consider the subcontractor as a competitor of the main contractor. See A. Musso, *La subfornitura* (Bologna/Roma: Scialoja-Branca, 2003) above n 12, 405. Moreover the disclosure has to be considered an unfair practice (see para 6 below).

45 See, in the US, *Lac Minerals Ltd* v *International Corona Resources Ltd* [1989] 2 SCR 574 [*Lac Minerals*] in which court states that Corona was vulnerable to Lac and this vulnerability was a factor deserving of considerable weight in the identification of a fiduciary

may deprive the transferor of legal protection. Therefore, the parties are expressly induced to identify the information that is shared with the other party.[46]

A principle of declaring the secrecy status of information shared with another party is also stated in the Draft Common Frame of Reference (DCFR). Therein confidential information is defined as 'information which, either from its nature or the circumstances in which it was obtained, the party receiving the information knows or could reasonably be expected to know is confidential to the other.'[47]

*Exclusive Dealing Arrangements and Covenants Not to Compete*

When dealing with secret knowledge, tacit knowledge acquires a special role. An example is *know-how.*[48] In Commission Regulation (EC) No 772/2004 of 27 April 2004 on the application of Article 81(3) of the Treaty to categories of technology transfer agreements, know-how is defined as secret, substantial, identified or

---

obligation. Given industry practice, Corona would not expect Lac to use this information to Corona's detriment. The fact that Corona did not protect itself with a confidentiality agreement, which would confirm what everyone knew, should not be reason to deny the existence of a fiduciary obligation. Confidentiality agreements should not be presumed where it is not established that the entering of confidentiality agreements is a common, usual or expected course of action, particularly when the law of fiduciary obligations can operate to protect the reasonable expectations of the parties. There was no reason to clutter normal business practice by requiring a contract.

See also *Baldwin* v *Von Micheroux*, 25 NYS 857 (Supreme Court, Special Term, NY County, 1893) (former partners of dissolved partnership became co-owners of secret process and each had the right to manufacture products using the process); see *B.F. Gladding & Co, Inc* v *Scientific Anglers, Inc*, 245 F2d 722, 729 (6th Cir 1957) (conclusion based in part on terms of agreement between the parties).

In European case law see the English precedent *Yovatt* v *Winyard*, 1 J and W 394 (1820).

46 See Moore, n 7 above, stating that 'Given the scarcity of precedent, it is essential that co-owners of a trade secret specify their respective rights by express agreement.'

47 See DCFR, 2009, II – 3:302 (Breach of confidentiality, co 2). Even the Unidroit principles state a duty of confidentiality in negotiations. See Unidroit Principles of International Commercial Contracts, 2004, Art 2.1.16. However the DCFR acknowledges a general duty also during the contract performance. See DCFR, 2009, IV E – 2:203 (Confidentiality).

48 The ideas of 'corporate secret' and 'know-how' are quite different. In fact, know-how may not be secret, while a corporate secret may concern information that does not confer a competitive advantage to the firm, unlike know-how which must always do so. In fact, a corporate secret is defined as any information designed not to be disclosed outside the firm. See, in Italy, Supreme Court 20 March 1991, n 3011. However, in practical terms, the two ideas often overlap since know-how is generally secret and is bound to remain so. Moreover, in order for contracts that transfer know-how to be valid, know-how must always confer a value to the firm and be secret. See, in Italy, Supreme Court 20 January 1992, n 659. See also Franchini Stufler, n 39 above, 41 *et seq*.

identifiable information.[49] The latter condition is satisfied where 'the licensed know-how is described in manuals or other written form'.[50] However, this is not possible in some cases as 'the licensed know-how may consist of practical knowledge possessed by the licensor's employees'.[51]

The protection of tacit knowledge becomes quite complex when regulating unfair competition, since the information must be the subject matter of measures that are designed to keep it secret.[52] Hence, such information must usually be expressly indicated.[53]

This problem especially arises in disputes concerning an employee's infringement of the secrets disclosed in the course of his employment. Some legal systems lay down a confidentiality obligation that applies during the employment relationship, though according to some scholars not thereafter.[54] However, even where there is a specific confidentiality provision, the boundary between information, which the worker is required to keep secret and information, which is

---

49 See Commission Regulation (EC) n 772/2004, Article 1, lett i). '"know-how" means a package of non-patented practical information, resulting from experience and testing, which is (i) secret, that is to say, not generally known or easily accessible, (ii) substantial, that is to say, significant and useful for the production of the contract products, and (iii) identified, that is to say, described in a sufficiently comprehensive manner so as to make it possible to verify that it fulfils the criteria of secrecy and substantiality'. In these cases, however, the definition differs in that there is no reference to economic value of know-how and no provisions about the relationship between the value and its secrecy.

50 See Guidelines, Commission Regulation (EC) n 772/2004 para 47.

51 See previous n.

52 See TRIPs (39.2) just quoted above.

53 See *Tyson Foods, Inc* v *Conagra, Inc, and ConAgra Poultry Co*, 349 Ark 469; 79 SW3d 326; 2002 Ark Lexis 391; 18 IER Cas (BNA) 1609. The appellate court found that the corporation failed to take any precautionary measures to protect its nutrient profile. Absent clear corporate action to protect the nutrient profile as a trade secret, a subjective belief of an individual employee that the information was confidential or even had value was irrelevant in the court's analysis. Relying on an ethical guide like the corporate code which failed to identify what was a trade secret or to mention the nutrient profile was not enough for the corporation to invoke trade-secret protection. Thus, the failure of a business to protect against the disclosure of information it considers to be secret following employment is critical to the appellate court's analysis and ultimate decision regarding whether the information is in fact a trade secret.

54 In the Italian legal system the confidentiality duty for the ex-employee is controversial both among scholars and jurisprudence. See, in favour of a standing duty, P. Auteri, 'Il segreto industriale', in A.A.V.V., *Il Segreto nella realtà giuridica italiana: Atti del convegno nazionale, Roma, 26–28 ottobre 1981* (Padova: Cedam, 1981) 313 *et seq*. See, among scholars who hold that the duty ceases for the ex-employee, P. Ichino, *Diritto alla riservatezza e diritto al segreto nel rapporto di lavoro* (Milano: Giuffrè, 1979) 130 *et seq.*, and, in case law, Supreme Court 11 October 2002, n 14479.

part of his personal knowledge and thus can be used freely is very subtle indeed. Similar problems may arise in inter-firm relationships.[55]

In these cases, the secrecy obligation may be strengthened by other devices that can prevent knowledge from being disclosed to third parties for a certain amount of time.

In case of a pending contractual relationship between firms, this role can be played by exclusive dealing arrangements, whereas non-competition covenants are usually drafted in such a way as to also apply after the termination of the contractual relationship.[56]

A firm signing an exclusive dealing arrangement is bound not to deal with a third firm performing an activity similar to that included in the contract relationship. Subscribing a covenant not to compete, the firm is engaged in not performing a competitive activity with the counterparty even once the contractual relationship with him ends. By limiting the possibility of performing a competitive activity, the firm cannot be able to use the knowledge beyond what is contractually allowed or to transfer it even accidentally.

These clauses, which are included by the parties in the contract or in a separate though connected agreement, typically play a different role that does not concern knowledge. For example, exclusive dealing provisions are widely used in the distribution of contracts to avoid the exclusive distributor from marketing goods that compete with the producer's. Exclusive dealing arrangements are also included in franchising contracts or in the distribution of contracts in order to reduce the inefficiencies stemming from the competition among independent distributors.[57]

Some authors have underlined the incentive nature of exclusive dealing arrangements in long-term contracts and in relational contracts concerning the

---

55 See R. Gilson, 'The legal infrastructure of high technology industrial districts: Silicon Valley, Route 128 and covenants not to compete' 74 (3) *New York University Law Review* 575 (1999).

56 An implicit not to compete duty is included in the first part of art 2105 of Italian civil code. See n 42 above.

57 See G. Hadfield, 'Problematic Relations: Franchising and the Law of Incomplete Contracts' 42 (4) *Stanford Law Review* 927 (1990); F. Lafontaine and E. Raynaud, 'Residual Claims and Self-enforcement as Incentive Mechanisms in Franchise Contracts: Substitutes or Complements?' in E. Brousseau and J.-M. Glachant, *The economics of contracts: theories and application* (Cambridge: Cambridge University Press, 2002) 315 *et seq.*; J. Asker, *Measuring Cost Advantages from Exclusive Dealing An Empirical Study of Beer Distribution* (Cambridge: Harvard University Press, 2004) *mimeo*.

parties' specific investments.[58] These devices may be granted a further role with regard to investments in knowledge.[59]

Non-competition covenants in labour relationships can prevent a firm from pursuing an activity with third parties that is similar to that performed with the other party, thus avoiding the disclosure of the information acquired during their relationship.[60] Exclusive dealing arrangements could be included so as to prevent one party from disclosing the knowledge provided by the counterparty as they limit the possibility of dealing with the competitors of the latter.[61]

---

58 See R. Scott, 'Principles of Relational Contracts' 67 (6) *Virginia Law Review* 1089 (1981); H. Marvel, 'Exclusive Dealing' 25 *Journal of Law and Economics* 1 (1982); B. Klein, 'Vertical Integration as Organizational Ownership: The Fisher Body-General Motors Relationship Revisited' 4 *Journal of Law, Economics and Organization* 199 (1988); S. Masten and E. Snyder, 'United States versus United Shoe Machinery Corporation: On the Merits' 36 *Journal of Law and Economics* 33 (1993); D. Besanko and M. Perry, 'Equilibrium Incentives for exclusive dealing in a differentiated products oligopoly' 24 (4) *RAND Journal of Economics* 646 (1993); I. Segal and M. Whinston, 'Exclusive Contracts and Protection of Investments' 31 (4) *RAND Journal of Economics* 603 (2000).

In *Standard Oil Co* v *United States*, 337 US 293, 306 (1949) ('Standard Stations'), the Supreme Court identified several procompetitive reasons for exclusive dealing arrangements: 'In the case of the buyer, they may assure supply, afford protection against rises in price, enable long-term planning on the basis of known costs, and obviate the expense and risk of storage in the quantity necessary for a commodity having fluctuating demand.' From the seller's perspective, output contracts may offer protection against price fluctuations and provide a more predictable market. Idem, at 306–307; see *Roland Machinery Co* v *Dresser Industries, Inc*, 749 F2d 380, 384-385 (7th Cir 1984) (elimination of divided loyalties among distributors; elimination of free riding).

59 Long-term contracts are usually regulated by resorting to several devices, each of which may serve different purposes. See Gilson, Sabel and Scott, n 19 above, 497: 'There are various governance tasks and various instruments for managing them. Each task can be addressed by more than one instrument, and each instrument can, alone or in combination with others, be used to address more than one task.' See B. Holmstrom and J. Roberts, 'The Boundaries of the Firm Revisited' 12 (4) *Journal of Economic Perspective* 73 (1998).

60 This is the so-called 'inevitable disclosure doctrine' which endorses the imposition of obligations on the former employer that prevent him from accepting similar assignments for a given amount of time, thus avoiding the disclosure of confidential information acquired by reason of his previous employment. See *BF Goodrich* v *Wohlgemuth* 192 NE 2nd 99 (1963); *Procter & Gamble Co* v *Storeham*, 747 NE2d 268 (2002); *Barilla America, Inc* v *Wright et al.*, 2002 WL 31165069 (2002).

61 See Nooteboom, n 30 above. See US Dep't of Justice & Federal Trade Comm'n, Antitrust Guidelines For the Licensing of Intellectual Property ('Intellectual Property Guidelines'), reprinted in 4 Trade Reg Rep (CCH) 13,132 (1995), available at http://www.usdoj.gov/atr/public/guidelines/0558.pdf, § 4.1.2: 'The fact that intellectual property may in some cases be misappropriated more easily than other forms of property, may justify the use of some restrictions [as exclusive dealing arrangements] that might be anti-competitive in other contexts.'

It is worth noting that some concerns arise about the circulation of knowledge. Such covenants may foster the transfer of knowledge to specific contractual partners, thus permitting the diffusion of knowledge otherwise kept secret within the boundaries of the holder's firm. However, competitors could raise similar barriers by including such covenants in contracts they enter with other firms (such as subcontractors or distributors), reducing the circulation of knowledge in the whole industry. Thus, among competitors, a firm should consider the trade-off between risks and benefits of knowledge flow.[62]

Moreover some antitrust concerns may also arise. For instance, exclusive dealing arrangements may restrict the access of upstream rivals to distributors. Competitors may be foreclosed from the market or can access the market with a higher cost. In either case, competition can be reduced.[63]

Thus, competition law can ban the use of such covenants in order to foster competition. In other cases it admits to some extent the restrictions the holder introduces on the knowledge transferred with the contract in order to prevent the diffusion among third parties.[64]

Quite clearly, the kind of incentive to the transfer of knowledge depends on the mode of enforcement of the other party's obligation. Enforcement costs may be high, both for monitoring compliance once the contractual relationship is over and for proving the eventual breach of the covenant.[65]

Nonetheless, subjected to these limits, a covenant not to compete or an exclusivity clause could provide better protection because they set up some restrictions over the behaviour that generates spillover.[66] A firm signing an exclusivity clause is bound

62 See Nooteboom, n 30 above, 8. See also considerations concerning the local economic systems of firms (as industrial districts) in the final paragraph.

63 See D. Melamed, 'Exclusive Dealing Arrangements and Other Exclusionary Conduct: Are There Unifying Principles' 73 (2) *Antitrust Law Journal* 375 (2006); see also E. Rasmussen, J. Ramseyer and J. Wiley, 'Naked Exclusion' 81 (5) *American Economics Review* 1137 (1991).

64 See para 4.1 below. More generally competition law performs the task of balancing between pro-competitive efficiencies and negative effects on competition. For instance, exclusionary conduct can be unambiguously anticompetitive or can provide, instead, some efficiency benefits that must be taken into account to determine whether the conduct, on balance, is anticompetitive and, thus, violates the antitrust laws. See Melamed, n 63 above, 377.

65 See J. Saulino, 'Locating Inevitable Disclosure's Place in Trade Secret Analysis' 100 *Michigan Law Review* 2002, 1195; S. Whaley, 'The Inevitable Disaster of Inevitable Disclosure' 67 *University of Cincinatti Law Review* 1999, 836.

66 See Gilson, n 55 above, 602. See also Segal and Whinston, n 58 above. Some models have been proposed, which introduce some compensation schemes on employees contingent on the qualities of its and the other firm's products. The employee receives lower payments when the products of the two firms are of the same or similar qualities, because such similarity indicates that information exchange could have taken place. See S. Severinov, 'On Information Sharing and Incentives in R&D' 3 *RAND Journal of Economics* 542 (2001).

not to perform a similar activity with a third firm.[67] Limiting the possibility of dealing with other competitors, the firm cannot be able to transfer knowledge even accidentally.

Furthermore, as has been underlined, tacit knowledge may be harder to transfer.[68] If the knowledge is tacit, the process of transfer is even longer and more costly. The transfer of knowledge calls for a learning process by the party that receives it. The ability to exploit it is a function of the level of prior related knowledge and of previous interactions.[69] So, the transfer of tacit knowledge is positively affected by contract duration and by the technical assistance provided by the holder.[70]

Contracts cannot realize an effective transfer of knowledge, even if they provide for the transfer or licence of property rights over knowledge where the latter is tacit;[71] in this last case it is necessary to include some obligations that make the transfer effective. For instance, specific provisions concerning the training of employees should be included. As also stated by the Commission Regulation 772/2004, 'the licensor's employees may possess secret and substantial knowledge about a certain production process which is passed on to the licensee in the form of training of the licensee's employees.'

Some evidence indicates that in licensing agreements technical assistance serves the purpose of an effective transmission of know-how as well as the aim of reducing the moral hazard of the licensee in the use of knowledge.[72] Some collaboration mechanisms that improve the investments in information while reducing the monitoring costs are also observed in a wide range of contracts across several industries.[73]

Despite this, the spillover risk also applies to tacit knowledge.[74] The kind of interactions taking place in inter-firm relationships for the production of goods or services or even for the organization of distribution activities usually require strong interactions between the firms involved, which also imply the transfer of

---

67 An exclusive dealing arrangement is vertical non-price restraint that precludes a firm for a period of time from establishing a business relationship (i.e. licensing, selling, distributing, or using) with competitors or owners of competing technology. See S. Russell, 'Analytical Framework for Antitrust Counseling on Intellectual Property Licensing' 2008 Practising Law Institute, Westlaw database.

68 See E. Kitch, 'The Law and Economics of Rights in Valuable Information' 9 *Journal of Legal Studies* 683 (1980) part 711.

69 See W. Cohen and D. Levinthal, 'Absorptive Capacity: A New Perspective on Learning and Innovation' 35 (1) *Administrative Science Quarterly* 128 *et seq.* (1990).

70 See P. Mendi, 'Contractual Implications of International Trade in Tacit Knowledge' 39 *Applied Economics* 1173 (2007).

71 See A. Arora, 'Contracting for Tacit Knowledge: The Provision of Technical Service in Technology Licensing Contracts' 50 *Journal of Development Economics* 233 (1995).

72 See Mendi, n 70 above, 1174.

73 See Gilson, Sabel and Scott, n 19 above; Sabel, n 19 above.

74 See Nooteboom, n 30 above.

tacit knowledge that may then be passed on to other firms too.[75] Moreover, these interactions contribute to codifying knowledge in inter-firm relationships, thus increasing the spillover risk.[76] Hence, the abovementioned considerations related to the disclosure risks of knowledge to the other party are to some extent actual even for not codified (or even not fully codified) knowledge.

## The Transfer of Knowledge in Production and Distribution Contracts: Applicable Provisions in European Law and in the DCFR

### *Production Contracts*

The transfer of knowledge in production contracts is affected by the economic transaction which the contract gives rise to. In the sale of goods, the good produced by the seller has standardized characteristics when compared to the products that are usually made by the latter. This means that the technical knowledge needed to produce the good is held by the seller and that the contract may merely transfer information as to the proper use of the good delivered to the buyer.[77]

---

75 See Gilson, Sabel and Scott, n 19 above, 496.

76 See Gilson, Sabel and Scott, n 19 above, 499.

77 The seller's communication obligations mainly concern information related to the good and its proper use and information on eventual defects of the good when compared to the buyer's legitimate expectations. This information has no technological content; rather, it reduces the information imbalance between the parties and protects the buyer, especially where he is a consumer.

Also the DCFR principles expressly consider this perspective. As for the first point, art IV A – 2:301 contains an explicit obligation of information in respect of the instructions required by the contract related to the use of the good. See DCFR, 2009, IV A – 2:301 (Conformity with the contract): 'The goods do not conform with the contract unless they … (c) are supplied along with any accessories, installation instructions or other instructions required by the contract.' These obligations are strengthened where the buyer is a consumer. (See DCFR, 2009, IV A – 2:304: Incorrect installation under a consumer contract for sale).

In other cases, the systems that promote the transfer of knowledge are centred on liability for the lack of conformity of the products. The DCFR endorses the principle that excludes the seller's liability where the buyer knew or could reasonably be assumed to have known of the lack of conformity, thus prompting the seller to transfer information prior to contractual execution. See DCFR, 2009, IV A – 2:307 (Buyer's knowledge of lack of conformity): '(1) The seller is not liable under IV A – 2:302 (Fitness for purpose, qualities, packaging), IV A – 2:305 (Third party rights or claims in general) or IV A – 2:306 (Third party rights or claims based on industrial property or other intellectual property) if, at the time of the conclusion of the contract, the buyer knew or could reasonably be assumed to have known of the lack of conformity).' However, the DCFR does not suitably deal with the consequences of the transfer of knowledge where the good is produced according to the buyer's instructions, which is typical of subcontracts. In this case, there are no specific

The second case concerns subcontracting agreements where '"the contractor", whether or not in consequence of a prior order from a third party, entrusts to another, called "the subcontractor", the manufacture of goods, the supply of services or the performance of work under the contractor's instructions, to be provided to the contractor or performed on his behalf'.[78] The contractor holds the information needed to produce the good, which is contractually transferred to the subcontractor, who will then see to producing the good.[79] The transfer of knowledge (and above all of non-proprietary knowledge) entails the problem of managing the risk that the subcontractor may unduly use the transferred information.

Production contracts in particular convey technical knowledge in different shapes. For instance, the contractor can give the subcontractor the right to use intellectual property rights, but he may also allow him to use drawings, data or equipment provided by the contractor. The knowledge could also be embedded in such physical goods and may not be protected by any intellectual property right.[80]

However, it is precisely the non-proprietary nature of transferred knowledge that makes it particularly difficult to identify the seller's or the subcontractor's eventual violation in using knowledge (see § 6 below). The possibility of binding the other party by a secrecy obligation certainly increases the transferor-firm's control of the knowledge flows, allowing the latter to have a longer competitive advantage and to contain the costs for limiting the use of the information transferred. In other words, the covenant reduces the spillover risk, fostering the transfer of knowledge. As seen above, this purpose may also be achieved by an exclusive dealing arrangement that reduces the subcontractor's possibility of using the contractor's knowledge in contractual relationships with a similar object.[81]

In the Commission notice of 18 December 1978, concerning its assessment of certain subcontracting agreements in relation to Article 85 (1) of the EEC Treaty, it is expressly said that 'in order to protect the economic value of technology or equipment of the contractor, the contractor may wish to restrict their use by the subcontractor to whatever is necessary for the purpose of the agreement.'[82] For this purpose, the clauses that limit the subcontractor's possibility of using

---

obligations that (i) identify the knowledge to be exchanged and (ii) the seller's use of the buyer's knowledge to produce the good.

78 See Commission notice of 18 December 1978 concerning its assessment of certain subcontracting agreements in relation to Article 85 (1) of the EEC Treaty, art 1.

79 In the DCFR, while the definition of a contract for sale does not expressly refer to the seller's option to produce the good according to the buyer's instructions, another article excludes the guarantee against third party rights in respect of third party claims based on intellectual property rights related to the good sold where the good is produced according to the buyer's technical drawings, designs, formulas or other specifications. See DCFR, 2009 IV A – 1:202 (Contract for sale) and IV A – 2:306 (Third party rights or claims based on industrial property or other intellectual property).

80 See Bessy, Brousseau and Saussier, n 25 above.

81 See para 3 above.

82 See Commission notice of 18 December 1978, art 1.

the contractor's knowledge when dealing with third parties or for purposes other than the contractual ones are exempted from the assessment of Article 85(1) EEC Treaty.[83] Secrecy agreements and exclusive dealing arrangements are expressly exempt, by reason of the role they have in protecting knowledge.[84] Knowledge also includes technical information that is not secret or protected by an intellectual property right.[85]

Similar provisions are included in the Commission Regulation (EC) No 772/2004 of 27 April 2004, on the application of Article 81(3) of the Treaty to categories of technology transfer agreements.[86]

A similar function may be performed by covenants not to compete that prohibit a party, upon contractual termination, to pursue similar activities to the ones performed during the life of the agreement. In the Commission Regulation (EC) No 2790/1999 of 22 December 1999 on the application of Article 81(3) of the Treaty to categories of vertical agreements and concerted practices, Article 5 states that exemption does not apply to 'any direct or indirect obligation causing the buyer, after termination of the agreement, not to manufacture, purchase, sell or resell goods or services, unless such obligation … is indispensable to protect know-how transferred by the supplier to the buyer'.[87]

We should remember that European regulations are not designed to introduce provisions related to contract law, but rather to promote competition. However, it

---

83 See Commission notice of 18 December 1978, art 2.

84 See Commission notice of 18 December 1978, art 3. The clauses are not exempted essentially in two cases:

(i) where the contractor's instructions are mere general indications and thus the subcontractor has at his disposal or could, under reasonable conditions, obtain access to the technology and equipment needed to produce the products, provide the services or carry out the works independently (see Commission notice of 18 December 1978, art 2).

(ii) in the event of any undertaking by the subcontractor regarding the right to dispose of the results of his own research and development where such results are capable of being used independently of the contractor's knowledge (see Commission notice of 18 December 1978, art 3).

85 See Commission notice of 18 December 1978, art 2.

86 See Commission Regulation (EC) No 772/2004 of 27 April 2004 on the application of Article 81(3), art 4. See also Guidelines, n 50 above, art 77, 92, 96.

87 See Commission Regulation (EC) n 2790/1999 of 22 December 1999 on the application of Article 81(3) of the Treaty to categories of vertical agreements and concerted practices, art 5, where in the same article is stated that 'this obligation is without prejudice to the possibility of imposing a restriction which is unlimited in time on the use and disclosure of know-how which has not entered the public domain.' The know-how is to be intended 'a package of non-patented practical information, resulting from experience and testing by the supplier, which is secret, substantial and identified.' See M. Griffiths, 'A Glorification of De Minimis – The Regulation on Vertical Agreements' *European Competition Law Review* 241 (2000).

is significant that they exempt given contractual clauses precisely in the light of their role in promoting the transfer of knowledge.

*Distribution Contracts*

Distribution contracts are entered into for the purpose of putting a party's products on the market through the other party's skills or of regulating a party's provision of services to final buyers according to the other party's instructions. Knowledge also circulates in respect to distribution contracts where the distributor relies on a number of instructions as to distribution where the distributor is given the opportunity of using intangible goods (e.g. a trademark) that are put at his disposal by the other party. For instance, in a franchising agreement, the franchisor's knowledge is transferred to the franchisee to allow the latter to pursue the distribution activities envisaged in their agreement.[88]

In other cases, distribution contracts do not imply the inclusion of a firm in a distribution system with characterizing and distinctive traits (like the manufacturer's trademark); rather, they simply regulate the supply of goods to the distributor and eventually govern the latter's relationship with other producers competing with the supplier (e.g. through exclusive dealing arrangements).

The information transferred in the first kind of contractual relationship is substantially different from that transferred in the second kind of arrangement. In contracts similar to franchising agreements, the transfer of technical knowledge and the licensing of the trademark are of the essence. In the second case, this information is not usually shared since it is not instrumental to putting the goods on the market. However, in both cases, useful information is transferred for further purposes, such as that of monitoring the distributor and of coordinating production and the ensuing distribution.

A party may be interested in keeping some information confidential. The parties may thus introduce clauses in the contract that require a confidential use of the information transferred. As seen above in respect to contracts for the production of goods, these provisions reduce the risk of a party's knowledge being disclosed to third parties and thus losing its value. The principle of confidentiality in distribution contracts is recognized in the general section of the DCFR dealing with distribution contracts and is confirmed when regulating franchising contracts.[89]

Other clauses may serve a similar purpose to that of secrecy provisions. In distribution contracts, exclusive dealing arrangements and non-competition

88 See European Franchising Association's Code of Ethics § 1.

89 See DCFR, 2009, IV E – 2:203 (Confidentiality): '(1) A party who receives confidential information from the other must keep such information confidential and must not disclose the information to third parties either during or after the period of the contractual relationship. (2) A party who receives confidential information from the other must not use such information for purposes other than the objectives of the contract.' See also Code of Ethics provided by European Franchise Federation, 2009, art 3.4.

covenants are mainly used for purposes other than the transfer of knowledge. Distribution contracts usually include a provision granting the distributor, the agent or the franchisee the right to operate in a territory on an exclusive basis. In return, these operators are usually required not to distribute products that compete with the producer's: this obligation is usually enforced by including exclusive dealing clauses and non-competition covenants in the same contract.[90] These provisions promote the parties' cooperation and specific investments.[91]

However, as shown above, where knowledge is secret and thus has an economic value, especially where it consists of a commercial formula (just like in franchising), the use of exclusive dealing arrangements or non-competition covenants that bind the distributor may also serve the purpose of limiting the use of such knowledge *vis-à-vis* third parties and thus of preserving its value, promoting its transfer.[92]

The DCFR takes exclusive dealing arrangements into account only when dealing with distribution contracts (not production contracts), though without mentioning their role.[93] Such clauses are not envisaged in franchising agreements, where they may also foster the circulation of knowledge. Moreover exclusive dealing arrangements imply lower monitoring costs when compared with secrecy provisions.[94]

In other cases, the transfer of knowledge also allows a party to coordinate and monitor the other party. Some contractual provisions are included in both parties' interest in attaining the contractual goal.[95] In agency and franchising agreements,

90 See case No IV/35.079/F3 Ð Whitbread, concerning beer distribution, in which it is stated that 'The exclusive purchasing obligation, together with a non-compete clause is indispensable to the advantages produced by beer supply agreements, as noted in recital 150. As described in recital 17 of the Regulation these advantages cannot otherwise be secured to the same extent and with the same degree of certainty.'

91 See C. Goetz and R. Scott, 'Principles of Relational Contracting' 67 *Virginia Law Review* 1089, 1091 (1981); B. Klein, 'The economics of franchise contracts' 2 *Journal of Corporate Finance* 9 *et seq.* (1995).

92 See D. Decker and M. Filipp, *Covenants not to Compete* (3rd edn, New York: Aspen Publisher, 2009) 239 *et seq.*

93 See DCFR, 2009, IV E – 5:101 (Scope and definitions of distributorship) …: '(2) An exclusive distribution contract is a distribution contract under which the supplier agrees to supply products to only one distributor within a certain territory or to a certain group of customers. … (4) An exclusive purchasing contract is a distribution contract under which the distributor agrees to purchase, or to take and pay for, products only from the supplier or from a party designated by the supplier.'

94 See Segal and Whinston, n 58 above. See also M. Granieri, *Il tempo e il contratto. Itinerario storico-comparativo sui contratti di durata* (Milano: Giuffrè, 2007) 250.

95 See DCFR, 2009, IV E – 2:202 (Information during the performance): 'During the period of the contractual relationship each party must provide the other in due time with all the information which the first party has and the second party needs in order to achieve the objectives of the contract.'

this interest mainly serves the principal's and the franchisor's interest in the business being conducted according to the instructions given thereby and in the network's common image.[96] Moreover, in agency contracts, the agent is required to follow the principal's instructions.[97] In other cases, the information is needed in order to allow for a party to monitor the other party's activities.[98]

The introduction of these provisions may also favour the coordination between production and distribution. In fact, the producer of final goods may enter into collaboration arrangements with firms that are entrusted with the material production of the goods (which is often outsourced) and with its distribution.[99] In other cases, it is the distribution that promotes the execution of contracts with the producers that create the goods according to the principal/distributor's instructions.[100] Therefore, the information drawn from the market has a direct impact on production since it allows for the goods to be suited to the consumers' requests or resolve functional problems that did not arise during the creation and realization of said product.

## Transfer of Knowledge and Inter-Firm Networks

Much of the economics literature on inter-firm networks has stressed that networks are superior to the market in exchanging information and producing knowledge, but it seems less clear how networks can pursue these goals.[101] As acknowledged

96 See DCFR, 2009, IV E – 3:307 (Information by principal during the performance): 'The obligation to inform requires the principal in particular to provide the commercial agent with information concerning: (a) characteristics of the goods or services; and (b) prices and conditions of sale or purchase.' See also DCFR, 2009, IV E – 5:202: Information by supplier during the performance, on distributorship.

97 See DCFR, 2009, IV E – 3:202 (Instructions): 'The commercial agent must follow the principal's reasonable instructions, provided they do not substantially affect the agent's independence.'

98 See DCFR, 2009, IV E – 3:203 (Information by agent during the performance) and IV E – 3:204 (Accounting concerning Commercial Agency); IV E – 4:302 (Information by franchisee during the performance on franchising); IV E – 5:302 (Information by distributor during the performance concerning distributorship).

99 These agreements are quite frequent where industrial production is de-localized to a country which is also that of distribution. Evidence was provided in L. Azzolina, G. Bosi and M. Gobbato, 'Le reti di imprese nel distretto dello Sportsystem di Montebelluna', in F. Cafaggi and P. Iamiceli (eds), *Reti di imprese tra crescita e innovazione organizzativa: riflessioni da una ricerca sul campo* (Bologna: Il Mulino, 2007) 85 *et seq.*

100 See the research on the furniture district: M. Gobbato and G. Zanchi, 'Le reti di imprese nel distretto dello Sportsystem di Montebelluna', in Cafaggi and Iamiceli (eds), n 99 above.

101 See Powell, n 4 above; C. Menard, 'The Economics of Hybrid Organizations' 3 *Journal of Instit. and Theor. Ec.* 345 *et seq.* (2004).

by legal scholars, even long-term relationships as well as inter-firm networks are characterized by cooperation and conflict dynamics which may hinder the exchange and the production of knowledge.[102] However, trade secret agreements, exclusive dealing arrangements and covenants not to compete may affect the possibility for a firm engaged in a network relationship to use knowledge outside of it. This can promote the circulation of non-codified knowledge among firms and avoid disruption of the cooperative structure of the network.

Within inter-firm networks, the value of knowledge is higher than in the market. Inter-firm networks are characterized by interdependences among the firms involved, also concerning the knowledge shared.[103] In other words, the knowledge is specific to the network of firms: within the network it has a higher value than in any other possible application in a relationship with a firm outside the network. This is also due to the long-term relationship characterizing contractual networks that reduces the costs of transferring knowledge.

But it also implies that the circulation of knowledge within the network increases its value because of complementarities. The overall value for the knowledge within the network is not the mere sum of the knowledge values of each firm involved in the network.[104] Because of the complementarities, each firm in the network evaluates the knowledge more than a firm engaged in a market relationship.

Typically in market relationships the value of knowledge decreases as it is diffused to a high number of firms. The transfer of knowledge within a network, instead, does not entail the loss of knowledge value, but promotes its enhancement.

Consider, for instance, the case of a franchising network. Thanks to vertical complementarities – between franchisor and each franchisee – and horizontal ones – among franchisees – the value of knowledge increases the value of intangible assets of the overall network such as a trademark or reputation. The intangible assets generate a value not accessible for market transactions.

---

102 See Goetz and Scott, n 91 above; R. Scott, 'Conflict and Cooperation in Long-Term Contracts' 75 (6) *California Law Review* 2005 (1987). See also G. Teubner, *Networks as Connected Contracts* (Oxford: Hart, 2011) (with and introduction by Hugh Collins) p. 32 *et seq*. See also M. Amstutz and G. Teubner, *Networks. Legal Issues of Multilateral Cooperation* (Cambridge: Hart Publishing, 2009).

103 See Powell, n 4 above; see also Teubner, n 102 above, 19: 'the communication of non-marketable knowledge is more deeply anchored within long-term inter-personal cooperative relations and is less dependent on individual acts of impersonal exchange (the latter being characteristic for the production and distribution of material or tangible goods). As a direct consequence, businesses have been forced to restructure themselves as network type arrangements, within which trust-based co-operation forms the basis for enduring informational relations, recursive reinterpretation of events and for the collective construction of knowledge.'

104 See Teubner, n 102 above.

Taking into account these statements, it should be recognized that it can be efficient to provide incentives in order to increase the circulation of knowledge within the network.

First of all, it should be considered whether the level of cooperation required for parties concerning the transfer of knowledge should be higher for the firms involved in network relationships. In franchising contracts, parties also take into account the network dimension aside from the single relationship. In general, the DCFR disregards the regulation of inter-firm networks.[105] Beyond a general provision of cooperation,[106] it only considers the information exchange aimed at sustaining the reputation and the value of intangible assets of the franchise network. In particular, it takes into account the horizontal coordination activity carried out by the franchisor in order to support the promotion of the franchise network and the obligations concerning the compliance to the franchisor's instruction in relation to business method and the maintenance of the reputation of the network.[107]

Therefore, some implications in terms of the scope of information obligations should be drawn specifically for inter-firm networks. For instance, if firm A enters into a contract with firm B, and the latter enters into a second contract with a third party C, the information obligations of firm A should be strengthened if both the contract A/B and contract B/C perform interdependent activities.

We could acknowledge the principle of retaining knowledge within the network in order to preserve the incentives for transfer. Therefore, a network calls for obligations concerning the transfer of knowledge and confidence during the performance but also after its resolution.[108] These duties can be legally based or stated by the parties themselves within contracts of the network.[109]

Case law provides rare examples of acknowledgement of the duty of confidence within inter-firm networks. According to a recent judgment passed by the Court of Turin, the transmission of patentable (but not yet patented) knowledge by one subcontractor to another one does not affect the novelty of the knowledge transmitted. Moreover, in the case of a 'supply chain' constituted by a contractor

105 See F. Cafaggi, 'Contractual Networks and the Small Business Act: Towards European Principles?' 4 *European Review of Contract Law* 494 (2008); Grundmann, n 29 above.

106 See DCFR, 2009, IV E – 2:201 (Co-operation): 'The parties to a contract within the scope of this Part of Book IV must collaborate actively and loyally and co-ordinate their respective efforts in order to achieve the objectives of the contract.'

107 See DCFR, 2009, IV E – 4:207 (Reputation of network and advertising). See also DCFR, 2009, IV E – 4:303 (Business method and instructions); IV E – 4:304 (Inspection) – '(1) The franchisee must grant the franchisor reasonable access to the franchisee's premises to enable the franchisor to check that the franchisee is complying with the franchisor's business method and instructions. (2) The franchise must grant the franchisor reasonable access to the accounting books of the franchisee.'

108 See Cafaggi, n 105 above. See also F. Cafaggi and M. Gobbato, 'Rischio e responsabilità nella rete', in F. Cafaggi (ed.), *Il contratto di rete* (Bologna: Il Mulino, 2009) 91 *et seq*.

109 See Castronovo, n 29 above.

and some subcontractors, the latter having a contractual relationship with the contractor, there is a confidential obligation concerning the patentable knowledge among firms involved in the same 'chain'.[110] Above all, the obligation is implicit, so it could be acknowledged even in the absence of explicit agreements or of obligations required by law because they are based on the good faith principle.[111]

Even if the Court does not provide a definition of 'supply chain' (without any reference to networks at all) and the decision concerns a patentable (but not yet patented) innovation, according to this principle all firms are bound not to disclose the knowledge transferred and produced within the supply chain to other enterprises. It seems that an implicit obligation stems from the interdependences between the activity of three subcontractors and the common main contractor so that the transfer of knowledge is necessary in order to produce the good by using the innovation.

Unfortunately courts, except for the above case, do not acknowledge any confidence duty within contractual networks. This is also due to the difficulty of acknowledging a common interest of the network itself (to retain the knowledge within the network), and to the preference for acknowledging each party's different interests (in using the knowledge) and for solving the potential conflicts among them in conformity with the privity principle.[112] So parties can introduce some covenants affecting the ability to use know-how and other immaterial assets only for the scope of the network's activity.

However, several knowledge distribution settings are possible within networks. One common setting is explained by franchising or by subcontracting. The same party enters into several autonomous, though interdependent contractual relationships ('star' networks). If the franchisor or the contractor is the owner of the relevant knowledge, he is interested in protecting it when transferring it to other parties, so it is sufficient for the owner to negotiate restrictions with each firm engaged in a relationship therewith. Provided that the various restrictions

---

110 See S. Pene Vidari, 'Commento a Trib Torino, 29 settembre 2005' 5 *Il Diritto Industriale* 2006, 419 *et seq*.

111 See Court of Turin, 29 September 2005, the confidentiality obligation stems from 'the same reasons that have determined the communication, from the common interest in keeping technical information confidential, from corporate practices or from obligations of proper behaviour and good faith, which are typical of any contractual relationship.' See also *Lac Minerals Ltd* v *International Corona Resources Ltd* [1989] 2 SCR 574 in which Corona had communicated private, unpublished information and, although the matter of confidence had not been raised, there was a mutual understanding between the parties that they were working towards a joint venture and that valuable information was communicated to Lac under circumstances giving rise to an obligation of confidence (without entering a confidentiality agreement). The information was misused by Lac and Corona sued Lac.

112 See M. Wellenhofer, 'Third Party Effects of Bilateral Contracts Within the Network', and C. Heldt, 'Internal Relations and Semi-spontaneous Order: The Case of Franchising and Construction Contracts', both included in Amstutz and Teubner, n 102 above, 119 and 137 respectively.

have the same content, the costs of negotiation are low since, as a matter of fact, the contracts are often standardized.

On the other hand, it is much more costly to link provisions concerning restrictions on the use of knowledge in each contract if the relevant knowledge to be transferred and to be protected is shared by the firms of the overall network. In such a case, it might be more efficient to enter into a multilateral agreement introducing general restrictions that provide incentives to the transfer of knowledge among the network's firms.

Such restrictions on the use of knowledge by the firms of the network might be included even in a framework contract. A multilateral contract as a framework contract could regulate some general provisions (and those concerning knowledge) whereas bilateral contracts regulate the specific elements of production or distribution activity.[113]

The new Italian regulation concerning network contracts considers the possibility for some firms to enter into a multilateral contract for pursuing one or more economic activities, together, with the aim of increasing their reciprocal innovative capabilities and their competitiveness on the market.[114]

The network contract allows firms to pursue an economic activity jointly. The regulation does not mention any duties concerning the transfer or the use of knowledge. However, it may be possible to acknowledge a confidence duty as well as other duties concerning restrictions in using knowledge, even if the regulation disregards them.[115] Such duties are encompassed in the good faith principle in relation to the common interest performed by the network contract and could just operate for some activities. They survive when the network ceases, even if within a reasonable time, and also in the case of withdrawal of just one party. Otherwise, the participation in the network would be undermined as parties would in advance be aware of the risk of disclosure of knowledge outside the network in the case of dissolution of the network or of withdrawal of a firm.

The restrictions about knowledge may concern the activity performed through the network contract itself even if the parties can enter into bilateral executory contracts that are collateral but connected to the main activity carried out by network contract. For instance, the contract can designate particular employees of each firm to be trained in and be responsible for the use of the knowledge needed to perform the joint activity, requiring the firms not to allow such employees to be involved in activities with third parties.[116]

---

113 See Cafaggi, n 105 above, 509.

114 See art 3, co 4-*ter* dl 5/09, converted into L 33/2009 and Cafaggi (ed.), n 108 above.

115 See Cafaggi and Gobbato, n 108 above, in which it is stated (94) that 'other than confidentiality obligations, ... further obligations related to the communication of information and eventually to the exclusive participation in the network's specific activities should be recognized.'

116 This example is provided also in the guidelines of the Commission Regulation 772/2004 at para 94 in which the restrictions on the activity performed by the licensee could

**Remedies Against Misappropriations and Enforceability of Clauses**

Monitoring the party who receives the knowledge within a bilateral contract relationship is even more important, also given the limited remedies available to the owner of non-proprietary knowledge in case of eventual misappropriation. The remedies perspective does not affect the validity of our considerations. Instead it brings awareness concerning the limits of protecting knowledge by means of the contractual devices mentioned.

Non-proprietary knowledge is generally protected by industrial and trade secret regime, within the framework of unfair competition.[117]

In the United States, the Uniform Trade Secrets Act states that the owner of a trade secret is entitled to injunctive relief for future use of the secret and remedies against misappropriation.[118] But the doctrine of misappropriation has not been much considered by the United States courts.[119]

Even if the TRIPS protects the subjective destination to secrecy that the owner attributes to knowledge, it is undoubted that TRIPS and the majority of European national legislation do not acknowledge trade secrets as the object of IPRs proper protection.[120] So no *erga omnes* protection is acknowledged. This means that the remedies may be activated only against the party who discloses the secret or enters a secrecy agreement stipulated with the owner or against the third party who induces such violation or at least consciously gains a competitive profit therefrom.

---

be limited to the requirement for the employee who has access to the licensor's know-how not to perform an activity with a third party.

117 This outcome is stated in art 39 of TRIPS agreements which ensure 'effective protection against unfair competition as provided in Article 10bis of the Paris Convention (1967).' The protection is accorded only to 'undisclosed information' as long as 'such information (a) is secret in the sense that it is not, as a body or in the precise configuration and assembly of its components, generally known among or readily accessible to persons within the circles that normally deal with the kind of information in question; (b) has commercial value because it is secret; and (c) has been subject to reasonable steps under the circumstances, by the person lawfully in control of the information, to keep it secret.'

118 See Uniform Trade Secrets Act, that defines trade secret as 'information, including a formula, pattern, compilation, program device, method, technique, or process, that: (i) derives independent economic value, actual or potential, from not being generally known to, and not being readily ascertainable by proper means by, other persons who can obtain economic value from its disclosure or use, and (ii) is the subject of efforts that are reasonable under the circumstances to maintain its secrecy.' The injunction should terminate as soon as the secret becomes public. For the meaning of misappropriation see UTSA, § 1. The injunction should terminate as soon as the secret becomes public. However, the courts sometimes allow the injunction to be valid for a 'limited, reasonable, time'. See Scotchmer, n 14 above, 81.

119 See W. Cornish, *Intellectual Property – Patents, Copyright, Trademarks, and Allied Rights* (London: Sweet & Maxwell, 2003) cap IV.

120 See Ghidini and Falce, n 26 above, 117 *et seq.*

Failing an uncompetitive misconduct, the accidental appropriation or the reverse engineering of the knowledge kept secret is lawful. So no remedy is recognized to the owner of a trade secret against a third party who acquires confidential information by his own or other people's lawful activities or by accident or even by a good faith purchase – so at the time of disclosure or use s/he did not know or had no reason to suspect that the knowledge was obtained by unlawful conduct.[121]

Moreover, the application of Article 10 of the Paris Convention, quoted in Article 39 of the TRIPS, entails an identification of common criteria of honest practices established in international trade.[122] The guiding principles of unfair competition have changed over the last years. From protectionist, corporative basis principles, these have moved to a more pro-competitive perspective so that unfair competition protection can no longer be considered an IPR-like protection.[123]

The protection of knowledge could be very difficult even in the case of unlawful behaviour of the contractual counterpart. In fact, in order to be awarded damages, it is necessary to demonstrate that there is an actual appropriation by the counterpart, that is to say that the counterpart used the knowledge stolen from the owner. This circumstance is not so straightforward, especially in the case of tacit or self-embodied knowledge.

In these cases, to some extent, a covenant not to compete or an exclusive dealing arrangement may provide better protection since they do not simply prohibit the disclosure or use of knowledge, but establish some restrictions on the mechanism through which spillover may occur.[124]

However, exclusive clauses and covenants not to compete are not always enforceable.[125] Even if the regulation framework changes across each jurisdiction,

121 See Kitch, n 68 above, 691; see Scotchmer, n 14 above, 79 *et seq*.

122 See G. Bodenhausen, *Guide to the Application of the Paris Convention for the Protection of Industrial Property* (Geneva: BIRPI, 1968) 144.

123 See G. Ghidini, *Intellectual Property and Competition Law. The Innovative Nexus* (Cheltenham: Elgar, 2007) 111 *et seq*.

124 See para 3 above and Gilson, n 55 above, 602. In any event, also in these cases, it might not be easy to distinguish between knowledge that can be freely used, being part of an individual's personal wealth of information, and knowledge drawn from another party.

125 For instance, in franchising, most courts have held that a franchise covenant is enforceable if, given the franchisor's interests to be protected, the covenant is reasonable in terms of geographic scope, duration, and activities prohibited. See *Bennigan's Franchising Company, LP* v *Swigonski*, 2007 WL 603370 (ND Tex Feb 27, 2007) (covenant against competition in a franchise agreement must be reasonable in geographic scope and duration, the restraint must be no greater than is required to protect a legitimate interest of the franchisor, it must not impose an undue hardship on the franchisee, and it must not be injurious to the public); *Gandolfo's Deli Boys, LLC* v *Holman, et al*, 490 F Supp 2d 1353 (ND Ga 2007) (noncompetition covenant is unreasonable where it precludes the franchisee from opening a broad array of restaurants, including those that did not target the same customers or directly compete with the franchisor); *Papa John's Intern, Inc* v *Rezko*, 2006 WL 1697134 (ND Ill June 14, 2006) (covenant against competition may be over-broad

exclusive clauses and covenants not to compete are subject both to antitrust legislation and to private law restraints. For instance, according to Commission Regulation No 2790/1999 in the case of vertical agreements containing exclusive supply obligations, 'the exemption provided ... shall apply on condition that the market share held by the buyer does not exceed 30 per cent of the relevant market on which it purchases the contract goods or services'.[126] Generally speaking, according to EU law, any provisions which violate the prohibitions in Article 81(1) of EC Treaty will automatically be unenforceable. If the agreement cannot operate without the restrictive clause or clauses, the entire agreement will be void.[127]

At the same time, covenants not to compete are reduced by several laws to certain limits of time and geographical extension, or, where they lack consideration, they are entirely unenforceable.[128]

The deficiencies of remedies are straightforward, given that the owner is not entitled to any remedy if the knowledge is acquired by a third party acting in good faith. In order to strengthen the remedies, some jurisdictions have recently granted trade secrets the same legal protection as IPRs.

For instance, the Legislative Degree no 30, of 10 February 2005, that introduced the Italian Code of Intellectual Property, grants confidential trade, commercial and technical information the same protection as an IPR, even in the absence of patent entitlement.[129] As shown, the information has to be secret, it must have an economic value as a result of being confidential and has to be the object of any reasonable measure to keep it confidential.

However, this protection has been criticized by some Italian lawyers because of the lack of certainty provided by an entitlement and, mainly, because an IPR concerning trade secrets grants protection even if the knowledge is not disclosed and even for non-patentable improvements in relation to social costs arising from the subtraction of the invention of the public domain.[130] Moreover, under the new regime the inventor may secure an absolute protection for a potentially unlimited period, regardless of the possible loss of novelty, thus discouraging patenting.[131]

---

as it may effectively limit franchisees' activities both in any region where they may have developed a positive reputation and in thousands of other locations where franchisees would have no advantage stemming from their status as former franchisees); *Smallbizpros, Inc* v *Court*, 414 F Supp 2d 1245 (MD Ga 2006); *In re Michael E. and Angela L. Ward, Debtors; The Maids International, Inc* v *Ward*, 194 BR 703 (Bankr D Mass 1996); *Allegra Network, LLC* v *AM Mktg, Inc*, Bus Franchise Guide (CCH) 12,136 (ED Mich 2001); *Domino's Pizza, Inc* v *El Tan, Inc*, 1995 WL 367893 (D Okla April 28, 1995).

126 See Commission Regulation (EC) No 772/2004 of 27 April 2004, art 3, co 2.

127 See J. Schrire, 'Intellectual Property Licences and EU Law', Practising Law Institute Patents, Copyrights, Trademarks, and Literary Property Course Handbook Series, PLI Order No 19037, February–April, 2009.

128 See Decker and Filipp, n 92 above, cap 11.

129 See Ghidini and Falce, n 26 above, 119.

130 See Ghidini and Falce, n 26 above, 119.

131 See Ghidini and Falce, n 26 above, 124 and *supra* para 3.

Without redefining the scope of the intellectual property regime, we may wonder whether the owner of knowledge is entitled to further remedies stemming from contract law against the third party which acquires the knowledge.

Generally speaking, the answer is no. According to the principle of privity of contract, obligations cannot be imposed on any person or agent other than the contractual parties. So, the owner of stolen knowledge can have access to contractual remedies only against the counterparty in the event of a breach of a specific secrecy agreement or remedies concerning the competitive misconduct. We may only suppose that in a contract between the party who accesses the owner's knowledge and the third party, an extension of the confidentiality agreement is included so that the third party is bound by the obligation.

However, in the case of inter-firm networks, we may wonder whether a general principle of confidentiality can be acknowledged. The abovementioned judgment by the Court of Turin provides an example of a general duty of confidence on the supply chain as a whole. The acknowledgement of such a duty is quite difficult in identifying the network and its scope (i.e. the firms involved in it and thus bound by the duty).

## Concluding Remarks

This chapter has tried to support the following thesis: that the transfer of non-proprietary, tacit knowledge requires long-term contracts and specific provisions in order to make the transfer effective. Moreover, the parties can use specific devices that introduce restrictions on the use of the knowledge transferred, thus fostering the transfer of the knowledge by the owner.

Restrictions on the use of exclusivity clauses and covenants not to compete reflect a trade-off between the wide benefits of knowledge spillovers and the costs of the parallel reduction in incentives for intellectual property investments and for the transfer of knowledge.[132] The enforcement of such covenants can be detrimental for territorial systems of firms (e.g. industrial districts), as it prevents the circulation of knowledge in the whole district, even if it fosters the transfer among the firms linked by contractual relationships. Some scholars addressed this problem by affirming that the legal regime for such covenants should be set up in a similar way to defining the scope of intellectual property rights.[133] Moreover courts should consider the public interest, the structure of industry, and the eventual economic agglomerations in deciding about the enforcing of such covenants.[134]

However, it should also be considered that, in any case, the diffusion of knowledge is not totally precluded: the inclusion of restrictions on the use of

132 See Gilson, n 55 above, 627. As noted by the author, the problem of setting the right legal regime for such covenants is similar to defining the scope of intellectual property rights.

133 See Gilson, n 55 above, 627 *et seq*.

134 See Gilson, n 55 above, 627 *et seq*.

knowledge may be useful in providing incentives to knowledge transfer that, even for a limited time, safeguard its economic value before entering in the public domain. Such covenants are usually considered valid for a limited period of time and, sometimes, for a specific geographical area. Thus, within the limits provided by each jurisdiction, the duration of such covenants might reflect the limited useful life of the knowledge for each industry.

Some legal scholars acknowledge that a full enforcement of such covenants and, mainly, of covenants not to compete, may hinder the technological progress of clusters or districts. However, some evidences show that a system of trade secret protection based on punitive damages, except in some extreme cases, increases profits, stimulates clustering, and is not an impediment to technology spillovers.[135]

The correct approach might be that of balancing the reciprocal benefits stemming from the disclosure of knowledge (even within the cluster or the district) while preserving the incentive to transfer knowledge.[136] The inclusion of these issues in contract law might be useful to foster collaboration among firms and preserve incentives for the transfer of knowledge.

---

135 See A. Fosfuri and C. Rondo, 'High-Tech Clusters, Technology Spillovers, and Trade Secret Laws' 22(1) *International Journal of Industrial Organization* 45 *et seq.* (2004).

136 See Gilson, n 55 above, 629. See also Guidelines on Vertical Restraints (2000/C 291/01), para 141 that expresses some flexibility in relation to the duration of covenants not to compete.

# PART V
# Remedies and Specific Governance Rules in Long-Term Relationships

# Chapter 11

# Contract Remedies – A Relational Perspective

Yehuda Adar and Moshe Gelbard*

## Introduction

One of the leading contemporary theories of contract is the relational theory. Notwithstanding its remarkable development since the fundamental works of Macaulay and Macneil[1] this body of literature has generally neglected the discussion of legal remedies.[2] Scholarly literature pertaining to the relational theory has typically focused on extra-legal or informal devices for the regulation of long-term contractual relations, such as: consensual adjustment of primary contractual arrangements in light of changing circumstances, informal incentives for performance and cooperation, the tendency to abstain from relying on formal rights and duties, and the frequent use of alternative dispute resolution mechanisms. Much less attention has been devoted to a different aspect: How, if at all, should the existence of a relational contract affect the basic rules governing the award

* The authors would like to thank the participants of the 2009 SECOLA annual conference, which took place in Florence, for their insightful comments on a previous draft of this chapter.

1 See below, n 3–4.

2 A recent exception is D. Campbell, 'The Relational Constitution of Remedy: Co-operation as the Implicit Second Principle of Remedies for Breach of Contract' 11 *Texas Wesleyan Law Review* 455 (2005) (relational theory to justify efficient breach of contract, and to rationalize the rules limiting both specific performance and compensatory damages). Campbell's approach is fascinatingly presented – and lightly criticized – in a recent article by S. Macaulay, 'Renegotiations and Settlements: Dr. Pangloss's notes on the Margins of David Campbell's Papers' 29 *Cardozo Law Review* 261 (2007). However, these articles do not offer a comprehensive look at the question of remedies in the relational context. Macneil's writings on remedies focused, mainly, on the limitations of formal remedies within the framework of the relational theory of contract. I.R. Macneil, 'Essays on the Nature of Contract' 10 *South Carolina Central Law Journal* 159 (1980). Macneil has also dealt with the weaknesses of the simplistic efficient-breach analysis: I.R. Macneil, 'Efficient Breach of Contract: Circles in the Sky' 68 *Virginia Law Review* 947 (1982); I.R. Macneil, 'Contract Remedies: A Need for a Better Efficiency Analysis' 144 *Journal of Institutional and Theoretical Economics* 6 (1988). See also Chapter 7 (*The Analysis of Remedies*) in D. Campbell (ed.), *The relational theory of contract: selected works of Ian MacNeil* (London: Sweet & Maxwell, 2001) 265. However, in none of these articles does Macneil discuss the need to adjust the legal rules of remedies to the relational context.

of remedies for breach of contract? To what extent, if at all, should the remedial response to the breach of a long-term relational contract differ from the ordinary or traditional legal response to contract breach?

The paucity of sources of detailed academic research on these questions is far from surprising. Relational contract theory categorizes the formal legal infrastructure governing the contractual relationship as being of secondary importance to informal norms of decency, solidarity and cooperation. According to generally accepted approaches to relational contracts, the primary obligations originating from a long-term relational contract are merely, at best, a basis for future adjustments and variations to be made by the parties. Consequently, breach or violation of such terms should not be viewed as a trigger for asserting secondary rights of remedy, but rather as an occasion for renegotiation, readjustment, compromise and settlement. This conventional understanding, resorting to the formal law of remedies upon breach, misses the mark. Instead of reflecting the parties' ongoing commitment to promoting their goals through cooperation and mutual agreement, such a move reflects a diametrically opposite set of values, of confrontation and antagonism. Hence it is assumed the formal law of remedies for breach of contract does – as it should – play a relatively marginal role in the context of relational contracts.

This chapter challenges this widely held assumption. It argues that marginalizing the importance of formal remedies in the relational contexts is unwarranted. Formal legal remedies play a significant role not only when a short-term one-shot contract is violated, but in the relational context as well. Furthermore, understanding the function remedies play in the relational context is crucial for the development of a full-scale relational theory of contract. In light of this basic assertion, the chapter proposes a theoretical model of relational remedies that would offer guidance to courts or other tribunals, whenever they are required to resolve relational contract disputes on a formal legal basis. This requires adaptation of some of the basic rules of contractual remedies to the distinct characteristics of relational contracts.

The chapter is structured in five parts. The second part discusses the reasons for the belief that, contrary to the implicit assumption of the relational theory literature, remedies do play an important role in the relational context. The third section consists of a few preliminary clarifications regarding the nature and purpose of the theoretical model proposed in this chapter. Part four outlines the model itself: it begins with a general presentation of the guiding principles offered by the model, and moves on to demonstrate its possible implications on the resolution of specific remedial questions. Part five then examines the extent to which the remedial provisions of the DCFR conform to the model offered in the article. The authors argue that while not explicitly distinguishing between relational and non-relational contracts as such, a considerable number of provisions in the DCFR reflect sensitivity to the unique nature of various types of relational contracts. In this respect, the DCFR may be seen as a first step towards recognizing the need to develop a relational theory of contract remedies.

## The Relevance of Remedies in the Relational Context

Today, 50 years after Macaulay's pioneering research into what he referred to as 'non-contractual business relations',[3] and 39 years after the publication of Macneil's seminal article on 'the many futures of contract',[4] it may safely be concluded that the relational theory is one of the richest and most influential contemporary theories of contract law.[5]

Although the exact content of the best relational theory is disputed – as are the appropriate definition and scope of such a theory[6] – authors who wrote about relational contracts seem to have held substantially similar presumptions regarding the role of remedies in long-term relational contracts. Under the traditional view legal rules, in general, and formal rules of remedy, in particular, play a marginal role in factual settings that fall under the purview of a 'relational contract'.[7] A variety of reasons are given for this. The most significant reason highlights the existence of more efficient and more attractive non-legal incentives for cooperation. Indeed, it has often been suggested that practical experience and empirical evidence

---

3 S. Macaulay, 'Non-Contractual Relations in Business: A Preliminary Study' 28 *American Sociological Review* (1963) 55; S. Macaulay, 'The Use and Non-Use of Contracts in the Manufacturing Industry' 9 *Practical Lawyer* 13 (1963); S. Macaulay, An Empirical View of Contract 1985, *Wisconsin Law Review* 465 (1985).

4 I.R. Macneil, 'The Many Futures of Contracts' 47 *South California Law Review* (1974) 691; I.R. Macneil, 'Contracts: Adjustment of Long-Term Economic Relations under Classical, Neoclassical, and Relational Contract Law' 72 *Northwestern University Law Review* (1978) 854; I.R. Macneil, *The New Social Contract* (New Haven: Yale University Press, 1979).

5 Although few books present comprehensive treatments of the relational theory, the literature dealing with aspects of the relational theory is rich and versatile. Important essays and collections include, inter alia: S. Nysten-Haarala, *The Long-Term Contract: Contract Law and Contracting* (Helsinki: Kauppakaari Oyi Finnish Lawyers Publishing, 1998); 'Symposium, Relational Contract Theory' (1985) *Wisconsin Law Review* 461–757; 'Symposium in Honor of Ian R. Macneil: Relational Contract Theory in Context' 94 *Northwestern University Law Review* 737 (2000); D. Campbell, H. Collins and J. Wightman, *Implicit Dimensions of Contract: Discrete, Relational and Network Contracts* (Oxford: Hart publishing, 2003). Campbell (ed.) (2001), n 2 above. For a survey of the literature see D. Campbell and S. Clay, *Long-Term Contracting: A Research Bibliography and Review of the Literature* (Oxford: Centre for socio-legal Studies, 1995). For a critique of relational contract theory see, e.g. R.E. Barnett, 'Conflicting Visions: A Critique of Ian Macneil's Relational Theory of Contract' 78 *Virginia Law Review* 1175 (1992); J.M. Feinman, 'Relational Contract Theory: Unanswered Questions' 94 *Northwestern University Law Review* 737 (2000).

6 See below, text to n 19–20.

7 'In a relational contract … it is suggested that legal remedies play a secondary role … and that non-legal factors … play a critical role in the resolution of disputes.' E. McKendrick, 'The Regulation of Long-Term Contracts in English Law', in J. Beatson and D. Friedman (eds) *Good Faith and Fault in Contract Law* (Oxford: Clarendon, 1995) 305, 309–10.

support the conclusion that the most salient feature of remedies in the context of a relational contract is their 'non-use' by parties to such contracts.[8]

In this chapter the aim is not to challenge the assumption, based on empirical evidence, that the actual use of formal remedies in cases of breach is fairly rare and limited.[9] However, it does question the traditional tendency to point to this phenomenon as proof of the marginal role played by formal or legal remedies in the context of a relational contract. A number of reasons lead to a belief that such a conclusion would be unwarranted.

First, even if only a comparatively small fraction of all relational contractual disputes reach the stage of formal litigation – an empirical assertion which is not challenged in this chapter – this fact alone should by no means belittle the crucial role of contractual remedies in resolving the numerous cases that do find their way every year to the courts or to formal arbitration procedures.[10] Furthermore, the well-known problems of access to justice and of costly litigation, which are major barriers to formal litigation, are not in any sense unique to the relational context. Thus, the general reluctance of businessmen to refrain from contract litigation cannot, in itself, be regarded as evidence for the marginal role of formal remedies in the particular context of long-term or relational contracts.[11]

Secondly, the authors are sceptical regarding the conventional assumption that the very existence of a long-term relationship would usually suffice to safeguard against resorting to formal remedies. True, in a typical relational contract the parties' relations would generally be characterized by cooperation, solidarity and

8 The phenomenon of abstaining from reliance on formal remedies was pointed out as early as 1975 in the work of H. Beale and T. Dugdale, 'Contracts between Businessmen: Planning and the Use of Contractual Remedies' 2 *The British Journal of Law & Society* 45, 53–9 (1975), whose conclusions generally stand in line with those reached by Macaulay's earlier research, n 3 above. The idea that contractual remedies are of virtually no use in the context of long-term relational contracts has become an underlying theme in the relational theory literature. This widely held view is presented and discussed in D. Harris, D. Campbell and R. Halson, *Remedies in Contract & Tort* (2nd edn, Cambridge: University Press, 2005) 27–8, 31–8: '… the overwhelming conclusion of empirical studies is that formal remedies are not used in continuing contractual relationships.' See, similarly, Campbell and Clay, n 5 above, 54–5.

9 However, this assumption requires re-examination and validation on the basis of fresh and updated empirical work. It is the authors' impression that legal disputes around the most typical relational contracts (employment, partnership and joint entrepreneurship, distribution, etc) today form a substantial part of contract litigation.

10 Arguably, it is reasonable to assume that most litigated cases – whether arising from a discrete transaction or a relational contract – are typically those involving weighty interests, the legal resolution of which is considered worthwhile by the respective parties.

11 See, e.g. the data regarding the paucity of litigated business contract disputes brought by Harris, Campbell and Halson, n 8 above, 31. This general data is brought as an example for the non-use of remedies in the relational context. However, it is unhelpful in establishing such a claim.

mutual consideration. But even so, crises may arise between the parties which will preclude the conciliatory function of the relational dynamic.

The return to a 'classic' pattern of confrontation following a crisis in the relationship is hardly surprising, if one recognizes that willingness to compromise and to cooperate does not necessarily reflect altruistic motives. In many instances, such conduct would originate in a party's recognition of his or her dependence on future performance by the other party. Hence, a party may decide to cooperate and give weight to the other party's interests, in fear that behaving otherwise (e.g. opportunistically or intolerantly) might lead to an unwelcome response.[12]

However, as the carrying out of a long-term relationship approaches its final stages, the fear of counter reaction in future 'rounds' of the relational game is naturally diminished. At this stage one would expect an increase in opportunistic or manipulative conduct on the part of some contracting parties. This in turn would naturally invite reciprocal reaction, thus eventually leading to a 'classic' legal dispute.

Third, one should recall that the traditional scheme of remedies offered by the law of contract includes not only judicial, but also a diverse set of self-help remedies. These self-administered remedies – such as termination, reduction of price, set-off and the right to withhold performance of an opposing obligation – do not, in principle, require any formal litigation. Furthermore, contrary to an action brought before a court, the use of such remedial mechanisms does not entail the infliction of any immediate reputational loss on the breaching promisor. It is for this reason that resorting to 'middle-way' self-help remedies may not hinder further negotiation and cooperation between the parties, and may even encourage cooperation in times of crisis. Although, admittedly, this feature of self-help remedies is not unique to relational contracts, it may cast doubt on the validity of arguments emphasizing the marginal role of formal remedies in long-term contractual relations – at least in so far as they are based upon empirical findings focusing solely or primarily on the use of judicial remedies.

Lastly, assuming – as the authors are willing to do – that explicit reliance on formal remedies is less frequent in the relational context, one cannot disregard the possibility that legal remedies have a significant – though indirect – influence on the conduct of the parties to relational contracts. Even parties to a fully functioning relational contract may act, consciously or unconsciously, under the influence of the implicit threat of being exposed to a legal sanction (i.e. a legal remedy) for failing to comply with one's contractual obligations. There seems to be no convincing reason to expect that the 'radiating effect' of legal rules, which

12 In this sense the conduct of the contractual parties to a relational contract may be seen as representing a series of 'prisoner's dilemmas'. Each party fears the counter-reaction of the other party in the future, and therefore has an incentive for cooperative conduct in the present.

has been emphasized by writers in other contexts,[13] will stop at the doors of the relational sphere. Here too, one should expect the well-recognized phenomenon of 'bargaining in the shadow of law'[14] to take place – both before and after a violation of the agreement has taken place.

If this expectation is realistic, the contracting parties' mutual expectations, their attitude towards their duty to perform their own obligations, and their reaction to any deviation from the contract by the other party are all influenced – at least to a degree – by their perception of the legal system's position vis-à-vis each of these aspects. Hence, it would be a mistake to ignore the possible impact of the formal law of remedies on contracting parties – not only in the prototypical case of a discrete one-shot bargain, but in long-term relational contracts as well.[15]

Such influence may be less evident in emotionally loaded relationships (e.g. financial agreements between married couples). However, in other contexts, especially business or commercial contracts, which serve primarily as a vehicle for the enhancement of economic gain, the radiating influence of formal remedies for breach – whether fixed by the contract itself or otherwise provided by the law – is probably substantial.

It is therefore the view of the authors that contrary to what is commonly assumed, the question of what the formal regime of remedies for breach offers the aggrieved party to a relational contract is by no means an irrelevant or unimportant issue. From both the standpoint of the parties to a relational contract and of the legal system itself, this question is a crucial one. In contract, as elsewhere in the law, awareness of the legal principles governing the award of remedies for breach of a primary right or duty arising from a legal relationship is vital for a full understanding of the nature of that relationship.

---

13 The argument that formal remedies are used as possible threats and that the parties' relations are conducted with these threats in the background has been advanced by M. Galanter, 'The Radiating Effects of Courts', in K. Boylum and A. Mather (eds), *Empirical Theories About Courts* (New York: Longman, 1983) 117, 121–4; C. Menkel-Meadow, 'Toward Another View of Legal Negotiation: The Structure of Problem Solving' 31 *University of California Los Angeles Law Review* 754, 764–94 (1984).

14 See R. Mnookin and L. Kornhauser, 'Bargaining in the Shadow of the Law: The Case of Divorce' 88 *Yale Law Journal* 950 (1979). For an application of the idea to the contractual area see S. Wheeler, *Reservation of Title Clauses: Impact and Implications* (Oxford: Clarendon, 1991).

15 A similar criticism was raised by the authors of an important treatise on contractual remedies. Discussing, in the relational context, the widely recognized phenomenon of non-use of formal remedies, they state: '... [the presumed] exceptional use [of remedies] is not, however, an entirely accurate account of the role of remedies ... Even in functioning relational contracts, the formal remedies remain as possible threats, and the parties' relations are conducted with these threats in the background ... The formal remedies may never be invoked, but they have a most important influence on the actions of the parties, for their existence ... radiates an influence on the nature of any settlement and on any continuing relationship.' Harris, Campbell and Halson, n 8 above, 34.

Furthermore, marginalizing the role of remedies in the field of relational contract entails a risk. Namely, it entails the risk of overlooking the possible necessary adjustments – internal rather than external, legal rather than non-legal – of the formal law of remedies to the relational context. Indeed, there is no reason to assume that the adjustment of the classical law of contract to the relational context should cease at the doors of the realm of remedies. Just as the need for adjustments has been recognized in other contexts (e.g. with regard to the rules on formation, interpretation, and adaptation of primary obligations to changing circumstances), here too one should expect certain adjustments of the general rules of remedy to the relational context.[16]

More specifically, the authors believe that judges and arbitrators resolving disputes between parties to relational contracts will often find a need to deviate from a traditional rule of remedy, or to apply it in a flexible way that will better suit the dynamic and long-lasting character of the relationship. Such adjustments may be necessary, if the remedy awarded is to properly serve its goal, i.e. to vindicate the distinct interest a party to a relational contract has in its performance, without imposing a disproportionate burden on the party in breach.

For example, recognizing the complex non-economic aspects of a certain contractual relationship may call for a more liberal application of certain remedies. On the other hand, the same characteristic feature of relational contracts may limit the desirability of other remedies, the award of which should raise no particular problems in the context of economically oriented bargaining.

In the remainder of this chapter the authors wish to provide some preliminary thoughts on what a desirable model of relational remedies should look like, i.e. on what kind of adjustments may be expected to take place when the general law of contract remedies is applied in the relational context. Such adjustments are not only natural and foreseeable; they are also justifiable on substantial grounds and with reference to various policy considerations. It should be noted that within the confines of this preliminary study it is not the aim to examine the possible justifications and policy arguments in any depth. Rather, the authors will try to demonstrate, by way of illustration, the need for certain adjustments in

16 As noted above, the literature on relational contracts has generally neglected the question of whether, and to what extent, the remedial rules of the classical law of contract should be altered or adjusted to suit the relational nature of a contract. Nevertheless, some authors have acknowledged the need for some adjustment of the law of remedies to the relational context. For example, Ewan McKendrick, though claiming that, apart from rules of interpretation, relational contracts do not require any distinctive regulation, remarked that 'consideration might usefully be given to the development of a more flexible remedial regime on the occurrence of a breach of contract …'. McKendrick, n 7 above, 333, n 92. A similar recommendation was made by the authors of Harris, Campbell and Halson, n 8 above, 37. While discussing the problems associated with the traditional use of formal remedies in the relational context, these authors noted that: '… it would appear necessary, from the point of view of the substantive law, to design remedies which facilitate more and hinder less the making of the necessary … modifications of obligations in relational contracts.'

the traditional rules. As can be seen, these adjustments directly derive from the nature of a relational contract and from certain prominent features that should influence decisions on the remedial level. Whether or not moral or economic rationales provide a justification for any specific adjustment recommended here (or for any change at all in the rules of contract remedies), is an important question which deserves separate treatment, and one the authors intend to deal with more systematically in a future article.[17]

## The Nature of the Required Model of Remedies: Some Preliminary Observations

Before going into the details of the model proposed in this chapter, a number of clarifications are necessary, regarding its nature and purpose.

A first comment concerns the general purpose of the theory advanced herein, and its relation to other possible theories of relational contracts. Legal theories – relational theories of contract are no exception – may vary in their nature and purpose. Positive or descriptive theories seek to faithfully describe a legal state of affairs, as reflected in a legal institution or a legal rule of law. A legal theory may instead, or in addition, aim to explain or justify the existing law, by reference to external values (moral, economic, political or cultural) in order to achieve better understanding of the law. Further still, a normative legal theory may wish to evaluate the desirability of an existing legal phenomenon, and – where needed – to recommend reform of a particular legal rule or institution. Finally, a legal theory may point out the desired approach to a legal problem, without necessarily making any judgment about the manner in which positive law actually treats that problem. The theory presented in this chapter falls into the last category. It purports neither to criticize existing rules of remedy, nor even to present them in any detail.[18] Rather, it aims to offer a systematic way of thinking about remedial issues in the context of relational contracts. As such, the model of remedies recommended

17 For example, the authors believe that the adjustments recommended in the rules regarding the right to terminate a contract upon breach (below, text to n 45–6) may be justified with reference to the reasonable expectations of the parties to a relational contract, namely, the expectation that each party will do its best to avoid the loss to the other party of that party's initial investment – even in the face of a serious violation on the part of that party. Similarly, the authors believe that the recommended adjustment in the rules on forseeability of damage (below, text to n 41–2) may be justified in terms of economic efficiency, as they may reduce transaction costs, and alleviate information problems.

18 The reason for that is twofold. First, reviewing the existing law in detail and examining the ways relational contracts are actually treated, is a descriptive mission, outside the scope of this chapter. Second, the law of remedies in different legal systems may approach this issue differently, from a methodological as well as conceptual point of view. This fact makes it difficult to discuss an 'existing law of remedies', within a project of a universal character such as ours.

here is universal in character. Its goal is to increase awareness – of courts and legislators – to the need to adjust general principles and rules of remedy to the particular features of the relational setting. In particular, the proposed model may assist judges and arbitrators, relying on the formal rules of remedy offered by contract law, to apply those rules in a manner that would best suit the relational character of the legal relationship between the disputing parties.

On a more concrete level, a further comment concerns the special character of the theoretical model proposed in this chapter. It should be clear from the outset that the authors do not argue for a new system of remedial principles to substitute for the traditional ones provided by the general law of contract remedies. They believe that such a far-reaching proposal is unwarranted in the relational context. In order to see why this is so, it is necessary to add a note regarding the nature and definition of a relational contract.

The concept of a relational contract has long been recognized as vague and elusive.[19] Even today, maybe even more than in the formative periods of the relational theory, there is no consensus regarding the scope and limit of the term 'relational contract'.[20] However, there does seem to be wide agreement among writers that this concept does not admit a rigid, categorical definition. In particular, the term 'relational contract' is not limited to certain types of contracts (at least insofar as 'type' is defined by the content or purpose of the contract). Scholars discussing relational contracts have generally eschewed any attempt to provide any such rigid definitions. It is generally accepted in the literature that whatever the best definition of a relational contract may be, it should be flexible enough to encompass, at least potentially, almost every kind of contractual bargain.

A brief overview of some common definitions should suffice to clarify this point. Take, for example, the view that associates a relational contract with a long-term contractual relationship.[21] Even according to this relatively 'thin'

19 '... although the phrase "relational contract" is regularly used in the literature, its meaning is not at all that easy to elucidate.' McKendrick, n 7 above, 307. One of the causes for this typical vagueness has been the tendency of leading relational theorists to refrain from a 'positive' definition of the constitutive elements of a relational contract. Instead, a 'negative' definition was commonly adopted, according to which a relational contract is a contract, the nature of which departs substantially from the nature of a discrete, one-shot commercial bargain (a concept which had not always been clearly defined). For a critical discussion of this phenomenon see, e.g. McKendrick, n 7 above, 307–8.

20 The inherent vagueness of the term is reflected in the fact that neither the legislation nor the courts implement the concept of a 'relational contract' to distinguish between different types of contracts. In this sense, a relational contract does not represent a formal legal category, but rather a theoretical or sociological concept. The point is made by J. Bell, 'The Effect of Changes in Circumstances on Long-Term Contracts', in D. Harris and D. Tallon, *Contract Law Today: Anglo-French Comparisons* (Oxford: Clarendon, 1989) 195, 195. See also McKendrick, n 7 above, 305 (same).

21 '... the phrase *long-term contracts* has become virtually a synonym for relational contracts.' M.E. Eisenberg, 'Relational Contracts', in Beatson and Friedman (eds), n 7 above,

definition,[22] any type of contractual bargain (including, for example, a sufficiently lengthy lease agreement or even a contract for the sale of goods, if the contract includes commitment of the seller to supply the goods over a lengthy period of time) may in principle fit into the relational context, as long as the duration of its performance extends over a substantial period of time. [23] A similar conclusion is in order regarding definitions focused on the incompleteness and indeterminacy of the reciprocal obligations of the parties, as the defining character of a relational contract.[24] It is evident that the presence of such features does not depend on the content of the party's obligations. Hence, relational contracts remain a wide and open-ended category, under which any type of transaction may fit.

According to a third view, the relational contract is distinguished not by its duration or by its incompleteness, but rather by the existence of a 'relationship' – in addition to a mere 'exchange' – between the parties. Under this approach, which the authors intuitively find the most appealing, the defining element of a relational contract is the existence of a personal interrelationship between the two sides of the exchange. Whenever such an interrelationship is present – and only then – should the bargain be classified as a relational contract.[25]

Here, as with the two other definitions mentioned earlier, it is obvious that the proposed classification does not attempt to exclude, a priori, any specific type of contract. It is rather the opposite that is true, namely, each of the proposed definitions is capable of encompassing any kind of contractual transaction, as long as the legal relationship created by the parties is lengthy enough, vague enough, or personal enough. Indeed, given these wide and flexible definitions of the relational phenomenon, it would not seem unreasonable to assume – as has been indeed

---

291, 293. Cf C.J. Goetz and R.E. Scott, 'Principles of Relational Contracts' 67 *Virginia Law Review* 1989, 1991 (1981).

22 For a criticism of such a definition of a relational contract see Eisenberg, n 21 above, 293–4 ('... long duration does not of itself make a contract relational, and short duration does not of itself make a contract discrete.').

23 This vague formulation has led one writer to adopt a more rigid test for distinguishing a long-term relational contract from a short-term discrete contract. See, e.g. T. Daintith, 'The Design and Performance of Long-Term Contracts', in T. Daintith and G. Teubner (eds), *Contract and Organisation; Legal Analysis in the Light of Economic and Social Theory* (Berlin: de Gruyter, 1986) 164, 175 proposing a five-year period of performance as the borderline between a long-term and a short-term contract.

24 Such an approach was professed by Goetz and Scott, n 21 above ('A contract is relational to the extent that the parties are incapable of reducing important terms of the arrangement to well-defined obligations.'). For a forceful critique of this definition see Eisenberg, n 21 above, 294–5. The incompleteness feature is discussed, among other features of relational contracts, in R. Speidel, 'The Characteristics and Challenges of Relational Contracts' 94 *Northwestern University Law Review* 823, 828–9 (2000).

25 Such a definition was proposed by Eisenberg, n 21 above, esp 296–8. The existence of personal relationship was also pointed to as a typical characteristic of a relational contract by Speidel, n 24 above, 830–31.

suggested by some authors – that in modern times most contracts are in fact – at least to some extent – relational in one sense or another.[26]

What are the implications of this insight and how does it affect the nature of the theoretical model proposed in this article? The response is simple: accepting that relational contracts is not a rigid category but rather an open-ended concept that emphasizes certain features of a contractual relationship leads inevitably to the conclusion that no manageable test exists for distinguishing, *ex ante* and *a priori*, between transactions that may fit the relational model of contracting and those which never will. If this is true, successful adjustment of any body of law to the relational context could therefore not be achieved by replacing that body of law with an alternative set of specific rules designed 'only' for relational contracts. Putting it differently, if any kind of contract is capable of being defined – either *ex ante* or *ex post* – as a relational contract, creating rigid rules of remedy that would suit all relational contracts is probably an impossible task.[27]

Indeed, some leading relational theorists have gone so far as to claim the distinction between transactional or regular contracts and relational contracts is not a factual one, but rather a purely analytical distinction. As such, it only underscores certain dimensions which in fact coexist, with other non-relational dimensions, in practically every contract.[28] In other words, all contracts are relational contracts and all contracts reflect varying permutations and degrees of relational characteristics with those of discrete transactions.

While rejecting this far-reaching conception as impracticable, this chapter does concede that, as explained above, the analytic category of relational contracts is

---

26 Such a conclusion was reached by Eisenberg, n 21 above, arguing that 'It is discrete contracts that are unusual, not relational contracts. The great bulk of contracts either create or reflect relationships. A contract to build something as simple as a fence creates a relationship. A contract to sell almost anything is likely to either create or reflect a relationship; even contracts on perfect spot markets are likely to be between traders of brokers who have continuing relationships of some sort, not between strangers.' (Idem, 297).

27 This has been acknowledged by a number of writers, who criticized mainstream relational theory for tacitly assuming that the recognition of a separate category of relational contracts entails the creation of special legal rules to deal with such contracts. For such a critique see, e.g. Eisenberg, n 21 above, 298–9, arguing that: 'Once relational contracts are properly defined … it is easy to see that they should not be governed by special rules … because most contracts are relational, the general principles of contract law – whatever those should be – must be catholic enough to govern relational contracts.' Eisenberg's approach is further explained in M. Eisenberg, 'Why There Is No Law of Relational Contracts' 94 *Northwestern University Law Review* 805 (2000). Cf McKendrick, n 7 above, arguing that although more flexibility is in place when interpreting relational contexts and adjusting them to changing circumstances, no formal category of 'relational contract' should be recognized by the law.

28 See e.g. D. Campbell, 'The Relational Constitution of the Discrete Contract', in D. Campbell and P. Vincent-Jones (eds), *Contracts and Economic Organisation: Socio-legal Initiatives* (Aldershot: Dartmouth, 1996) 40.

neither rigid nor limited in its scope. Thus, it concedes that every kind of contract may – depending on the facts of the transaction and of the relationship – assume certain features that endow it with a relational character.

In summation, the amorphous character of the very concept of a relational contract dictates the adoption of a flexible theoretical model that will be elastic enough to be useful in every contractual dispute involving relational elements. This in turn calls for the construction of a model of contract remedies that will guarantee correlation between the typical features of relational contracts on the one hand, and the unique character of the remedy provided for by the law of contract on the other hand. In order to do that, a theory is needed that will enable the court ordering a remedy (or assessing the lawfulness of a party's use of a self-help remedy) in any given case to take into account, and give effect to, the distinctive characteristics of the relationship between the disputing parties. Such an approach was professed, as a general approach to relational theory, by Elizabeth Mertz:

> ... relational contract does not rely on a picture of rigidly distinct treatments for hermetically sealed compartments containing kinds of contract or types of law (discrete v relational), but rather on a range of contextually responsive tools capable of being deployed where (and to the degree) appropriate. ... The core inquiry would not center on a yes or no answer to the question of whether a contract is relational, but rather on determining what kinds of relational aspects to the contract might require contextual analysis by the court in order to reach optimal results.[29]

The remainder of the chapter offers a theoretical model of relational remedies that answers these demands.

## The Model at Work: Theory and Practical Implications

### *The First Step: Identifying the Pertinent Features of the Relational Contract*

The usefulness of a relational theory of remedies does not depend on which definition one adopts for a 'relational contract'. However, it does seem vital for any such theory to single out the most relevant features of a relational contract,

29 E. Mertz, 'An Afterword: Tapping the Promise of Relational Contract Theory – "Real" Legal Language and A New Legal Realism' 94 *Northwestern University Law Review* 909, 914–15 (2000). Cf Eisenberg, n 21 above, 303: '... although different types of economic relationships present different kinds of economic problems ... these problems do not derive from the fact that the contracts are relational, but from the specific attributes of the proposed relationship.'

i.e. those features which should be expected to have substantial impact on the application of general remedial rules in the relational context.[30]

In a review of the literature, three features of relational contracts that should have a major influence at the remedial stage – and therefore deserve close attention – have been identified.

The first feature, although not necessarily the most important one, is the duration of the contractual relationship.[31] Whether explicitly agreed upon or not, the fixing of a lengthy period of performance naturally results in difficulties of foreseeing future events. Thus, long duration creates difficulties of assessing the possible impact of such events on both the ability of each party to perform its obligations and the expected profit from performance.

Such uncertainty, inherent in any long-term contractual relationship, has long been recognized in the literature as justifying significant adjustments (to the relational context) of traditional rules of interpretation, as well as rules providing an excuse for non-performance due to an unexpected change of circumstance.[32] Less attention, however, has been devoted to the possible impact of such inherent uncertainty at the remedial level. As will be demonstrated shortly, such influence is indeed expected not only when determining the primary rights and duties of the parties, but when determining their respective secondary (remedial) rights as well.

A second feature, which is of paramount importance at the remedial level, is the 'personal relationship' feature of relational contracts.[33] Close and direct personal interrelationship between parties to a contract should have an enormous influence on the remedial reaction in case of breach. This is the case regardless of when the relationship was created. Whether preceding the formation of the contract (e.g. a relationship between a regular customer and a retailer preceding a simple sale), coinciding with and created by it (such as in the case of a contract of employment), or following subsequent events (e.g. when a one-night hotel reservation turns gradually into a two-month lease agreement) – the existence of a

---

30 The following discussion will assume that a 'relational contract' has been identified. However, it is noteworthy that the applicability of the model outlined here does not necessitate such a presumption. It is equally useful and relevant, even under the premise – adopted by some relational theorists – that no manageable test can properly distinguish between a relational and a non-relational contract (since every contract is both relational and non-relational to some extent). Even if that were the case (and this is not being said here), drawing attention to the features examined would be useful, since it will facilitate the adjustment of existing rules and principles concerning remedies to the specific characteristics of the relationship under examination.

31 This feature is discussed above, text to n 21–3.

32 The issue has received wide attention in the relational theory literature. D. Campbell and D. Harris, 'Flexibility in Long-Term Contractual Relationships: The Role of Co-Operation' 20 *Journal of Law & Society* 166 (1993); P.D.V. Marsh, *Contract negotiation handbook* (3rd edn, Aldershot: Gower, 2001) ch 5 (Adjustment of Long-term Contracts) 19–22.

33 See above, text to n 25.

truly personal relationship between the parties should definitely affect the reaction of the law of remedies to the breach of the contract.

Third, attention should be given to another distinct feature. Some authors have argued that the most important feature of relational contracts concerns the nature and extent of the investment the contract requires from each of the parties (hereinafter: the investment factor). More specifically, it has been suggested that a relational contract is a contract in which the nature and extent of the initial investment made by each of the parties to the transaction (or the one each party undertakes to make in the future) make the costs of withdrawing from it prohibitively high. As a consequence, the parties to a relational contract may be regarded as being practically 'locked into the relationship', as they realize that a complete withdrawal from the bargain will be harmful to both.[34]

Each of the three factors discussed above represents a central and dominant aspect of relational contracts. Furthermore, and more importantly for the purposes of this chapter, these typical characteristics of relational contracts all play a crucial role in the determination of the remedial rights of parties to a violated relational contract.[35]

*The Second Step: Highlighting the Remedial Implications of the Pertinent Features of the Relational Contract*

As has just been explained, in the context of the proposed theoretical model, a judge or an arbitrator applying the formal law of contract remedies to a relational contract is required to focus attention on three distinct characteristics of such a contract. These are:

a. The extent to which the contract defines – or necessitates – a lengthy period of performance;

---

34 The connection between the 'investment factor' and the relational structure of a business contract was first emphasized and developed as an economic insight by Oliver Williamson. Williamson argued that initially high transaction costs – when they do not prevent contracting – typically create relational characteristics between the parties to an economic bargain. O.E. Williamson, 'Transaction Cost Economics: The Governance of Contractual Relations' 22 *Journal of Law & Economic* 233 (1979). The investment factor has been recognized as a typical feature of relational contracts by legal scholars. See e.g. McKendrick, n 7 above, 310, mentioning the phenomenon of parties to a relational contract investing '... so heavily in the relationship that they are effectively locked in to each other.'

35 At the same time, it should be clear that the authors do not hold the view that a contract must reflect each and every one of these three elements in order to be considered relational. On the contrary: under their understanding of the concept of a relational contract, a contract that lacks one, or even two of the three characteristics, would still rightly be considered relational, as long as at least one of the features (long duration, personal relationship or heavy investment) is clearly present. On the other hand, when none of these characteristics is present, the contractual relationship should be defined as non-relational, or what sometimes is called 'transactional' or 'discrete'.

b. The extent to which the contract creates an intensive interpersonal relationship, or is carried out in the framework of such an existing relationship;
c. The extent to which entering into the contract requires a substantial investment, which would make the retreat or withdrawal from the contract very costly or very risky for one of the parties, or for both.

What are the potential implications of each of these three traits of the relational contract at the remedial level? In other words, in what specific ways should each of these three characteristics affect the remedies of the aggrieved party? More concretely, how, if at all, does each of the features affect the choice of remedy? To what extent does each of them influence the operational rules relating to any of the specific remedies to which a plaintiff may be entitled following a violation of the contract? In addition, what can be said of the interrelationships between the three features? Do they all operate in the same remedial direction, or is it possible for them to work in different or even contradictory directions?

This chapter does not purport to answer any of these questions in a detailed and systematic manner. To do so would require further research. At this stage of the development of the theory, it will suffice to lay out, by way of illustration, some preliminary thoughts regarding the possible remedial implications of each of the pertinent characteristics of relational contracts.[36]

In doing so, it would be useful to distinguish between two types of influence. First, on a very general level, each of the three characteristics discussed may influence the *choice of remedy* – a fundamental issue for the law of remedies in any legal system.[37] Namely, each of the features may operate as a limitation on the freedom of the aggrieved party to choose freely among the remedial venues available to him upon breach. Second, on a more concrete level, each of the features may have a more subtle influence on the internal doctrinal rules pertaining to any given remedy, to which the aggrieved party is entitled.

The following lines highlight some of these influences, in order to illustrate the possible implications of the relational model of remedies advanced in this chapter.

*Extended period of performance* As pointed out earlier, an extended period of performance increases the probability that unexpected and unplanned events will occur, which would significantly raise the costs of performance, and thus reduce the profitability of the bargain from the standpoint of one of the parties,

36 And, in addition, to discuss the possible integrated influence of the different features, in cases where they coexist at a single relationship. This will be done in the next subsection.

37 The choice of remedy is the first question to arise whenever a party to a contract suffers a violation and considers resorting to a formal remedy. It is not exclusive to the relational context. Nevertheless, as will be seen in the context of relational contracts, the resolution of the choice of remedy requires special attention and raises an array of difficult questions which may not arise in non-relational transactions.

or both. Of course, such 'change of circumstance' may justify a variation of the contract itself, i.e. an adjustment of the primary rights and duties of the parties as reflected in the original agreement.[38] This, however, is not a question of remedies. A different question needs to be addressed, namely, assuming that the change of circumstance does not amount to an excuse for the non-performance of a pre-determined obligation, in what respect may such a change in circumstance affect the remedial rights of the parties?

A first possible implication concerns the choice of remedy. More specifically it concerns the choice between remedies that seek to literally enforce the violated transaction and those which merely seek to provide the party suffering the breach with a right to compensation (most typically through an award of compensatory damages). It is submitted that an extended period of performance should in most cases justify a sympathetic approach towards a plaintiff's claim for enforcement (i.e. specific performance or an injunction). The reason lies in the difficulty of assessing and quantifying – at the moment the damages are computed – the benefit of which the aggrieved party has been deprived as a result of the breach. This inherent difficulty makes the computation of damages uncertain and conjectural, a fact that undermines the ability of monetary compensation to protect the plaintiff's expectation interest. In this sense, an extended period of performance should generally be seen as supporting a plaintiff's claim for specific enforcement of the contract.

Second, on a more tangible level, an extended period of performance may influence the operational rules of specific remedies to which the plaintiff may be entitled. For example, a change of circumstance (which is a common occasion in a long-term contractual relationship) may result in the plaintiff being denied the right to specific enforcement – due to its becoming impossible or unjust. Alternatively, such a change of circumstance – occurring between the formation of the contract and the judicial determination of the defendant's liability – may persuade the court, at the plaintiff's request, to apply a doctrine of approximated enforcement (sometimes known as *cy près*).[39]

Extended duration may also affect the rules for assessing compensatory damages. To start with, due to the conjectural nature of long-term ventures, one should expect the courts to demonstrate considerable tolerance towards plaintiffs who have not succeeded in proving their loss – or the extent of their loss – with reasonable certainty. In light of the inherent difficulties of computation typical in such contracts, courts should be expected to relax traditional requirements of proof,

---

38 See Introduction, above.

39 Doctrines allowing approximated enforcement of contractual obligations have been endorsed by a number of legal systems. They usually require, as a precondition for awarding such a remedy, that the deviation from the original obligation be minimal or trivial. However, it is submitted that in the relational context, especially when the contract is characterized by a lengthy period of performance, such remedies would be administered more liberally, that is, more frequently, even in cases where the deviation from the original obligation is significant.

especially when specific enforcement of the transaction would be unreasonable or impossible.[40]

In addition, some adjustments may be required with regard to the rules on legal causation and remoteness. For example, under the English rule of *Hadley v Baxendale*[41] a precondition of liability in damages is the forseeability of the loss, the existence of which is examined at the time of contracting. However entrenched, it is argued that such a rule may not be justified in the context of a long-term relational agreement. Here, unlike under a one-shot discrete transaction, each party should be expected to foresee – or at least to take into account – the possibility that further events might change the nature and extent of the other party's loss from non-performance. Hence, it is not at all obvious that a defendant should be exempt from liability for the (foreseeable) loss caused by his breach of the contract, just because at some time in the distant past (i.e. upon formation) that loss could not have been expected to result from future non-performance.[42]

*Intensive interpersonal relationship* Similarly to the preceding feature, this feature may influence both the choice of remedy, and specific rules pertaining to particular remedies.

At the basic level, one should expect the law of remedies to respond to the intensive interpersonal factor in two somewhat contradictory ways. On the one hand, the non-economic character of the relationship may lead a court to look favourably at the aggrieved party's claim for enforcement (when such a claim is made). On the other hand, the very existence of such a personal relationship would in most cases present a serious obstacle from the standpoint of a party seeking to enforce the contract. This arises from the fact that in most western legal systems the remedy of enforcement will not be granted when it requires the giving – or receiving – of a personal service. Thus, in a somewhat paradoxical way, the closer the relationship between the parties before the breach, the more problematic it is to enforce their mutual obligations after its occurrence.

On the other hand, the same factor would work in the opposite direction in respect to the remedy of termination. A failure to perform an obligation arising from a close interpersonal relationship may frequently involve a breach of trust or of a fiduciary duty (not necessarily in the technical sense). As such, it may support the conclusion that the non-performance constituted a fundamental breach, and

40 When specific enforcement is available, a question arises as to the plaintiff's right to choose between enforcing the contract and terminating it due to the breach. This problem is discussed below, see sub-section 'Intensive interpersonal relationship'.

41 [1854] 9 Exch 341.

42 For further discussion of the possible implications of a long-term relationship on the rules of remoteness and the rules on damages more generally see recently: Campbell, n 2 above.

as such endowed the aggrieved party the right to terminate, i.e. to unilaterally withdraw from the bargain.

Second, on a more specific level, interpersonal relations may also require some adjustments in the traditional rules of damages. For example, the traditional reluctance of courts to compensate victims for non-pecuniary losses resulting from breach of contract may not be justified. This would certainly be the case when the loss complained of originates in a breach of an interpersonal relationship of trust and interdependence.[43] In these cases the law of damages should be applied more flexibly, to the extent that it does not recognize the right to non-pecuniary damages. The law of damages should be altered so as to adequately express the emotional, non-financial dimensions of relational contracts.

This more liberal approach may also be applied towards claims for extra-compensatory damages (e.g. disgorgement damages or punitive damages), at least in cases where the violation has been deemed inexcusable or opportunistic.[44]

*Heavy investment and high costs of retreat* How should heavy investment and high costs of retreat, typical characteristics of relational contracts, affect the remedial rights of the parties in case of breach?

It is argued that their main impact should be reflected in a tendency, on the part of the legal system, to limit the right of the aggrieved party to terminate the contract following its breach.

Thus, when other proactive measures are available to the victim in a relational contract of this sort, he may be expected – even in the face of a fundamental breach of contract – to refrain from exercising his legal right to terminate it. Indeed, as a general rule, the victim of breach should not be allowed to terminate a relational contract in which this characteristic features highly, without first resorting to less drastic remedies, such as reduction of price, and – most importantly – the right to withhold performance. These two moderate, middle-way remedies enable the aggrieved party to protect his legitimate interests, without renouncing the entire legal and commercial relationship – a step that would jeopardize the other party's interest in the performance of the contract.[45]

---

43 Such a result may be formally justified by reference to the idea that in a relational contract of this sort, mental distress should be regarded as a foreseeable consequence of breach.

44 Indeed, American case law seems to be moving in this direction in recent decades, in terms of widening the scope of the right to collect non-pecuniary and punitive damages. See, e.g. *Parker Chapin Flattau & Klimpl, LLP* v *Bamira*, 803 NYS 2d 19 (2005), where an award of $5 million in punitive damages was affirmed in the appellate court against an individual (and a law firm that acted as his agent) for breach of fiduciary relationship by the defendant arising out of a commercial partnership with the plaintiff. For a summary of the (unpublished) decision in the first instance see, e.g. http://www.lpklaw.com/showarticle.php?aid=104&desc=1 (accessed 2.6.09).

45 As mentioned earlier, the ability to use non-judicial remedies, such as reduction of price, withholding performance and – as a last resort – termination, plays a significant role in preserving the relational context, in the sense that they do not entail the opening of

Furthermore, whenever the victim is aware of the heavy investment made by the other party, he should not be allowed to terminate without first giving the former a reasonable opportunity to rectify the breach.[46] In the special context of a relational contract with the feature here discussed, this principle should not be regarded as a mere recommendation, but as a binding legal rule which forms part of the formal law of remedies.

### *The Final Step: Integrating the Remedial Implications*

What is the interrelation between the three relational features we discussed in the preceding sections? And how are their influences at the remedial stage to be integrated in any specific case? Having examined the remedial implications of the individual features separately, we will now consider the impact of their unified influence.

The answer proposed here is, in theory, relatively simple. The concrete answer to any of the remedial questions that may arise following the breach of a relational contract should be the result of a process of balancing the implications of each of the remedial features present in the relational contract at hand.

Yet, in practice, the balancing is not always a simple task. For example, when a particular relational contract features only one of the three characteristics, applying the appropriate rule of remedy will necessitate adjusting the relevant principles and rules provided by the law of contract remedies – whatever form they may take – to this unique feature. On the other hand, where a contract features a number of characteristics, the needed adjustments will have to be considered in light of the combined and simultaneous influence of all those characteristics. Even this may not pose great difficulty, when the different features work in the same remedial direction, i.e. when giving weight to their remedial implications provides similar answers to the remedial issue in question.

However, as already seen, this is not always the case. At times, the various characteristics, operating simultaneously in a contractual setting, may work in different and even conflicting directions. For example, where the relational contract is characterized by both a prolonged duration, and a heavy investment on the part of the breaching party, these features will frequently 'work together', at least as far as the choice between enforcement and termination is concerned.[47] On the other hand, the same question may be much more difficult to answer, when

---

a formal, judicially imposed, resolution of the dispute. See section above (the third reason for the relevance of traditional remedies in the relational context).

46 The authors would, though, leave an exception for cases of opportunistic and inexcusable violations, which by their very nature reduce the possibility of future cooperation.

47 As has been seen, the first feature will usually justify a sympathetic approach towards a plaintiff's claim for specific performance of the contract, while the second feature usually operates as a restrain on the right to terminate, thus indirectly supporting the preservation of the contractual relationship (i.e. ongoing performance). See above, fourth

the third relational feature (heavy investment) is present alongside the 'intensive interpersonal relationship' factor. The reason should be obvious by now: while the former feature generally supports the right to demand enforcement of the agreement, the latter feature presents a serious obstacle to such a claim.[48]

Needless to say, the influences of each of the factors or features need not be of the same weight in any given case. Correct balancing should therefore entail not only the determination of the existence (or non-existence) of any of the factors, but also their respective relative weight. This, in turn, requires a complex intellectual process that takes all the relevant implications into account, gives each their appropriate normative weight, and finally balances them against each other.

## Concluding Remarks: The Relational Theory of Remedies and the DCFR

A reader expecting to find in this chapter a comprehensive code laying out, in detail, new rules of remedy for relational contracts would probably be disappointed. The reason for this was explained above. Relational contracts do not constitute a clearly differentiated category of contracts. Rather, they represent a broad and open-ended category, ranging from transactions bearing some of the features of relational contracts (in various degrees), to transactions reflecting all the typical characteristics of a non-discrete contract (e.g. partnerships, contracts of marriage, long-term distribution contracts, etc).

Accordingly, it would be impossible to create a closed list of remedial rules – designed only for relational contracts – which would suit each and every relational contract. Instead the chapter proposed a theoretical model to guide courts and legislators seeking to adjust existing rules and principles so that they can best suit the relational context. The main purpose has been to develop a principled way of thinking about remedies in relational contracts. It is submitted that this way of thinking is relevant and useful, whether or not one adheres to the relational theory of contract, and whether or not one professes a clearly defined distinction between relational and discrete contracts. A further advantage of the proposed relational theory of remedies lies in its universal character, which makes it applicable to any sophisticated legal system. Furthermore, implementing the theory does not necessitate legislative intervention. It can be effectively applied on a case by case basis, through judicial application of the flexible principles of the law of remedies.[49]

section, under sub-headings 'Extended period of performance' and 'Heavy investment and high costs of retreat' respectively.

48 See above, fourth section, under sub-headings 'Heavy investment and high costs of retreat' and Intensive interpersonal relationship' respectively.

49 However, the authors do believe that the general principles proposed in this article can be usefully incorporated into the framework of an existing (or a proposed) civil code, or more specific legislation concerning contractual remedies. Such legislative initiative may facilitate judicial efforts to adapt remedial rules to the relational context.

Indeed, even assuming that in the classical period of contract law remedies were tailored to suit only discrete (non-relational) contracts (and that is unlikely), this is clearly not the situation today. In modern times, the law of remedies is characterized by tremendous flexibility, significant broadening of the range of remedies, and by judicial discretionary powers to decide issues concerning the choice of remedies, their availability, as well as their scope and extent. There has been wide recognition of the need to relax rigid rules and to subject contractual rights to principles of justice, reasonableness, and decency.[50] Hence, what is necessary today in order to give effect to the relational theory of remedies is nothing more than awareness to its existence, and to the possible need to adjust certain rules of remedy to suit the relational context. To exemplify this, suffice it to take a brief look at some of the remedial provisions of the European Draft Common Frame of Reference (DCFR).

First, while the DCFR does not explicitly relate to the relational contract theory, the document as a whole employs a number of relational notions, such as solidarity, cooperation, and the contractual validation of consensual norms of conduct.[51] This is expressed both in the general principal of good faith interspersed among its various sections[52] and in other contexts, such as contractually validating practices endorsed by the parties in the course of the contract[53] and imposing the obligation of cooperation between the parties to the contract (both on the general level[54] and in specific contractual contexts[55]). A striking example of the function played by the relational theory in the DCFR framework is found in section III-1:110. This section regulates the court's authority to alter the contract, or to terminate it, in the wake of a change in circumstances. To begin, sub-section (1) lays down the basic principle of the duty of fulfilling contractual obligations even in the face of changing circumstances.[56] Notwithstanding sub-section (2) specifically addresses situations, in which the performance of the original obligation would be unjust due

---

50 The principle of good faith is not recognized as a general rule of direct application in the Common Law jurisdictions. However, even the Common Law systems contain many particular rules that are functionally equivalent to good faith: DCFR Interim Outline Edition (2008) Introduction §73 (35).

51 For the core aims and underlying values of the DCFR see: DCFR Interim Outline Edition (2008) Introduction §15–36 (10–18).

52 See, e.g. art I-1:102(3)(b), II-3:301, II-8:102(1)(g), III-1:103(1).

53 See art II-1:104(1): 'The parties to a contract are bound … by any practice they have established between themselves.'

54 Art III-1:104.

55 Art IV.C.-2:103 (Services), art IV.C.-2:101 (Mandate), art IV.E.-2:201 (Commercial agency, franchise and distributorship). It clearly stands out that the 'obligation to co-operate' articles within the chapter of specific contracts appear particularly in those types of contracts that are usually characterized as relational contracts.

56 'An obligation must be performed even if performance has become more onerous, whether because the cost of performance has increased or because the value of what is to be received in return has diminished.'

to a change in circumstances. In those situations the court is authorized to change the substance of the obligation in order to render it reasonable and fair, or, under certain circumstances, to terminate the contract subject to the conditions set forth by the court.[57] Without a doubt, this section reflects insights based on the theory of relational contracts. However, as is standard practice within the framework of that theory, the contract is dealt with on the level of its primary obligations rather than on the level of remedies. The remedies chapter of the DCFR does not contain a similar, general arrangement, but, as clarified above, the space for judicial discretion is broad enough to enable most of the required adjustments even within the existing framework.

This point will be briefly demonstrated here. The general obligation of good faith, which also applies to remedies,[58] allows a sufficiently broad margin for the exercise of judicial discretion. This discretion may influence both the choice of remedies and the internal rules governing the administration of specific remedies (for example, rules limiting the extent of compensation). On the first level, broad discretion has been granted the courts on both the question of when enforcement should be available and the question of whether 'the debtor's non-performance is excused'.[59] If the court determines that this is indeed the situation, the aggrieved party will be entitled to all other remedies, apart from enforcement and indemnification.[60] This broad discretion regarding the enforcement remedy is also found in the framework of the internal limitations on the remedy of enforcement.[61] The section in the DCFR dealing with enforcement lacks a provision to grant courts the general authority to make an injunction subject to conditions fixed by the court. A provision of this sort would allow greater flexibility in the adjustments required when granting an enfordement order. The remedy of rescission is also subject to wide judicial discretion. Rescission is only an option in the case of a fundamental breach,[62] while the definition of fundamental breach leaves relatively

57 'If, however, performance of contractual obligations ... becomes so onerous because of an exceptional change of circumstances that it would be manifestly unjust to hold the debtor to the obligation a court may: (a) vary the obligation in order to make it reasonable and equitable in the new circumstances, or (b) terminate the obligation at a date and on terms to be determined by the court.'

58 Art III-1:103(1): 'A person has a duty to act in accordance with good faith and fair dealing ... in pursuing or defending a remedy for non performance...'

59 Art III-3:104(1) sets the conditions, leaving room for wide judicial discretion: 'A debtor's non-performance of an obligation is excused if it is due to an impediment beyond the debtor's control and if the debtor could not reasonably be expected to have avoided or overcome the impediment or its consequences.'

60 Art III-3:101(2).

61 Art III-3:302(3).

62 Art III-3:502(1). Termination is also possible in case of delay in performance, which does not amount to a fundamental breach. However, this would be possible only if the creditor gives the debtor a notice fixing an additional period of time for performance. See art III-3:503(1).

broad margins for judicial discretion.[63] The discretion regarding the availability and scope of damages finds expression in the requirement of forseeability, according to which the party in breach must indemnify the aggrieved party only for loss which the debtor foresaw or could reasonably have foreseen at the time when the obligation was incurred[64] as a likely result of the non-performance.[65]

Finally, the DCFR recognizes remedies of a more moderate nature, which may be applied without any judicial intervention. These arrangements (such as withholding performance,[66] price reduction[67] and the ability to fix an additional period for performance[68]) add a further dimension to the usefulness of the DCFR in the context of relational contracts.

Academic writing in the fascinating field of relational contracts has, to date, focused almost exclusively on the impact of the relational context on the primary obligations of the parties (via interpretation, renegotiation and settlement, and alternative dispute resolution mechanisms). However, there has been little discussion of the possible influence of the relational nature of the contract on the secondary rights of the parties, namely, on their remedial rights. This chapter has argued that the formal law of remedies plays a significant role in the relational context, both before and after the eruption of a legal dispute. This chapter reflects the authors' effort to direct attention to this, as of yet, virgin territory of contract law. It is a first endeavor, hopefully to be followed by others, to explore the subtle interface between the law of remedies and the relational theory of contract.

---

63 Art III-3:502(2).

64 See supra text to n 41–2.

65 Art III-3:703.

66 Art III-3:401.

67 Art III-3:601.

68 Art III-3:103.

# Chapter 12

# Contract Governance within Corporate Governance: A Lesson from the Global Financial Crisis

Florian Möslein[1]

This chapter was first drafted in 2009, the year which marked the thirtieth anniversary of research of governance as a widespread academic exercise. The term and idea of governance are, of course, much older, as one can see when reading Plato's *Euthydemus*,[2] or, even more vividly, when visiting the Palazzo Pubblico in Siena, where Ambrogio Lorenzetti painted his wonderful frescoes 'Cattivo governo ed effetti del buon governo', in the fourteenth century.[3] These pictures illustrate in a wonderful manner what governance is all about.[4]

It was only three decades ago, however, that Oliver Williamson published his seminal article that is widely acknowledged as the starting point of modern discussions of governance.[5] Under the subtitle 'The Governance of Contractual Relations', Williamson compared markets, long-term contracts and corporate organizations as alternative governance structures. Despite Williamson's clear

---

1 The present article is an updated version of a lecture that I have given at the Secola Conference in Florence on June 6th 2009. The original contribution has been published in IUP Journal of Governance and Public Policy VI 2 (2011), 7-25 (cf. also, in German: Juristenzeitung [JZ] 2010, 72-80).

2 See Plato, *Euthydemus* (380 BC), para 291d: 'Here obviously was the very art which we were seeking – the art which is the source of good government, and which may be described, in the language of Aeschylus, as alone sitting at the helm of the vessel of state, piloting and governing all things, and utilizing them' (transl by Benjamin Jowett, available at http://classics.mit.edu/Plato/euthydemus.html).

3 On the interpretation of these paintings, from the perspective of history of arts: Q. Skinner, 'Ambrogio Lorenzetti: The Artist as Political Philosopher' *Proceedings of the British Academy* 72 (1986), 1 *et seq.*; U. Feldges-Henning, 'The Pictorial Programme of the Sala della Pace – A New Interpretation' *Journal of the Warburg and Courtauld Institutes* 35 (1972) 145 *et seq.*

4 Similar is D. Tarschys, 'Wealth, Values, Institutions: Trends in Government and Governance', in OECD (ed.), *Governance in the 21st Century – Future Studies* (Paris: OECD Publishing, 2001) 27, 39 *et seq.* ('The message of Lorenzetti still holds: Governance matters').

5 O. Williamson, 'Transaction-Cost Economics: The *Governance* of *Contractual* Relations' *Journal of Law and Economics* 22 (1979) 233 *et seq.*

focus on contracts in general and on long-term contracts in particular, governance research has not received much attention in contract law theory,[6] at least as opposed to academic discourse in corporate law,[7] let alone in national and international public and administrative law.[8]

This contribution therefore tries to explain why research into contract governance is of crucial importance in that area of tension between exchange and cooperation that is debated in this volume. More specifically, it will discuss contracts and organizations as two forms of governance that not only provide functional alternatives, but indeed operate as closely interacting and interdependent governance mechanisms.[9] First of all, however, this author wishes to explain why he believes it is particularly important to start such a discussion about contract governance more than 30 years after Williamson's article. The argument is that in the wake of the global financial crisis, contract governance is urgently required as a tool for lawmaking and research of contract law alike.

## Crisis and Innovation

Banks have been struggling; companies have gone bankrupt; more and more people have been losing their jobs: the global economy has just experienced one of its fiercest crises ever.[10] Governments have been accumulating incredibly huge

6 For a first step see F. Möslein and K. Riesenhuber, 'Contract Governance – A Draft Research Agenda' *European Review of Contract Law* (*ERCL*) 5 (2009) 248 *et seq*; with a somewhat different focus P. Vincent-Jones, 'Contractual Governance: Institutional and Organizational Analysis' *Oxford Journal of Legal Studies* 20 (2000) 317 *et seq.*; P. Zumbansen, 'The Law of Society: Governance through Contract' *Indiana Journal of Global Legal Studies* Jul 14 (2007) 191 *et seq.* and the contributions in *European Law Journal* (*ELJ*) 15 (2009) 155–276 (special issue on 'Regulating Markets and Social Europe: New Governance in the EU'). On the merits also H. Collins, *Regulating Contract* (Oxford: Oxford University Press, 1999) 225 *et seq.*

7 Recent surveys: P. Leyens, 'Corporate Governance: Grundsatzfragen und Forschungsperspektiven' *Juristen-Zeitung* (*JZ*) 2007 1061 *et seq.*; and T. Clarke, *International Corporate Governance – A Comparative Approach* (New York: Routledge, 2007) esp. 228 *et seq.* ('The Globalisation of Corporate Governance').

8 On governance research in general, see the surveys by S. Burries, M. Kempa and C. Shearing, 'Changes in Governance: A Cross-Disciplinary Review of Current Scholarship' *Akron Law Review* 41 (2008) 1, 7–12; A.M. Kjaer, *Governance* (Cambridge: Polity Press, 2004) 3–7, with further references; J. Pierre, 'Introduction: Understanding Governance', in idem (ed.), *Debating Governance* (Oxford: Oxford University Press, 2002) 1, 3 *et seq.*; and the contributions in G. Schuppert (ed.), *Governance-Forschung: Vergewisserung über Stand und Entwicklungslinien* (2nd edn, Baden-Baden: Nomos, 2006).

9 See below, sub III (Governance in the 'Nexus of Contracts').

10 Comprehensively on its origins and implications: S. Grundmann, C. Hofmann and F. Möslein (eds), *Finanzkrise und Wirtschaftsordnung* (Berlin: de Gruyter, 2009); R. Posner, *A Failure of Capitalism: The Crisis of '08 and the Descent into Depression*

debts in order to combat the economic downturn, but their options were limited: the more money they pumped into the financial and economic system, the lower – apparently – the effect, and the narrower their future scope of action.[11] Market participants were increasingly lacking mutual trust. Even worse, confidence in our economic order also threatened to evaporate.[12]

*Creative Destruction and Smart Regulation*

Not every crisis, however, ends in disaster. According to the literal meaning of the term's Greek origin, a crisis may also be a turning point,[13] providing an opportunity to trace its causes, to change structures and to improve a system in the long run, in particular, to make it more stable. In this perspective, each crisis offers chances to innovate. The Austrian lawyer, economist and politician Joseph Schumpeter brought this idea to a head when he used the keyword 'creative destruction' in his book *Capitalism, Socialism and Democracy*.[14] (By the way: this book was originally published in 1942, just a few years after Schumpeter had lost his entire fortune by driving the private bank M. L. Biedermann & Co Bankaktiengesellschaft into bankruptcy.[15]) Schumpeter's central hypothesis is that capitalism is subject to a permanent process of industrial change, a process

(Cambridge/Mass: Harvard University, 2009); R. Shiller, *The Subprime Solution: How Today's Global Financial Crisis Happened, and What to Do about It* (Princeton: Princeton University Press, 2008).

11 For critical assessments of policy responses, see V. Acharya and M. Richardson (eds), *Restoring Financial Stability: How to Repair a Failed System* (Hoboken: Wiley, 2009); J. Taylor, *Getting Off Track: How Government Actions and Interventions Caused, Prolonged, and Worsened the Financial Crisis* (Stanford: Hoover Institution Press, 2009).

12 Similar F. Roth, 'The Effect of the Financial Crisis on Systemic Trust' *Intereconomics* 44 (2009) 203 *et seq*, stating a particular sharp decline of confidence in European institutions. More generally on the role of trust and confidence in economic life, and their relevance to the recent financial crisis: T. Earle, 'Trust, Confidence, and the 2008 Global Financial Crisis' *Risk Analysis* 29 (2009) 785 *et seq.*; F. Tonkiss, 'Trust, Confidence and Economic Crisis' *Intereconomics* 44 (2009) 196 *et seq.*

13 In ancient Greek, κρίσις (krísis, today κρήση, krísi) initially referred to decision, determination or judgment, but has later increasingly been understood in this broader sense. In general on the phenomenon that small events can trigger an epidemic of change: M. Gladwell, *The Tipping Point: How Little Things Can Make a Big Difference* (New York: Back Bay Books, 2002).

14 J. Schumpeter, *Capitalism, socialism and democracy* (London: Routledge, 1994) 81 *et seq.* ('The Process of Creative Destruction').

15 More extensively on this experience and its influence on Schumpeter's academic thinking: R. Allen, *Opening Doors: the Life and Work of Joseph Schumpeter, vol 1: Europe* (New Brunswick: Transaction Publishers, 1991) 183–200; T. McCraw, *Prophet of innovation: Joseph Schumpeter and creative destruction* (Cambridge/Mass: Belknap Press, 2007) 105–12.

'that incessantly revolutionizes the economic structure *from within*, incessantly destroying the old one, incessantly creating a new one'.[16]

This process of creative destruction not only leads to new products and businesses, but also to changes in the framework of market economy: every crisis of the economic system offers opportunities to rethink, to reform and to renew structures and institutions, rules and standards.[17] Schumpeter therefore provides a hopeful message for today: our social market economy can survive the global financial crisis, it may even emerge in better shape, but it must be open to scrutiny or even to reinventing itself.[18] Such an evolutionary process of innovation is now already in full swing: advisory boards such as the Issing, the Turner and the Larosière Committee have developed reform proposals at the national and European level.[19] Many of these have at least been drafted as legislative proposals.[20] At the international level, we can discern a new global financial architecture in the aftermath of the financial crisis.[21] This recent history can therefore teach important lessons about the regulation of financial markets and, more generally, of governance structures.[22] Reforms in periods of crisis, however, always tend to

16 Schumpeter, n 14 above, 83, emphasis in the original.

17 Hence *Schumpeter* is regarded as a pioneer of the study of economic evolution: E. Andersen, *Evolutionary Economics: Post-Schumpeterian Contributions* (London: Pinter, 2005) 1; see also J. Metcalfe, *Evolutionary Economics and Creative Destruction* (London: Routledge, 1998).

18 For an extensive account of examples illustrating that good design of a market is crucial to its success, that a market develops over time by trial and error, and that government plays an indispensable role in providing public goods and acting as rule setter and referee, see J. MacMillan, *Reinventing the Bazaar: A Natural History of Markets* (New York: Norton, 2002).

19 *New Financial Order – Recommendations by the Issing Committee* (February 2009), available at http://www.bundesregierung.de/Content/DE/StatischeSeiten/Breg/G8G20/Anlagen/bericht-issing-london.pdf?__blob=publicationFile; *The Turner Review – A regulatory response to the global banking crisis* (March 2009), available at http://www.fsa.gov.uk/pubs/other/turner_review.pdf; and *Report of the High-Level Group on Financial Supervision in the EU* (February 2009, chaired by Jacques de Larosière), available at http://ec.europa.eu/internal_market/finances/docs/de_larosiere_report_en.pdf (all last visited on 12 July 2013).

20 See, for instance, on the European level: *Communication from the Commission for the Spring European Council on Driving European Recovery* of 4 March 2009, COM(2009) 114 final; and, more specifically, *Communication from the Commission on European Financial Supervision* of 25 May 2009, COM(2009) 252 final. See also references n 112.

21 The London G-20 summit has been the starting point for this reform: *The Global Plan for Recovery and Reform*, Final communiqué of 2 April 2009 and, more specifically *Communiqué of the Meeting of Finance Ministers and Central Bank Governors* of 14 March 2009, available at http://www.g20.org/load/780979548 (last visited on 12 July 2013).

22 See, inter alia: K. Alexander and N. Moloney (eds.), *Law Reform and Financial Markets* (Cheltenham: Edward Elgar, 2011); S. Grundmann and Y. Atamer (eds.), *Financial Services, Financial Crisis and General European Contract Law* (Alphen: Kluwer, 2011);

embody overreactions. Klaus Hopt strongly warns against 'the danger of over-regulation, a plethora of standards and a new protectionist wave'.[23]

Hence crisis and innovation are a real challenge, not least for legal scholarship, and namely in three respects: in the first, numerous new rules simply widen the scope for jurisprudential discussion and sometimes even open up entirely new fields of law, for example, at the crossroads of stabilization measures, financial supervision and international law.[24] Second, we have to face questions of legal policy, namely to identify dangers of over-regulation, to advise against them in a timely fashion, and to develop principles of smart regulation.[25] Third and last, legal scholarship itself might be forced to rethink its own methods and approaches in specific disciplines, in order to meet these first two challenges.[26]

### *The Innovation of Corporate Governance*

Corporate governance provides a prime example for this innovation process of creative destruction.[27] The main trigger was the last major financial and economic crisis, the so-called Asian flu, which mainly hit local emerging markets between 1997 and 1999 to an extent that was hitherto unknown.[28] In 2002, the bankruptcies

---

W. Sun, J. Stewart and D. Pollard (eds.), *Corporate Governance and the Global Financial Crisis* (Cambridge: Cambridge University Press, 2011); E. Wymeersch, K. Hopt and G. Ferrarini (eds.), *Financial Regulation and Supervision: A Post-Crisis Analysis* (Oxford: Oxford University Press, 2012).

23 K.J. Hopt, 'Gefahr einer Überregulierung' *Handelsblatt* (2 January 2009), 12 (interview, translation mine).

24 A. von Aaken and J. Kurtz, 'Prudence or Discrimination? Emergency Measures, the Global Financial Crisis and International Economic Law', *Journal of International Economic Law* 12 (2009) 859 *et seq*. See also K. Alexander, 'The International Supervisory Framework for Financial Services: An Emerging Regime of Transnational Supervision' *Journal of International Banking Regulation* 1 (2000) 33 *et seq*.; D. Singer, *Regulating capital: setting standards for the international financial system* (Ithaca: Cornell University Press, 2007).

25 C. Kirchner, 'Prinzipien für eine kluge Regulierung' *Frankfurter Allgemeine Zeitung* (26 March 2009) 14. The term and concept have been developed in a different area: N. Gunningham and P. Grabosky, *Smart Regulation – Designing Environmental Policy* (Oxford: Clarendon Press, 1998).

26 More generally on the influence of economic change on legal reasoning: M. Amstutz, *Evolutorisches Wirtschaftsrecht* (Baden-Baden: Nomos, 2001), D. Wielsch, *Freiheit und Funktion: zur Struktur- und Theoriegeschichte des Rechts der Wirtschaftsgesellschaft* (Baden-Baden: Nomos, 2001).

27 At a glance: Clarke, n 7 above, 1–32 ('cycles of governance'); comprehensively P. MacAvoy and I. Millstein, *Recurrent Crisis in Corporate Governance* (Basingstoke: Palgrave Macmillan, 2003).

28 OECD, *Principles of Corporate Governance* (1st edn, Paris: OECD Publishing, 1999) 7: 'The recent financial crises in Asia ... have made amply clear ... why the issues of transparency and accountability in corporate governance are so important to investor

of Enron (according to its own slogan 'The World's Greatest Company') and Worldcom gave additional impetus.[29] They brought about the two biggest corporate scandals that the United States had ever experienced. Since then, the corporate governance movement has been a tremendous success all over the world, a success that is reflected in a sharp increase of practical corporate governance rules, but also in many academic research projects and publications.[30] The triumph of corporate governance is now so impressive that it is no exaggeration to claim that traditional legal scholarship of corporate entities, of corporate management and control has reinvented itself at its very core.[31]

From an academic point of view, the innovation of corporate governance is displayed mainly in examining well-known questions in a new, sometimes much broader research perspective. This observation can be unfolded in four different dimensions.[32] First of all, corporate governance is not limited to the internal structures of companies, but takes their market-drivenness into account.[33] This twofold perspective is often referred to as internal and external corporate

---

confidence and to overall national economic performance'. Comprehensively on that crisis and its implications: M. Goldstein, *The Asian Financial Crisis: Causes, Cures, and Systemic Implications* (Washington DC: Institute for International Economics, 1998); and the contributions in G. Noble and J. Ravenhill (eds), *The Asian Financial Crisis and the Architecture of Global Finance* (Cambridge: Cambridge University Press, 2000).

29 P. Ali and G. Gregoriou (eds), *International Corporate Governance After Sarbanes-Oxley* (Hoboken: Wiley, 2006); J. Armour and J. McCahery (eds), *After Enron: Improving Corporate Law And Modernising Securities Regulation in Europe And the US* (Oxford: Hart Publishing, 2006); see also D. Branson, 'Enron – When All Systems Fail: Creative Destruction or Roadmap to Corporate Governance Reform?' *Villanova Law Review* 48 (2003) 989 *et seq*.

30 See references n 7 above; more specifically, for instance: K.J. Hopt, 'Die rechtlichen Rahmenbedingungen der Corporate Governance', in P. Hommelhoff, K.J. Hopt and A. von Werder (eds), *Handbuch Corporate Governance* (Stuttgart: Schäffer-Poeschel, 2003) 29, 31, and, in more detail; K.J. Hopt, 'Corporate Governance: Aufsichtsrat oder Markt? – Überlegungen zu einem internationalen und interdisziplinären Thema', in P. Hommelhoff, H. Rowedder and P. Ulmer (eds), *Max Hachenburg, Dritte Gedächtnisvorlesung 1998* (Heidelberg: Müller, 2000) 9, 10 *et seq* and 14–24.

31 Similar S. Grundmann and P.O. Mülbert, 'Corporate Governance – Europäische Perspektiven' *Zeitschrift für Unternehmens- und Gesellschaftsrecht* (*ZGR*) 2001, 215, 217; K.J. Hopt (2003), n 30 above, 29, 31 *et seq*.; M. Lutter, 'Vergleichende Corporate Governance – Die deutsche Sicht' *Zeitschrift für Unternehmens- und Gesellschaftsrecht* (*ZGR*) 2001, 224, 225 ('rank of a distinctive field of legal research', translation mine). On the subject matter itself, very comprehensively: K.J. Hopt, E. Wymeersch, H. Kanda and H. Baum (eds), *Corporate Governance in Context* (Oxford: Oxford University Press, 2006).

32 In more detail on these aspects: Möslein and Riesenhuber, n 6 above, 252–6.

33 F. Möslein, *Grenzen unternehmerischer Leitungsmacht im marktoffenen Verband* (Berlin: de Gruyter, 2007) in particular at 2.

governance.[34] This perspective is not entirely new, but is gaining influence where companies are increasingly financed through capital markets. Second, corporate governance implies modifications to rule-making: standards of behaviour are no longer decreed by the legislator alone, but by a whole range of different, partly private rule-makers.[35] Moreover, they are no longer conceptualized as a rigid list of legal obligations, but as 'soft law',[36] allowing for deviations only if sufficiently justified (*comply or explain*). In the third place, corporate governance and internationalization are closely interrelated.[37] Corporate governance is essentially based on the globalization of financial and capital markets, which requires a higher degree of cross-border transparency of standards of good corporate governance. On the other hand, corporate governance provides a common language that makes it easier to compare rules and legal facts, and that is ultimately required for a truly global research on so-called comparative corporate governance.[38] Fourth,

---

34 E.g. S. Grundmann and F. Möslein, *European Company Law* (Antwerpen: Intersentia, 2007) § 14; K.J. Hopt, 'Common Principles of Corporate Governance in Europe?', in B.S. Markesinis (ed.), *The Clifford Chance Millennium Lectures – The Coming Together of the Common Law and the Civil Law* (Oxford: Hart Publishing, 2000) 105, 106 *et seq.*; Hopt (2003), n 30 above, 34–6; C. Teichmann, 'Corporate Governance in Europa' *Zeitschrift für Unternehmens- und Gesellschaftsrecht* (*ZGR*) 2001, 645, 646 *et seq.*; and now also the monograph by A. Naciri, *Internal and External Aspects of Corporate Governance* (New York: Routledge, 2009).

35 See, for instance, R. Aguilera and A. Cuervo-Cazurra, 'Codes of Good Governance Worldwide: What is the Trigger?' *Organization Studies* 25 (2004) 417–46; for a survey on the most important rule-books cf Grundmann and Möslein, n 34 above, para 476 *et seq.*; Möslein, n 33 above, 414, and extensively: Weil, Gotshal and Manges LLP (eds), *Comparative Study of Corporate Governance Codes Relevant to the European Union and Its Member States – Final Report* (Brussels, 2002), available at http://ec.europa.eu/internal_market/company/docs/corpgov/corp-gov-codes-rpt-pat1_en.pdf; an index with links to all codes is available at http://www.ecgi.org/codes (both last visited on 12 July 2013). Regulatory diversity is increasingly perceived as a specific characteristic of European Company law as such: S. Deakin, 'Reflexive Governance and European Company Law' *European Law Journal* (*ELJ*) 15 (2009) 224 *et seq.*; P. Zumbansen, '"New Governance" in European Corporate Law Regulation as Transnational Pluralism' *European Law Journal* (*ELJ*) 15 (2009) 246 *et seq.*

36 Cf., e.g. K.J. Hopt, 'Corporate Governance in Europa: Neue Regelungsaufgaben und soft law' *Der Gesellschafter – Zeitschrift für Gesellschafts- und Unternehmensrecht* (*GesRZ*) 2002 special issue, 4 *et seq.*; Lutter, n 31 above, 224, 225, E. Vetter, 'Der Deutsche Corporate Governance Kodex – nur ein zahnloser Tiger?' *Neue Zeitschrift für Gesellschaftsrecht* (NZG) 2008, 121, 128 (qualifying); Zumbansen, n 35 above, 12–21 and 47 *et seq.*; with respect to the notion and the concept: U. Ehricke, '"Soft Law" – Aspekte einer neuen Rechtsquelle' *Neue Juristische Wochenschrift* (*NJW*) 1989, 1906 *et seq.*; U. Mörth (ed.), *Soft Law in Governance and Regulation* (Cheltenham: Elgar, 2004).

37 Grundmann and Mülbert, n 31 above, 215, 217 *et seq.*

38 See, in particular: K.J. Hopt, H. Kanda, M.J. Roe, E. Wymeersch and S. Prigge (eds), *Comparative Corporate Governance – the State of the Art and Emerging Research*

corporate governance inspires interdisciplinary research.[39] It covers issues of corporate finance, corporate culture and corporate law.[40] Only a functional perspective allows for a truly comprehensive discussion across disciplines, among economists, lawyers and social scientists.

## Governance Lessons of the Global Financial Crisis

### *Instability of Markets, not Organizations*

The recent crisis had much to do with governance, but *corporate* governance did not play a central role.[41] The most important reports, documents and declarations barely mentioned corporate governance: it was not addressed in the recommendations of the US-American President's Group on Financial Markets,[42] neither in the reports of the Financial Stability Forum[43] and the International Monetary Fund,[44] the Washington nor in the London Declaration of the G20.[45]

---

(Oxford: Oxford University Press, 1998); K.J. Hopt and E. Wymeersch (eds), *Comparative Corporate Governance – Essays and Materials* (Berlin: de Gruyter, 1997).

39 Grundmann and Mülbert, n 31 above, 215, 217.

40 To this effect Lutter, n 31 above, 224, 225 *et seq.*; B. Rudolph, 'Unternehmensfinanzierung und Corporate-Governance-Entwicklungen und weiterer Anpassungsbedarf' *Betriebs-Berater* (*BB*) 2003, 2053 *et seq.*; see also S. Rudolf, 'Entwicklungen im Kapitalmarkt in Deutschland', in M. Habersack, P.O. Mülbert and M. Schlitt (eds), *Unternehmensfinanzierung am Kapitalmarkt* (2nd edn, Munich: Beck, 2008) § 1 para 13 *et seq.*

41 Similar P.O. Mülbert, 'Corporate Governance of Banks' *European Business Organization Law Review* (*EBOR*) 10 (2009), 411, 417 'After the beginning of the financial turbulences in summer 2007, the issue of banks' corporate governance, with the notable exception of remuneration, went out of focus for some time'. See, however, M. Isaksson and G. Kirkpatrick, 'Corporate governance: Lessons from the financial crisis' *OECD Observer* No 273 (June 2009), 11: 'If there is one major lesson to draw from the financial crisis, it is that corporate governance matters'. For a general account, see F. Möslein, 'The focus of regulatory reforms in Europe after the global financial crisis: from corporate to contract governance', in: Sun, Stewart and Pollard, n 22 above, 284 *et seq.*

42 The President's Working Group on Financial Markets, *Policy Statement on Financial Markets* (March 2008), available at http://www.law.du.edu/images/uploads/presidents-working-group.pdf (last visited 12 July 2013).

43 Financial Stability Forum, *Report of the Financial Stability Forum on Enhancing Market and Institutional Resilience* (April 2008), available at http://www.financialstabilityboard.org/publications/r_0804.pdf (last visited 12 July 2013).

44 International Monetary Fund, *The Recent Financial Turmoil – Initial Assessment, Policy Lessons, and Implications for Fund Surveillance* (April 2008), available at http://www.imf.org/external/np/pp/eng/2008/040908.pdf (last visited 12 July 2013).

45 G-20 Declaration of the Summit in Financial Markets and the World Economy, Action Plan to implement Principles for Reform (November 2008), available at http://www.

In Great Britain, the Turner report was a bit more fruitful;[46] in particular as complemented by the so-called Walker Commission which deals specifically with bank governance arrangements.[47] The European Larosière report even called corporate governance 'one of the most important failures of the present crisis'.[48] Under this heading, however, the report mainly criticized general incentive mechanisms on markets which promote short-term profit-orientation. Only the reform proposals on remuneration and risk management were more specifically related to corporate governance as such. Even the OECD, the world's leading rule-setter in corporate governance issues,[49] called for corresponding reforms and launched an ambitious action plan, but its analysis mainly concentrated on the same two aspects.[50] Moreover, the OECD called for better implementation and enforcement mechanisms, but did not propose any substantive revision of the current corporate governance principles.[51]

Indeed, the recent crisis had many causes. Systematic failure of corporate governance, however, was not of key importance.[52] This crisis did not primarily emerge due to specific corporate structures, but was rooted in the instability of markets: as is well known, subprime loans in the US were often approved

---

mofa.go.jp/policy/economy/g20_summit/2008/declaration.pdf (last visited 12 July 2013); and reference n 21 above.

46 *The Turner Review*, n 19 above, 78 ('Regulation can and should address issues relating to the proper governance and conduct of rating agencies and the management of conflict of interest'), and 93 ('Achieving high standards of risk management and governance in all banks is therefore essential').

47 The final report has been published in November 2009: *A review of corporate governance in UK banks and other financial industry entities*, available at visithttp://webarchive.nationalarchives.gov.uk/20130129110402/http://www.hm-treasury.gov.uk/d/walker_review_261109.pdf (last ed 12 July 2013)..

48 *Report of the High-Level Group on Financial Supervision in the EU*, n 19 above, 29.

49 See reference in n 28 above. A revised edition of the OECD Principles (as of 2004) is available at www.oecd.org/daf/corporateaffairs (last visited 12 July 2013).

50 OECD (ed.), *The Corporate Governance Lessons from the Financial Crisis*, Working Paper by Grant Kirkpatrick (February 2009), available ibid. Two additional, but closely related aspects are the performance of boards and the exercise of shareholder rights.

51 OECD (ed.), *Corporate Governance and the Financial Crisis – Key Findings and Main Messages* (June 2009), available ibid.

52 P.O. Mülbert, 'Corporate Governance von Banken' *Zeitschrift für das gesamte Handelsrecht und Wirtschaftsrecht* (*ZHR*) 173 (2009) 1, 3-5 ('Irrelevanzthese'); similar E. Wymeersch, *Corporate Governance and Financial Stability*, Financial Law Institute Working Paper No 11 (2008), 1, available at www.ssrn.com, abstract_id=1288631: 'Corporate Governance and Financial stability is an odd couple'. See also L. van den Berghe, *To What Extent is the Financial Crisis a Governance Crisis? From Diagnosis to Possible Remedies*, Working Paper (2009), available ibid, abstract_id=1410455 (both last visited 12 July 2013).

regardless of financial standing and equity contribution.[53] Corresponding risks were collateralized with insufficient security because mortgages were not transparent, or they were transferred by virtue of loan insurances.[54] Personal claims against real estate credit users were almost impossible, for legal or practical reasons. Low and partly variable mortgage rates and the expectation of rising house prices created further incentives to borrow more money than appropriate with respect to personal solvency.[55] On the opposite side of the market there was no incentive for responsible lending either, because through securitization, transfer and bundling credit risks could be transferred almost at will, and without any real chance for the purchasers to evaluate these risks themselves.[56] Instead, they had to count on the information of rating agencies, who themselves had little incentive to reduce the profitable source of income of the securitization business by poor ratings.[57] More generally, remuneration incentives fostered the dynamics that led to this crisis. This means not just remuneration packages of company directors, but above all the bonuses of investment bankers and even commissions of loan and investment advisors: in other words, compensations in the operational business.[58]

53 S. Grundmann, C. Hofmann and F. Möslein, 'Finanzkrise und Wirtschaftsordnung: Krisenursachen, Finanzmarktstabilisierung, Finanzmarktstabilität', in idem, n 10 above, 1, 3 *et seq.*, with further references.

54 Ibid., 3 *et seq.* and 8–10; see also M. Richardson, 'Causes of the Financial Crisis of 2007–2009', in Acharya and Richardson (eds), n 11 above, 57, 61–3.

55 Grundmann, Hofmann and Möslein, n 53 above, 7 *et seq.*; for illustrative figures see M. Zandi, *Financial Shock: A 360 Degree Look at the Subprime Mortgage Implosion, and How to Avoid the Next Financial Crisis* (Upper Saddle River: Pearson Education, 2009) 45–77; comprehensively J. Barth, *The Rise and Fall of the US Mortgage and Credit Markets* (Hoboken: Wiley & Sons, 2009).

56 Despite early warnings, see, for instance: Center for Responsible Lending (ed.), *Losing Ground: Foreclosures in the Subprime Market and Their Cost to Homeowners*, Working Paper by E. Schloemer et al. (December 2006), available at http://www.responsiblelending.org (last visited 12 July 2013). At a glance on the merits: Grundmann, Hofmann and Möslein, n 53 above, 8–12.

57 H.-P. Schwintowski, 'Finanzmarktkrise: Ursachen, Grundsatzfragen, institutionelle Konsequenzen', in Grundmann, Hofmann and Möslein (eds), n 10 above, 41, 45 *et seq.*; for a more thorough analysis, see: P. Hosp, 'Problematic Practices of Credit Rating Agencies: The Neglected Risks of Mortgage-Backed Securities', in E. Kolb (ed.), *Lessons from the Financial Crisis: Insights and Analysis from Today's Leading Minds* (Hoboken: Wiley, 2010); and J. Mason and J. Rosner, *Where Did the Risk Go? How Misapplied Bond Ratings Cause Mortgage Backed Securities and Collateralized Debt Obligation Market Disruptions*, Working Paper (2007), available at www.ssrn.com, abstract_id=1027475 (last visited 12 July 2013). In general: R.M. Levich, G. Majnoni and C. Reinhart (eds), *Ratings, Rating Agencies and the Global Financial System* (Boston/Mass: Kluwer Academic Publinshing, 2002).

58 See, for instance, OECD (ed.), n 49 above, 14–16. For an extensive account of (non-executive) remuneration practices in the City of London before the crisis, see House of

This short outline demonstrates that the global financial crisis had its roots in the allocation of risks and in a lack of transparency. This crisis mainly had to do with certain incentives for market participants.[59] Loans were granted, securitized and rated in a legal and social framework that allocated risks and chances in a manner which created incentives for transactions that destabilized the whole system in the long term. As an aside, most of the contracts in question were long-term relationships – loan contracts, bond contracts and loan insurance contracts. Such relationships are by nature more likely to provide strong and steady incentives than simple spot contracts.[60] For a thorough understanding of the market instability that was at the heart of the financial crisis, it is, in any event, crucial to analyse the steering effects of all different public, but also social, mechanisms that had an impact on the autonomous interaction of the various players – central banks, borrowers and private banks, insurance companies and credit-rating agencies. It is necessary to understand the entirety of collective, not only hierarchical influences on a specific social system. This is precisely the task that governance research is all about.[61] Yet the social system that is primarily concerned is the market, not the internal organization of corporations.[62] What we have to explore and to improve is the institutional framework of contractual (rather than intra-organizational) relations.[63] Not corporate governance, but contract governance is primarily in demand today.

*Market Stability and Contract Governance*

The notion of contract governance was only used rather sporadically until recently, usually with a view to worker participation agreements in corporations, that is, in

---

Commons – Treasury Committee (ed.), *Banking Crisis: Reforming Corporate Governance and Pay in the City*, Ninth Report of Session 2008–2009 (2009), 10–17.

59 For a similar conclusion, see Wymeersch, n 52 above, 13: 'The relationship between corporate governance and financial stability is an indirect one, as the stability of firms and markets are essential elements for maintaining financial stability. Corporate governance tools do contribute to the intermediate objectives at the firm level, but not directly to financial stability'.

60 This is one of the central arguments of Williamson, n 5 above, 233, 247–54; see also O. Williamson, *The Mechanisms of Governance* (New York: Oxford University Press, 1996) 145–70.

61 J. Köndgen, 'Privatisierung des Rechts' *Archiv für die civilistische Praxis* (*AcP*) 206 (2006) 477, 514, following the approach of M. Hill and P. Hupe, *Implementing Public Policy – Governance in Theory and in Practice* (London: Sage, 2002) 13 *et seq.*

62 This fits the concept of governance as defined, for instance, in O. Williamson, 'The Economics of Governance' *American Economic Review* 95/2 (2005) 1 *et seq.*

63 For a very similar approach, yet from a purely economic perspective, see the research programme of the Collaborative Research Centre (Sonderforschungsbereich) Transregio 15, *Governance and the Efficiency of Economic Systems* (coordinated by Urs Schweizer), available at http://www.sfbtr15.de/ (last visited 12 July 2013).

terms of corporate governance on a contractual basis.[64] Yet contract governance has a much wider scope than this corporate context alone: contract governance provides a research approach that deals with the institutional framework of contractual relations on markets and examines whether their legal, social, cultural or otherwise agreed conditions generate coordination or steering effects for market participants.[65] This approach is consistent with the picture of contract law as an auxiliary infrastructure.[66] However, it also takes into account that structural conditions may have an impact on the result. Compare this with other infrastructures – roads, traffic signs and traffic lights – that allow for the individual freedom to move, in the first place, but that also have a potential to coordinate and steer the traffic and thereby prevent the traffic from collapsing. The objective of contract governance is therefore to allow market players as much freedom of contract as possible, while also providing for long-term stability of markets.[67]

Contract governance will only be able to provide new solutions for preventing future systemic crises if this research approach can indeed offer useful innovations for legal scholarship. In this author's opinion, such a change of perspectives promises new insights indeed, at least in a threefold sense.

In the first place, the perspective on contractual and legal rules changes from the usual *ex post*- to an *ex ante*-perspective: contract governance understands rules not primarily as an instrument of dispute resolution, but as a mechanism

64 C. Windbichler, 'Cheers and Boos for Employee Involvement: Co-Determination as Corporate Governance Conundrum' *European Business Organization Law Review* (*EBOR*) 6 (2005) 507, 529 and 533 *et seq.*; C. Windbichler, 'Arbeitnehmerinteressen im Unternehmen und gegenüber dem Unternehmen – Eine Zwischenbilanz' *Die Aktiengesellschaft* (*AG*) 2004, 190, 195 *et seq.*; similar H. Eidenmüller, 'Forschungsperspektiven im Unternehmensrecht' *Juristen-Zeitung* (*JZ*) 2007, 487, 493.

65 In detail: Möslein and Riesenhuber, n 6 above, 248.

66 G. Bachmann, 'Privatrecht als Organisationsrecht', in C.-H. Witt et al. (eds), *Jahrbuch Junger Zivilrechtswissenschaftler 2002 – Die Privatisierung des Privatrechts* (2003) 9; 20 *et seq.*; S. Grundmann, 'Regulating Breach of Contract – The Right to Reject Performance by the Party in Breach' *European Review of Contract Law* (*ERCL*) 3 (2007) 121, 143; C. Windbichler, 'Neue Vertriebsformen und ihr Einfluss auf das Kaufrecht' *Archiv für die civilistische Praxis* (*AcP*) 198 (1998) 261, 271; with respect to company law H. Fleischer, 'Gesetz und Vertrag als alternative Problemlösungsmodelle im Gesellschaftsrecht' *Zeitschrift für das gesamte Handelsrecht und Wirtschaftsrecht* (*ZHR*) 168 (2004) 673, 707. Similar from the perspective of (institutional) economics ('facilitative law'): E.G. Furubotn and R. Richter, *Institutions and Economic Theory – The Contribution of New Institutional Economics* (2nd edn, Michigan: University of Michigan Press, 2005) 12 *et seq.*; R.C. Clark, 'Agency Costs versus Fiduciary Duties', in J.W. Pratt and R.J. Zeckhauser (eds), *Principals and Agents – the Structure of Business* (Boston/Mass: Harvard Business School Press, 1985) 55, 60–72.

67 In a similar direction, already prior to the present crisis: K. Alexander, R. Dhumale and J. Eatwell, *Global Governance of Financial Systems: The International Regulation of Systemic Risk* (Oxford: Oxford University Press, 2006).

of steering and coordinating human behaviour.[68] Legal scholars have examined the steering effects of private law rules before, but not systematically and mainly with respect to tort law.[69] In contract law, this perspective can help to analyse the effects of incentives, for example, to better understand the impact of contractual bonus or malus arrangements on the behaviour of the involved parties. However, legal scholarship itself lacks a specific model of human behaviour. Such analysis, therefore, requires a more intense dialogue with other disciplines – not just economics, but social sciences more generally, in particular sciences of human behaviour, including neurobiology.[70] Experience shows that governance provides a common language which greatly facilitates this dialogue, maybe henceforth also for contract law.[71]

Second, contract governance widens the perspective. The contractual relationship between two persons, the bilateral 'privity of contract', represents the focus of classical contract law scholarship.[72] Networks and chains of contracts have only quite recently become a subject of contract law discussion,

---

68 Möslein and Riesenhuber, n 6 above, 248, 257.

69 In detail on the legitimacy of preventive and regulatory functions of private law: G. Wagner, 'Prävention und Verhaltenssteuerung durch Privatrecht – Anmaßung oder legitime Aufgabe?' *Archiv für die civilistische Praxis* (*AcP*) 206 (2006) 352 *et seq.*; criticizing, for instance, H. Honsell, 'Die Erosion des Privatrechts durch das Europarecht' *Zeitschrift für Wirtschaftsrecht* (*ZIP*) 2008, 621, 626 *et seq.*

70 As Contract Governance concerns the behaviour of market actors, behavioural law and economics appears as an indispensable complementary discipline. Seminal D. Kahneman and A. Tversky, 'Prospect Theory – An Analysis of Decision under Risk' *Econometrica* 47 (1979) 263 *et seq.*; further C.F. Camerer, G. Lowenstein and M. Rabin (eds), *Advances in Behavioral Economics* (Princeton: Princeton University Press, 2004); C.R. Sunstein (ed.), *Behavioral Law and Economics* (Cambridge: Cambridge University Press, 2000); in German mainly H. Eidenmüller, 'Der homo oeconomicus und das Schuldrecht – Herausforderungen durch Behavioral Law and Economics' *Juristen-Zeitung* (*JZ*) 2005, 216 *et seq.*; C. Engel, M. Englerth, J. Lüdemann and I. Spiecker gen Döhmann (eds), *Recht und Verhalten* (Tübingen: Mohr Siebeck, 2007); H. Fleischer, 'Behavioral Law and Economics im Gesellschafts- und Kapitalmarktrecht – ein Werkstattbericht', in A. Fuchs, H.-P. Schwintowski and D. Zimmer (ed.), *Festschrift for Immenga* (Munich: Beck, 2004) 575 *et seq.*

71 On 'Governance als Brückenbegriff' (Governance as a conceptual bridge) see W. Hoffmann-Riem, 'Methoden einer anwendungsorientierten Verwaltungsrechtswissenschaft', in W. Hoffmann-Riem and E. Schmidt-Aßmann (eds), *Methoden der Verwaltungsrechtswissenschaft* (Baden-Baden: Nomos, 2004) 9, 11; G.F. Schuppert, 'Governance im Spiegel der Wissenschaftsdisziplinen', in Schuppert (ed.), n 8 above, 371, 373 *et seq.*; in substance to the same effect already G.F. Schuppert, 'Schlüsselbegriffe der Perspektivenverklammerung von Verwaltungsrecht und Verwaltungswissenschaft' *Die Verwaltung (Verw)* supplement 2/1999 (Werkstattgespräch aus Anlass des 60. Geburtstags von Eberhard Schmidt-Aßmann) 103 *et seq.*

72 On externalities as a conceptual problem for traditional contract law: M. Trebilcock, *The Limits of Freedom of Contract* (Cambridge/Mass: Harvard University Press, 1993) 58–77.

the importance of which we can perceive in this volume.[73] Governance research promises to be a suitable tool for such analysis, given that it looks by nature at social systems as a whole.[74] More generally, contract governance focuses on markets, not only on individual contracts.[75] This is particularly important with respect to the recent crisis because the question of whether specific contractual arrangements represent a systemic risk can only be assessed with a view to the entire system, much like domino effects that cannot be predicted by looking at one individual domino alone.[76] Take bonus arrangements as an example again. From the perspective of traditional contract law, these arrangements do not give rise to any real concern because they usually do not harm legitimate interests of any contracting party.[77] They can only develop a dangerous dynamic once they are employed on a comprehensive basis, virtually covering an entire market. To predict this risk naturally requires a system-wide, market-oriented perspective.[78] As is generally known, it was the competition for skilled workers (investment bankers)

73 Furthermore: S. Grundmann, 'Die Dogmatik der Vertragsnetze' *Archiv für die civilistische Praxis* (*AcP*) 207 (2007) 718 *et seq.*; S. Grundmann, 'Vertragsnetz und Wegfall der Geschäftsgrundlage', in L. Aderhold, B. Grunewald, D. Klingberg and W.G. Paefgen (eds), *Festschrift for H.P. Westermann* (Cologne: Schmidt, 2008) 227 *et seq.*; G. Teubner, 'Hybrid Laws – Constitutionalizing Private Governance Networks', in R.A. Kagan and K. Winston (eds), *Legality and Community* (Lanham: Rowman & Littlefield, 2002) 311 *et seq.*; see also: F. Cafaggi, 'Contractual Networks and the Small Business Act: Toward European Principles' *European Contract Law Review* (*ERCL*) 4 (2008) 493 *et seq.*

74 See, for instance, R. Mayntz, 'Von der Steuerungstheorie zu Global Governance', in G.F. Schuppert and M. Zürn (eds), 'Governance in einer sich wandelnden Welt' *Politische Vierteljahresschrift*, special edition 41 (2008) 43, 46 ('institutions in a double sense', translation mine).

75 Similar to the traditional approach of economic law; very much to the point K.J. Hopt, 'Rechtssoziologische und rechtsinformatorische Aspekte im Wirtschaftsrecht' *Betriebs-Berater* (*BB*) 1972, 1017, 1019 ('Nicht das einzelne Rädchen, das Räderwerk ist gemeint'). Similar, for instance, E. Schwark, *Anlegerschutz durch Wirtschaftsrecht* (Munich: Beck, 1979) 64-66; and already F. Böhm, *Wettbewerb und Monopolkampf – Eine Untersuchung zur Frage des wirtschaftlichen Kampfrechts und zur Frage der rechtlichen Struktur der geltenden Wirtschaftsordnung* (Berlin: Heymann, 1933) 189 (economic law as an aggregate of rules 'serving social order and the steering of the collective economic process', translation mine).

76 Similar: National Research Council (ed.), *New Directions for Understanding Systemic Risk* (New York: 2007) esp 2–6 (transition 'from a bank-based to a market-based financial system', report written by J. Kambhu, S. Weidman and N. Krishnan).

77 Still uncritical (alignment of interests), for example: D.A. Becher, T. Campbell and M. Frye, 'Incentive Compensation for Bank Directors: The Impact of Deregulation' *Journal of Business* 78 (2005) 1753 *et seq.* For a broader evaluation of management incentives: A. von Werder, 'Persönliche Managementverantwortung aus betriebswirtschaftlicher Sicht', in Grundmann, Hofmann and Möslein (eds), n 10 above, 87 *et seq.*

78 Wymeersch, n 52 above, 8–10.

that led to the stipulation of such bonus rules on a huge scale.[79] An analytic tool to identify such systemic risks could be risk maps, for example, as have initially been proposed by the Issing Committee for purposes of financial supervision.[80] On the other hand, individual needs of protection often appear less relevant once not only the bilateral contractual relationship, but also alternatives on markets are taken into account.[81] Similar to corporate governance, contract governance therefore includes an internal and an external dimension, thereby linking contract and competition law considerations more closely together.[82]

Third, the broader, result-oriented perspective of contract governance can contribute to a contract law theory of rule-making, thus going beyond the mere application of rules.[83] Strategic advice for legislators, especially with respect to techniques and intensity of regulation, becomes even more important during times in which uniform statute books are increasingly supplemented and substituted by various regulatory instruments at different regulatory levels.[84] Such need is quite well known in corporate and labour law, where multiple layers of regulation are nothing new, but it now also gains importance in contract law,[85] especially in anticipation of a possible Optional European Sales Law (CESL).[86] By taking

79 See, for instance, C. Kirchner, 'Wege aus der internationalen Finanzmarktkrise' *Wirtschaftsdienst* 7 (2009) 1 et *seq*.

80 *New Financial Order*, n 19 above, 10–16.

81 Möslein and Riesenhuber, n 6 above, 248, 259.

82 Ibid, 248, 270 and 288.

83 Eidenmüller, n 64 above, 487, 490 *et seq*.

84 On this development G.-P. Calliess, J. Freiling and M. Renner, 'Law, the State, and Private Ordering' *German Law Journal* 9 (2008) 397; G.-P. Calliess, *Grenzüberschreitende Verbraucherverträge – Rechtssicherheit und Gerechtigkeit auf dem elektronischen Weltmarktplatz* (Tübingen: Mohr Siebeck, 2006); G.-P. Calliess, 'Weiter-gehende Übereinstimmung und laufendes Programm – Zur Legitimation von Privatrecht im Zeitalter der Globalisierung', in K. Riesenhuber and K. Takayama (eds), *Rechtsangleichung – Grundlagen, Methoden und Inhalte* (Berlin: de Gruyter, 2006) 115 *et seq*.; R. Michaels and N. Jansen, 'Private Law Beyond the State? Europeanization, Globalization, Privatization' *The American Journal of Comparative Law* 54 (2006) 843, 868 *et seq*.; for a stock-taking, see Köndgen, n 61 above, 477, 479 *et seq*. See also N. Winkler, 'Private Ordering: Harmonisierung des Unternehmensvertragsrechts ohne Europäischen Regelgeber?', in K. Riesenhuber (ed.), *Perspektiven des Europäischen Schuldvertragsrechts* (Berlin: de Gruyter, 2008) 43 *et seq*.; M.A. Wiegand, 'Die Auflösung des Staatsbegriffs in internationalen Rechtsverhältnissen', in Riesenhuber and Takayma (eds), op.cit., 83 *et seq*.

85 See e.g. G. Bachmann, *Private Ordnung* (Tübingen: Mohr Siebeck, 2006) 359 *et seq*.; G. Bachmann, 'Optionsmodelle im Privatrecht' *Juristen-Zeitung* (*JZ*) 2007, 11, 19 *et seq*.; Eidenmüller, n 70 above, 216 *et seq*. and 223.

86 S. Grundmann, 'Costs and benefits of an optional European sales law (CESL)' *Common Market Law Review* (*CMLR*) 50 (2013), 225 *et seq*; K. Riesenhuber, 'A Competitive Approach to EU Contract Law' *European Contract Law Review* (*ERCL*) 7 (2011) 115 *et seq*. More generally F. Cafaggi and H. Muir-Watt (eds), *Making European Private Law: Governance Design* (Cheltenham: Elgar, 2008); see also F. Möslein, 'Legal Innovation

incentives and patterns of behaviour into consideration, governance research can contribute to a better understanding of steering mechanisms which may be well known, but have been used rather intuitively by legislators so far. Contract governance can be an eye-opener for 'softer' steering instruments and for mechanisms of self-control.[87] It can, for example, assess whether default rules or non-binding standards can be taken into consideration as an effective alternative to mandatory law.[88] Contract governance may thus help in preserving individual freedom and contribute to smarter, less intrusive regulation – a contribution that seems particularly important in times of crisis, given the danger of over-regulation.

## Governance in the 'Nexus of Contracts'

However, contract governance does not offer a substitute for corporate governance. Both mechanisms rather supplement each other, for they are closely linked and interact in a variety of ways. This interaction inspires many contributions in this volume about networks and long-term relationships, about similarities and differences between exchange and cooperation.[89] However, it has not been the focus of governance theory in recent years.

### *Contracts and Organizations as Alternative Forms of Governance*

Exchange and cooperation are, of course, fundamentally different mechanisms, but they are nonetheless often equally suitable to reach specific goals. This idea is the actual starting point of governance research in Williamson's above-mentioned article;[90] it also defines a key decision problem in economic theory.[91] The most important difference between contract and organization is that contracts

in European Contract Law: Within and Beyond the Common Frame of Reference', in W. Micklitz and F. Cafaggi (eds), *European Private Law after the Common Frame of Reference* (Cheltenham: Elgar, 2010).

87 Möslein and Riesenhuber, n 6 above, 248, 288 *et seq*.

88 See F. Möslein, 'Governance by Default: Dispositives Recht als Entdeckungs- und Koordinationsverfahren', in S. Grundmann, H. Merkt and P.O. Mülbert (eds), *Festschrift for K.J. Hopt* (Berlin: de Gruyter, 2010); F. Möslein, *Dispositives Recht: Zwecke, Strukturen und Methoden* (Tübingen: Mohr Siebeck, 2011).

89 For instance, F. Cafaggi, S. Grundmann and G. Vettori, 'The Contractual Basis of Long-Term Organisation – The Overall Architecture', and C. Gillette and R. Scott, 'Contractual Networks, Contract Design, and Contract Interpretation – The Case of Credit Cards', both in this volume. Moreover, see S. Grundmann, 'On the Unity of Private Law – From a Formal to a Substance Based Concept of Private Law' *European Review of Private Law* 2010, 1055-1078.

90 Reference above n 5.

91 Path-breaking R.H. Coase, 'The Nature of the Firm' *Economica* 4 (1937) 386 *et seq.*; cf. furthermore: O. Williamson, *The Economic Institutions of Capitalism* (New York: Free

are typically concluded *pari passu* on markets, wheras business organizations are characterized by a hierarchical order.[92] Decision-making power and risk bearing can diverge in instances of majority and management decisions.[93] It is mainly because of this divergence that a corporate governance framework is required, which makes decision-making procedures more transparent and provides incentives for decision makers to act in the best interest of the corporate organization.[94]

With respect to contractual relationships, however, not all relevant questions are decided by mutual consent either. Particularly in long-term contracts and contractual networks we can also track 'hierarchical' decision-making mechanisms.[95] Moreover, even the market mechanism does not always provide for equitable solutions (*Richtigkeitsgewähr*).[96] In these cases, alternative governance structures may be required, which are contractual in nature, but feature, depending on their specific design, more or less similarity to corporate governance.[97] This smooth transition between contract and corporate governance corresponds with the insight of business administrations that corporate boundaries are not in every respect fixed. Rather, the choice between corporate and contractual structures is one of the central challenges for management that has to optimally allocate the various areas of entrepreneurial activity. Due to the advancements of information

---

Press, 1985) 32–4, 60–2 and *passim*; for a survey H. Eidenmüller, 'Kapitalgesellschaftsrecht im Spiegel der ökonomischen Theorie' *Juristen-Zeitung* (*JZ*) 2001, 1041, 1042.

92 Möslein and Riesenhuber, n 6 above, 248, 258.

93 On this mechanism, see in detail P. Behrens, *Die ökonomischen Grundlagen des Rechts* (Tübingen: Mohr, 1986) 110–277.

94 On this divergence cf again Williamson, n 5 above, 233 *et seq*; on other mechanisms of coordination (such as clans, federations, networks), see the survey by R. Mayntz, 'Governance-Theorie als fortentwickelte Steuerungstheorie?', in Schuppert (ed.), n 8 above, 11, 14 with further references.

95 On this phenomenon, see in detail Behrens, n 93 above, 491, 493 *et seq*.

96 German legal scholars tend to speak, more cautiously, of *Richtigkeitschance* instead of *Richtigkeitsgewähr:* A chance rather than a guarantee of just solutions inherent in the contract mechanism; W. Schmidt-Rimpler, 'Grundfragen einer Erneuerung des Vertragsrechts' *Archiv für die civilistische Praxis* (*AcP*) 147 (1941) 130 *et seq*.; W. Schmidt-Rimpler, 'Zum Vertragsproblem', in F. Baur, J. Esser, F. Kübler and E. Steindorff (eds), *Festschrift for Raiser* (Tübingen: Mohr, 1974) 1; recently C.-W. Canaris, *Die Bedeutung der Iustitia Distributiva im deutschen Vertragsrecht* (Munich: Beck, 1997) 48–51; C.-W. Canaris, 'Verfassungs- und europarechtliche Aspekte der Vertragsfreiheit in der Privatrechtsgesellschaft', in P. Badura and R. Scholz (eds), *Festschrift for Lerche* (Munich: Beck, 1993) 873, 883 *et seq*.; R. Singer, *Selbstbestimmung und Verkehrsschutz im Recht der Willenserklärungen* (Munich: Beck, 1995) 9–12.

97 One example is so-called 'cooperative governance', increasingly studied by economists, see various contributions in T. Theurl (ed.), *Economics of Interfirm Networks* (Tübingen: Mohr Siebeck, 2005); T. Theurl and A. Schweinsberg, *Neue kooperative Ökonomie: moderne genossenschaftliche Goverancestrukturen* (Tübingen: Mohr Siebeck, 2004); in a broader framework subject of a recent congress of the prestigious 'Verein für Socialpolitik' (under the heading *Governance in economic policy*).

technologies, outsourcing has gained much importance in recent years so that management experts aptly speak of an 'expansion of corporate boundaries'.[98] Corporate boundaries are blurred in many directions, also with respect to financing, where creditors are often granted a similar degree of influence as shareholders by means of contractual covenants.[99] The outsourcing of risks on special-purpose entities or by securitization can be conceptualized as a similar development in the banking business (as a step to banks without boundaries, so to speak).[100] Due to this blurring of corporate boundaries the often-cited 'nexus of contracts' is not only a law-and-economics metaphor for the corporate entities,[101] but becomes business reality in a very literal sense. If governance research really wants to take a look at social systems as a whole, it cannot focus exclusively on the single corporate entity but needs to analyse the whole contractual network in which corporations are embedded.[102] In other words: 'Contracting for control' needs to be taken into account.[103]

---

98 R. Wigand, A. Picot and R. Reichwald (eds), *Information, Organization and Management – Expanding Markets and Corporate Boundaries* (Chichester: Wiley, 1997).

99 See the recent monograph by W. Servatius, *Gläubigereinfluss durch Covenants* (Tübingen: Mohr Siebeck, 2008); furthermore: K. Krolop, 'Covenants in loan agreements as "legal transplant" from the US to the European continent and their impact in Corporate Governance: Indispensable tool of creditor protection or threat to the position of shareholders?' *Law and Economy* 5 (2008) 203 *et seq.*; J.A. McCahery and E. Vermeulen, *Corporate Governance of Non-Listed Companies* (Oxford: Oxford University Press, 2008) 189 *et seq.*

100 Cf. L. Obay, *Financial innovation in the banking industry: the case of asset securitization* (New York: Garland, 2000).

101 Seminal M.C. Jensen and W.H. Meckling, 'Theory of the Firm, Managerial Behaviour, Agency Costs and Ownership Structure' *Journal of Financial Economics* 5 (1976) 305, 311 ('The private firm is simply a form of legal fiction which serves as a nexus for contracting relationships'); see also F.H. Easterbrook and D.R. Fischel, 'The Corporate Contract' *Columbia Law Review* 89 (1989) 1416 *et seq.*; M. Eisenberg, 'The Conception that the Corporation is a Nexus of Contracts, and the Dual Nature of the Firm' 24 *The Journal of Corporation Law* 819 (1998); in German and with further references: Eidenmüller, n 91 above, 1041, 1042 *et seq.*; M. Ruffner, *Die ökonomischen Grundlagen eines Rechts der Publikumsgesellschaft* (Zurich: Schulthess, 2000), 129 *et seq.*

102 Similar B. Deffains and D. Demougin, 'Governance: Who Controls Matters' *Zeitschrift für Betriebswirtschaft* (*ZfB*), Special Issue 5 (2006) 1, 7 (with references to respective research in organizational economics at 4 *et seq.*).

103 G. Baker, R. Gibbons and K.J. Murphy, *Contracting for Control*, Working Paper (2006), available at http://www.stanford.edu/group/SITE/archive/SITE_2006/Web%20Session%206/Gibbons.pdf (last visited 12 July 2013). In a similar vein the recent economic literature on (long-term) 'contracts as reference points': O. Hart and J. Moore, *Quarterly Journal of Economics* 123 (2008) 1–48; E. Fehr, O. Hart and C. Zehnder, 'Contracts, Reference Points, and Competition – Behavioral Effects of The Fundamental Transformation' *Journal of the European Economic Association* 7 (2009) 561–572.

*Linkages between Contract and Corporate Governance*

The tricky question, however, turns out to be where social systems 'without boundaries' actually end. As a subject matter of academic research, they can by their very nature hardly be dissolved from their surrounding environment.[104] Therefore, corporate governance and contract governance are not only two alternatives with certain similarities. Instead, these two mechanisms are closely interwoven. Contract governance can therefore reflexively give new ideas to corporate governance research. Two major linkages between contract and corporate governance are indicated in the above-mentioned Larosière report and in the action plan of the OECD,[105] and they both have already induced regulatory activity at various levels.

*Remuneration schemes* A first linkage concerns employment contracts, binding decision makers to the company. Their incentive structures, especially their remuneration schemes, are of a contractual nature, but they have an impact on corporate strategy and success. The most prominent example is the policy of management compensation, namely the question of whether bonuses depend on short- or long-term performance targets.[106] The Impact Assessment that the European Commission published in order to complement its two recommendations on the remuneration of directors of listed companies and on remuneration policies in the financial services sector,[107] accurately states that 'there is a general consensus that badly designed [remuneration] policy and schemes at all levels in the financial services industry contributed to "short-termism" and excessive risk-taking without adequate regard to long-term global performance … The problem addressed is not how much directors are paid, but the mismatch between pay and performance'.[108]

104 The disappearance of (national) boundaries has indeed been the starting point for (global) governance research: J. Rosenau, 'Governance, Order, and Change in World Politics', in J. Rosenau and E.-O. Czempiel (eds), *Governance without Government – Order and Change in World Politics* (Cambridge: Cambridge University Press, 1992) 1.

105 References n 19 and n 50 *et seq*.

106 Comprehensively L.A. Bebchuk and J. Fried, *Pay without Performance: The Unfulfilled Promise of Executive Compensation* (Cambridge/Mass: Harvard University Press, 2004).

107 Commission Recommendation complementing Recommendations 2004/913/EC and 2005/162/EC as regards the regime for the remuneration of directors of listed companies, C(2009) 3177 ('Recommendation on remuneration of directors'), and on remuneration policies in the financial services sector, C(2009) 3159, both of 30 April 2009.

108 Commission Staff Working Document accompanying the Commission Recommendation complementing Recommendations 2004/913/EC and 2005/162/EC as regards the regime for the remuneration of directors of listed companies and the Commission Recommendation on remuneration policies in the financial services sector ('Impact Assessment'), C(2009) 3159, of 30 April 2009, 3. See also the accompanying Communication, COM(2009) 211 final, *passim*.

Executive remuneration depends on contractual arrangements between companies and their employees; it often comprises not only a fixed salary, but also variable elements such as annual bonuses, long-term cash incentives or stock options, and possibly even severance payments. The contractual structure of these elements creates incentives that have an impact on management actions and can, as the Commission states, 'affect the long-term performance and sustainability of the companies and therefore also affect investor confidence, employment, competitiveness and long-term economic growth'.[109] In other words, the contract governance of remuneration schemes is of crucial importance for the corporate governance of the company.

On the other hand, there is also a close interaction in the opposite direction, because the structure of the contractual design largely depends on the procedural setting within the corporation, more specifically on the question of which corporate body is competent and accountable to decide on such arrangements: a board committee, the board itself, or, increasingly at least in a consulting role, the General Assembly.[110] The importance of appropriate corporate governance structures and corresponding disclosure rules[111] for the contract governance of remuneration agreements has triggered respective legislative reforms in various Member States.[112] Moreover, this linkage is explicitly acknowledged in the above-mentioned recommendations of the European Commission: They aim at improving shareholders' oversight of remuneration policies, at strengthening the role and accountability of remuneration committees and at ensuring independence for remuneration consultants.[113] With respect to the financial sector, the Commission proposes more specific mechanisms of internal transparency, control and review as well as an allocation of the responsibility for remunerations policy to the board instead of a remuneration committee.[114] Above all, the Commission recommends these measures not only for company directors, but for 'those categories of staff whose professional activities have a material impact on the risk profile of the financial undertaking'.[115] Given that remuneration incentives in the operational

109 Impact Assessment, previous n, 7.

110 For a comparative survey, see Möslein, n 33 above, 101 *et seq.*

111 Ibid., 71 et seq.

112 In Germany, for instance: Gesetz zur Angemessenheit der Vorstandsvergütung (VorstAG) of 31 July 2009, *Bundesgesetzblatt* I (2009) 2509. For a recent analysis of the regulatory framework and remuneration practices in Europe, see G. Ferrarini, N. Moloney and M.-C. Ungureanu, *Understanding Directors' Pay in Europe: A Comparative and Empirical Analysis*, ECGI Law Working Paper Nr 126 (2009), available at www.ssrn.com (last visited 12 July 2013).

113 Recitals 10 to 12 of the Recommendation on remuneration of directors; cf also accompanying Communication, n 108 above, 3.

114 Recommendation on remuneration policies in the financial services sector, sub 6 and Section III.

115 Recommendation on remuneration policies in the financial services sector, sub 1.2 and Recital 13.

business of investment banks were much more relevant for the recent crisis than the remuneration of company directors, this wide scope of application is entirely plausible and it had, indeed, been recommended before, by the Larosière report[116] and by the OECD.[117] Such coverage of ordinary employment contracts shows very clearly that remuneration policy is not only a question of corporate governance, but also, and maybe primarily, of contract governance.[118] However, this linkage is not restricted to the financial and banking sector, but applies in principle to every corporation that is embedded in a nexus of employment contracts.[119]

*Risk management* The second linkage between contract governance and corporate governance is structurally similar to the first one, but has a more general nature: it concerns corporate risk management, in other words, the systematic identification, assessment, and prioritization of risks.[120] Since the financial crisis, the focus is mainly on external, namely systemic risks, i.e. on market risks that originate in contractual arrangements.[121] Again, the linkage is of a twofold nature. On the one hand, contractual risks and incentive structures can have a crucial impact on corporate strategy and corporate success. The financial crisis has dramatically shown the importance of a comprehensive understanding and assessment of such contractual risks: while most major banks failed to anticipate the development of the housing market, there was a marked difference in how intensely they were affected, depending on their exposure to certain financial instruments.[122] Understanding and controlling over contractual risks therefore turned out to be decisive for surviving the financial turmoil. This aspect of risk

116 *Report of the High-Level Group on Financial Supervision in the EU*, n 19 above, 31 (Recommendation 11: '… the same principles should apply to proprietary traders and asset managers').

117 OECD (ed.), n 49 above, 14 ('Remuneration problems also exist at the sales and trading function level'). This concern was also shared by the Financial Stability Forum, n 43 above, 20.

118 Quite explicitly OECD (ed.), n 50 above, 17: Incentives at lower levels beyond 'the usual focus of corporate governance debates'.

119 For some well-known examples see OECD (ed.), n 50 above, 17 (Metallgesellschaft, Sumitomo Corporation, etc).

120 D.W. Hubbard, *The Failure of Risk Management* (Hoboken: Wiley, 2009) 10; comprehensively: D.H. Chew, *Corporate Risk Management* (New York: Columbia Business School Publishing, 2008); T. Merna and F. Al-Thani, *Corporate Risk Management* (2nd edn, Chichester: Wiley, 2008).

121 See, for instance Senior Supervisors Group, *Observations on Risk Management Practices during the Recent Market Turbulence* (March 2008), 12 *et seq.*, available at http://www.newyorkfed.org/newsevents/news/banking/2008/SSG_Risk_Mgt_doc_final.pdf (last visited 12 July 2013); see also OECD (ed.), n 50 above, 8 *et seq.*

122 Senior Supervisors Group, previous n 3 *et seq.* and *passim*; cf. also OECD (ed.), n 49 above, 7 *et seq.* For an empirical study of the 25 largest European banks see D. Ladipo and S. Nestor, *Bank Boards and the Financial Crisis* (London: Nestor Advisors, 2009).

management is, in turn, very much sector-specific, given that the relevance of contractual risks crucially depends on the complexity of contracts, which tends to be much higher with respect to financial services and other long-term relationships than with respect to spot contracts for the exchange of goods.[123]

On the other hand, the rank of risk management in the internal corporate governance structure may well have an impact on the structure and design of these contractual relationships, thereby affecting contract governance. Accordingly, the Larosière report proposed an independent risk management at senior management level with direct access to the board.[124] Such risk management should be competent for stress-test exercises in order to assess the incentive and risk structures of all substantive contractual relationships of the financial firm in question. Moreover, the Basel Committee on Banking Supervision published its *Principles for sound stress-testing practices and supervision*, advocating a stronger integration in banks' risk governance and capital planning.[125] The above-mentioned OECD paper went even further and emphasized the importance of future-oriented stress tests in a very general manner, not only with respect to the financial sector: 'Stress testing must form an integral part of the management culture so that results have a meaningful impact on business decisions'.[126] In other words, contract governance, the forward-looking assessment of long-term contractual relationships, is meant to become a key management responsibility for corporate boards in general.

## Conclusion

Williamson once defined governance as 'an effort to implement the "study of good order and workable arrangements", where good order includes both spontaneous order in the market … and intentional order'.[127] Even though corporate governance has been studied quite well over the last decades, the recent financial crisis revealed important weaknesses in governance mechanisms. Yet this crisis did not primarily emerge due to specific corporate structures, but rather had its roots in the instability of markets. From now on, the study of good order and workable arrangements needs to take markets into account as well: contract governance is an important lesson of this crisis. By this token, the destruction of financial values might again have created an innovation, posing new challenges not only for regulators and

123 More in detail OECD (ed.), n 51 above, 31 *et seq*.

124 *Report of the High-Level Group on Financial Supervision in the EU*, n 19 above, 32 *et seq*.

125 Basel Committee on Banking Supervision, *Principles for sound stress testing practices and supervision* (January 2009), available at http://www.bis.org/publ/bcbs147.pdf (last visited 12 July 2013).

126 OECD (ed.), n 49 above, 10; with potential impact on future corporate governance standards: OECD (ed.), n 50 above, 33–40.

127 Reference n 62 above.

legal academics, but also for management practice. Contract governance provides for an important link between the corporation and its contractual environment. By virtue of this link, such approach can contribute to avoid future crises and to make the system of market economy more stable in the long run.

# PART VI
# Towards Legislation?

# Chapter 13

# The Nemesis of European Private Law: Contractual Nexus as a Legislative Conundrum

Marc Amstutz

Is contractual nexus[1] the nemesis of European private law? This chapter will argue that this is the case – yet in a very specific sense. The thesis is as follows: *Contractual networks render obvious the methodological shortcomings of the legislative tools thus far employed in European private law for coming to terms with emerging structures of private governance.* Or, to put it more positively: the rising importance of networks of contracts may be seen as an opportunity for developing new legislative tools for enabling European private law to comprehend modern forms of private governance.

Stefan Grundmann, in a recent paper, raises some questions as to the underlying concept behind the Draft Common Frame of Reference (DCFR) for European private law, which was prepared at the behest of the European Commission.[2]

---

1 For the purposes of the present article, the term 'contractual nexus' is used in a non-technical sense to refer to the relationship that exists between linked contracts. There are a number of different means by which the linkage can be achieved, some of which will be considered more closely in this chapter. The terminology used for the general phenomenon is not fixed, and the terms 'network of contracts', 'network contracts', 'linked contracts', 'interlinked contracts' etc, are used here more or less interchangeably to refer to the broad notion of contractual nexus.

2 See C. von Bar and E. Clive (eds), *Principles, Definitions and Model Rules of European Private Law: Draft Common Frame of Reference (DCFR), Full Edition, prepared by the Study Group on a European Civil Code and the Research Group on EC Private Law (Acquis Group)* (Munich: Sellier, 2009). This article is based on the case-law and literature available at the end of the year 2009. For further information on the recent evolution of European contract law (including the Commission's 2011 Proposal for a Regulation of the European Parliament and of the Council on a Common European Sales Law, COM[2011] 635 final), see G. Dannemann and S. Vogenauer (eds), *The Common European Sales Law in Context: Interactions with English and German Law* (Oxford: OUP, 2013); L. Moccia (ed.), *The Making of European Private Law: Why, How, What, Who* (Munich: Sellier, 2013). On linked contracts in particular, see T. Dang Vu, Linked contracts in the DCFR, the Consumer Rights Directive and the Draft Optional Instrument, in: I. Samoy and M.B.M. Loos (eds), *Linked Contracts* (Cambridge: Intersentia, 2012) 115 *et seq.*

Grundmann argues that the DCFR's methodology is not entirely consistent with today's market reality; he compares the effort of the Draft authors with trying to manufacture a Mac computer by adding parts to a PC, or attempting to produce a Ferrari engine by tinkering with a standard commuter car.[3] In explaining his misgivings, Grundmann provides an illuminating analysis of the DCFR's basic approach. The central difficulty, as he sees it, lies in the failure of the DCFR to draw a fundamental distinction between contracts dealing with those types of performance that are already fully definable when the contract is drawn up, and those types for which this is not possible because the subject of the contract is something that will come into being only in the future and remain mutable:

> The DCFR, in its general part, does not distinguish between definition, in the contract, of a quality owed and a defining of governance mechanisms on how to reach decisions within the ongoing (long-term) relationship.[4]

This criticism touches on a crucial point that must be kept in mind when considering the conceptual basis for a European private law of contractual networks. Grundmann is saying, in effect, that the DCFR is trying to use the methodology of twentieth- or even nineteenth-century contract law to deal with twenty-first-century phenomena and, this being the case, its chances for success are severely limited. Why? Because networks of contracts are a phenomenon involving legal issues that do not fit the concepts developed by traditional contract law. The reason for this lies in the increasing complexity of contractual nexus: *the interdependencies of contemporary contractual networks allow bilateral contracts to generate entirely new orders of expectations, which arise over time as several, sometimes very large numbers of actors are selectively interacting with each other* (as, for instance, in franchising agreements or payment networks). Traditional law of contract is blind to these new expectations.

But how – using what methodology – can we design appropriate rules for the contracts that make up such networks? This is clearly the *real issue* at the core of constructing a European law of contracts that can also be applied effectively to contractual networks. One of the first issues that needs to be resolved, before we even begin, is whether we should focus our attention, from the outset, on the actual formulation of rules, or whether it might not be wiser to first reflect on certain preliminary steps, such as collecting the data that will need to be analysed in order to come up with a workable set of contractual network rules. Even if we should manage to agree on this second approach, however, it is still unclear what methodology should be used. Should we retain the traditional methods of legal analysis, or should we move beyond the bounds of legal science and look to the other social sciences for assistance?

---

3 S. Grundmann, 'The Structure of the DCFR – Which Approach for Today's Contract Law?' *European Review of Contract Law* 2008, 246.

4 Grundmann, n 3 above, 243.

The chapter begins by elaborating on these issues, reviewing some of the legislative instruments currently in use in European private law and assessing their usefulness in unravelling the conundrum of contractual nexus. It then attempts to articulate some of the inferences that can be drawn from these findings for the development of an analytical methodology capable of comprehending legal realities not foreseen by the tradition that currently shapes our legal codes.

## Law's Reality: Evolutionary Semantics

### *Overcoming Legal Formalism*

It is well known that the DCFR was the product of efforts based on two related, but nevertheless distinct, methodological steps: on the one hand, a comparative study of the existing legal regimes of the member states was conducted;[5] on the other, the so-called *acquis communautaire* was subjected to a thorough analysis.[6] It is important to note, however, that the Commission itself never made the effort to clearly define its methodological approach.[7] It decreed simply that the DCFR should be based 'on the EC acquis and on best solutions identified as common to member states' legal orders.'[8] What this in fact calls for is two separate stages of preparation, each of which requires its own methodology: the first is the search for a common core – the *acquis communautaire*; the second is the search for 'best solutions'. At the same time, there is a suggestion that a solution found in the legal order of one or more of the member states may not be accepted as a 'best solution' where it is 'not common to Member States' legal orders'.[9]

This raises the question as to the criteria according to which any given solution should be considered the 'best solution', and as to criteria for determining whether the solution in question is 'common' to the member states.[10] Neither the Action Plan,[11] nor the subsequent Communications on contract law issued by the European

5 M. Oderkerk, 'The CFR and the Method(s) of Comparative Legal Research' *European Review of Contract Law* 2007, 321.

6 R. Schulze, 'Die "Acquis-Grundregeln" und der Gemeinsame Referenzrahmen' *Zeitschrift für Europäisches Privatrecht* 2007, 731 *et seq.*; H.-W. Micklitz, 'Grundfragen: (Selbst-)Reflektionen über die wissenschaftlichen Ansätze zur Vorbereitung' *Zeitschrift für Gemeinschaftsprivatrecht* 2007, 10 *et seq.*

7 Oderkerk, n 5 above, 321 *et seq.*

8 Oderkerk, n 5 above, 321.

9 Oderkerk, n 5 above, 321.

10 Oderkerk, n 5 above, 316, 321 *et seq.*

11 R. Schulze, 'Informationspflichten und Vertragsschluss im Acquis Communautaire', in R. Schulze (ed.), *Der Acquis communautaire und die Entwicklung des Europäischen Vertragsrechts* (Tübingen: Mohr-Siebeck, 2003) 3 *et seq.*; Oderkerk, n 5 above, 320; S. Grundmann, 'The Optional European Code on the Basis of the Acquis Communautaire – Starting Point and Trends' *European Law Journal* 2004, 699.

Commission[12] provide any explicit answers to these questions. The documents do, however, contain statements from which the Commission's opinions on certain matters can be deduced. Thus, two issues to which the Commission unquestionably attaches importance are the preservation of (1) the principle of freedom of contract, and (2) the overall coherence of the DCFR.[13] In reviewing the *acquis*, the following criteria are mentioned as meriting particular attention: reasonableness, simplicity, consistency, completeness, a high degree of protection for consumers, predictability, and a balance between what is required in terms of consumer protection and what is needed in order to maintain the competitiveness of enterprises.[14] These criteria have been left by the Commission 'to speak for themselves'.[15] Their precise meaning, in other words, is a matter that is to be determined discursively by the stakeholders in European private law. For the time being, the definition of these criteria remains rather fuzzy.

Insofar as it concerns contractual networks, however, this point is not of vital importance, in the sense that the definition of such terms is a matter of traditional legal methodology. Their use as criteria in determining 'best' and 'common' solutions is not particularly problematic once it has been established that there exists, in the legal regimes of the member states and in the *acquis*, a set of rules from which a viable selection can be made. Rules dealing with contractual networks, however, are rare and, where they do exist, are not only very dissimilar from Member State to Member State, but also tend to be greatly in dispute.[16] Similarly, they are almost entirely absent in the *acquis*. The conclusion would thus appear inescapable that for the development of legislative proposals for provisions on contractual networks, the methodologies employed by the Study Group and by the Acquis Group (and thus underlying the Full Edition of the DCFR) are not adequate. A certain corroboration of this finding can be seen in the proposals thus far submitted

12 Communication from the Commission to the Council and the European Parliament on European contract law, COM(2001) 398 final, OJEC C 255/13.9.2001; Communication from the Commission of 12 February 2003 to the European Parliament and the Council – A more coherent European contract law – An action plan, COM(2003) 68 final, *OJEC* C 63/15.3.2003; Communication from the Commission of 11 October 2004 to the European Parliament and the Council – European Contract Law and the revision of the acquis: the way forward, COM(2004) 651 final. See also: Commission Report of 23 September 2005: First Annual Progress Report on European Contract Law and the Acquis Review, COM(2005) 456 final; Commission Report of 25 July 2007: Second Progress Report on the Common Frame of Reference, COM(2007) 447 final.

13 Von Bar and Clive, n 2 above, DCFR I, 37 *et seq*.

14 Oderkerk, n 5 above, 323 *et seq*.

15 Oderkerk, n 5 above, 321.

16 See F. Cafaggi, 'Contractual Networks and the Small Business Act: Towards European Principles?' *European Review of Contract Law* 2008, 493 *et seq*.

by the Study Group and the Acquis Group for dealing with certain types of contracts for which the existence of a contractual nexus is an essential issue.[17]

17 Two actual examples may illustrate this point. The first is found in art II-5:106 DFCR, which deals with B2C contracts (von Bar and Clive, n 2 above, DCFR II-5:106, 381 *et seq.*). It provides that the effects of a consumer's withdrawal from a contract for the supply of goods or services from a business extend to any linked contract, a linked contract being defined as objectively forming an economic unit (von Bar and Clive, n 2 above, DCFR II-5:106, 383). Paragraph (2) gives a non-exhaustive list of certain criteria that may aid in determining whether or not the contracts in question form such an economic unit. It is particularly noteworthy that the article treats the existence of an economic unit formed by the contracts in question as being an objectively determinable fact. This concept of contractual interdependence, as defined in art II-5:106 DCFR, is flawed in several respects. The principal difficulty is that it rests on the assumption of an objectively existing entity – that is: of a fully integrated unity – and does not allow for a taking into account of the reasons – subjective or objective – that led the parties to conclude two separate contracts and to institute an articulated relationship based on links and nodes. It may well be that linked contracts should sometimes be treated as an entity, but situations are nonetheless conceivable, in which the division of an agreement into a number of autonomous covenants reflects a specific logic of action which should not be automatically overridden with no further ado. The provisions of art II-5:106 DCFR were quite obviously the result of convention and not of a differentiated analysis of the reality of contractual networks. A second example is provided by the rules proposed for franchises, which involve B2B contracts. In Part IV E the term 'network' is used several times. First, a 'franchise network' is defined in comment F on art IV E-4:101 as consisting of 'a franchisor and the group of all franchisees that operate the same business method and the existing liaison among them' (von Bar and Clive, n 2 above, DCFR IV E-4:101, 2382 *et seq.*). The term appears again in art IV E-4:102(1) (von Bar and Clive, n 2 above, DCFR IV E-4:102, 2387 *et seq.*) and IV E-4:205(b) (von Bar and Clive, n 2 above, DCFR IV E-4:205, 2406 *et seq.*), both relating to information on the network structure and on the network's commercial result. Then, the network concept can also be found in art IV E-4:207 (von Bar and Clive, n 2 above, DCFR IV E-4:207, 2412 *et seq.*), which deals with the duty of the franchisor to make reasonable efforts to promote and maintain the reputation of the network. Lastly, it is mentioned once more in art IV E-4:303(2) and (3) (von Bar and Clive, n 2 above, DCFR IV E-4:303, 2419 *et seq.*), which provides for an obligation on the part of the franchisee to maintain the reputation of the network and not to cause harm to the network. On closer examination, however, it becomes clear that the notion of 'network' in these provisions does not have any substantive consequences. Its function is one of mere description. Not only this, but the concept of 'network', employed by the Study Group also appears to confuse two opposing concepts: hierarchy on the one hand, and heterarchy on the other. Comment A on art IV E-4:207 explains the meaning of the reputation maintenance duty by stressing that it 'depends on the extent to which uniformity is preserved'. It then goes on to say that, 'such uniformity is achieved when all the members within the network follow the common guidelines for conducting the business. All these aspects, pursuant to this provision, fall under the franchisor's control' (von Bar and Clive, n 2 above, DCFR IV E-4:207, 2412). Here we have a clear suggestion that a 'network' (= heterarchy), at least as it is implicitly understood in the DCFR, is a strongly hierarchical concept – as inferable, in

The finding that the methodological approach of the Study Group and of the Acquis Group is, for the reasons given, not suited for comprehending the way in which contractual networks operate, brings us back to our first question: using what method would it be possible to design an adequate legal treatment of this phenomenon in European private law? Since existing legal systems lack the required precedents (that is, 'common' and 'best solutions') for dealing with contemporary forms of contractual networks, any efforts to devise a legislative means of filling this lacuna would probably do well to attempt an *interdisciplinary* approach. There is, quite simply, no exclusively legal source to guide lawmakers in this question. Unfortunately, this need to look outside the law, in order to devise laws, gives rise to a further dilemma. As Gunther Teubner has put it: 'It is a scientistic misconception of the law to believe that empirical results or theoretical insights from the social sciences can guide law to any significant degree.'[18]

The dilemma lies in the fact that the science of (private) law must find a way of maintaining a sufficient degree of distance from its fellow disciplines while, at the same time, exploiting the results of their research.[19] In other words, the required methodology for analysing contractual networks – for the purpose of developing proposals for codifying European private law in the matter – would consist of *prudently* integrating insights drawn from the other social sciences into legal analysis. But how is this to be accomplished? What, precisely, is meant by the term 'prudent'? In order to answer these questions, certain historical considerations may be of use:

### *Understanding Law's Understanding*

The dominant tendency in private law theory in the twentieth century was characterized by a view focused almost exclusively on the legal and institutional 'superstructure' of life. As a result, the operations of the legal system have detached themselves from the system's environment. Taking the Roman concept 'quod non est in actis non est in mundo' in its most literal sense, law simply ignores society. The high degree of autonomy that is typical of modern law is a consequence of this systemic closure, and is one further example of the functional differentiation that

---

particular, from the use of the terms 'uniformity' and to 'franchisor's control'. The network concept advanced by the DCFR would thus appear to be closely related to the concept of an organization. However, although that may be the case, it is clear from these examples that the complexity of contractual networks cannot fully be comprehended by the logic of traditional legal methodology.

18 G. Teubner, '*Coincidentia Oppositorum:* Hybrid Networks Beyond Contract and Organization', in M. Amstutz and G. Teubner (eds), *Networks: Legal Issues of Multilateral Co-operation* (Oxford/Portland: Hart 2009) 4.

19 See M. Amstutz, V. Karavas and G. Teubner, 'Preface', in Amstutz and Teubner (eds), n 18 above, ix *et seq.*

defines today's social environment and which has been the subject of extensive investigation for decades now.[20]

Under these historical circumstances, the operational closure of the legal system does not render it dysfunctional. When differentiated social systems, such as the economy, sports, the arts or religion reach the limits of their capabilities in coping with inner systemic conflicts and turn to the law for assistance, it would be incongruous for the law to seek a settlement to the dispute by relying on the specific logic of the social system in which it arose.[21] It was precisely the inability of that system's logic to resolve the conflict on its own that caused it to turn to the law for a solution. What is expected of the law is that it considers the dispute that has been handed over to it 'with different eyes'. It is asked to 'dissociate' the dispute from the particular social system in which it first arose.[22] This access to a resolution mechanism, not available to it within its own structures, provides the social system in question with an instrument for overcoming the blockage of its operations that was occasioned by the dispute. Newly articulated in the terms of the law, the dispute takes on a new 'meaning' – one that allows a restoration of the blocked system's ability to function. The law's capacity for creating new social meaning in this way is a direct function of the legal system's high level of autonomy.[23]

This being the case, how to explain the persistent, relatively high level of popular dissatisfaction with the legal system, as documented over time, by sources ranging from Roscoe Pound's famous article on the subject[24] to Christie's provocative thesis[25] and various recent opinion surveys?[26] If the diverse systems that make up society, overstrained by internal disputes, turn to the law for an 'alien' view of things, how does it happen that legal decisions are accepted only

20 On the functional differentiation of society, see below, third section, under sub heading 'The Social Multi-Dimensionality of Contracts'.

21 A fuller presentation of this argument can be found in M. Amstutz, 'The Constitution of Contractual Networks', in Amstutz and Teubner (eds), n 18 above, 310.

22 Perhaps this is the systems theoretical explanation for the blindfold on Lady Justice: she is blind to the subjective internal operational logic of the systems whose disputes she judges – so as better to see by the light of the law's own logic.

23 See G. Teubner and P. Zumbansen, 'Rechtsentfremdungen: Zum gesellschaftlichen Mehrwert des zwölften Kamels' *Zeitschrift für Rechtssoziologie* 2000, 189; see also G. Teubner, 'Zur Eigenständigkeit des Rechts in der Weltgesellschaft: Eine Problemskizze', in R.J. Schweizer et al. (eds), *Festschrift für Jean Nicolas Druey* (Zurich: Schulthess, 2002) 149; M. Amstutz, 'Das Gesetz', in P. Gauch and P. Pichonnaz (eds), *Rechtsfiguren: K(l)eine Festschrift für Pierre Tercier* (Zurich: Schulthess, 2003) 160 *et seq.*

24 R. Pound, 'The Causes of Popular Dissatisfaction with the Administration of Justice' *American Law Review* 1906, 729 *et seq.*

25 N. Christie, 'Conflict as Property', in C.E. Reasons and R.M. Rich (eds), *The Sociology of Law: A Conflict Perspective* (Toronto: Buttersworth, 1978) 295.

26 See, e.g. K.F. Röhl and H.C. Röhl, *Allgemeine Rechtslehre* (3rd edn, Cologne/ Munich: Heymanns, 2008) 336 *et seq.*

sometimes, and are sometimes rejected?[27] Evidently, it not sufficient simply to 'dissociate' the *social* conflict from its native environment and convert it into a *legal* dispute.[28] Whether or not that process leads to a successful conclusion – that is, whether or not new social meaning is in fact created – would appear to be contingent on certain conditions. But what are those conditions?

The answer to this question must, of course, be sought not in the legal system itself, but in the social systems in which the conflicts submitted for legal resolution first arise, and by which the solution provided by the legal system must be accepted. This paradoxical situation, in which the legal system is both fully autonomous and, at the same time, dependent on the internal operations of the other social systems that comprise its environment, is a second consequence of the differentiation of society: each system is capable of performing its operations only on its own terms. The conversion of a social conflict into a legal dispute allows the law to seek a solution autonomously, by means of exclusively legal operations; in order for that solution to be 'successful', however, it must be converted back into an element of the system in which the problem originated. The situation is comparable to that of a physician prescribing a cure, which, according to the rules of classical medicine, is expected to choose the appropriate remedy solely on the basis of medical science: whether or not that remedy is effective, however, depends solely on the patient's response. So also is the effectiveness of a legal solution dependent upon its reception by the autological forces of the disrupted system that has turned to the law for assistance. This being the case, the next question that arises is: does this circumstance inevitably imply that the law has no other choice but to abandon itself to its fate – or is there an alternative, one that would allow the legal system to overcome this dependency?

If it is correct that legal operations can be socially effective only when integrated into the operations of the social system that has suffered a disruption, then any attempt to influence this outcome will necessarily have to be based on the logic of *second-order observation*[29]: in order to effectively resolve conflict, the solution provided by the law must function in such a way as to sensitize the malfunctioning system to its 'blind spots'. In other words, the system in question must be rendered cognizant of the misperceptions from which it suffers in the

27 On the social consequences of faulty legal decisions, see R. Nobles and D. Schiff, *Understanding Miscarriages of Justice: Law, the Media, and the Inevitability of Crisis* (Oxford: Oxford University Press, 2000).

28 See N. Luhmann, *Law as a Social System* (Oxford: Oxford University Press, 2004) 76: 'The concept of positivity suggests that it can be understood through the concept of decision. Positive law is supposed to be validated through decisions. This leads to the charge of 'decionism' in the sense of a possibility to decide in an arbitrary fashion, dependent only on the coercive force behind such decisions. *Thus, this leads in fact to a dead-end; after all, everybody knows that in law decisions are never simply made arbitrarily*' (italics added).

29 See, e.g. H. von Foerster, *Understanding Understanding: Essays on Cybernetics and Cognition* (New York: Springer, 2003) 211 *et seq*.

observation of its own environment – so that, based on this newfound awareness, it can better adapt its behaviour to that environment and thus reduce the sources of conflict. In order for the law to devise solutions of this kind, however, it must first raise the level of its own awareness of the systems that make up its environment: it must venture out into the society within whose midst it exists. Only if the law learns to look at society 'from within' will it be able to discover the opportunities that exist for helping other social systems to recognize their 'blind spots'. In order to perform this function, however, the legal system first requires a suitable means of gathering reconnaissance from its environment.

### *Legal Ontogeny vs. Legal Ontology*

One possible beginning might lie in a change in the way law looks at itself – in its abandoning descriptions of its own nature and operations in the causal or teleological terms that are more or less markedly intrinsic to orthodox legal theories, by making use, in their stead, of what may be termed '*evolutionary semantics*'.[30] Heinz von Foerster has indicated with exemplary simplicity the epistemological usefulness of such an approach:

> What is ontologically inexplicable may prove to be an ontogenic necessity. The navel is an ontological joke, a whimsical ornament, a grotesque riddle, on one's own belly. Ontogenetically, however, we could not exist without it. Evolutionists and creationists are in similar fashion seeking an ontogenic explanation for an otherwise inexplicable phenomenon: we are here![31]

There can be little doubt that it is just this new perspective that has provided the impetus for the recent renaissance of evolutionary theory in the social sciences, often referred to as an 'interdisciplinary paradigm shift'.[32]

At first glance, it may not be immediately apparent how this shift can contribute to attempts to provide law with a more 'realistic' approach to society. In contrast with traditional epistemological approaches, what is being proposed here is the renunciation of all aspirations to 'explain the world' – on the assumption that the

30 M. Heilmann, 'Angepasste Selbstbeschreibung: Zu Niklas Luhmann "Evolution der Evolution"', in T. Wägenbaur (ed.), *Blinde Emergenz? Interdisziplinäre Beiträge zu Fragen kultureller Evolution* (Heidelberg: Synchron, 2000) 145.

31 Von Foerster, n 29 above, 370.

32 D.G. Shaw, 'An Interdisciplinary Paradigm Shift', in P. Pomper and D.G. Shaw (eds), *The Return of Science: Evolution, History and Theory* (Lanham: Rowman & Littlefield, 2002) 1; M.T. Fögen, *Römische Rechtsgeschichten: Über Ursprung und Evolution eines sozialen Systems* (Göttingen: Vandenhoeck & Ruprecht 2002) 14 *et seq.*; R. Moser, 'Evolutionismus in den Kulturwissenschaften', in A. Dieckmann and R. Moser (eds), *Evolution in den Natur-, Sozial- und Geisteswissenschaften: Referate einer Vorlesungsreihe des Collegium generale der Universität Bern im Sommersemester 2000* (Bern: Haupt, 2003) 217.

voluntary waiver of any such claim may offer new heuristic opportunities. What is meant by this can perhaps best be explained by the example of the natural sciences. For many years, the social sciences took their orientation from the 'mechanistic' (deterministic) conception of reality that, under Cartesian and Newtonian influence, had for centuries informed natural scientific study.[33] The underlying assumption was that there exists, in all areas of life, something analogous to *unalterable truths*, and that it was this fact that rendered social processes of all kinds – whether historical, economic, sociological, legal, or other – inherently predictable. This illusion has gradually been dispelled, however.[34] Indeterminacy slowly edged its way into science's vision of reality, and this in the form of what McNeill has aptly termed 'evolutionary uncertainty'.[35] The assumption that the elements of a system of knowledge and the regularities that can be deduced from them were limited in number has been recognized as false. In reality, the possibilities are infinite.[36] The consequence of this realization was the abandonment of the idea that any phenomenon could be comprehensively explained in generalized terms. It was replaced by an understanding that everything that can be 'known' can be done so only situationally, piecemeal, and relative to a specific time and context.

For the social sciences in general, and for legal science in particular, this 'discovery' has quite specific implications, articulated perhaps most precisely by T. Meleghy in recent years. This author points out that evolutionary theory contains no universal laws of any kind. Rather, it attempts to describe a mechanism

33 Perhaps the most impressive analysis of these references (on the example of the relation between economics and physics) is given by N. Georgescu-Roegen, *The Entropy Law and the Economic Process* (Cambridge/London: Harvard University Press, 1971); see also, regarding the example of law & economics: M. Amstutz, *Kollektive Marktbeherrschung im europäischen Wettbewerbsrecht: Eine evolutorische Perspektive* (Tübingen: Mohr-Siebeck, 1999); see also the excellent, and more recent, concise survey of epistemological interaction between the natural and social sciences in W.H. McNeill, 'History and the Scientific Worldview', in Pomper and Shaw (eds), n 32 above, 13.

34 See W.V. Quine, *The Ways of Paradox* (Cambridge/London: Harvard University Press, 1976); D.G. Hofstadter, *Gödel, Escher, Bach: An Eternal Golden Braid* (New York: Basic Books, 1979).

35 McNeill, n 33 above, 23, who also provides a vivid description of the process: 'Whatever its start, the regime that prevails among the complex molecules now constituting earth's biomass soon imposed new balances on the earth's physico-chemical system. Forests, for example, altered rainfall patterns on land, while decaying organic matter laid down strata of limestone under the sea. On a global scale, plants eventually transformed the earth's atmosphere by releasing oxygen, making the earth hospitable to animals, who ate the plants and one another, establishing a series of ecological equilibria across geological time, each of which gave way to its successor in bursts of change whose precise provocation remain unclear.' It should be made clear that references to 'evolutionary uncertainty' in the present essay are in no way connected with the evolutionary theories of knowledge proposed by Popper and others (see, e.g. K.R. Popper, *Objective Knowledge: An Evolutionary Approach* (New York: Oxford University Press, 1972)).

36 See, e.g. I. Prigogine, *Les lois du chaos* (Paris: Flammarion, 1994) 16 *et seq.*

(or algorithm) that should, in principle, be as capable of replicating the purposeful, rational actions of humans, as it is of imitating the planned, deliberate actions of a creator.[37] For law, the advantage offered by an evolutionary epistemology is that it opens the way for overcoming the trauma that was occasioned by the realization, in the late nineteenth and early twentieth centuries, that the legal system does not rest upon any fixed constant, be it in heaven or on earth – that is, that law is not an absolute and that neither God, reason, the logic of efficiency, or anything else for that matter, can make it so.[38] The relativity of law, and its resultant ineffectiveness as an instrument of 'social planning', is no longer really a matter of dispute among legal scholars – with the possible exception of legal positivists, who use various fictions, such as 'the legislator', 'the lawmaker's intent', or the 'purpose of the law', as a fig leaf behind which to hide the embarrassing reality.

The discomfiture of legal scholars following the discovery of law's relativity derived primarily from the need to demonstrate that waiving the claim to absoluteness did not automatically imply that legal systems had been granted license to operate arbitrarily in their relations with other social systems. And it is precisely here that an evolutionary epistemological approach can provide the needed solution. Seen from an evolutionary perspective, it becomes clear that legal systems are inherently constrained to respect certain *regularities* (or 'conditions') – if for no other reason than that their own continued existence depends on their ability to keep up with the evolutionary pace of the society within which they operate – on the maintenance, that is, of a 'reciprocally produced homeostasis'. In order to maintain this symbiosis, the law must find a way to adjust the lenses through which it observes the subjects of its operations, and begin to see not only itself, but them, as well, from an 'evolutionary' perspective. The question is: how?

37 T. Meleghy, 'Methodologische Grundlagen einer evolutionären Soziologie', in T. Meleghy and H.J. Niedenzu (eds), *Soziale Evolution: Die Evolutionstheorie und die Sozialwissenschaften* (Wiesbaden: Westdeutscher Verlag, 2003) 132: 'Darwin showed us that the mechanism of natural selection can, in principle, imitate the purposeful, planned activity of a creator, and similarly also rational, purpose- or objective-oriented human actions'; see also A. Dieckmann and R. Moser, 'Vorwort', in Dieckmann and Moser (eds), n 32 above, VI.

38 Modern paradoxologists have also taught us why this is so: because the law cannot apply its prime distinction, between (legally) right and wrong, to that distinction itself; see G. Teubner, 'Dealing with paradoxes of Law: Derrida, Luhmann, Wiethölter', in O. Perez and G. Teubner (eds), *On Paradoxes and Inconsistencies in Law* (Oxford: Hart, 2006) 41 *et seq.*

## The Real World of Contractual Nexus

### *A Framework for Evolutionary Analysis*

There are a number of theoretical paradigms available in contemporary evolutionary thought that could serve as models for adjusting law's analytical perspective.[39] One of the most useful ones in this context is the framework developed by Stephen Jay Gould in his magnum opus, *The Structure of Evolutionary Theory*,[40] as the analytical criteria on which it is based are particularly useful in the present context. Gould's model sets up three parameters – to which he assigns the terms 'Agency', 'Efficacy' and 'Scope'[41] – for evaluating the validity of a given evolutionary explanation:

1. *Agency*: at what 'level' do evolutionary forces work? Evolution requires a 'locus of action',[42] commonly referred to as a 'unit of selection'. Darwin assumed that, in biological evolution, this locus was the individual organism. More recent evolutionary theory has come to realize that there are also other units of selection, at both higher and lower organic levels (genes, cells, organs, or else groups, species, etc) and that evolution takes place simultaneously at multiple levels, giving rise to both *micro-evolutionary* and *macro-evolutionary* phenomena.[43] The social sciences in general, and

39 An overview from a social-science viewpoint can be found in T. Meleghy and H.J. Niedenzu, 'Einleitung: Die Evolutionstheorie und die Sozialwissenschaften', in Meleghy and Niedenzu (eds), n 37 above, 11.

40 S.J. Gould, *The Structure of Evolutionary Theory* (Cambridge/London: Belknap, 2002).

41 This trichotomy provides the structure for Gould's entire book; it is briefly explained in Gould, n 40 above, 14 *et seq*.

42 Gould, n 40 above, 14.

43 The assumption that selection takes place at multiple, hierarchically ordered levels of selection derives, in particular, from the fact that the logic of certain selection processes is indiscernible at the level of the organism, the unit of selection posited by classical Darwinism; see D.J. Depew and B.H. Weber, *Darwinism Evolving: Systems Dynamics and the Genealogy of Natural Selection* (Cambridge: MIT, 1996) 381: '[T]here can … be some sort of higher-order selection … in which the spatiotemporally individuated species of the modern synthesis are said to stand to the overall direction in whole clades (branching phylogenetic lineages, from Greek for "branch") as variation among individual organisms stands to the adaptedness in populations … In this event, direction in a clade will be the result of a sorting process in which characteristics of the clade itself have the statistical edge. These might include higher speciation rates, lower extinction rates, or other traits that cannot be reduced to the adaptive prowess of individual members of the component species of a lineage.' Because selection is taking place simultaneously at various levels, certain selective processes may inevitably find themselves in contradiction with each other; see D.S. Wilson, 'Group Selection', in E.F. Keller and E.A. Lloyd (eds), *Keywords in Evolutionary Biology* (Cambridge/London: Harvard University Press, 1992) 145: 'Because adaptations

legal science in particular, would do well to consider this model of multi-level selection in the analysis of ongoing social processes, taking at all times into consideration the evolutionary forces simultaneously at work at the various levels of social grouping and within the individual sub-systems of society.

2. *Efficacy*: In addition to the mechanisms of natural selection, are there other factors that need to be understood in order to explain the evolutionary process? Classical Darwinism rejects this idea, arguing that where there is sufficient variation over time, the slow and steady (gradualist) process of eliminating individual organisms poorly adapted to their environment is a force strong enough to guarantee the production of new life-forms that are better fitted for survival.[44] By contrast, modern evolutionary biology emphasizes the importance of so-called 'constraints': Darwinism's 'external' perspective is certainly valid, but it remains incomplete, since organisms also possess 'internal' developmental constraints that play an important role in the evolutionary process. To put it simply: even after millions of years of variation and selection an elephant will still not have turned into a cat. In Darwin's own terms, 'unity of type'[45] rules out such a process.[46] Clearly, such 'constraints' are also a factor in social evolution, where the history or structure of a given society may cause the selective forces at work in it to wind off in seemingly unpredictable directions.[47] It is perhaps here that we should seek the explanation for interest in

---

can occur at a variety of levels … what is adaptive at one level may be maladaptive at another. It is adaptive for predators to capture prey, but if they are too successful the predator population can overexploit its prey and itself go extinct. It is adaptive for a group of monkeys to post sentries to watch for predators, but maladaptive for the individual sentry who must watch while its fellows eat.' By accepting the hypothesis that there is a hierarchy of selective forces at work, it becomes possible to discern the highly complex interplay of their effects; on the entire subject, see also M. Lenzen, *Evolutionstheorien in den Natur- und Sozialwissenschaften* (Frankfurt a.M./New York: Campus, 2003) 79 *et seq.*

44 See S.J. Gould, 'Darwinism and the Expansion of Evolutionary Theory' *Science* 1982, 381.

45 C. Darwin, *The Origin of Species by Means of Natural Selection or the Preservation of favoured Races in the Struggle for Life* (London: John Murray, 1859) 206.

46 On this, in greater detail, see M. Amstutz, *Evolutorisches Wirtschaftsrecht: Vorstudien zum Recht und seiner Methode in den Diskurskollisionen der Marktgesellschaft* (Baden-Baden: Nomos, 2001) 266 *et seq.*

47 For law, see, e.g. J.B. Ruhl, 'The Fitness of Law: Using Complexity Theory to Describe the Evolution of Law and Society and its Practical Meaning for Democracy' *Vanderbilt Law Review* 1996, 1428; for economics, see, e.g. V. Vanberg, 'Institutional Evolution Within Constraints', *JITE* 1996, 690.

path dependency that has recently begun to find expression in the social sciences.[48]

3. *Scope*: Are the mechanisms of Darwinian micro-evolution alone sufficient to explain the vast diversity of nature? What then is the role of such 'non-evolutionary' (or non-algorithmic) phenomena such as climate change, volcanic eruptions or large meteorite impacts? These are the questions at the centre of the controversy that divides evolutionary theorists. For uniformitarians, natural selection, in the strict Darwinian sense, is the sole cause of ecological diversity; for the catastrophists, that same diversity can be explained only by taking other causes and, in particular, cataclysmic events, into account.[49] In current evolutionary theory, it is the catastrophist viewpoint that has gained the upper hand, and there is no reason not to apply it analogously as a means of explaining social evolutionary developments as well. Because social systems are structurally linked, mutually dependent on elements in each other's structures – the economy on the existence of legal contracts, for example, or the political system on the existence of codified law – 'jumps' that occur in one social system may have enormous evolutionary consequences for the others. Examples of these are numerous, particularly in the area of technological development – one need think only of the social consequences of the invention of writing, of money, of the printing press, of the railway or of the Internet, to name but a few.[50]

In the following, this analytical method is first applied in a consideration of the phenomenon of contractual networks as it actually occurs ('externally' to the legal system, as it were). In doing so, it is assumed that there is a direct connection between the increasing occurrence of this phenomenon in the business world and the emergence of laws intended to deal with it, that is, of attempts by the legal system to come to terms with the nexus-of-contracts phenomenon 'internally'.[51]

48 See, e.g. O.A. Hathaway, 'Path Dependency in the Law: The Course and Pattern of Legal Change in a Common Law System' *Iowa Law Review* 2001, 601 *et seq.*

49 For a concise overview of the history of the uniformitarian/catastrophist debate, see Depew and Weber, n 43 above, 95 *et seq.*

50 Efforts to explain this phenomenon generally tend to involve attempts to identify rules of co-evolution; see, for example, Fögen, n 32 above, 18. Thus far, however, social co-evolution has remained a riddle. Gould's concept of 'scope' is arguably a cogent approach to at least some aspects of the problem.

51 No attempt will be made here to examine the precise nature of the connection between network phenomena at social level and contractual networks at legal level. The working assumption will be that Teubner is correct in positing that the two phenomena are 'forcibly linked'; for further detail, see G. Teubner, 'Beyond Contract and Organization? The External Liability of Franchising Systems in German Law', in C. Joerges (ed.), *Franchising and the Law: Theoretical and Comparative Approaches in Europe and the United States* (Baden-Baden: Nomos, 1991) 105 *et seq.*; G. Teubner, 'Piercing the Contractual Veil? The Social Responsibility of Contractual Networks', in T. Wilhelmsson (ed.), *Perspectives of*

At a later stage, there is consideration of the ways in which the internal structures of the legal system *ought* to respond to this phenomenon. To begin, a few recent examples from German case law are discussed in order to illustrate some of the socio-legal practices that have evolved in connection with contractual networks. The use of examples from national law is necessitated by the fact that external observation of the law requires an analysis of the judicial (re-)interpretation of taken legislative or doctrinal norms. Non-national jurisprudence on the law of linked contracts is largely lacking in the case of the DCFR. However, this is not of any particular relevance for an evaluation of the adequacy of the evolutionary method proposed here.

### *Network Analysis I: The Problem of Multi-Level Complexity*

The first ruling to be examined has been chosen for its usefulness in demonstrating how variations that contribute to the institutional evolution do not occur at one level alone. Just as, in nature, evolutionary processes operate not only at the level of the individual organism, social evolution also takes place at several levels simultaneously. The changes that take place in private autonomous sub-systems – contractual relations, companies, etc – may have effects at higher levels of the overall system to which they belong. In order to observe these effects, however, Gould's concept of agency must be taken into account.[52] The way in which this multi-level complexity arises can be seen quite clearly by considering the contractual networks created through the use of cashless payment instruments and, in particular, of giro transfers, on which the German High Court has had repeated occasions to pronounce.[53]

Giro transfers involve rarely three, most often four, and occasionally even larger numbers of parties connected to each other in a chain of transactions. The first link in the chain is the person making a payment to a creditor in settlement of a debt. The debtor–creditor relationship – referred to in German law, in this context, as the 'valuta-relationship' (*Valutaverhältnis*) – provides the legal basis for the transaction. In order to effect payment, the debtor instructs his bank to debit a given amount from his account and credit it to that of the creditor. The relationship between the debtor and his bank, the so-called 'coverage relationship' (*Deckungsverhältnis*) is ruled by a funds transfer agreement between them, a giro

*Critical Contract Law* (London: Dartmouth, 1992) 211 *et seq.*; G. Teubner, 'Hybrid Laws: Constitutionalizing Private Governance Networks', in R. Kagan and K. Winston (eds), *Legality and Community: On the Intellectual Legacy of Philip Selznick* (Berkeley: Berkeley Public Policy Press, 2002) 311 *et seq.*

52 Gould's criterion of 'agency' is, of course, only one possible means for making 'derived' variation and selection discernible. There is no intention to imply here that similar results could not be achieved by other means.

53 For an overview of the jurisprudence, see M. Rohe, *Netzverträge: Rechtsprobleme komplexer Vertragsverbindungen* (Tübingen: Mohr-Siebeck, 1998) 14 *et seq.*

contract, pursuant to which the debtor issues individual payment orders to the bank.[54] Where both debtor and creditor use the same bank, payment is effected by the bank by means of an *internal* transfer of funds from one account held by the bank to another. This gives rise to a tripartite chain, the bank and the creditor also being linked directly through a giro contract, whereby the relationship between them in the event of payments being credited to the client's account is referred to as a 'collection relationship' (*Inkassoverhältnis*). Often, however, the payer and the payee will have their accounts at different banks. In such cases, the payment chain that connects them is lengthened by (at least) one further link – namely, the payee's bank. The transaction involved is then referred to as an *external* transfer of funds.[55] In order to effect the transfer of funds, as instructed by the payer, the debtor's bank enters into an interbank relationship with that of the creditor, a relationship which governs the modalities of the fund transfer.[56]

It is important to note that in the contractual network just described, where an external transfer of funds is involved, there is no direct contractual relationship between the debtor's bank and the creditor, nor is there one between creditor's bank and the debtor. It is precisely this circumstance that often leads to legal uncertainties when one party to such a payment network (a client), suffers purely economic damages caused by another party to the network (a bank or the payee), where no direct contractual relationship between the two parties exists and there is a need to provide the injured party with a claim against the injuring party for the damages. Non-contractual claims for purely economic damages will generally fail for lack of a specific protective law.[57] This legal situation is particularly

54 Opinions are divided as to whether each individual payment order represents a unilateral legal transaction, an instruction, carried out within the framework of the giro contract, or whether it is a bilateral legal transaction, a fund transfer agreement, the conclusion of which rests on the preexistence of a giro (master) agreement. The literature is, however, unanimous in assuming the existence of a contractual relationship of one sort or another between the payer and his bank. For the purposes of the present remarks, this is sufficient, so that a more thorough discussion of the question is not required here. For an overview of the current state of the debate in the German literature, see K. Hopt, 'Bankgeschäfte', in A. Baumbach (ed.), *Handelsgesetzbuch* (33rd edn, Munich: Beck, 2007) 1647 *et seq.*

55 On the distinction between internal and external fund transfers, see H. Sprau, '§ 676a', in O. Palandt (ed.), *Bürgerliches Gesetzbuch* (68th edn, Munich: Beck, 2009) 1056–1057 N 4 *et seq.*

56 These may vary, depending on whether domestic or cross-border transactions are involved, or whether other correspondence banks are also involved as intermediaries between the debtor's bank and that of the creditor. The precise details of such transactions have no particular relevance to the arguments here presented; for further details, see Sprau, n 55 above, 1057 N 7; O. Fehrenbacher, '§ 676a', in H. Prütting, G. Wegen and G. Weinreich (eds), *BGB Kommentar* (4th edn, Cologne et al.: Luchterhand, 2009) 1368 N 4 *et seq.*

57 See e.g. R. Schaub, '§ 823', in Prütting, Wegen and Weinreich (eds), n 56 above, 1661 N 214.

dissatisfying in view of the fact that in the case of an internal transfer of funds a contractual basis for the claim does exist. It is unacceptable that the difference in the injured party's position should be the result of pure coincidence, that is, of whether debtor and creditor are, or – as is more often the case – are not, clients of the same bank.

This would also appear to be the thinking of Germany's Federal High Court, the Bundesgerichtshof (BGH), in its rulings in such matters. Based on its decisions on payment networks, it is clear that the Court is seeking legal solutions that take into account the economic nexus that arises out of the several contracts of which payment chains are composed – solutions that are adequate to situations in which the interests in conflict are not exclusively those of the parties to a single contract. While maintaining the bipartite model that underlies traditional contract law, in defining the duties and obligations arising therefrom the BGH nevertheless draws inferences from the linkage between the individual contracts. And it is by this means, as we will see, that the Court succeeds in coming to terms with the multi-level structures that are typical of emerging orders of contractual networks.

Particularly instructive in this regard is the High Court ruling of 6 May 2008, which deals with the *contractual* duty of banks to warn their customers and other banks.[58] The case in question centred on a company that had been newly founded for the sole purpose of providing asset management services. Defendant in the case was the bank at which the company had opened a giro account in its own name. The account was used for the receipt of payments from the sale of high return investment strategies that were marketed by telephone. The damages suffered by investors were the result of acts of embezzlement. In order to pursue their claims, a large number of the injured investors formed a company, which acted as plaintiff in the suit against the bank. Over the five-month period during which the bank had held the asset management company's giro account, the members of the plaintiff company – who represented only a part of all injured investors – had made payments to the account amounting to a total of just under €1 million. To make these payments, the investors had availed themselves of various means: *internal* fund transfers, *external* fund transfers, cash deposits, and checks.[59] These payments, booked for the most part as 'deposits', were embezzled by the directors of the asset management company and their authorized agents. They did so by making numerous cash withdrawals from the account, in varying amounts, up to five times per day. This unusual behaviour came to the bank's attention some two months after the account had been opened. The bank thereupon opened an internal investigation. Four months later – not until one month after the closing of the account, that is – it filed a criminal complaint. During the roughly three months

58 BGH, 6 May 2008 – XI ZR 56/07.

59 The questions that arise in connection with these last two payment forms are beyond the scope of the present remarks; see, on this, Sprau, n 55 above, 1056–1057 N 4 *et seq.*; see also below, second section under sub-heading 'Network Analysis II: The Problem of Internal Constraints'.

that followed the first arousal of suspicion of criminal activity, up to the time of the closing of the account, transactions on the account continued to be carried out, without the bank's having provided any warning to its clients or to other banks regarding the advisability of making any further payments to the account. In the last four weeks alone, just prior to the closing of the account, some €300,000 were embezzled by transferring funds, in tranches, to an account held in Turkey by the director of the asset management company.

In its ruling on the case, the BGH held that, with regard to fund transfers, a bank's *duty to warn* exists only vis-à-vis its clients (in the case of internal fund transfers) and other banks (in the case of external fund transfers), that is, only vis-à-vis those parties in a payment chain with whom the bank has a direct contractual relationship. The ruling is highly significant, in the sense that it implicitly rejects the analogous application, in such cases, of the principle of third-party beneficiary contracts *(Vertrag mit Schutzwirkung zugunsten Dritter)*, which until that time had regularly been seen by the lower courts in Germany as a *contractual* basis for the claims of injured third parties against banks with whom they had no direct contractual relationship, where cashless fund transfers were at issue.[60] In a reversal of precedent,[61] the BGH chose to ground its decision on the principle of third-party damage *(Drittschadensliquidation)*, which provided it with a means of helping those payers in the payment chain who had no direct contractual link with the receiving bank to arrive at a settlement of the claims they held arising out of that bank's failure to perform its duty of warning. The difference in the principles underlying claims based on third-party beneficiary contracts and those arising from third-party damage lies in the fact that the former involves the injured party's *own* contractual rights whereas the latter involves rights of *another party*, which are then *assigned* to the injured party.[62] In holding the bank liable for third-party damage, the BGH reasoned that in such constellations as this, in which there was a relationship of indirect representation (acting in one's own name for the account of a third party) of the investors by the asset management company, the receiving bank must be deemed to have a duty to warn as to the possible presence of criminal activity against its contractual partners where the relationship of indirect representation is known to it and it becomes cognizant of the fact that acts of embezzlement have occurred or, on the basis of solid, objective grounds for suspicion, ought to have been cognizant thereof.[63]

---

60 See E. Theewen, 'Zur Bankenhaftung im bargeldlosen Zahlungsverkehr – Urteilsanmerkung zu BGH XI ZR 56/07' *Zeitschrift für Bank- und Kapitalmarktrecht* 2008, 387 *et seq.*, 389.

61 BGH, n 58 above, para 32.

62 See D. Medicus, '§ 249', in Prütting, Wegen and Weinreich (eds), n 56 above, 393 N 92.

63 BGH, n 58 above, para 15 und 35; on the concept of a 'duty to warn' in connection with contractual nexus, see S. Grundmann, 'Die Dogmatik der Vertragsnetze' *Archiv für die civilistische Praxis* 2007, 718 *et seq.*, 757–8 (who suggests that, in franchising contracts,

The ruling is remarkable in several respects. First, because what it establishes, in essence, is that the liability of banks towards their clients cannot be made contingent upon the particularities of a given transaction, that is, specifically, on whether an internal or an external fund transfer is involved. Secondly, this principle of equal treatment of both clients and non-clients of the receiving bank was then grounded not on the doctrine of third-party beneficiary *protection* – as had hitherto been the usual practice in German law in matters of cashless payments[64] – but on the basis of claims arising out of third-party *damages*. The grounds and the reasoning behind this reversal of precedent are of particular interest in the context of the present remarks. The change in the Court's position relates to the fact that, as an injured third party, the client of the paying bank, although he has no contractual relationship with the receiving bank, is nevertheless deemed to have a right to the assignment of his own bank's liability claims against that receiving bank.[65]

Only briefly alluded to by the BGH is the issue of whether and how any coincident transfer of damages from the paying bank to the payer, the usual grounds admitted for third-party damage claims, actually took place.[66] The German literature on this point is divided. There are, in fact, good reasons to doubt whether the damages coincidentally transferred to the client could have originally arisen to the bank. The question is whether the bank is even capable of suffering such damages.[67] The BGH apparently lacked the courage to dispense entirely with such standard arguments as third-party damage or, previously, third-party beneficiary protection, as grounds for awarding damages and to devise new (judicial) norms for coming to terms with the specificities of contractual nexus disputes. The Court chose to see the transaction between the paying bank and the receiving bank in the case of external fund transfers as another instance of indirect representation. The paying bank acts, as the Court (rightly) held, in its own name but on the client's behalf. It is possible, however, to conceive of the notion of indirect representation as extending one step further. Ultimately, the intent of the contracting parties relates to the particularities of the network of which the individual contract is an element. In contrast with strictly bipolar contractual relationships, the operations of which do not depend on those of third parties, the formation of contractual networks often leads to situations in which the performance of an individual

claims against third parties require the construction of a *Drittschadensliquidation)*; the concept of a 'duty to warn' in banking is explained in Hopt, n 54 above, 1631 N A/10, 1633 *et seq.* N A/16 *et seq.*, 1637 N A/30 *et seq.* und 1655 N C/10.

64 For an overview of the jurisprudence, see Rohe, n 53 above, 21 *et seq.*; Theewen, n 60 above, 389 *et seq.*

65 BGH, n 58 above, para 35; the same principles apply in the case of a payment chain involving more than two banks provided that a 'multiple assignment' agreement *(Kettenzession)* was concluded. The BGH says next to nothing with regard to causality in the transfer of damages, which is usually required by the courts in cases of third-party damages; on this issue, see Rohe, n 53 above, 20–21.

66 See Rohe, n 53 above, 20–21.

67 Rohe, n 53 above, 21.

contract in the network depends on the collaboration of partners who are not formally parties to that contract. In this context, Teubner distinguishes three phases in the life of a contract: (1) negotiation, (2) conclusion, and (3) performance.[68] In classical legal theory, only those parties who participate in the second phase, the conclusion of the contract, are actually considered as parties to the contract. Where contractual networks are formed, however, disputes often arise from the fact that participants in the other two phases fail to meet their obligations. Seen in this way, the provisions of § 358 BGB, in which the collaboration (in the broadest sense) of a third party lender is taken into account, represent a recognition of the lender as a 'material' party to the purchase agreement during the negotiation phase (phase (1)). In the same light, the problem of warning duties in cashless payment chains can be considered as one of taking into account the conduct of the receiving bank as a 'material' party to performance (phase (3)). Teubner has shown that, with regard to prospectus liability, there are already cases in which the distinction between the various phases in the life of a contract has been taken into account.[69] It is possible that also in respect of cashless payment networks this approach would be more fruitful than that based on third-party damages.

The BGH decision is compatible – if unintentionally – with the notion of contractual nexus also in another respect The resolution of the case via the principle of third-party damage places a client who is party to an external transfer of funds in precisely the same position as that of a party to an internal transfer, with the concomitant result that he remains subject to his bank's rights of set-off, retention and/or lien. This, as the Court explicitly points out, would not be the case if the client were entitled to protection as a third-party beneficiary,[70] since the contract from which a third party benefits creates no reciprocal contractual obligations on his part towards the parties between whom it was concluded. He is outside of the contractual loop, as it were.[71] By contrast, where third-party damage is assumed, the injured client (the payer) is linked to the network through his giro relationship with the paying bank.[72] This provides a contractual basis for his claims, which consist, *in the first place*, in his right to the assignment of the paying bank's damage claims against the receiving bank. The basis for those claims, in turn, is the contractual relationship between the two banks. As a contracting party, in the formal sense, the client thus remains subject to any counterclaims the bank may hold against him. The Court's position, according to which only parties linked to the payment network by a synallagmatic contractual relationship are entitled to claims arising out of network malfunctions, has since found legislative

68 G. Teubner, *Networks as Connected Contracts. With an Introduction by Hugh Collins* (Oxford: Hart, 2011) 255 *et seq*. (Baden-Baden: Nomos, 2004) 236.

69 Teubner, n 68 above, 254 *et seq*.

70 BGH, n 58 above, para 37.

71 See also Theewen, n 60 above, 391.

72 The legal nature of the contractual relationship between the customer and the bank is the subject of a doctrinal controversy; on this, see the references in n 54 above.

confirmation with the introduction of §§ 676a *et seq*. BGB governing cashless fund transfers. These provisions were not yet in force at the time of the ruling.[73]

What is interesting about the reasoning developed by the BGH in this case, from an evolutionary legal point of view, is the manner in which it analyses the contractual relations involved in cashless payments: although the payment chain is made up exclusively of bipartite contractual relationships, it is the way in which these relationships are functionally connected with each other that determines the legal position of the parties. The linkage between the parties must stand the test of synallagmatic 'nexus'.[74] In other words, the law is here observing and operating not only at the primary level of the individual agreements involved, but also at the secondary level of the overall network created by the linkage of those individual agreements. In evolutionary terms, the unit of selection at which the Court's reversal of precedent operates is no longer that of the individual organism: there is no change in the terms of the individual contracts. The variation here is at the level of the network, that is, in the relationship between the contracts. The law, in other words, has moved from 'lower order' to 'higher order' selection.

*Network Analysis II: The Problem of Internal Constraints*

If we now alter our perspective and consider the same BGH ruling of 6 May 2008, not in terms of Gould's principle of 'agency', but applying this time his concept of 'efficacy', it becomes possible to recognize another crucial factor intrinsic to contractual networks. The ruling shows that contractual networks have certain 'constraints', whose effect is precisely as described by Gould. They work to channel the forces of selection in the legal system in a specific direction. It is a feature of contractual networks that they resist being 'atomized' into individual contracts. Their nature is such that they consistently confound the efforts of classical contract law in its attempts to break down complex realities into discrete legal units of individual bipartite contractual relationships without regard to their place in a larger network of contracts. The effect of these constraints is that the law, however unwilling, is obliged to deal with contractual networks as unified wholes, and not as mere assortments of individual contracts, each as a discrete, self-sufficient unit unto itself. Unable to ignore the phenomenon of contractual networks, Continental legal theory has invented a loose set of undefined terms with which to allude to it. Reference is made, in German, to the 'inner linkage'

73 BGH, n 58 above, para 37.

74 See also Grundmann, n 63 above, 735 *et seq*., 754, who has a similar preference for such legal constructions based on the model of the links of a chain.

or 'internal connection' of unitary contracts;[75] or to a 'final nexus'[76] or a situation of 'multilateral synallagma'.[77] Authors writing in French speak of 'groups' or 'ensembles' of contracts supposedly recognizable by their *identité d'objet, communauté de cause*,[78] or the *indivisibilité objective ou subjective des contrats*,[79] etc. These are the equivalents of what is sometimes referred to in common law as 'contractual nexus'. While all of these expressions cannot be said to be entirely devoid of meaning, they are, nevertheless, only approximative in nature. The question remains as to what, precisely, they are intended to denote.

As discussed above, the German Federal Court in its ruling of 6 May 2008 found that the bank's liability in connection with cashless payments could not be made contingent upon whether the payment was effected via internal or external transfers. All clients were to receive equal treatment regardless of whether the payer's bank and the payee's bank were identical or not. The decision, as described above, involved a reversal of precedent, in that it was based on the notion of third-party damage rather than that of third-party beneficiary protection. While this is, obviously, only a first step in the development of a law of contractual (payment) networks, it is nevertheless crucial, as it recognizes, for the first time, that *the intent of the parties is not decisive in determining whether or not two (or more) contracts are interlinked*: in rejecting the principle of third-party beneficiary protection as a basis for client claims, the Court simultaneously rejected the principle that the protection of third parties is dependent upon the intent of the contracting parties. Prior to this decision, German precedent[80] had required that the inclusion of third parties within the 'protective sphere' of a contract be in conformity with the hypothetical *intent of the parties*, as deduced from the court's interpretation of

75 J. Gernhuber, 'Austausch und Kredit im rechtsgeschäftlichen Verbund: Zur Lehre von den Vertragsverbindungen', in G. Paulus (ed.), *Festschrift für Karl Larenz zum 70. Geburtstag* (Munich: Beck, 1973) 472; see also E. Kramer, 'Art 19–22 OR', in A. Meier-Hayoz (ed.), *Berner Kommentar: Das Obligationenrecht, Band VI / 1.Abteilung / 2. Teilband / Unterteilband 1a: Inhalt des Vertrags* (Bern: Stämpfli, 1991) 33 N 64.

76 Gernhuber, n 75 above, 469 *et seq.*; similarly, J. Gernhuber, *Das Schuldverhältnis: Begründung und Änderung, Pflichten und Strukturen, Drittwirkungen* (Tübingen: Mohr-Siebeck, 1989) 710 *et seq.*

77 P.W. Heermann, *Drittfinanzierte Erwerbsgeschäfte: Entwicklung der Rechtsfigur des trilateralen Synallagmas auf der Grundlage deutscher und U.S.-amerikanischer Rechtsentwicklungen* (Tübingen: Mohr-Siebeck, 1998) 138 *et seq.*; P.W. Heermann, 'Ringtausch, Tauschringe und multilaterales Bartering' *Juristenzeitung* 1999, 183; see also P.W. Heermann, 'Verbundene Geschäfte im Sinne des § 9 Abs 1 VerbrKrG' *Archiv für die civilistische Praxis* 2000, 19.

78 B. Teyssié, *Les groupes de contrats* (Paris: LGDJ, 1975) 295; F. Chaix, *Le contrat de sous-traitance en droit Suisse: Limites du principe de la relativité des conventions* (Basel: Helbing & Lichtenhahn, 1995) 47 *et seq.*

79 See C. Aubert de Vincelles, 'Réflexions sur les ensembles contractuels: Un droit en devenir' *Revue des Contrats* 2007, 985, 988.

80 BGHZ 56, 269.

the contract.[81] In the ruling here under discussion, however, the BGH has now explicitly stated that this rule is not applicable to the individual contracts involved in cashless payments, which banks execute in bulk.[82] Indeed, it was precisely the fact that external fund transfers, as an instance of indirect representation, do not require any consent on the client's part, which contributed to the Court's preference for applying the notion of third-party damage.[83] As this ruling is hardly intended to entirely eliminate party intent as a factor in determining liability where one of the parties to the payment network fails to perform, it can only be assumed that the High Court preferred to recognize the existence of a 'nexus' that links the individual contracts 'in substance'. In other words, the circumstances surrounding the conclusion of the contract(s) create a situation in which the individual contracts combine to form a whole. But what is the nature of this 'nexus'? The answer provided by the BGH ruling of 6 May 2008 appears to be clear: *only to the extent that an overall 'enterprise' undertaken on the basis of a number of bilateral promises is of such nature that an essential condition of its fulfilment resides in the performance, without exception, of all of the promises undertaken (or the payment of all damages resulting from failure to perform) is it permissible to deviate from a linear conception of contractual relationships in favour of the presumption of a contractual 'network' relationship.* From these observations, certain important conclusions concerning the ontogenesis of contractual nexus may be derived.

It is only in such cases, where both the intent of the parties and the circumstances surrounding the agreements they enter into create a situation in which the fulfilment of each individual contract is contingent upon the fulfilment of the others, that this multi-contract 'network' as a whole can be said to create 'constraints'. These constraints may well be in conflict with, or neutralize the effects of, such 'environmental' factors as contribute to the selective processes involved in the formation of the individual contracts of which the network is made. These 'constraints' result from the fact that each contract, in becoming a part of a network of transactions, must relinquish a certain degree of its independence, as a contribution to the stability of the whole (the nature of which nevertheless remains essentially unstable, due the competing interests involved in the formation of the individual agreements).[84] The individual contracts – much like the individual members of a social group – no longer exist merely as self-contained units, the purpose of whose existence lies solely in their own fulfilment, as is otherwise the rule in contract formation. The individual contracts that make up a contractual network – again, like the members of a social grouping – are seen as elements contributing to the 'higher' purpose of fulfilling the intent that lay behind the creation of the network, an intent that goes beyond, and may even come into conflict

81 See C. Grüneberg, '§ 328', in Palandt (ed.), n 55 above, 539–40 N 14 *et seq*.

82 Cf BGH, n 80 above, para 33.

83 See above, second section, under sub-heading 'Network Analysis I: The Problem of Multi-Level Complexity'.

84 See V. Lemieux, *Les réseaux d'acteurs sociaux* (Paris: PUF, 1999) 17 *et seq*.

with, the immediate intent of the individual contracts. As such networks are able to function only if a certain degree of stability is maintained, the 'stabilization contributions' provided by the individual contracts can be seen as a result of higher order legal evolutionary forces, analogous to the 'constraints' posited by Gould as functioning simultaneously with the natural forces of Darwinian selection. In this view, contractual networks of various kinds can be said to exist as a legal reality, functioning in their own right as complex institutionalized arrangements – similar to associations, corporations, franchise groups, etc – whose relative viability will be established over time, as they adapt competitively to their changing environmental circumstances.

### *Network Analysis III: The Problem of Contractual 'Heterarchization'*

An adequate explanation of the phenomenon of contractual networks in terms of evolutionary theory must also take Gould's third principle into account: 'scope'. As Gould points out, in the process of evolution, non-evolutionary phenomena (such as catastrophes, natural or other) can sometimes exert a decisive influence on the way in which various forms of life develop. The possibility of such cataclysmic events occurring must also be taken into consideration in describing the ontogenesis of contractual networks. The key here is what is coming to be known as the *network revolution*.[85] For some time now there has been a veritable explosion of heterarchically structured activity in all areas of social organization. Contract law, however, is not simply one further example of an area in which this phenomenon can be observed. It would appear that the process of 'heterarchization' in certain areas of social activity is serving as a catalyst to an exceedingly rapid increase in the use of contractual networks as a means of imposing acceptance of the new organizational structure as a permanent and inevitable feature of legal relations.

Evidence of this is provided in exemplary form by a decision of the BGH dated 16 November 2006,[86] dealing with the question of value-added services. The facts of the case, briefly, were as follows: the plaintiff operates a telecommunications network through which it provides clients, such as the defendant, with telephone

85 See, e.g. M. Fassler, *Netzwerke: Einführung in die Netzstrukturen, Netzkulturen und verteilte Gesellschaftlichkeit* (Munich: Fink, 2001) 119 *et seq.*; A.-L. Barabaási, *Linked: How Everything is Connected to Everything Else and What it Means for Business, Science, and Everyday Life* (New York: Plume, 2003); T. Stonier, 'The Wealth of Information and the Emerging Global Community', in H. Eichmann et al. (eds), *Netzwerke: Kooperation in Arbeit, Wirtschaft und Verwaltung* (Vienna: Falter, 2000) 13 *et seq.*; an informative survey of various network theories in the sociological and economic area can be found in S. Dinter, *Netzwerke: Eine Organisationsform moderner Gesellschaften?* (Marburg: Tectum, 2001); A. Brand, *Funktion und Auftreten von Unternehmensnetzwerken aus der Sicht der Neuen Institutionenökonomie und soziologische Ansätze: Welche Rolle spielt die Informationstechnik?* (Stuttgart: Ibidem Verlag, 2002).

86 BGH vom 16.11.2006 – III ZR 58/06.

access and connections. At the same time it also makes its network available to so-called value-added service providers, who provide, independently of the network operator, telephone connections at their own rates (0900 numbers). The defendant was billed by the plaintiff for the telephone access and for calls. The overwhelming majority of the calls billed were made through value-added service providers, so that the services billed were provided, for the most part, not by the plaintiff itself but by a third party network participant. The plaintiff sued for payment in its own right not only for the services it provided itself, but also for those provided by the value-added service providers, based on the existence of a community of creditors (§ 428 BGB) as provided in the General Terms and Conditions. The BGH notes first, that the contractual establishment of a community of creditors is indeed possible. It then goes into an analysis of the relevant legal relationships:

> 1. Where the user of a telephone connection makes use of a value-added service by dialing by telephone or by computer a specific number … beginning with the … series of digits … 0900 … there are, as a rule, two legal relationships involved: a) on the one hand, there is the telephone service agreement, which is to be qualified as a continuing obligation, by which the network operator … undertakes to provide the client with access to the public telecommunications network and, by establishing outgoing and receiving incoming telephone connections, to enable him to exchange spoken or other data communications with other participants in the fixed or mobile telephone network … b) This is supplemented by an additional legal relationship with the provider of a further service … in the present case with the respective value-added service provider …
>
> 2. It does not, however, result therefrom that the network operator cannot have grounds for a claim in its own right for the portion of the compensation due for the use of a third party value-added service. a) On the contrary, an obligation of this nature on the part of the subscriber to the telephone line can arise out of the telephone service contract … Where the network operator and the subscriber conclude such an agreement, the service provider and the network operator form a community of creditors pursuant to § 428 BGB …[87]

At this point, however, the Court turns with a critical eye to the fact that the terms in question were contained within the General Terms and Conditions, and reaches what would at first appear to be an unambiguous conclusion:

> While it is true that similar clauses would certainly be unusual in ordinary business relations and thus unexpected, so that they would not constitute an element of the agreement (§ 305c para 1 BGB …). Moreover, they would be incompatible with essential underlying principles of the legal provisions – the

87 BGH, n 86 above, para 12 *et seq.* (author's translation).

> privity of contractual obligations – with the consequence that they would in any event be without effect (§ 307 para 1 and para 2 no 1 BGB).[88]

Were it not for the use of the conditional in these formulations, there would be no reason to doubt that the Court had thus decided to rule in favour of the plaintiff. At this point, however, comes a surprising, even revolutionary, reversal.

What is extraordinary about the decision is not that the Court, in the end, allows the validity of an agreement on the formation of a community of creditors between the network operator and the value-added service provider included in the General Terms and Conditions. The astonishing thing is that its reasoning is based not on *legal* argumentation, but on *practical necessity* deriving from the nature of the legal relationship and the legal structures specific to the telecommunications industry. Such references to practical requirements are anything but commonplace in German Supreme Court rulings, particularly where they serve, as in the ruling here discussed, as *rationes decidendi.* The decisive passage reads as follows:

> *The specificities of telecommunications law, however, render admissible a divergent interpretation.* § 15 para 1 clause 1 of the Telecommunications Ordinance [TKV] already foresees that, barring any agreement to the contrary, that client dealings in all billing matters are conducted solely with the network operator, even where compensation for the services of another operator is owed. The right and the obligation of the network operator to bill third party claims is further extended in § 15 para 1 clause 4 of the TKV to the point that the client may make payments to the former with effect of discharge. In actual practice, subscribers, as a rule, make use of this and make payment of their telephone bills to the network operator. In addition, value-added service providers and connection network providers often grant to the subscriber network operators payment collection powers or direct debiting authorization, or assign their claims for collection purposes … *It is, therefore, common, in legal relations in the telecommunications sector, for billing and payment operations to be handled solely by the subscriber network operator, even where the claims of third party providers are asserted.* The recognition of an independent claim on the part of the subscriber network operator – in contrast to the situation with regard to a connection network operator, whose role in the establishment of the connection is not made outwardly visible … – thus represents, in spite of the possibility that the subscriber network provider may further appear as an additional creditor, only a minor deterioration in the subscriber's legal position. This is justified in consideration of the interests of the subscriber network provider, which are worthy of recognition, as set forth in the following considerations regarding the arguments raised by the subscriber. *The handling of payments in the*

88 BGH, n 86 above, para 13 (author's translation).

> *telecommunications branch involves bulk transactions, for which there exists a justified interest in maximum simplification and standardization of procedures.*[89]

From a legal point of view, the justification of the claim allowed by the judges is obviously quite vague. In particular, while mention is made of the fact that this decision has a bearing on German law regarding General Terms and Conditions, there is no final ruling in that regard. What matters for our purposes here, however, is the fact that the German Federal Court evidently felt that whatever the solution may be, it must be sought not at the level of individual contracts, as in classical legal theory, but at the emergent level of contractual networks. From an evolutionary point of view, it would appear that a 'catastrophic event' has occurred: *in the final analysis the possibility of resolving the case with the traditional arguments known to Continental law of obligations no longer even existed; it had been 'wiped out' by the actual practices developed by the value-added service branch.*[90] The ruling handed down on 16 November 2006 thus provides us with evidence to suggest that the emergence of contractual networks as a legal phenomenon may be the result not only of the gradual selective effects of environmental forces and 'constraints', but also of rapid and radical transformations in the surrounding economic reality. In this sense, it may be said that 'catastrophism' also plays a role in the evolution of institutional arrangements.

## The Constitution of Contractual Nexus

### *Deficiencies in the Law of Contracts*

In the foregoing, there was an examination of some of the attempts encountered in the recent jurisprudence to develop the legal argumentative tools needed for dealing with business arrangements built on a plurality of linked contracts. Observing the issue through the looking-glass of evolutionary theory, and with the aid of Gould's analytical framework based on the principles of *agency, efficacy, scope*, three basic preliminary conclusions were drawn: (1) The interlinkage of individual contracts may give rise to the emergence of new orders, which differ from the orders instituted by individual 'bipolar' contracts, and which function according to a logic of their own – a 'network' logic.[91] (2) The business constructs that emerge out of this nexus of contracts are nevertheless subject (inter alia) to the selective pressures of existing contract law, which tends to approach the

89 BGH, n 86 above, para 19 *et seq.* (author's translation).

90 A detailed discussion of this point – specifically the deficits of the classical law-of-obligations models in coping with defaults in performance extending beyond a contract – can be found in Rohe, n 53 above, 65 *et seq.*

91 See above, second section, under sub-heading 'Network Analysis I: The Problem of Multi-Level Complexity'.

individual contracts on which such networks are built not as interlinked elements of a whole but as, independent, autonomous units. At the same time, however, it is possible for such interlinked contracts to reach a level of interdependence, of organizational density, as it were, that the true meaning of the agreement reached by the parties can no longer be deduced from the declarations of intent contained in each of the individual contracts; it can only be inferred by considering them in conjunction with each other, as elements in a *contractual network*. When this occurs, such networks form 'constraints' on the law and can effectively block the synallagmatic reflex of traditional contract law. This occurs, in particular, where there is a 'project' to be accomplished, the success of which inevitably depends on the correct performance of the obligations set forth in the individual contracts linked to each other by this 'common' purpose.[92] (3) In some domains today, socio-economic or technological developments have reached a point where, in fact, there is no longer any alternative to the formation of contractual networks. In such 'catastrophist' cases, it is no longer possible to treat the individual contracts involved as existing in their own right. As elements in a nexus of contracts they have 'forfeited' their autonomy to the network they combined to create. It is to this situation that the law must respond.

In the following an attempt will be made to outline such a possible response. The approach taken consists of two steps:

1. To begin with, it will be useful to recall the reasons for the difficulties of traditional concepts of contract law to comprehend the modern constructions of contractual networks. We have already established that the core of the problem lies in the (historically conditioned) tendency to reduce all complex contractual relations to their simplest form by interpreting them as a series of individual and independent legal transactions. This can be observed when we consider the law of obligations by looking at it from the outside, as we did in the previous section. The object now is to consider the law of obligations from the 'inside': why do the internal operations of contract law appear to be so confused when confronted with the phenomenon of contractual nexus? Why are the courts constrained to seek solutions for which the accepted doctrines of the classical theory of contracts are unable to provide convincing justification – as we have seen, for example, in the BGH decision of 16 November 2006?
2. The next step will be to examine the possibilities for putting the insights we have gained from taking an evolutionary view of interdependent contracts to use: what theoretical constructs do these insights suggest as a means of adapting legal doctrine to fit emerging legal realities?

---

92 The term 'common' is in no way meant to imply that the parties are pursuing a common purpose (in the company-law sense). This very feature is alien to contractual networks, since they are formed through bipolar contracts. In short, *the 'common' project referred to in the text is one structurally upheld by the contracts, not by all the parties*.

*The Social Multi-Dimensionality of Contracts*

In explaining the difficulties of current theories of contract law in coming to terms with contractual networks, the working hypothesis will be that the rise of such networks is directly connected with the functional differentiation of modern society, an ongoing and increasingly complex process that, among other things, has now strained traditional contract theory to its limits.[93] The underlying assumption is that the functional differentiation of society – entirely in the classic sense – has given rise to new social formations, the increasing dominance of which is causing a restructuring of modern society in such a way that it is becoming polycentric – with neither top nor bottom, nor even a centre.[94] The relationship between this phenomenon and the law of contracts, as will be seen, is best explained with the aid of systems theory.

From a systems theoretical point of view, contracts are not, as generally defined in law, agreements between two or more parties to perform or refrain from specific acts. Rather, they are what is termed a structural coupling between the different functional systems of which society is made up (the economy, the legal and educational systems, etc).[95] What this means, in essence, is that contracts supply the means by which the systems in question are able to observe and describe each other.[96] This is made possible by virtue of the fact that every contract (as a form of structural coupling) contains within it a repertoire of possibilities that serves to inform each of the systems that are party to the contract as to the functional mechanisms of the other. With regard to the question as to how, precisely, the information derived from the contract is put to use by the respective systems, it has rightly been pointed out that such information has a constitutive effect for a social system in that it converts latent expectations into actual obligations, mere

---

93 See in detail, M. Amstutz, 'Vertragskollisionen: Fragmente für eine Lehre der Vertragsverbindung', in H. Honsell et al. (eds), *Aktuelle Aspekte des Schuld- und Sachenrechts: Festschrift für Heinz Rey zum 60. Geburtstag* (Zurich: Schulthess, 2003) 165; see also N. Luhmann, *Organisation und Entscheidung* (Opladen/Wiesbaden: Westdeutscher Verlag, 2000) 411.

94 N. Luhmann, *Politische Theorie im Wohlfahrtsstaat* (Munich: Olzog, 1981) 22.

95 See, e.g. Luhmann, n 28 above, 440 *et seq.*; G.-P. Calliess, 'Das Tetralemma des Rechts: Zur Möglichkeit der Selbstbeschränkung des Kommunikationssystem Recht' *Zeitschrift für Rechtssoziologie* 2000, 296; D. Wielsch, *Freiheit und Funktion: Zur Struktur- und Theoriegeschichte des Rechts der Wirtschaftsgesellschaft* (Baden-Baden: Nomos, 2001) 56 and 59 *et seq.*; P. Zumbansen, *Ordnungsmuster im modernen Wohlfahrtsstaat: Lernerfahrungen zwischen Staat, Gesellschaft, Vertrag* (Baden-Baden: Nomos, 2000) 206; T. Lieckweg, *Das Recht der Weltgesellschaft: Systemtheoretische Perspektiven auf die Globalisierung des Rechts am Beispiel der lex mercatoria* (Stuttgart: Lucius & Lucius, 2003) 45 *et seq.*

96 Zumbansen, n 95 above, 206; Lieckweg, n 95 above, 46 *et seq.*

projections into operational ties.[97] To put it in different terms, the information produces the structures of a sub-system that 'press for fulfilment of the contract's purpose' in the functional system concerned.[98] And it is here, in the production of such ad hoc structures, that the role of contracts in the process of social differentiation lies: they allow each of the systems to continue to function according to its own intrinsic logic and nevertheless form a link with the other – this is the substance of contracts. The specific nature of the transactions that each contract makes possible is then a function of the systems that are involved in the contractual link. Within the economic system, the agreement leads to an organized procedure for *resource allocation*;[99] within the legal system, the contract may provide a 'governance structure' through which a *normative discourse* is made possible;[100] where other functional systems are involved (the sciences, the arts, medicine, education, etc) a *project* may be defined, which, in its communicative implementation, alters the processes by which the system produces its respective results (increased knowledge, aesthetic value, improved health, enhanced socialization and technical skills, etc).[101] As facilitators not only of individual transactions, but also – and simultaneously – of intersystemic discourse, each contract thus takes on a social 'multi-dimensionality',[102] which, in the event of an interlinkage between several individual contracts, creates a level of complexity that traditional theories of contract law are no longer able to comprehend. As components of a larger network, through which various functionally differentiated social systems are linked in an ongoing discourse, network contracts no longer serve solely the simple purpose of facilitating interaction,[103] but also promote the complex reflective processes that enable nascent systems to complete the process of self-differentiation and evolve into autonomous autopoietic sub-systems.[104] The plausibility of this construction is most clearly seen where contracts of extended duration are involved, in which the relationship created between the parties is

97 G. Teubner, 'Contracting Worlds: The Many Autonomies of Private Law' *Social & Legal Studies* 2000, 409.

98 Ibid., 249.

99 Lieckweg, n 95 above, 46.

100 O. Williamson, 'Transaction Cost Economics and Organization Theory', in N.J. Smelser and R. Swedberg (eds), *The Handbook of Economic Sociology* (Princeton/New York: Princeton University Press/Russell Sage, 1994) 77.

101 See G. Teubner, 'Im blinden Fleck der Systeme: Die Hybridisierung des Vertrages' *Soziale Systeme* 1997, 313; a good example is given by Teubner, n 97 above, 249 *et seq.*: 'When a medical operation is to be done, a technical project carried out or a complex service provided, the contractual relation actualizes this potential and converts it into the mandatory structure of a social system, an obligatory discourse and the real performance of a social dynamic.'

102 Teubner, n 97 above, 314.

103 On this concept, see, e.g. H. Willke, *Systemtheorie I: Grundlagen* (7th edn, Stuttgart: Lucius & Lucius, 2006) 72 *et seq.*

104 See Willke, n 103 above, 99 *et seq.*

no longer confined to the limited, short-term effects of spot transactions. The cooperative mechanisms that come to characterize the relationship created by the structural coupling embodied in such long-term contracts allow for both the observation and the reflection of the environment in which the emergent (sub) system conducts its operations. By this means the contractually initiated system is able to anticipate possible conflicts between its own structurally coupled sub-systems and the systems that constitute their external environment. Such potential conflicts are assessed with a view to predicting their consequences, in order to steer the system in such a way as to avoid them. The complexity of this reflexive discourse increases exponentially where each of the systems that are structurally coupled through one contract are simultaneously coupled with other such systems. The discourse conducted in each of the contractual sub-systems becomes linked to those of the other sub-systems in reflexive loops thus giving rise to a kind of *perpetuum mobile* with which traditional notions of contract law are ill equipped to deal. The language of law has simply not yet invented a conceptual term for the reflexive loops through which the network discourse is conducted. Because of this, the law attempts to 'translate' the new phenomenon into such terms as it is capable of comprehending.

In our analysis of recent attempts by the German High Court to deal with the phenomenon of contractual nexus, we saw that the law reconstructs the complex reciprocal discursive relationship that arises between other social systems through the interplay of individual, contractually initiated sub-systems as a '*contractual network*'. However, by construing reflexive, interlooped discourse (as it is described in more sociologically oriented approaches) in the more lawyerly terms of 'contractual nexus', a loss in translation occurs, which, from a systems theoretical standpoint, is also inevitable: as a system, the law is able to conceive of the reality it observes beyond its own confines only in its own terms. For the law, conflicts occur only within the discourse of the individual, discrete sub-systems created by contract. The source of any friction that arises in the uninterrupted discursive flow created through the interlinking of contractual sub-systems must therefore be assigned to a conflict in one of them. The reality, however, is that each contractual discourse in the network observes and adapts to the conflict on its own terms, according to its own *calculus*, creating a greater or lesser degree of friction throughout the entire overall system. It is this diffuse, ubiquitous 'presence' of the conflict throughout the network that remains unintelligible to the law in its attempts to assign it to contract A, contract B or contract C. The notion of 'contractual nexus' is useful in the sense that it provides the problem with a name. It is worth recalling, however, that it is only a diagnosis, not a solution.

This is precisely the difficulty that the BGH was faced with in its decision of 16 November 2006, discussed above. Ultimately, it remained unclear, both from a practical and from a legal theoretical point of view, whether the conflict over the payment for value-added services arose out of the contractual relationship between the client (subscriber) and the value-added service provider, or out of the contract between the client and the subscriber network provider. The response was, necessarily, enigmatic: from neither alone, but from both together! As the Court itself was forced to recognize, attempting to deal with the phenomenon of contractual networks at the level of the individual contracts leads to an unavoidable paradox, the solution to which can be found only by moving to a 'higher order' of legal organization.

### *'Constitutionalizing' Contractual Networks: Network-Functional Criteria*

A number of approaches have already been suggested for overcoming the difficulty faced by legal theory in dealing with the evolutionary phenomenon of contractual networks. Some authors have proposed considering mutually linked legal transactions as emanating from a multiparty consensus. In this view, the existence of a 'network contract' *(Netzvertrag)* is to be assumed, which functions as a kind of master contract pulling all the various threads of the network together, and to which all of the 'network participants' have (implicitly) declared their intent to be parties.[105] Others seek various means by which to analogously apply the principles of company law or even conglomerate law to contractual networks of all types.[106] To date, the most sophisticated and most convincing attempt to devise a legal methodology for dealing with combinations of contracts in such a way as to account for the specificities of such arrangements has been suggested by Teubner. He proposes the use of a specific technique for attributing rights and duties to the various parties to a contractual network. This involves (1) the designation of enhanced loyalty duties to the network as such; (2) the development of contractual patterns of liability so as to account legally for the differentiation of areas of competition and areas of cooperation within the contractual network and define the relationship between participants who are not direct contractual partners; and (3) the selective double attribution of network acts both to individual contracting parties and to the network as a whole ('network share liability'), so as to define legal consequences appropriate to the network structure.[107]

The evolutionary view of contractual networks, as outlined above, suggests a different approach to designing a 'constitution' or 'code' for contractual networks. The foundations of such an approach would rely on the same regular patterns of behaviour (algorithms) that, in the economy, give rise to the evolutionary tendency to form contractual networks. If it is correct to assume that contractual networks lead to the creation of a new, emergent order of expectations, to a 'higher' order that operates according to a 'network logic', the first question we must ask ourselves is whether the rules that are applied *ex lege* at the lower level of individual contracts can possibly be extrapolated to networks formed out of such contracts. The emergence of a higher order of expectations would then

105 W. Möschel, 'Dogmatische Strukturen des bargeldlosen Zahlungsverkehrs' *Archiv für die civilistische Praxis* 1987, 211.

106 See the survey in Teubner, n 68 above, 116 *et seq* and 133 *et seq*.

107 Teubner, n 68 above, 145 *et seq*.

correspond to the emergence of a higher legal order, founded upon the same legal rules that apply to the individual contracts that combine to form the network. The suggestion is that an emergent legal order to deal with contractual networks could be derived from the rules of classical contract law. Rather than constructing an entirely new code of network law, based on doctrinal elements hitherto unknown to the law of obligations, the norms for 'incorporating' individual contracts into networks would serve as the building blocks for a legal constitution for the whole complex.[108] The only remaining question, then, relates to the method by which such an 'extrapolation' of classical contract law to contractual networks could be effected. A helpful approach, in a nutshell, would consist in the assumption that the subsumption of 'network conflicts' under rules that apply to conflicts arising in individual contracts requires the addition of a *second (emergent) dimension* to those rules. What is needed is a new set of criteria governing their application – criteria not relevant to their application to bipolar contracts. One legal technique that could prove useful in providing such a criterion is the *conflict-of-laws method.*[109]

To explain this suggestion, let us begin by comparing some of the basic issues involved in contractual networks with those that arise in conflicts of laws. Obviously, in the case of contractual networks, it is not a multinational but a *multi-contract* situation. In both instances, however, we are faced with the same fundamental question: *by what 'governing law'* (in conflict of laws, by which national legal system; in the case of connected contracts, by the terms of which contract in the network) is the conflict at hand to be decided? In the case of contractual networks, the issue can be reduced to a determination of how, by what criteria, based on the 'logic' of the network in question, the conflicts that arise in that network can be assigned to the 'jurisdiction' of one of its constituent contracts. If such criteria could be determined, the same norms that are applicable at the level of individual contracts would take on the added dimension needed to 'elevate' them to the higher, network level – qua rules of conflict of laws – and fit them into a legal constitution governing the whole. One possibility of determining the criteria we are seeking would be to apply the principle of functional connection, as proposed by Schnitzer, who posits that the decisive element in the classification of a legal relationship is the *function* of that relationship in society. The argument is based on the idea that the ordering of the rights and obligations of the parties to a legal

108 The pattern on which this constitutional process (in the active sense of the term: the act of constituting) takes place, which *mutatis mutandis* also applies to contractual networks, is described by G. Teubner, 'Societal Constitutionalism: Alternatives to State-centred Constitutional Theory?', in C. Joerges, I.-J. Sand and G. Teubner (eds), *Constitutionalism and Transnational Governance* (Oxford: Hart, 2004) 19: 'Constitution always starts as the linking of two real processes: from the viewpoint of law it is the production of legal norms intimately interwoven with basic structures of the social system; from the viewpoint of the constituted social system it is the production of basic structures of the social order, which at the same time inform the law and are in turn normed by the law.'

109 For a more detailed treatment of this issue, see Amstutz, n 93 above, 170 *et seq.*

relationship has a functional significance, that is, that the rights and obligations themselves perform a certain function in the given social context.[110]

It follows from the application of this thesis to contractual networks that in attributing a conflict to one of the individual contracts of which the network is constituted, the determining factor would be the *function* performed by the individual contracts within the overall network. In other words, the decisive criterion to be articulated in a conflict-of-laws rule for contractual networks would be the *capacity of the contractual network to fulfil its role (function) in the economy or in society in general.* A possible way of formulating the rule would be to say that *a conflict arising in a contractual network is governed by the provisions of that individual contract whose terms, in the case at hand, ensure the ability of the overall network to continue functioning.*

Has the German High Court already adumbrated such a rule? Do the criteria we have suggested help in supplying the theoretical underpinnings to the vague construction applied by the BGH in its decision of 16 November 2006? In short, can it be said that that decision represents a step in the right direction towards a new 'network doctrine' in the law of obligations? *Ex facto ius oritur?* One thing, in any event, is certain: in the end, the fundamental legal issue involved in the case, the question of the value-added service provider's contractual right to payment, was resolved according to the terms of an agreement, to which the value-added service provider itself was not a party – the subscription agreement between the subscriber and the network operator. That such a solution was chosen can only mean that, ultimately, it was only by taking recourse to conflict of law rules that the Court was able to reach its judgment.

### *The 'Network-Functional' Calculus in Statutory Law of Contracts*

Any attempt to follow up on this proposal to 'constitutionalize' contractual networks through a functional conflict-of-laws rule, in the sense just suggested, will, admittedly, first have to deal with the question of how, in actual practice, the 'function of the contractual network' is to be determined. This is obviously a question to which no general response is possible. It is safe to assume that reality produces an enormous number of contractual network types, each of which fulfils a different function in its own particular way.[111] A phenomenological study of all of the forms in which such networks can manifest themselves is certainly beyond the scope of the present remarks. With regard to certain typical instances of interlinked contracts, however, it is nevertheless possible to demonstrate that

110 A.F. Schnitzer, 'Die funktionelle Anknüpfung im internationalen Vertragsrecht', in Rechts-, wirtschafts-, sozialwissenschaftliche Fakultät der Universität Freiburg (ed.), *Festgabe für Wilhelm Schönenberger* (Freiburg [Schweiz]: Universitätsverlag, 1969) 397.

111 See, for example, P. Hessinger, *Vernetzte Wirtschaft und ökonomische Entwicklung: Organisatorischer Wandel, institutionelle Einbettung, zivilgesellschaftliche Perspektive* (Wiesbaden: Westdeutscher Verlag, 2001) 196 *et seq.*

codified German law has already begun to make use of *network-functional criteria* to resolve questions of the sort discussed here and, thus, to provide contractual networks with a statutory foundation under the law of obligations. In other words, it would appear that the solution here developed already fits quite seamlessly into existing German contract law. By way of example,[112] we will conclude here with a brief discussion of § 358 BGB, which provides an interesting paradigm for a codification of contractual network law based on the conflict-of-laws mechanism.

Consumer rights of withdrawal from purchases that are fully or partially financed with consumer loans are governed by § 358 BGB. The two contracts involved in such transactions are considered to be *linked*, provided that the purpose of the loan is the financing of the acquisition agreement and that the two contracts form a functional complex – a higher order based on operations coupling – a condition which arises, in particular, where the seller and the lender are identical (bilateral arrangement) or the seller facilitates the financing through one or more third parties (multilateral arrangement).[113] Where the contracts are considered to be linked, withdrawal from one of them automatically entails the avoidance of the other, and this regardless of which of the contracts has been withdrawn from.[114] There is, however, still some controversy as to whether this rule is in conformity with the consumer protection objective of the provision in those cases where the contract with regard to which the consumer exercises his right of withdrawal is the loan agreement. Certain authors would prefer to leave to the consumer the choice as to whether or not the withdrawal from the loan agreement should automatically entail the avoidance of the purchase transaction; others oppose this suggestion.[115]

As concerns the conflict-of-laws mechanism for dealing with contractual nexus, a solution of particular interest is that proposed by German lawmakers in § 358 (4) clause 3 BGB, with regard to a purchase agreement concluded in a multilateral arrangement from which the consumer withdraws *after* the amount of the loan has already been transferred to the seller: in such a constellation, the

---

112 For a survey of the other potentially relevant provisions – i.e. § 311 (3), 328, 278, 434 (1) clause 2, 478 *et seq.*, 676b and 676c BGB – see Grundmann, n 68 above, 733 *et seq.*; see also, above, second section, under sub-heading 'Network Analysis I: The Problem of Multi-Level Complexity'; in the BGH ruling XI ZR 56/07 of 6 May 2008, dealing with the contractual duty to warn on the part of banks in the context of cashless payment transactions, the court refers to § 676a *et seq* BGB.

113 Cf M. Habersack, '§ 358', in F.J. Säcker and R. Rixecker (eds), *Münchener Kommentar zum Bürgerlichen Gesetzbuch, Band 2 Schuldrecht Allgemeiner Teil* (5th edn, Munich: Beck, 2007) 2287 *et seq.* N 36 *et seq.*; D. Medicus, '§ 358', in Prütting, Wegen and Weinreich (eds), n 56 above, 630 N 5–6; C. Grüneberg, '§ 358', in Palandt (ed.), n 55 above, 565–6 N 10 *et seq.*; R. Schulze, '§ 358', in R. Schulze (ed.), *Bürgerliches Gesetzbuch – Handkommentar* (4th edn, Baden-Baden: Nomos, 2005) 464–5 N 6 *et seq.*

114 This German construction is referred to as the '*Widerrufsdurchgriff*', a borrowing from the concept of 'lifting of the corporate veil'.

115 An overview of the literature on the question can be found in Habersack, n 113 above, 2281 N 22; Medicus, n 113 above, 632 N 19.

rights and obligations of the seller, with regard to the consumer, pass to the lender, so that the former can unwind both of the agreements bilaterally, addressing himself solely to the lender. The lender, for its part, receives from the consumer the goods purchased and must then recover the purchase price from the seller.[116] This provision is questionable in three respects. Firstly, because the lender is obliged to take on the product deterioration risk for the goods purchased,[117] a situation that is likely to be particularly problematic where moveable goods are involved. This is a risk over which the lender, who does not have possession of the goods, has no influence, while the consumer, who does have possession, bears no risk. Secondly, the provisions of § 358 (4) clause 3 BGB thus lead to a situation in which the consumer is freed from the deterioration risk only where the purchase is paid for through a *loan*, since it is only in this situation that he can exercise his right of withdrawal against the lender. In consequence, a consumer making a purchase with his own funds finds himself in a worse position than a consumer who finances his purchase through loans.[118] Thirdly, the legal situation becomes even more dubious if one considers that the lender also bears the risk of the seller's insolvency;[119] a risk which is normally borne by the consumer when exercising his right of withdrawal for goods paid for with his own funds. Freeing the consumer from both the risk of product deterioration and that of seller insolvency during the withdrawal period acts, in effect, as an incentive for him to buy on credit. Pursuant to § 355 (2) BGB, the withdrawal period begins only after the consumer has been *clearly* informed by the entrepreneur, in writing (by letter or electronically), with regard to this right in connection with the conclusion of the agreement and, pursuant to § 355 (1) clause 2 BGB, is of two weeks' duration. *The withdrawal period is, however, not limited in time, according to § 355 (3) clause 3 BGB, where the entrepreneur fails to properly inform the consumer.*[120] According to a recent BGH decision, handed down on 3 October 2009,[121] the protection granted to a consumer who makes a purchase partly with his own funds and partly on credit extends even to that part of the purchase price that came from his own funds, in that on exercising his right of withdrawal he is entitled to be reimbursed for this amount, by the lender, even though the latter was not the source of the funds. It follows that, as a consumer, one is well advised to buy at least partially on credit,

116 See, on this, Habersack, n 113 above, 2302 *et seq.* N 82 *et seq.*; Medicus, n 113 above, 631 N 15; Grüneberg, n 113, 566–7 N 20; Schulze, n 113, 465–6 N 11.

117 Medicus, n 113 above, 631 N 15.

118 Medicus, n 113 above,, 631 N 15.

119 On this, in detail, see Heermann (1998), n 68 above, 267 *et seq.*; cf. also Habersack, n 113 above, 2288 N 40.

120 On this unnecessarily complicated and generally incomprehensible provision see, in lieu of others, D. Medicus, '§ 355', in Prütting, Wegen and Weinreich (eds), n 56 above, 622–3 N 5 *et seq.*, which includes a copy of a sample right of withdrawal notice, issued by the German Federal Ministry of Justice, at N 14.

121 BGH ruling XI ZR 33/08 of 10 October 2009.

wherever there is any doubt as to the solidity of the purchase being made. By borrowing at least a part of the purchase price, the consumer is, in effect, 'insured' by the lender for the total amount, including his own capital outlays.

The significance of § 358 (4) clause 3 BGB in the present context lies, in particular, in the fact that the reallocation of risk that the provision engenders – by the Court's construing the consumer's bilateral right of withdrawal in this fashion – is brought about through a bundling and functionally conditioned modification of the debtor and creditor roles of the three (or more) parties involved in the multilateral transaction. At the outset, the position of each of the parties as the debtor or creditor in a bilateral transaction is clear, even though that transaction is part of a contractual network. The seller is a party both to the purchase transaction and to an agreement with the lender, who will often pay him a commission for having brokered the loan agreement.[122] Where there is no relationship between the seller and the lender, the two transactions are not considered to be linked, so that there is no 'functional complex' between them and § 358 BGB remains inapplicable. The consumer is both the purchaser and the borrower. The lender, in addition to its role in the credit transaction, is originally also party to a contractual relationship with the seller, which, as noted, creates the necessary economic unity of the two consumer transactions involving the consumer. In the situation foreseen in § 358 (4) clause 3 BGB, that is, where the funds have already passed to the seller, however, the original roles of the parties are reallocated, for *network-functional* reasons. As the consumer's rights and obligations vis-à-vis the seller pass to the lender, who is now responsible for the unwinding of both transactions, their nature is modified. What began as a *trilateral* transaction for all of the parties remains so only for the lender, while for both the seller and the consumer it is now merely *bilateral* – the relationship between them having been severed, since the lender now assumes both the role of the consumer (in relation to the seller) and of the seller (in relation to the consumer). The Court has thus decided in favour of a solution which, in spite of its somewhat dubious consequences with regard to the elimination of consumer risk in purchases on credit, must nevertheless be seen as an attempt to institute a viable mechanism for the unwinding of such transactions in a manner that fulfils the provision's ostensible purpose: protecting the consumer. From a structural point of view, the objective may, however, be described differently: to maintain the contractual network's ability to function for as long as is necessary in order to permit the unwinding of the transactions.

By laying bare the 'network-functional' calculus underlying the provisions of § 358 BGB, it becomes possible to recognize the significance of this provision as a step towards the codification of contractual network law: it has introduced the principle of functionality as the central criterion on which to base the application of contract law to contractual networks. By applying this criterion, using a conflict-of-laws approach, the courts are now in a position to determine, in each case, to

122 As was the case in the BGH ruling mentioned, n 121 above, para 2; on the relationship between the seller and the lender, see Habersack, n 113 above, 2304–5 N 87–8.

which of the network contracts a given dispute is to be attributed. In this way, the maintenance of network functionality becomes a question not only of systems theoretical sociology, but also one of law.

## Coda

The purpose of the foregoing remarks has been to test a new methodological approach – taking German case law as an example – for developing legal rules to deal with the phenomenon of contractual nexus. As we have seen, it would appear that, at the current stage in the development of European contract law, there remains a need for a preliminary phase of reflection on the fundamental issues involved in framing laws on contractual networks before the actual legislative work can begin. Given the emphatically sociological perspective that informs the methodology proposed here, wide divergences from the legislative principles that presently guide the drafting of European private law are, of course, inevitable. It is worth keeping in mind, however, that those principles are based largely on models of civil society that mirrored the social and economic realities of the nineteenth and twentieth centuries. The rapidly expanding use and significance of contractual networks, on the other hand, is a relatively new phenomenon, characteristic of the current state in the evolution of European – and global – social, economic and legal structures. In this sense, there is, and will presumably continue to be, increasing pressure on European private law to innovate and adapt its legislative instruments to the changing environment in which it operates. Under these circumstances the potential advantages of an evolutionary methodological approach, as here proposed, should, perhaps, not lightly be overlooked.

## Chapter 14

# Towards a Legal Framework for Transnational European Networks?

Fabrizio Cafaggi and Stefan Grundmann

### Contractual Business Networks

Forms of collaboration among European enterprises can occur at different levels and for various purposes. While collaboration among large enterprises has been in place for a long time, the collaboration of European SMEs both within global supply chains and among them is significantly low. This lack of interaction translates into a low rate of intra-community trade and the inability to jointly access global value chains.

A European legal model of inter-firm collaboration does not exist. The most common model deployed in several areas is the consortium agreement which will be briefly examined below. The national landscapes are quite diverse. In regulated markets network models have been implicitly or explicitly regulated. One can find references in telecom, electricity, gas and transport, primarily associated with the management of the material infrastructure. The management of the network can operate via different instruments, from ownership, with obligations towards the users and the final customers, to contractual agreements between the different users to define common rules about use, entry and exit. The purpose of network creation is often to ensure interconnectedness among the different operators and ever more to enable risk management. References to the network form are also linked to financial markets, ranging from the field of payments to that of trading stocks and bonds. Here again the use of contractual networks may be associated with different functions: granting customers interoperability or coordinating risk management. Much less rich is the legal landscape for forms of collaboration between firms in unregulated markets, especially for SMEs.

The role of small and medium enterprises (SMEs) in Europe has become central for growth. Agenda 2020 places a significant emphasis on the development of SMEs and their relationship.[1] The increase of European cross-border trade and the deep restructuring of global value chains are affecting the choices faced by European entrepreneurs to tackle global competition. SMEs are often family owned and not inclined to merge, although willing to engage in cooperative, even long-term projects. The creation of trans-European networks (TENs) is one possible

---

1 See Agenda 2020 at www.ec.europa.eu/europe2020/

option to facilitate both internal cross-border trade and to increase competitiveness of European industrial systems. But which legal models are available? Are they adequate for fostering internationalization of SMEs? How can they be financed? The proposed regulation regarding COSME (Competitiveness of Enterprises and SMEs) tries to address this gap but the link between industrial policies, innovation and trans-European networks (TENs) is still underdeveloped.[2] More broadly the authors believe that insufficient attention has been given to the legal instruments that can promote inter-firm collaboration at a European level.

National legal models differ quite substantially and it is unclear whether any type of alternative option is available, unlike the case of bilateral contracts where regulatory competition among national legal systems exists. Consortia are diffuse in southern European countries, GIE (groupement d'intérêt économique) is very popular in France, and multiparty contracts are available in northern European countries, but these models are hardly comparable. They differ across a number of determinants that can be clustered around two macro variables:

1. Governance structure: In some cases governance is non-existent and decisions are made on the basis of the unanimity criterion by all signatories; in other instances a heavy governance body is in place with a clear-cut distinction between contractual design and implementation of the collaborative project delegated to an executive committee. The latter model presents a high degree of delegation either via mandate or agency or via conventional company law techniques. Delegation can even be attributed to a company whose main task is to manage the contractual network.
2. Liability: The partition between contractual and organizational networks is often associated with the limitation of liability. It is clear that, even from a conventional perspective, companies, unlike contracts, present different degrees of limitation from none to high. As the asset partitioning literature has suggested, however, the question is more complex and the difference between affirmative and negative asset partitioning might affect the taxonomy of organizational forms and the boundaries between contracts and companies.

## Redrafting the Boundaries Between Contract and Company Law in Designing European Networks of Enterprises

Forms of collaboration may vary according to purpose, to degree and intensity of collaboration and its relevance for the participants, to the number of participants;

2 See annex II where in relation to the improvement of SMEs financing two instruments are devised: The equity facility growth (EFG) and the Loan Guarantee Facility (LGF). The LGF has two main purposes: to address a lack of sufficient available collateral and securitization of debt finance portfolios.

and to the level of investment, generic or specific. In other words the strategic or non-strategic nature of the collaboration will affect the form and scope of the network. Networks also vary in relation to the size of firms. Collaboration may occur between large or small firms, or often along the supply chain between several SMEs and one or two large enterprises. Collaborative models can take the organizational or contractual forms with a wide range of intermediate models sharing features of both. While the legal partition at member states level is still quite strongly organized around the alternative between the two, practices and empirical research show that frequently the models, especially multiparty contracts, borrow from company law. Contractual networks are represented by two main structural models:

a. Multiparty contracts
b. Linked bilateral contracts.

These share some aspects but often they are used for different purposes. Multiparty contracts are deployed for horizontal agreements among producers or distributors. More rarely are they seen in vertical collaboration. However the increasing regulatory functions of supply chains are multiplying instances where multiparty contracts are used to coordinate safety or quality management vertically. This is the famous 'from farm to fork' model in agri-food businesses. The collaborative projects are often characterized by a higher level of risk sharing than those typically associated with bilateral contracts and with bilateral linked contracts forming a network. Networks are characterized by high level of interdependence among participants which can be generated by complementarity of input factors, complementarity of output factors, or both. Often collaboration is undertaken to do things that cannot be done alone or that would require much higher costs. Collaboration entails economies of complementarities embedded into specialization. These complementarities exist at the outset when firms decide to collaborate and they may persist or decline over time after collaboration has taken place. Clearly the complementarities require forms of risk sharing and an allocation of risk which can hardly be compared with the forms deployed in bilateral contracting where exchanges entail risk allocation rather than sharing according to the conventional view.

Collaborative work generates a common interest in the project between participants. Often such common interest might even exist when the project is not successful but has generated information and practices that can be usefully applied to similar projects. The protection of common interest(s) characterizes the governance features of the networks. Even if one emphasizes the cooperative aspects of exchange contracts, networks generally go well beyond the level of cooperation required in exchange contracts. The common interest imposes obligations among the parties and provides (limited) powers against third parties that want to infringe it, as is the case when the network reputation is harmed by competitors or when the trademark or other types of common rights are infringed.

The existence of such common interest impinges on the governance structure, on the degree of risk sharing and contributes to defining the boundaries with pure bilateral exchange contracts. It also affects the criteria for distributing profits and losses. But what makes the difference between contractual and organizational networks is much more subtle. Distinguishing between a network of firms that collaborate through a multiparty contract and one that decides to create a 'newco' (new company) among enterprises that want to pursue a common project is not an easy task and differences across legal systems on how to draw these boundaries are relevant. Contractual networks are generally defined by unlimited joint and several liability towards third parties with the possibility of reallocating the burdens internally via indemnification; they are characterized by unanimity rules which can be modified, and each participant is expected to contribute actively to the implementation of the project supplying not only capital but also expertise, knowledge and other production factors. Profits and losses are shared according to various criteria generally based on the activity rather than the amount of resources initially allocated.

The existence of a common aim often represents the specificity of a company and a distinction between a common aim and a shared interest is deployed to make the distinction between organizational and contractual forms. It is a matter of degree and has served to specialize different legal instruments all directed at favouring collaboration among firms. Should European law reflect the current ways in which national legal systems partition the functions of legal instruments or should they take a functional approach to networks and make the juxtaposition organizational versus contractual a relatively minor feature? Should we go back to the determinants of this distinction such as limitation of liability, effects on third parties, governance features and rethink the logics of boundaries? These authors believe that this should be the case and a European approach should build on less rigid boundaries between company and contract laws moving towards hybridization when necessary or towards more radical innovative schemes. They propose a functional rather than a structural approach based on the nature and the scope of collaboration among the enterprises which takes due account of the initial allocation of bargaining power and the potential modifications resulting from the nature of each participant's contribution. A relevant feature is the degree of stability both in terms of composition of the network and in terms of duration, which affects financing and more generally the design architecture.

### Financing Contractual Networks: Governance by Covenants? The Links Between Financial Contracts and Inter-Firm Collaboration

The lack of clear legal models poses daunting challenges for financing TENs. Often financial institutions tend to favour standardization in order to increase predictability and risk-control. Clearly they have to identify the risks of both participants and projects. Should TENs be financed at the national or European level, if so, how, and which legal framework will best promote access to credit? Traditionally banks and financial institutions have enjoyed privileged forms of collaboration through company law models. But contractual networks are certainly not unknown. Well-known in the area of distribution with franchising, dealerships and other forms of collaboration, networks have also developed in the area of research and development, especially among those firms which cannot produce in-house innovation. It is not uncommon that collaborative projects in the areas of R&D are financed even without the creation of a newco. Conventionally in this case the use of collaterals and guarantees has prevailed over covenants requiring specific governance or asset partitioning features. This seems to be the strategy also envisioned by the proposal for regulation currently discussed by the European Parliament.[3] There is however some sign of change emerging from national experiences. Financial institutions are currently designing minimum requirements that firms have to meet in order to access financing. How do current national practices affect the financing of TENs? Should the same logics apply to trans-European networks or is a different institutional framework needed?

In multiparty contracts the interest of financial institutions is manifold. The strategic question on contractual design is: what is the combination between covenants and collaterals in order to ensure adequate *ex ante* monitoring, promote peer monitoring and efficient risk sharing? Rules concerning access, exit composition and implementation of the industrial project are as important or even more important than those concerning liability and the design of asset partitioning between the assets dedicated to the collaborative project and those assigned to the enterprise. Often, given that these enterprises are family owned, a third factor complicates the matter when the personal and business assets of the entrepreneur are not well defined.

The financial contractual design aims at combining two different types of risks: those associated with the (previous behaviour of) financed parties and those associated with the financed submitted project(s). The current debate in some member states is whether the network or the individual participants should be financed. In the latter case the financing will be directed to the common project ensuring that each participant will not deploy the resources for alternative uses. This solution is a second best and increases monitoring costs. The first best is clearly financing the project and the network and if more than one project is at stake devise financing lines distinguished by projects. In either case the evaluation should encompass both the riskiness of the project and of individual participants. Emphasis on one or the other component rather than a comprehensive approach risks undermining the efficient monitoring of financial institutions. In order to maximize the effectiveness of financing the choice between covenants and collaterals has to be made dependent upon the nature of the project, the degree of

3 See Research, Innovation and Competitiveness package. Proposal for a regulation establishing a program for the competitiveness of Enterprises and small and medium enterprises (2014–2020). Brussels 30.11.2011. COM (2011), 834 final (hereinafter Cosme).

uncertainty and the factors that can control the risks. These factors are governance of the network, rules about its stability, that is, (1) by whom and how are entry and exit controlled; (2) the extent to which personal changes affect asset (in) stability; (3) the monitoring structure; and (4) the level of delegation in the implementation of multiproject networks. All these factors play a significant role. Increasingly national financial institutions design general guidelines for firms which define minimum governance requirements moving from individual to collective requirements. It is too early to determine whether banks are converging over benchmarking the most important governance features to be included in contractual covenants implemented via contractual networks. There is a trend having a significant impact at the European level where coordination among banks over these forms of lending contracts can facilitate the creation or consolidation of inter-firm networks.

Clearly individual multi-country banks can afford to finance the network themselves but for the majority it is likely that inter-firm collaboration may require inter-bank collaboration. How should this collaboration take place?

We envisage different possibilities: an agreement among European banks over terms that should occur when multiparty contractual networks with firms in various European countries are financed for the same project by different banks – this solution would probably be problematic from the competition perspective. Alternatively a system of mutual recognition is proposed which would prevent banks from denying access to credit when the terms are functionally equivalent according to the metric agreed upon within mutual recognition guidelines for financing TENs. Each bank or trade associations could define minimum requirements and a common metric could serve the purpose of evaluating if the required features exist across countries.

Recognition of the role of financial institutions has two implications on the diffusion of TENs:

a. Direct implications. Collaborations among financial institutions at EU level can increase the number and quality of SME collaborations by generating some degree of standardization in order to measure the risks.
b. Indirect implications. The increasing importance of covenants in loan contracts and more in general in financial instruments concerning governance and reporting will influence the design of European contractual governance. Covenants requiring minimum governance features to access credit will influence choices of parties and force a rethink of the external factors influencing private autonomy.

The recognition of the importance of governance covenants in financial contracts calls for a European legal framework which considers the potential influence of external factors in the governance design. If increasingly banks ask to meet governance requirements to access credit then clearly it will be important to establish legal rules to 'link' financial instruments and contractual networks and, from a policy perspective, to promote the active role of financial institutions in the formation and consolidation of inter-firm collaboration.

The financial influence on networks is not limited to B2B but affects also B2C networks where consumers' transactions are financed by banks or other financial institutions.

**Where are Consumers?**

The policy and scholarly debate has focused primarily on networks among enterprises. As mentioned at the outset little has been said about contractual networks in regulated markets where already a European legal framework exists. But even less has been said about consumers' contractual networks. Consumers can create their own contractual network when they cooperate vis-à-vis a supplier of goods or services. Clearly the most common model is the cooperative which deploys the organizational infrastructure to buy goods and/or services but flexibility might call for lighter forms of contractual collaboration between consumers and enterprises as is the case where networks of consumers are created within e-commerce platforms. Integrated supply of services to consumers constitutes possibly the most common example where a network of firms agrees to offer a 'package' of complementary services to an indefinite number of consumers which are asked to join the network in order to profit from the integrated offer.

Consumers can thence become part of business networks as the examples of airlines or credit cards show. In these cases multiple enterprises and multiple customers, including firms and consumers can join the contractual networks with circles of obligations that may differ according to the status of the participant. Typically the network form generates the so-called network effects which increase the benefits of participation with the growing number of members.

EU consumer contract law has neglected this dimension limiting the analysis to bilateral contracts. The collective dimension has been limited to the recognition of contractual standardization. Some pale sign of contractual interdependence can be found in the consumer credit directive where the trilateral structure of the relationship between the bank, the supplier and the consumer has received some attention. But the collective dimension of consumer contracting goes well beyond trilateral or multilateral transactions functionally linked! The collective dimension of mass contracts has been recognized at a remedial rather than a substantive level with little or no recognition of its governance dimension. Standard contracts can be used to create networks where each participant is held to the same obligations and holds the same rights.

We believe that European contract law, including both consumer and business law, should incorporate contractual networks in its different instances that exist in practice but are not fully recognized by the law.

## Contractual Networks and Private-Public Partnerships

Contractual networks have developed in many private-public partnerships and even more in collaborative ventures among research institutions, regardless of their public/private nature. The most widespread instrument has been the consortium agreement, a multiparty contract where a coordinator is selected to facilitate the relationship with the funding institution, often the European commission.[4] In consortium agreements the collaborative nature implies a relatively high degree of risk sharing and the risk of default by individual participants is borne by the other members with some significant limitations.

Two models have been used depending on the complexity of the project. For simple projects the governance is left to the signatories and the coordinator who interfaces with the funding institution. For the more complex models the general assembly is combined with an executive board. In either case the role of the coordinator is crucial since in interfacing with the funder she/he has to monitor performances and ensure compliance even if it does not have direct sanctioning power in case of breach.

Liability against the network and towards each of the participants is explicitly regulated by the contract and remedies for breach include termination but are limited to direct damages. A clause concerning exclusion of consequential damages is often inserted.

Different types of networks mimicking more an associational than a contractual model, but lacking legal personality, have also been deployed to foster coordination among national regulatory authorities. These models have been extensively used in the last 20 years. Some of them have evolved into an administrative agency, others have kept the nature of private law, combining associational and contractual features with performance of regulatory functions.[5]

## Sketching the New Architecture of Contractual Networks

The use of contractual networks in European law is much more widespread than is currently acknowledged. It operates in regulated markets, it has been used with some variation with the associational model in the coordination of national administrative bodies. But contractual networks used to implement many European projects via consortium agreements are possibly the most widespread form of

4 The model has developed in relation to framework project programmes and is based on the regulations that define these programmes. Over time they have changed and evolved but they certainly represent an important example of European contractual/associational network.

5 The paradigmatic example is that of financial markets with the evolution of CESB, Ceiops and SESR into EBA. But many other examples exist in other fields where we go from purely private-style EPRA in media to hybrid-style BEREC in telecoms or CEER in energy.

European contractual network. Yet European legislators seem to be unaware of the common features of these instruments for collaborative tasks and are unable to devise similar tools to promote collaboration among enterprises, and between them and consumers.

A divergence is observed between the emphasis in industrial and regional policies on inter-firm collaboration and the lack of legal instruments reflected in the design of the most recent proposals concerning European contract law. This contribution aims at filling this gap, proposing specific contractual instruments aimed at facilitating inter-firm collaboration especially, but not exclusively, directed at SMEs. Network forms can be applied not only to B2B but also to B2C relations. In addition the network forms can be, in fact already are, fruitfully deployed in public-private partnerships and can be further deployed in partnerships among universities, research centres and firms by creating innovation platforms.

A new legal framework is needed that presents common features for contractual networks in regulated and unregulated markets. Common principles should then be articulated along four different variables:

a. Regulated and unregulated markets, in particular markets where a material infrastructure is needed and markets where only interoperability has to be ensured;
b. Business to business and business to consumer relations should be differentiated but the possibility of vertical networks that encompass the whole supply chain should also be considered;
c. The private or public nature of participants, especially when they are only private or only public. It is beyond the scope of this chapter, but clearly the network model deployed in European administrative law for coordination should be part of the institutional design;
d. The for-profit or non-profit nature of the participants and the consequences for governance and liability in creating, managing and dissolving the network.

The contractual network form is certainly compatible with all the above variables but each of the four requires specific rules on the basis of the purpose of the network and the identity of the participants. The authors suggest that the first step should be the definition of what is already in place at EU level and a comparative analysis with the models deployed at the national level.

Very likely the new architecture will overcome the traditional disciplinary boundaries between contract and company law and between private and administrative law to accommodate new forms of partnerships and collaboration that can foster European integration and competitiveness.

# Index

For Product Safety Concerns and Information please contact our EU representative GPSR@taylorandfrancis.com Taylor & Francis Verlag GmbH, Kaufingerstraße 24, 80331 München, Germany